D1564622

Sidney Hook
Philosopher of Democracy and Humanism

Sidney Hook
Philosopher of Democracy and Humanism

edited by Paul Kurtz

PROMETHEUS BOOKS

Buffalo, New York

Published 1983 by
Prometheus Books
700 East Amherst Street, Buffalo, NY 14215

Library of Congress Catalog Card Number: 82-62459
ISBN: 0-87975-191-6

Printed in the United States of America

CONTENTS

SIDNEY HOOK

Born: December 20, 1902

B.S.: City College of New York (student of Morris R. Cohen)

M.A.: Columbia University, 1926

Ph.D.: Columbia University, 1927

Married: Ann Zinken

Children: John Bertrand
        Ernest Benjamin
        Susan Ann

Teacher: New York public schools, 1923-28

Lecturer: Columbia University (summer session), 1927, 1930

Instructor: Washington Square College, New York University, 1927-32

Assistant Professor: Washington Square College, New York University, 1932-34

Associate Professor: Department of Philosophy, New York University, 1934-39

Professor: Department of Philosophy, New York University, 1939-63

Head: Department of Philosophy, New York University, 1948-69

Chairman: Washington Square College, New York University, until 1969

Professor Emeritus: New York University, 1969-

Senior Research Fellow: Hoover Institution of War, Revolution and Peace, Stanford University

Visiting Professor: Harvard, 1961; University of California at San Diego, 1975

Regents Professor: University of California at Santa Barbara, 1966

Organizer: Conference on Methods in Philosophy and Science
        Conference on Scientific Spirit and Democratic Faith
        American Committee for Cultural Freedom
        Congress for Cultural Freedoms
        University Centers for Rational Alternatives
        New York University Institute of Philosophy

President and Treasurer: John Dewey Foundation

Guggenheim Fellow: 1928-29, 1961-62

Fellow: American Academy of Arts and Sciences
       American Academy of Education
       Committee for the Scientific Investigation of Claims of the Paranormal

Member: American Philosophical Association (President, Eastern Division, 1959)
       National Endowment for the Humanities (Council, 1972-78)
       League for Industrial Democracy (Vice-President)

Contributing Editor: *Free Inquiry* magazine

PREFACE

The Impact of Sidney Hook in the Twentieth Century

What is the measure of the greatness of a man? If it is the influence of his personality and ideas upon his immediate circle of friends and colleagues, his impact upon the world, and his effect upon both his contemporaries and the future, then the greatness of Sidney Hook is abundantly clear.

This volume is published to honor Sidney Hook on his eightieth birthday. In preparing this *Festschrift*, I have been impressed by the devotion, the loyalty, and the affection that his thought and character have inspired in so many leading intellectuals. Those who have known him have expressed profound admiration for his wisdom and humanity. All of the contributors to this book are distinguished in their own fields, whether philosophy or sociology, politics or law, education or the social sciences. Each of them has testified, either in print or privately, to the strong influence of his illuminating insights, his prodigious energy and brilliance of thought, and his basic moral concern.

Those who have attacked Sidney Hook professionally have rarely failed to appreciate his keen mind, but they have not understood his abiding normative interest. His critics no doubt are legion, for he is one of the outstanding social critics and polemicists of our time. Like Socrates, he is a gadfly, focusing on the contradictions and hypocrisies, the fads and fallacies of the reigning orthodoxies in the marketplace of ideas. As a great teacher and a prolific writer, Hook thrives on the provocative clash of ideas, hoping that out of creative controversy truth will emerge. He has known and debated many of the leading thinkers of the twentieth century, such as Max Eastman, Bertrand Russell, Albert Einstein, Jacques Maritain, Mortimer Adler, Robert Hutchins, Paul Tillich, Noam Chomsky, and John Kenneth Galbraith. As a democrat, Hook is committed to the philosophy of freedom and to studying the implications of freedom in actual practice. Indeed, throughout his career he has been the leading exponent of the democratic philosophy. As a humanist, Hook believes that ethics can be grounded in reflective intelligence.

The contributors to this volume have focused either on Sidney Hook's philosophy or on subjects related to his interests. Some agree with Hook; several differ with him in the spirit of constructive criticism. The essays are wide-ranging in scope; but, then, so is Hook's work, now spanning half a century. From his earliest days—first at City College, where he studied with Morris R. Cohen, and then as a student of John Dewey at Columbia University—to the present, Hook has demonstrated his consummate skill as both a theoretician and a dialectician.

Early in his life he became interested in Marxist ideas. They influenced him, as they have successive generations of intellectuals. But Hook has always been one step ahead of his time, able to wrestle with, define, and clarify key issues, to work out their implications virtually before anyone else, and to suggest possible solutions. An early defender of Marxism, Hook became its most persistent and sustained critic, especially regarding its revolutionary and totalitarian manifestations. A lifelong social democrat, he has always defended majority rule, civil liberties, and the open society. As a result he has been the *bête noir* of Leninists, Stalinists, and sundry New Leftists throughout the world. Hook attempted to make sense out of Marx and to interpret him in pragmatic terms; he has always sought to judge ideas by their observed consequences in human behavior. But first and foremost he has been a defender of democracy, not simply democracy *of* the people or *for* the people but *by* the people, based upon freely given consent. Not given to rhetoric or cant or deception, Hook has remained true to the principles of democracy, even when many of his socialist, leftist, and liberal friends have sought to compromise these principles in the name of equality, welfare, or some other ideal end and have criticized him for abandoning the faith.

Sidney Hook is the chief heir to John Dewey and the pragmatic tradition in American philosophy. He has excelled in *applied* intelligence, especially in the ethical, political, and social domain. Never given to empty philosophical abstractions or a cloistered existence, he has always sought to relate thought to concrete subject matter. Thus he is perhaps the preeminent normative philosopher of our time, not only dealing with speculative metaethics but eager to confront the genuine issues of human concern with facts, specific facts, which are always relevant to value questions. He has commented on most of the major issues of the day. In the nineteen-thirties he criticized the rise of fascism, communism, Leninism, Stalinism, and Trotskyism. After World War II he turned his attention to other problems. He has consistently defended the Western democracies from attacks by less critical intellectuals, not because these Western societies are perfect, but because they are far preferable when compared with the available alternatives. He has criticized the easy willingness of some to resort to civil disobedience. He has questioned the Supreme Court's usurpation of the powers of elected legislatures and the Congress. He has defended the rights of the victims of crime. In the late sixties and in the seventies Sidney Hook, perhaps more than anyone in the world, strongly defended the integrity of universities against the barbarians of virtue who were willing to sacrifice institutions of higher learning at the altar of political expedience. Academic freedom, he insisted, needs to be defined and defended, as do the chief functions of the university: the cultivation of excellence in teaching and the search for truth. An advocate of the rights of minorities and the principles of equality in a democracy, Hook nevertheless spoke out strongly against affirmative-action programs when others were fearful to do so.

In recent years, Hook has been identified with the establishment; some have even called him a "neo-conservative." But he has denied this appellation; indeed, he resists all labeling, for he has always been committed to the application of critical inquiry, treating each new problem with candor and an open mind. If it is sometimes difficult to predict which side of a question Hook will be on, one thing is sure: it will always be in defense of freedom, in a nondoctrinaire and meaningful way.

Hook is a secular humanist, perhaps the leading philosophical representative of that position at a time when it is being subjected to severe criticism from right-wing conservatives and fundamentalists. A scientific naturalist, committed to the use of the methods of science as the best way to understand nature and solve problems, he is also a skeptic concerning the quest for "Being" and the search for "divine purpose" in the universe. He believes that an ethic based upon critical intelligence need not have a divine source for its justification. Moral principles cannot be derived from the fatherhood of God, nor need the democratic philosophy be derived from metaphysical presuppositions or a doctrine of natural rights. Religion, he argues, should be a private matter and should require no public declaration. He has defended the rights of believers and nonbelievers alike, and maintains that the proper way to change attitudes and beliefs is through rational persuasion, mediation, and negotiation. Humanism, as he defines it, is an ethical philosophy. It encompasses everyone who believes in the separation of church and state, the secularization of values, and the view that morality can be based upon experience and reflection.

Hook has been attacked by the partisans of the extreme left for his courageous defense of a free society. Ritualistic liberals have condemned him for straying from their pat formulas and nostrums, and for his uncompromising defense of democracy against totalitarian forces everywhere. They have deplored his exposing the double standard of condemning right-wing authoritarian regimes while tacitly supporting brutal left-wing dictatorships. Reactionaries of the right have castigated his "irreligion" and his defense of a democratic welfare-state based upon an "equality of concern" for the needs of others. Hook has never accepted the uncritical faith of the libertarians in free enterprise and the sanctity of free market competition. He has consistently maintained that we must judge economic and social systems by their demonstrated contributions to the good life of the ordinary man.

For Hook, the central issue of the twentieth century is the contest between totalitarianism and democracy, not between the competing economic systems of capitalism and socialism. He has warned that, if democracy is to be wedded to a religious doctrine or to the Judeo-Christian tradition, it may never succeed in defending free societies against the assault of the ideologies of tyranny. He believes that we need to justify the democratic faith in secular-humanist and empirical terms. Hook exemplifies, perhaps better than anyone else in this century, the two key humanist virtues: critical intelligence and moral courage. Unlike many of his contemporaries, Hook's philosophy expresses a continued confidence in human intelligence and optimism that, with its application, we can resolve many, if not all, of the world's problems. In this regard he is a unique figure in American life.

For their help in preparing this volume, my thanks go to Nicholas Capaldi and David Sidorsky, who served on the original editorial committee. I wish to especially thank Doris Doyle, senior editor of Prometheus Books, for her expert assistance, and also Gregory Vigrass, Steven L. Mitchell, Victor Gulotta, and Lynette Nisbet of the Prometheus staff. Finally, I would like to express my appreciation to the many contributors, all busy individuals, who, in spite of a short deadline, managed to prepare their papers in time to present this volume to Sidney Hook at the dinner given in his honor at the St. Regis Hotel in New York City on October 29, 1982.

PAUL KURTZ

PART I

Sidney Hook the Man

MILTON R. KONVITZ

Sidney Hook: Philosopher of the Moral-Critical Intelligence

I

Reflecting upon his own intellectual life, soon after he had passed his seventieth birthday, Sidney Hook wrote:

> I have, to be sure, learned a great deal about man and society during the half-century almost that has elapsed since reaching philosophical self-consciousness. It has led me time and again to rethink my basic commitment to the pragmatic philosophy and hopefully to a more nuanced and subtle expression of my views. Nonetheless I have found no adequate ground for abandoning or radically modifying my basic position.

Then quickly followed an afterthought. Turning away from looking into his own intellectual history, and looking out on the state of the world about him, he added, with an obvious sadness of conviction, that he and his philosophical colleagues had "assumed too easily that the achievement of intellectual conviction carried with it the moral courage to act on it. Unfortunately, this has not been the case, especially in recent years."

We, however, surveying the same scene, and having before us the record of Sidney Hook's half-century of thought and action, can readily affirm that Hook has himself been an exception to the fact which he so correctly observed. In a singular and towering way, he has had the moral courage to act on his intellectual convictions. His mind, no less than his heart, has always been touched with fire. Thought and action have always been linked, not only in his pragmatic philosophy, but in his life from day to day. As I look upon that life that Sidney Hook has lived, and fortunately continues to live, I cannot help but

3

hear in my mind the words spoken by Justice Holmes in a Memorial Day address a century ago: "I think that, as life is action and passion [but Hook would say "thought" rather than "passion"], it is required of a man that he should share the passion and action of his time at peril of being judged not to have lived." No one will ever be able to say that Sidney Hook has not lived. The reasonable man, he has written, "has impulses but is not impulsive, has emotions but is not emotional, and understands what William James meant about the importance of moral holidays." But Hook himself has not taken moral holidays—or intellectual holidays, or any other holidays. Perhaps even outdoing the watcher of Israel, Sidney Hook neither slumbers nor sleeps. Many of us would ourselves have been more wakeful and more watchful had there been no Sidney Hook out there proving to us that "the achievement of intellectual conviction carried with it the moral courage to act on it." There has been great reliance on him as a surrogate who would effectively expose abuses and usurpations, injuries and oppressions; and the widespread trust in the messenger and his message has never been misplaced. He seems to be blessed with endless vitality; his writings have never revealed a weariness of thought, a slackening of intellectual energy or moral concern. One is tempted to apply to Hook the words of Jeremiah, "great in counsel and mighty in work, whose eyes are open upon all the ways of the sons of men." Readers of his many books and countless articles know that, in one way or another, Sidney Hook has the compulsion and the genius always to point to the higher values, to touch the mainsprings of one's better self, to propel one toward a fuller life and the more enduring joys of life.

More than any other contemporary American, Sidney Hook can be classified among the *philosophes,* thinkers who not only study the world but also try to change it; thinkers who act upon the moral, intellectual, and spiritual world that is the subject of their study; thinkers whose concern with the eternal or ultimate questions does not keep them from a concern with the immediate and intermediate questions that they, together with the rest of mankind, face. Hook reminds us that it is not necessary for people to agree about the meaning of ethical terms before they can determine the best moral policy "with respect to, for example, health care, the reduction of poverty, or treatment of crime." Our value problems, he says, are specific, and "if we take them one at a time, we do not have to settle questions about so-called ultimate values or goals. Our problem is always what to do in this particular case; if I discover that this action rather than another will win friendship (or health or knowledge or money), I do not have to inquire what these are good for or whether they are worth having." But of course, like Plato or Aristotle, like Kant or Hegel, Hook knows how and when to raise questions about ultimate values or goals; but what sets him apart from the conventional professional philosophers is that he is equally at home in the realm of practicalities as in the realm of abstractions. "I do not," he says, "have to be in possession of an ultimate or absolute value in order to choose what is desirable among possible alternatives.'' Many solutions are quite acceptable even though they fall short of being ideal.

Thus, while freely at home in the community of fellow philosophers— Hook was President of the American Philosophical Association (Eastern Division) 1959-60—he is unique among them in enjoying a worldwide audience for his articles in the *New York Times Magazine, Commentary, Encounter, American Scholar, Free Inquiry,* and other journals of public opinion and public affairs, and as a founder and leader of the Conference on Methods in Philosophy and Science, the American Committee for Cultural Freedom, the Conference on Scientific Spirit and Democratic Faith, the University Centers for Rational Alternatives, and the League for Industrial Democracy. When intellectuals in Europe, Latin America, Japan, or Israel try to think of a colleague in contemporary America, in most cases one of the first names that will come to them is that of Sidney Hook.

A poignant example of how ultimate and immediate problems and values are interlocked in the mind 'of Hook is the statement he has written for his biography in *Who's Who in America* as a reflection upon his principles and ideals:

> It is better to be a live jackal than a dead lion—for jackals, not men. Men who have the moral courage to fight intelligently for freedom have the best prospects of avoiding the fate of both live jackals and dead lions. Survival is not the be-all and end-all of a life worthy of man. Sometimes the worst thing we can know about a man is that he has survived. Those who say life is worth living at any cost have already written for themselves an epitaph of infamy, for there is no cause and no person they will not betray to stay alive. Man's vocation should be the use of the arts of intelligence in behalf of human freedom.

II

Born in New York in 1902 and brought up in working-class areas of the city, Hook at an early age discovered in himself a strong social interest which almost naturally propelled him toward the writings of Marx and Engels. But also in his youth he was fascinated by philosophical inquiry—he recalls how his imagination was fired by the amateur epistemological discussion in Jack London's *Martin Eden.* Early in his life, too, he was exposed to the books by Henry Charles Lea, William Edward Lecky, and John W. Draper, and thus found himself in a rationalistic revolt against superstition and organized religion, a position that was strengthened as he experienced or observed religious intolerance and discrimination.

At the College of the City of New York, Hook studied under Morris Raphael Cohen, whom he later described as the first critical mind he had encountered in the educational wilderness, and who gave him a sense for logical method and evidence. The study of logic led Hook to metaphysics and to the works of Bertrand Russell. As a graduate student at Columbia, he first came under the influence of Frederick J. E. Woodbridge, from whose "modified Aristotelianism" he was led away by John Dewey, who had the most enduring intellectual and personal influence on Hook.

One must exercise caution, however, in speaking of intellectual influences on a person who by temperament is unable to be a follower. Hook can be a friend but not a disciple. He selected from Marx and Engels, from Cohen and Russell, from Woodbridge and Dewey only those elements in their thoughts and ways of thinking that appealed to him and could meet the tests imposed by his own critical faculty. His own temperament played crucial selective and directive roles in the way his thoughts developed and the lines of action he chose to take from time to time. Hook himself has written that there is a connection between temperament and thought. The former, he wrote,

> which loves peace above all other values and sees in the ordered routines of professional, social and personal life the best methods of achieving it is likely to embrace in thought the calm options of eternity and invariance, if not the consolations of outright theology. The temperament which enjoys battle, for which variety is a genuine good, which values the perplexities that attend the pursuit of incompatible goods as the opportunities for creative action, is likely to follow the vital option of experimentalism.

He has also noted that, at least in extreme situations, reason alone does not determine the course of action. Character and habit, among other things, also play a role.

No one, of course, Hook has noted, has a temperament that loves only peace or only battle, but the dominant pattern will assert itself. There can be little doubt that by temperament Hook loves battle, variety, coping with the perplexities that attend the confrontation between competing values, and that the path he generally follows is that of experimentalism.

III

Hook has variously described or named his *Weltanschauung* as experimentalism, or experimental naturalism, or pragmatic naturalism. Most recently, however, he has called it simply pragmatism, or "the philosophy of pragmatism in the tradition of Charles Peirce and John Dewey." His basic conviction is that "there is only one reliable method of reaching the truth about the nature of things anywhere and at any time" and that "this reliable method comes to full fruition in the methods of science." Most recently Hook has written that, in its broadest sense as a philosophy of life, pragmatism "holds that the logic and ethics of scientific method can and should be applied to human affairs." This implies, he went on to say, "that one can make warranted assertions about values as well as facts." Although Hook's pragmatism recognizes that there are differences between questions of fact and questions of value, and that the latter require the use of different methods of inquiry and testing in ascertaining objective knowledge about them, nonetheless pragmatism "holds that it is possible to gain objective knowledge not only about the best means available to achieve given ends—something freely granted—but also about the best ends in the problematic situations in which the ends are disputed or become objects of conflict."

However, despite his repeated stress on scientific method and his claims for its far-reaching relevance and applicability, Hook generally succeeds in avoiding the charge of scientism, which critics are prone to make, by recognizing the legitimacy of "reason," "intelligence," or "common sense." Even though the scientific method is of supreme importance, it is not an "absolute." There is a legitimate place for even "good sense," which, "like a sense of tact or humor," has "as deep a root in our generic structure as in our learned behavior." What it all comes down to is that there may be so many relevant factors entering a decision, "regardless of whether the issue is political, personal or scientific, that one cannot formulate a rule prescribing reasonable behavior in all conceivable circumstances. What seems warranted is the assertion that, given the concrete circumstances of any decision, investigation will show that all possible decisions are not equally justifiable, that some are better than others."

The important point to be noted here is that Hook's pragmatism includes more—far more—than dedication to the scientific method. It includes the use of and reliance on intelligence, reason, common sense, good sense, and, as evidenced by his *Who's Who* statement of belief as well as by other statements to which we will soon refer, a strong commitment to certain ideals of life which a decent person will hold even in the face of death.

Hook's pragmatism effectively limits his naturalism and scientific temper. Hook emphasizes that man lives in an open universe in which our own ideas and actions play a creative role. What we choose to do makes a difference. We can influence events. There is no foreordination that should make us optimists or pessimists. With William James, Hook believes that a melioristic attitude toward life and the world is justified. Man is not powerless as he faces the world, for the outer world is not closed but is an open world, an unfinished world, one that man can, by his own actions, make better or worse. Pragmatism, as formulated by Hook, "denies nothing about the world or man which one truly finds in them, but it sees in men something which is at once . . . more wonderful and more terrible than anything else in the universe—the power to make themselves and the world around them better or worse." Against every cult of inevitability—whether it be a form of religious Providence or predestination, or a form of Marxist historical materialism, or Bertrand Russell's "free man's" or Stoic quietism—Sidney Hook consistently and insistently teaches the moral necessity to think for oneself, to act knowingly, to give to challenges that we face a total intellectual, moral, and spiritual response.

For ideas are not mere consolations. They are that, but ideas are also tools that must be used, that can be vindicated, that must be tested. The scientific method is generally the best way we have to subject ideas to the test of experience. And to do this, Hook maintains, is a *moral duty*. The scientific testing of ideas is morally responsible action.

It is hard to tell from his writing whether Hook intends to place his main emphasis on the moral necessity to use the scientific method or on his belief in man's freedom to make the world better or worse. The two ideas are, of course, interdependent, and this, I think, is where Hook would choose to place the emphasis. It is a moral imperative to extend the use of the scientific method to man and society, because it is through the application of the scientific method that the frontiers of knowledge and truth are extended, and because it is through the application of the scientific method that man can best assert his freedom to bring about a better, richer, more wholesome and fuller life for himself and humanity, and thus man may succeed to extend the frontiers of his freedom—freedom from ignorance, freedom from what Bertrand Russell spoke of as Fate.

It would be wrong, however, to suggest that Hook believes that man's freedom is an absolute one. We are only relatively free. Our options are not limitless. We act within limits. But within these limits, we *are* free to act. Were our options limitless, the world would be an anarchic place. We would need an infinite time to choose among infinite possibilities—under such circumstances, the will would in effect be paralyzed, there would be no room for action at all.

IV

Man's relative freedom does not move in a vacuum. There are values that beckon for recognition and selection. And one does not "have to be in possession of an ultimate or absolute value in order to choose what is desirable among possible alternatives. . . . We have *many* 'ultimate' values: love, work, knowledge, family, friendship, art, country. Our problems result because they conflict with each other." Some values are compatible with each other, some are incompatible. Some differences can be resolved by reason, some only by conflict. What is demanded is reasonableness; however, reasonableness "is not synonymous with sweet compliance nor does it exclude the judicious use of force. What it requires only is the offer . . . to negotiate conflict in the hope of reaching an acceptable, even if not ideal, solution." The process of reasoning cannot be expected to go on indefinitely. A reasonable man must know when it is time to stop reasoning; and reason "is the judge of its own legitimate use and limitation. Reason is not so much *reasoning* as it is good sense."

Values—or principles—"are a necessary but not a sufficient guide, for the simple reason that more than one principle is involved." And the number of factors that almost invariably enter into a decision are so many—whether the issue is political, personal, or scientific—"that one cannot formulate a rule prescribing reasonable behavior in all conceivable circumstances." There is no

Golden Rule, Hook would say, unless it be the commandment or necessity to be reasonable.

> What seems warranted is the assertion that, given the concrete circumstances of any decision, investigation will show that all possible decisions are not equally justifiable, that some are better than others . . .

In the most important decisions we are called upon to make, as well as in the ordinary affairs of each day,

> reason never operates alone but always in relation to our fears and hopes, desires and passions. But it [i.e., reason] is not their slave because . . . its insight and foresight give us some power to reconstruct them [i.e., our fears and hopes, desires and passions] and to modify the attitudes we bring to the assessment of fact. There is a continuum of ends and means in our attempt to think our way out of our predicaments. The means we select to realize our ends redetermine the ends which in turn lead us to modify the means. . . . Means are not merely means but integral parts of the end."

Reason, then, always faces alternatives, among which it must make a choice, a decision. There are many "ultimate" values; none among them is absolute; each makes its own bid for recognition and choice. The fanatic is one who knows what his goal or end is and is willing to sacrifice everything else to it, "to repudiate all the other ends of life for the sake of one overriding concern or supreme end. No matter how exalted the supreme end may be— whether knowledge or art, love or friendship, pleasure or purity, justice or glory—whoever is prepared to sacrifice all other ends to it is a moral monster."

It is not clear, however, how this last statement is consistent with Hook's formulation in *Who's Who,* which forcefully asserts that in an extreme situation a decent person should choose to die rather than betray a cause. To me this means that a moral person may feel compelled, in an extreme case, to act as a "fanatic," and that Hook would approve, and even commend, such an action. Thomas More chose to become a dead lion rather than to continue to live as a live jackal. As he walked to his death, Thomas More was no "fanatic" in a pejorative sense. In his own honorable way, he made his substantial contribution to human freedom. There are, then, situations in which a person must be prepared to sacrifice all other ends to a supreme end that is so exalted that he is willing and ready to give up even his life for it.

In a war, is not every fighting soldier in such a situation? Whether or not he has reasoned his way into his condition, he is in it nonetheless. In a non-pejorative sense, every soldier ready to sacrifice his life for his country is a "fanatic," and somehow relates himself with Thomas More, Giordano Bruno, Socrates, and countless other martyrs, named and nameless, who, not without reason, chose to become dead lions rather than be guilty of an unthinkable betrayal. There are, indeed, times when a man must feel compelled to say, with Luther, *Ich kann nicht anders.* At such a time he acts *as if* there is a supreme end, an absolute, a Golden Rule, an ultimate ideal, a commandment that he *must* obey, no matter at what cost. He has reached a point at which reasoning has terminated, even if it means that his life, too, must then terminate.

This does not necessarily mean that there are values which all men will agree are ultimate or absolute; but perhaps all will agree that every person ought to believe that there are, indeed, some values or ideals which he may one day feel compelled to vindicate at the cost of his life *as if* they ought to be universally considered ultimate or absolute. "Few human beings will contest the statements," says Hook, "that sight is better than blindness, knowledge better than ignorance, health than illness, and freedom than slavery, and that as a rule truthfulness, gratitude, fidelity, sincerity, friendship, kindness, and so on, are preferable to their opposites." "With rare exceptions," Hook has written, "human beings are not so simply organized that they can live at peace with themselves if, for the sake of survival, they betray friends, family, country, and the very ideals and values that are integral to their personalities." "We have," Hook has said, "*many* 'ultimate' values: love, work, knowledge, family, friendship, art, country." It is true, of course, that our "problems result because they conflict with each other." But when the conflict is resolved, when one value comes out as the victor, then is it not, then and there, *ultimate* without quotation marks?

This point should not be taken in any way that would minimize the fact, insistently made by Hook, that our moral predicament arises because our values are competitive. Our inner struggles are seldom between good and evil; more often they are between one good and another: between work and play, between truthfulness and kindness, between prudence and generosity. We pray, "Lead us not into temptation." But the temptation is often not an evil but a lesser good—the instant gratification of a lesser good in place of a deferred gratification of a more enduring good. Our agony of choice, Hook has observed, "results from the realization that right conflicts with right, good with good and sometimes the right with the good. We want both security and adventure and can't have both. We want to be just but discover we cannot be just without being cruel. We want to be loyal, but if we are, we can't be truthful and vice versa. We want to be free to live our life but find that we cannot do so except on the ruins of another's life. These are typical moral dilemmas. To the extent that we resolve moral conflicts, one right or good is sacrificed to another." Sidney Hook is altogether right in placing stress on this point, which is at the heart of the human predicament and so often the cause of heartbreak.

But when Hook goes beyond this and asserts categorically that "there is no one *alleinseligmachende Wert*—no specific all-sanctifying value—that one upholds at all costs in all circumstances," one feels compelled to recall his poignant—and commendable—statement in *Who's Who.*

V

Professor Hook raises the question, "Is it at all plausible to hold that, although ethically there can be no absolute human rights, there can or should be absolute constitutional rights, political or juridical freedoms, that may never be abridged in any circumstances?" Hook has addressed this question repeatedly over the years, in many of his writings, and one of his most important contributions to constitutional thought has been his concern with and resolution of this deeply significant problem.

Those who regard themselves as absolutists have, says Hook, overlooked a number of important considerations: (1) The concept of freedom cannot be totally open-ended. Obviously we must limit the freedom of criminals and madmen. (The jury verdict and the court's judgment in the case of John W. Hinckley, Jr., who attempted to assassinate President Reagan, has dramatically focused attention on this aspect of the problem of freedom.) Not all freedoms can be enjoyed or are desirable. "The cry for freedom is always a demand for a specific freedom, . . . for something that can be defended as reasonable, for a justified claim. It is inescapably normative." (2) A demand for a specific freedom entails a restriction on another person's freedom. If I am to have freedom of speech, then others are not free to demand that I be prevented from speaking. If the union is free to strike, then others are not free to enjoin or punish the strikers. (3) Our freedoms are often incompatible. Freedom of speech may affect a man's right to a fair trial. Freedom of knowledge may be an invasion of another's right of privacy.

On the central problem of freedom of speech and communication, Hook takes his stand with the position of Justices Holmes and Brandeis, one which he characterizes as "realistic liberalism." In brief, the position is that freedom of speech in a democratic society is of strategic importance. But, though this freedom has central importance, we must recognize "that at certain times, places, and occasions, in the interest of preserving the whole cluster of freedoms essential to a functioning democracy, some expressions may have to be curbed. I do not believe that one criterion or test can be found that will satisfy our reflective moral sense in all situations where some limit on expression is justified." There are times and occasions when "reasonable and temporary" limitation on speech is necessary and justified, in behalf of other human rights. If talk may not literally kill, "it can trigger the action that does kill." Sometimes, 'in the interest of preserving the entire structure of our desirable freedoms, we may be compelled to abridge one or another of our strategic freedoms for a limited time or in a limited place."

Since the problem that we face is one presented by the competition of different freedoms, Justice Frankfurter's notion of "balancing" is relevant and useful. Professor Hook, after a careful analysis of the arguments against "balancing" that have been offered by Justice Black and others, concludes that in the end they turn out to be "variations of the view that it is dangerous and ultimately disastrous to make exceptions to general rules. Many effective replies can be made to these arguments, but it is enough to say that, granting the danger of making exceptions to general rules, it is sometimes more dangerous and harmful not to make exceptions.''

In another context, Hook has said: "If the talk is likely to precipitate violence in consequence of the speaker's incitement, he should be barred. The line may be hard to draw but it is the precise task of intelligence to draw it. . . . *Sometimes* it is necessary to pass a red light to avoid a disastrous accident, and to fight fire with fire.'' In another essay, he asks, "After all, what is our intelligence for, if not to find appropriate stopping places?'' Perhaps more than any other philosopher or critic in our time, Professor Hook has exposed the flimsiness and foolishness of the slippery-pole argument: If you give an inch, how do you know where to stop? If one were to take the slippery-pole argument seriously, one would never shake hands, or hold hands, or start eating or drinking, or start a lecture. One recalls the statement of Justice Holmes, which reaches out far beyond the limits of the case before him: "The power to tax is not the power to destroy while this court sits.'' This is not to say that it is always easy to know where to draw the line. Every legislator, every judge, every parent, every neighbor, every friend, every person—if he is not criminally corrupt or insane—continually faces this problem, and continually resolves the problem. It is a lifelong process, which ends only with the end of life itself.

It should be noted, however, that Justice Frankfurter's "balancing'' process no longer plays a significant role in the Supreme Court's jurisprudence, at least not on the expressed or ostensible level of adjudication. It has been largely displaced by the "compelling interest'' and "strict scrutiny'' approach. When a right or an interest is involved, such as the Court has found to be a "fundamental'' right—a term that encompasses more than what Hook means by "strategic'' right—or when the legislation or action attacked is such as to adversely affect a "discrete and insular'' minority, constituting a "suspect'' classification, then the action or legislation under attack is subject to "strict scrutiny'' by the Court. For example, in *Shapiro* v. *Thompson* (1969), the Supreme Court had before it statutes under which welfare assistance was denied to persons who had not resided within their jurisdictions for at least one year. The Court, using the "compelling interest'' test, held these acts unconstitutional as an impingement upon the affected persons' "fundamental right'' to travel freely from state to state. These statutes were "suspect'' for the reason that the classification "touched on the fundamental right of interstate movement.'' The Court said: "Since the clasification here touches on the fundamental right of interstate movement, its constitutionality must be judged by the stricter standard of whether it promotes a *compelling* state interest.''

The new test of constitutionality, which has been used by the Court since the 1960s, does not change the fact that what the Court is called upon to do is to make a choice between two competing rights or interests. On the one hand, there was the reasonable fear of states that the elimination of a reasonable residence requirement would result in a heavy influx of individuals into the states providing the most generous welfare benefits. On the other hand, there was the contention that all citizens are constitutionally free to travel throughout the length and breadth of the land uninhibited by laws that impose burdens on needy persons. The argument of the states that the waiting period of one year facilitates the planning of the welfare budget was not such a "compelling governmental interest" as to override the exercise of the needy person's fundamental right to travel. In a sense, one may argue, the Court was still engaged in a "balancing" process; but the process is one that is much more weighted in favor of fundamental rights as against a conventional governmental right. The new process involves the principle that some rights, denominated as "fundamental," are of a higher dignity than other rights; that legislation curtailing such fundamental rights must be subjected, in judicial review, to a scrutiny that is "strict"; that such legislation will not pass such an examination in the absence of the state's establishing, to the Court's satisfaction, that the statute reasonably advances the state's "compelling interest," and that it is narrowly tailored to serve that interest. I think that it can be safely said that Justice Frankfurter, who died in 1965, would not have accepted the new constitutional development, for he strongly believed that the Court must exercise stern self-restraint in interfering with the popular will as expressed in legislation enacted by the people's representatives. He thought that in this respect he was following in the footsteps of Justice Holmes, the Court's most vigorous proponent of the philosophy of "judicial restraint." He did not agree that some constitutional rights or liberties enjoyed a "preferred" place, or that some issues justified "strict scrutiny." Frankfurter considered that the "enduring contribution of Mr. Justice Holmes to American history is his constitutional philosophy." This judgment is still valid, but it is doubtful that one could make the same judgment about Justice Frankfurter's own contribution, for not much of it promises to endure.

While all this, I submit, needed to be said, it does not lessen Sidney Hook's contribution to American constitutional philosophy. His emphasis on the point that while some rights may be of "strategic" importance, none can be considered as an absolute, and his argument that rights do not appear in isolation but in contest one with the other, are lessons that constantly need to be freshly learned. How these lessons are to be applied in constitutional adjudication depends on many factors. As case follows case, and as one member of the Court succeeds another, and as the dominant forces of our society shift and change, and as new values emerge, the public law undergoes development, introducing higher levels of sophistication and complexity. For Holmes, as Frankfurter said, "the Constitution was not primarily a text for dialectic but a means of ordering the life of a progressive people." The ordering of that life calls for new insights no less than for past reason, the recognition of new needs as well as enduring ideals.

To be sure, Hook has written:

the weight of experience is behind the moral injunctions and ideals expressed in
the testaments and commandments of the great religious and ethical systems of
the past. But they cannot all be categorical in all situations because they obviously
conflict. . . . The only absolute is, in John Erskine's phrase, echoing a thought of
John Dewey, 'the moral obligation to be intelligent' in the choice of that course
of conduct among possible alternatives whose consequences will strengthen the
structure of the reflective values that define our philosophy of life.

The logic of Sidney Hook's thought on freedom, I think, brings him close
to the new position of the Supreme Court, which has replaced the "balancing"
test of Frankfurter. "By freedom," Hook has written, "I do not mean the
right to do anything one pleases . . . but the strategic freedoms of speech,
press, assembly, independent trade unions and [an independent] judiciary, and
the cluster of rights associated with democracy in its widest sense. Although
they are interrelated, there is an order of priority in freedoms to guide us when
they conflict." That order of priorities, I assume, can be determined only by
the reflective, critical intelligence, case by case, from time to time. No voice
out of Sinai will be heard to resolve such conflicts, but only the still small voice
of reason.

VI

As Hook applies his pragmatic philosophy to social organization, he sees
himself as a socialist or as a social democrat. He does not hold to the theory of
historical materialism; he is no economic determinist. In our own era, since at
least World War I, Hook has said, "the mode of political decision seems to me
to have had at least as much influence on our culture as the mode of economic
production. This," he added, "is not a matter that can be established by conceptual analysis but by empirical, social, and historical inquiry."

Hook is not afraid that governmental intervention in economic affairs
must necessarily lead to totalitarianism. There are today socialized economies
in totalitarian, despotic countries, but Hook maintains that in all these cases
political democracy was destroyed *before* the economy was socialized.
Moreover, he has noted, "There is not a single democratic country where the
public sector of the economy has grown substantially over the years, either
through socialization or through governmental controls and subsidies
(whether it be England, Sweden, Norway, Holland, or the United States), in
which the dire predictions concerning the extinction or even the radical restrictions of democratic freedoms have been realized." The control or regulation
of the economy in the United States has not led to a diminution of the political
or cultural freedoms. While in welfare states the people have voted the governing political party out of power, not a single Communist country has allowed
its people to institute democracy. Although there can be a terroristic regime in

the absence of Communism, the absolute control of the economy by a Communist party enables it "to reinforce a kind of terror beyond anything previously known in human history, and to use the bread-card and the work-card to enforce conformity." From history and the world as we know it today, Hook concludes that the collectivization of major industries has in it the potential to transform the economy into a powerful engine of human repression, with the consequential loss of political freedom. "Therefore," Hook says, "in the interests of freedom, it is wiser and safer to limit carefully the extent of socialization." In the interests of human rights and freedoms, it is important to preserve a private sector, to encourage considerable private enterprise, to have some regulated industries and some public corporations, to encourage cooperatives, increased worker participation in the operation of industrial plants as well as in the boards of directors of large corporations, and to develop other means of multiplying centers of economic power.

Hook's socialism is, quite obviously, an economic system that operates within a democratic order. It is democratic socialism—hardly, or but barely, an *ism*. It is free from dogmatism. It contemplates a mixed economy, in which the mixing is determined by considerations of welfare and freedom. "The emphasis," says Hook, "must be placed not so much on the *legal form* of property relations but on the moral ideals of democracy as a way of life, conceived as an equality of concern for all citizens of the community to develop themselves as persons to their full growth. The economy should be considered a means to that end."

Again we see that, to Professor Hook, moral and political concerns are primary. He does not endorse a free enterprise uncontrolled economy. Neither Adam Smith nor Karl Marx is his prophet. What will best serve the nation is an economic order that will preserve our basic democratic values and yet maximize the individual's opportunities for self-development—an order that allows "the judicious development of the democratic welfare state pruned of its bureaucratic excrescences." "Morality," Hook has written, "must have primacy over all social phenomena."

VII

As we have seen, Sidney Hook has not hesitated to redefine and reinterpret such terms as pragmatism and socialism. The use and abuse of such and other terms by obscurantists and fanatics have not driven him to invent his own vocabulary—a device often resorted to by philosophers, only to add new obscurities and compound the difficulties of understanding. Yet Hook would not reinterpret "God," and in the list of strategic freedoms, which we quoted above, there is a noticeable absence of "religion." In this matter, Hook chooses a path other than that taken by William James and John Dewey. Perhaps in this he is wiser than most of us? "God," said St. Augustine, "is best known in not knowing Him." And Maimonides said essentially the same.

There is a respectable tradition for God as *deus absconditus.* I would not venture to speak for God, but it is hard to repress the thought that God wishes that the world had more persons who are uncertain of Him in the way of Sidney Hook, and less of those who claim to know Him by name, address, occupation, relatives, friends, enemies. There are gentle religions that teach that God finds most acceptable not those who call on Him by name but those who follow the paths of peace, freedom, and righteousness. God may well be the greatest pragmatist of all, judging ideas and men not by their presuppositions but by their consequences, by their fruit. "We say," Emerson wrote, "that every man is entitled to be valued by his best moment. We measure our friends so." It is thus that we measure Sidney Hook. Would God do less?

NICHOLAS CAPALDI

Sidney Hook
A Personal Portrait

Legend and Myth

For Americans, this is a time of much soul-searching. It is a time when it is difficult to find an idea, not to say an ideal, that can be taken seriously—one not dismissed as intellectually partisan, one not the product of fad or of commercial exploitation—an idea that can stand on its own, without MSG so to speak. Symptomatic of this state of affairs is the special sigh of relief that intellectuals have learned to breathe when all those books that blaze across the pages of the *New York Times Book Review* pass, like comets, before we are obliged to read them. In the absence of serious ideas, perhaps we should look for a serious mind. I have a candidate to recommend—Sidney Hook.

Sidney Hook is both a legend and a myth. Although it is flattering to be a living legend, there is also a price to be paid for it. Legends exist in the realm of fiction and pre-history, so in time we find it inconvenient to take them seriously. For those of us who do daily battle with intellectual pygmies, it is easy to ignore that Hook slew dragons. But even his detractors grudgingly must admit that they enjoy certain privileges because of battles he fought and won before they were old enough to write for, or even to read, the *New York Review of Books*.

Hook is admired by his friends, peers, and students for his brilliance, his courage, and his seemingly unlimited energy in the service of causes to which he is dedicated. He is feared by his enemies because of his polemical skills and his ability to see through rhetoric to the naked ideas within. Yet in the light of all of these dazzling attributes we are in danger of losing sight of the profundity and the integrity of one of the greatest American minds of the twentieth century. The passion that animates his thought is not the product of unscarred youthful enthusiasm but the inexhaustible strength that flows from a mind that has

17

ruthlessly plumbed its own presuppositions. Hook's thought has never lost contact with life.

The myth of Sidney Hook is quite another matter. That myth is a historical drama whose genesis was Hook's endorsement in 1932 of the Communist candidate for the presidency of the United States (in opposition to Roosevelt and Hoover) and whose climax is Hook's presence at the Hoover Institution, considered the most prestigious conservative think tank. This mythical movement from Left to Right is a collective concoction of all those individuals who at one time or another found themselves in the same trench but who now find themselves not only at odds with Hook but the targets of his recent critiques. His former allies wish that the myth were true, but they shrink from analyzing the basis of their wishes. They think that it is they who have kept the faith and that it is Hook who has betrayed it. On the contrary, Hook is one of the few who has consistently adhered to the cause of liberation, and it is his critics who are guilty of a false consciousness. The point of exposing the myth is not to settle old scores but to identify Hook's unique contribution to American intellectual heritage.

"More important than any belief a man holds is the *way* he holds it."

The Philosophy of Liberation

Hook is the most distinguished of John Dewey's students and the greatest living embodiment of the American pragmatic mode of thought. But it is hard to imagine Hook as a mere disciple. He was also the first Marxist professor in America and at a time when it was hardly fashionable. Here again, Hook was no follower, rather he saw in Marx the liberating possibilities that Marx himself had failed to appreciate. One way of making this point is to say that Hook saw the continuity between Marxism and pragmatism at least thirty years before anyone else. More important is the novel way in which Hook combined and understood pragmatism and Marxism, producing an ideology-resistant hybrid philosophy that transcends both of its sources. In short, it is the cross-fertilization of Dewey and Marx that makes Hook the most significant American social and political philosopher of the twentieth century.

Let us first sketch the starting point in Dewey and then add the contribution of Marx. The basic tenet of pragmatism is that action is more fundamental than thought. Efficient practice always precedes theory: and theory both emerges from the practice and modifies it. Failure to ground theory in prior practice produces sterile intellectualism and dangerous utopian schemes. The second tenet is that action cannot be comprehended by mechanistic models but must be understood organically. Neither ideas nor practices are constructed in modules but result from exchanges with their surroundings. In the course of these exchanges or transactions, ideas and practices are qualitatively changed; so the history of these transactions is therefore as crucial as the logic of their momentary structure. Regression to mechanical models makes a mystery of the thought process, including creative problem-solving, and leads to the treating of agents as responding wholly to external causes instead of as responsible beings able to do things. Public policies constructed mechanically lead to bureaucratic technological control instead of liberation.

The theory of values contained in Dewey's pragmatism is neither reactionary nor revolutionary; it is a pivotal reconstruction of Western civilization. Norms are always implicit in previous practice. The application of norms and the reevaluation of norms themselves occurs in a social context, a community of shared values. The shared values or norms are furthered by this reevaluation—in the process we both discover and transform the norms. The process is never final but continuously self-corrective. From this it follows that there can be no elites who possess the final truth or the sole means of access to it—there can be no value-free social science; that democracy is the form of government that most clearly captures the self-corrective element and has the added function of aiding in moral development; that education, as opposed to indoctrination or job-training, is a reconstruction or reevaluation of norms, which, if successful, develops moral character.

There is a strong tendency on the part of popularizers to vulgarize pragmatism into either mindless optimism or a total disregard for principle. The tendency to do the former is a throwback to the teleology and historicism inherent in Hegel, the belief that there are objective built-in goals. Of course, if there is a built-in goal, then something like ultimate fulfillment is possible under certain conditions. On the social level, the belief in built-in goals encourages misguided notions like the convergence theory, the belief that technological developments will eventually lead the Soviet Union to become a humane state. Neither Dewey nor Hook will have anything to do with this. There is no inner teleology, no final moment of fruition. The inability to encompass all goods uncovers the need to make moral choices. This is what Hook argued so passionately in his *Pragmatism and the Tragic Sense of Life*. It is because conflicts are real that moral principles must be taken seriously, that there are ultimately no technical solutions to moral problems. To believe otherwise is to believe that the end justifies any means. The finitude of pragmatism is in standing opposition to such moral self-deception.

Although pragmatism recognizes the crucial importance of the social dimension, it cannot be said that Dewey had any well-worked-out theory of the social world. Dewey was more at home as a psychologist stressing the individual and the organic dimension. Perhaps this is why so much of the literature of pragmatism sounds like unfocused methodology. It is this lack that is supplied by Marx's insights.

Unlike other organisms, human beings do not have a specific nature acquired before birth. Our transactions with nature are mediated by culture. Instead of conceiving transactions along the lines of what "I do," we must take into account that we act in relation to other people—"I and you do" ("we," in anything other than an editorial sense, is a fallacious hypostatization of culture). There is therefore an important break between the cultural and the natural. The cultural (social, historical) dimension certainly contains organic systems within it (just as organic systems may contain mechanical subsystems), but it is not reducible or explainable in wholly organic terms.

In Hook's philosophy, the leap to the foregoing position culminates in a brilliant and novel conception of dialectic that both supplements pragmatism with a powerful capacity for social analysis and avoids the absurdities of dogmatic Marxism. The new concept of dialectic accounts for how culture mediates man's relationships both with the world and with man. The dialectic method sees in all thought the "implicit prediction that certain consequences will follow upon certain actions, and its truth or falsity is established by the set of actions that realizes or fails to realize the predicted consequences" (*The Meaning of Marx,* 1934). The very meaning of an intellectual construct and the realization of its truth requires action. Before we can test a theory, even in so-called hard science, we must first know what it would be like to act consistently with that theory.

Dialectic

Dialectic in Marx is the relation between mind and social history. How we think is always in part a reflection of our cultural history. But, since there are changes both in history and in how we think, the question is raised of the reciprocal relation between mind and social history. Thought about the social world leads to action that changes the social world, which in turn leads to new thoughts. The relation as expressed by Marx is ambiguous. Orthodox Marxists tend to see the relation in such a way that thought is always caused by underlying conditions (material, economic, etc.) so that even when thought seems to direct action it is really a mediate cause rather than an ultimate cause. Despite its function, thought is always derivative.

In Hook's novel version, thought is more creative. Thought guides action in such a way that no social theory can be considered valid unless it is confirmed by subsequent action. Social theories not only describe but prescribe so that action must be taken to confirm the consequences. In performing the action we arrive at crucial self-knowledge. More important, thought is not the mere product of other objective conditions, and that is why change is not cumulative, incremental, and unidirectional (progressive). All change involves choice and redirection. Human action is goal-directed in such a way that it must be consistent with norms shared by others. That is the only way we can coordinate our action with others. Unlike animals who deal directly with nature, we must keep in mind that our action maintains or modifies our culture. Hence any theory we formulate about what we did or are doing can be reflexively developed to decide what to do in the future. This is how acting out a theory can lead us to discover who we are and extend who we are, but it is always done through other human beings as well. In the acting out we become more self-conscious of our reasons and can therefore perform the actions more deliberately. In so doing, we can assume greater responsibility for what we do. This makes social theories ongoing modifications/corrections of our practice.

The dialectical method is applicable to the three broad areas of physical science, social science, and ethics. First, in our understanding of physical science we must realize that it is guided by the aim of technical control over the environment as a way of enhancing survival, the survival of the culture. This is but one instance of how culture mediates between man and world. Second, in the social world theories help us to understand the meaning of our traditions, both preserving and expanding them by creating a consensus among social agents. That is why all social theories are both descriptive and prescriptive. Here culture mediates between man and man. Third, this implies that in ethics what we seek is rational agreement on goals, but such a consensus is only possible among rational and autonomous agents. Thus, at its highest level, the dialectical method reveals how to achieve true liberation by showing that it is implicit in all rational activity. Our dignity emerges not in tying reason to the mere survival of an organism but in recognizing that survival is but one value that expresses a *way* of life.

Hook is the first philosopher to stand dialectic on its head. The great tradition of Western thought, including Marx, looks for permanent structures, no matter how dynamically conceived, and then attempts to mold man to the structure. That is why most social theories abort in some kind of reduction of the social and moral realms to something else. Not so in Hook. By recognizing the break between the cultural and the organic, Hook is able to see that the belief in certain kinds of structure is itself a reflection of the inherent autonomy of man himself. Man can be free and transcend mere survival only in the ultimate self-reflection that he is himself a self-structured and structuring agent. It is the breakthrough provided by this insight that allowed Hook to transcend the illusion of objectivism, the intransigent positivism of the intellectual world, and the fanaticism of other social reformers.

The fundamental character of the social world is that it is an "I and you do" ("we") structure. Any attempt to understand it from a mere "I think" or a mere "I do" perspective distorts both the theory and the reality. The perversion of human relationships may reflect in part the adoption of such abstract starting points. The further mistake of construing the "I" mechanically leads in action to bureaucratic totalitarianism, and when construed just organically it leads to utopian historicism. Historicism, whether Marxist or ritualistically liberal, is to social science what positivism is to natural science—it is an attempt to see the world as a permanent structure. It makes no sense of the moral dimension of life and reduces freedom to the status of a means. The convergence theory is just such a truncated social theory; and the advocacy of pacifism or the silent practice of treason, the hoped for mechanical means of bringing it about. When Hook warns us of the danger of pacifism and disputes the convergence theory, he is not the lackey of capitalist imperialism. This is to forget Hook's critique of the equally implausible myth of a free-market structure. Rather he is a lone voice attacking an inadequate if not insane social theory and pleading the cause of genuine autonony and liberation.

"Those who say life is worth living at any cost have already written for themselves an epitaph of infamy, for there is no cause and no person they will not betray to stay alive. Man's vocation should be the use of the art of intelligence in behalf of freedom."

Hook vs. the Philosophers

The power of Hook's social analysis is its grounding in a philosophy. From the very beginning Hook has argued that the liberation of human thinking is the mainspring of pragmatism's great vitality, and from the very beginning he has had to defend pragmatism from its mindless critics and against the ingrained philosophical tradition. The central metaphysical claim of pragmatism is that the structure of the world is not complete. It is open to new possibilities. That is why we are not the victims of fate, not confined to accept the status quo, and not destined for an inevitable future (rosy or otherwise). To be sure, the world has some structure, otherwise it would be impossible to use any tool: but, if the world had an immutable structure, it would be impervious to instrumental transformation. The major tradition of Western thought is a quest for permanent structure, a quest ironically to which orthodox Marxists are committed. Revolution for them is part of the inherent structure.

Hook's belief in a structured world without complete or completed or completable structure puts him squarely at odds with just about everybody. He is at odds with the Aristotelian notion of substance, and therefore at odds with Thomism, and that explains his opposition to the Hutchins neo-Aristotelian clique in both education and social theory. He is in standing opposition to the positivism and analysis of professional philosophers who pretend that they are engaged in an attempt to arrive at pre-philosophical knowledge that is norm-free.

Hook's professional critics keep confining the pragmatic insight to the trivial contention that reason is an organ of adaptation. At the same time, they continually confuse dialectic with its degenerate version, the sociology of knowledge. But, as Hook has continually pointed out, a radical critique of knowledge is only possible by recognizing that the cultural mediation between man and world goes beyond mere adaptation and survival. All critique is meaningful only in the light of previously accepted social and intellectual norms. Instead of elevating and mystifying technical science as the model of all knowledge, Hook has argued that the scientific method grows out of common sense and is unintelligible without its home base. Perhaps that is why, at a time when so many members of the profession have lost faith in what they do, Hook's students have no such identity crisis.

How can someone who has disagreed so long with just about everybody nevertheless be a beloved, respected, and feared member of the academy? Part of the answer has to do with the false consciousness of professional life. Philosophers tend to deify the notion of an argument as a formal structure just as they tend to reduce all knowledge to technical physical science and fail to see the implicit norms within it. On the other hand, the business of life, including professional life, cannot be made intelligible and operate from that perspective. Instead of telling us what the final structure of a good argument is, Hook demonstrates in the very air he breathes the consummate skills of a polemicist, a controversialist, and a persuader. It is because in real life one has to ferret out the norms in order to get down to business. No one dares to argue with Hook for very long, and when the profession has to defend the validity of its own enterprise it turns to Hook. He practices what he preaches, and he preaches what he practices. Therein lies his advantage over others. There is an old-fashioned expression for this attribute: intellectual integrity.

Hook as Social Gadfly

Because of his conception of dialectic, Hook is able to provide an account of the social world and man's place within it that puts to shame the whole gamut of contemporary dogmatisms. Because culture, understood dialectically, is the medium through which man approaches the world and man himself, it follows that culture is not reducible either to abstract man or to abstract nature. Culture is not, first of all, a reflection of innate teleology. Hence the social world cannot be inferred from a collection of frozen psychological facts. It is also why Hook rejects any strictly conservative view seeking to immunize some alleged core that is not to be tampered with. Culture, moreover, is not the simple by-product of instrumental reason. As we have already seen, instrumental reason is itself unintelligible without culture. This means that social life is not the residue of coping with the environment. That is why Hook rejects all forms of determinism—historical, economic, and environmental. He can equally criticize both classical liberals and Marxists who try to make all human values mere reflections of economic forces. On the one hand, he can criticize obsolete power structures and, on the other hand, he can criticize ritualistic liberals for destroying the very cultural foundations that permit liberation by treating them as objects to other means. As a pragmatist Hook can recognize how technological progress increases the prospects of survival, and as a dialectician he can recognize that it is not mere survival, but the survival of a particular way of life, that is important. Most of all it is Hook's conception of dialectic that frees reflection of self-consciousness so that it becomes a form of moral autonomy. He is the sworn enemy of those theorists who see all social problems as resolvable through technical-bureaucratic means rather than through rational action. As against the old guard, Hook can recognize that you do not improve a man's life simply by increasing his paycheck. As against the new radicals, he sees that the quality of social life does not change simply by putting new faces into the power structure or on postage stamps. His object is not just to change the world but to make it more free. Shunning all labels, it is easy to predict where Hook will be on the next big issue; he will be on the side of freedom.

Rational solutions to social problems require communal agreement on goals and purposes. Such agreement is not possible except among creatures whose autonomy and sense of responsibility are the result of acquiring that knowledge or wisdom that transcends mere survival. Radicals, old and new, cannot really believe in autonomy because they do not understand it. Autonomy cannot be caused by economic conditions and still be autonomy. To understand autonomy requires a recognition that culture is not a by-product, and to recognize this is to confront all of the moral dilemmas that mere technical reason cannot solve. This underscores more than anything else the importance of education, because it is in our educational institutions that we are supposed to advance to the wisdom of autonomy and responsibility. Radicals and ritualistic liberals are so busy fretting over conditions or improving conditions that they fail to deal with how to make people aware of their autonomy and sense of responsibility.

A common story in the twentieth century is the story of those radicals who have come to see the moral blindness of radicalism, who recognize the failure of technocratic solutions to moral problems, but who then drift into the old irrational faiths. The drift from one form of dogmatism to another is understandable. The eventual recognition that life must have a moral dimension is commendable. The crucial question is why do these thinkers, including the noble Solzhenitsyn, believe that man needs something outside of himself? Sidney Hook is the best known secular humanist of our time. He has always recognized the moral dimension, and he has never subscribed to the cult of hedonistic fulfillment. I suspect that the reason for this difference is that most of those who have placed man in nature, at the center of nature in fact, have given man a fixed structure. Given a fixed structure, it then becomes impossible to explain how such a fixed structure could develop a sense of moral autonomy. What distinguishes Hook's theory and what enables him to avoid the degradation that Solzhenitsyn warns us about is the insight about dialectic that we have stressed. We all recognize the evil done by a false self-image, and we all strive to arrive at a true one. But a true self-image is not the grasping through pure theory of a permanent structure either inside or outside of man. Man's relationship to the world and to other men is always mediated by the prior norms of our culture. We never arrive at the Archimedian point of norm-free vision even when we revise our norms. But herein lies our autonomy! That we are always responsible for the interpretation and reinterpretation without appeal to anything else is our autonomy.

Although many individuals are familiar with Hook's activity as an anti-communist, few are aware of the principled basis upon which this activity operates. Perhaps the best example and expression of this principled approach is Hook's condemnation of Senator McCarthy in a letter to the *New York Times* (May 8, 1953). Let me quote from the letter in defense of Kaghan and Wechsler. "Even those who, for reasons of their own, are inclined to be silent about Senator McCarthy's methods must be aware of the incalculable harm he is doing to the reputation of the United States abroad. The evidence mounts daily that he is a heavy liability to the friends of American democracy and international freedom, and an obstacle to all efforts to counteract Communist lies about the true nature of American society . . . hounding former Communists who are now actively engaged in the defense of liberty against the totalitarian threat . . . The time has come to organize a national movement of men and women of all political parties to retire Senator McCarthy from public life."

Seemingly, the most paradoxical element in Hook's thought is his socialism. Perhaps one way of removing the paradox is to ask the question, "Is Hook a democratic socialist or is he a social democrat?" I think he is the latter. There is nothing more deeply ingrained than Hook's commitment to democracy, and that is why he is so resented by radicals, lunatics, and extremists who would gladly sacrifice democracy on the altar of some utopian scheme. More to the point is Hook's conception of socialism. He never believed in a bureaucratically central-ized economy, nor does he subscribe to the naively deterministic view that economic conditions are the cause of all other social affairs. Hook's notion of socialism, like J. S. Mill's, is a repudiation of the crude social Darwinism of the turn of the century, a plea for a decent minimum standard of humane living (but recall that, since Hook does not believe in ultimate fulfillment, this is not some-thing the state or anything else can provide), but most of all it exemplifies the thesis that *the social world is something we jointly create with others*. There is thus a special sense in which we must assume some responsibility for it. This is another consequence of Hook's conception of dialectic, in which we structure our future but only in negotiating it with others. The human level of existence does not emerge from the natural by the movement of abstractions like economic man or the forces of history, rather it is a product mediated by culture. In a truly liberated society of autonomous and responsible citizens we would have a nonauthoritarian consensus. This does not mean that we accept the naive assumption that all dialogue in a democracy is honest, but it does maintain that without democratic dialogue we cannot obtain autonomy and responsibility. Finally, when we come to recognize the difference between the paternalism of being our brother's keeper and the respect for the autonomy of others, we shall have progressed from liberalism to liberation.

Hook is now engaged in one of the most important battles of his life, the fight against affirmative action, the latest and most dangerous of all ritualistic liberal shibboleths. Affirmative action is the policy of delivering dignity to people by bureaucratic means. It is the ultimate contradiction of asking, "What can we do to make other people feel self-respect?" This policy threatens to destroy the bastion of our culture, namely, the university. It is the policy of treating education as a determinant of social mobility rather than as an opportunity for the pursuit of wisdom as moral autonomy. If the university falls, there will be no place from which the reevaluation of norms can take place.

If this battle were not so serious we could pause to enjoy a delicious irony. Many of those who recognize the dangers of the new authoritarianism are unable to combat it effectively. These other members of the academy, including social scientists who advise presidents and kings, these experts on the social world, have not the slightest idea of how to organize an opposition. So, to whom do they turn in time of trouble, to Sidney Hook. The problem cannot be solved with graphs, nor will the skills of petty bureaucracy handle a moral confrontation. The social world is not a technical abstraction, but it is the field of dialectic, *par excellence*. It is because he first formulated the requisite sense of dialectic that Hook is able to lead us out of the technological and moral barbarism that lies on all sides.

Although his closest friends believe him to be indestructible, we must raise the question of what happens after he is gone. The future is not bright. It is of little comfort to be reminded of how many clever people there are in the world. Clever is not profound. Nor is much comfort to be derived from a survey of the great philosophical minds of the twentieth century. Other than Hook, there has not been a single eminent philosopher who has so distinguished himself. There is, more accurately, no one other than Hook whose social philosophy is so indissolubly linked with his philosophy as a whole. Despite all of his well-publicized stances, Bertrand Russell denied any connection between philosophy and morality. He will also be remembered for his indiscretion that red is better than dead. In the case of Heidegger, it is not the Nazi blunder that shakes us but rather his failure ever to write an ethical treatise. Did the man ever think any ethical issue through to the end? Finally, it is difficult to fathom the connection between Sartre's ersatz Marxism and the pitiful image of the philosopher distributing leaflets on the street. Sartre found it difficult too, perhaps, and never wrote the promised second volume about his social theory. No doubt there are those who draw a firm line between theory and practice. But I strongly suspect that this is why no meaningful change will ever be attributed to them. In the case of Sidney Hook the world is different because of him. Some of us would add, it is also better.

IRVING KRISTOL

Life with Sidney: A Memoir

My first published article was an attack on Sidney Hook. I was twenty-one. It was an act of the rankest ingratitude, though not, I suppose, entirely unexpected in a young man of ideological pretensions and more intellectual arrogance than, he would later realize, he was entitled to.

The ingratitude derived from the fact that for the previous four years (1938–1941) Sidney had been the thinker and writer who had had the most decisive influence on me. He was not, alas, my teacher in the literal sense. He was at New York University, I was at CCNY, and I did not have the pleasure of meeting him, and of forming a deep, lasting friendship, until the late 1940s. But his books and articles were revelations to me.

The books were *From Hegel to Marx* and, especially, *Toward the Understanding of Karl Marx.* (The latter book I must have re-read at least half a dozen times.) The articles were in the *Marxist Quarterly* and *Partisan Review.* I was at that time a Trotskyist sympathizer and, consequently, a Marxist—but a Marxist who was constantly chafing at Marxist orthodoxy. Various aspects of Marxist doctrine troubled me; such authoritative expositors of Marxism as Plekhanov and Kautsky (in their earlier years, of course) seemed to me to be awfully simple-minded; Lenin struck me as repellingly dogmatic; Trotsky was dizzyingly brilliant but one was never absolutely certain of his intellectual rectitude. It was in the midst of these festering uncertainties—sure portents of future heterodoxy—that Sidney unwittingly moved me to a quick liberation from Marxism entirely.

I still vividly recall the first moment of liberating illumination. I was sitting at a table in the main reading room of the New York Public Library, reading a bound volume of the *Marxist Quarterly,* in which Sidney had published a devastating critique of Engels's dialectical materialism, especially as applied to the laws of nature. I was immediately and absolutely persuaded. One of the

27

pillars of Marxist orthodoxy vanished into nothingness before my very eyes. And if Engels (with Marx's approval) could be so incredibly silly about dialectical materialism, might not both these Founding Fathers be just as wrong on other, equally important matters? Only a few years later, Leon Trotsky, in a polemic against James Burnham, declaimed that "he who says 'A' must say 'B'"—that is, the rejection of dialectical materialism would mark the undoing of a Marxist, a process that would inexorably lead to an ultimate secession from socialism itself. Trotsky's logic, as Sidney pointed out at the time, was radically defective. But Trotsky's insight into the psychology of Marxists was quite astute. A minor operation on a totalistic *Weltanschauung* could cause the whole structure to crumble, sometimes slowly, sometimes rapidly. In my case, the process moved far more rapidly than even I anticipated. A year or so later, having distanced myself from the Trotskyists but still regarding myself as "a kind of democratic socialist," I was in fact well on the way to entertaining all sorts of "counterrevolutionary" ideas.

In this process, too, Sidney played a crucial role, though this time of a more positive kind. His writings taught me how to think analytically, provided me with at least a veneer of sophistication in logic, scientific method, and philosophical analysis. His *Toward the Understanding of Karl Marx* was, for me, less an exposition of Marxism than an introduction to Dewey's pragmatism, just as his *Marxist Quarterly* essay introduced me to contemporary philosophy of science. After a few months of feverish reading, and discussion with like-minded friends, I was convinced that, though Marxism held many important truths, it made more sense to incorporate these truths into a non-Marxist social philosophy than—as Sidney was then trying to do—incorporate all non-Marxist truths into a fundamentally revised edition of Marxian socialism. From that point on, as Trotsky would say, it was downhill all the way. By the time World War II came to an end, I couldn't see that there were any "Marxist truths" at all. All of the criticisms of modern capitalism I wished to make—for I then still thought of myself as vaguely left of center—needed no reference to the Marxist canon, and indeed could be much better made without such reference.

To return to that first essay of mine: in addition to being impudent, it clearly contained the seeds of future "deviation." My critique of Sidney was twofold. The first part, from a conventional "left" perspective, was a critique of Sidney for daring to favor the intervention of the United States in World War II, then in its earliest stages. It was a routine critique, of a kind also made by Norman Thomas and Dwight Macdonald, and it is not worth mentioning except to note that Sidney was right and I was wrong. But the second part of my criticism was devoted to Sidney's philosophy—to his "rationalism," his "pragmatism," which I found too thin a gruel for my developing philosophical appetite. For by then I had moved beyond Dewey to Reinhold Niebuhr and Paul Tillich and had concluded that no satisfactory social philosophy could be based on Dewey's secularist, rationalist pragmatism, since its conception of human nature was too bland and superficial.

How was it possible that Dewey, so important in freeing me from Marxism, so soon lost his hold over me? Well, it does seem to be the case that, ever since my adolescence, I have had the kind of permanent metaphysical itch that favorably predisposed me to religion (or at least religiosity) in general, and made it impossible for me ever to take secular humanism seriously as an intellectual option. Even while I tried to be a Marxist, I was reading Plato and actually liking his transcendental approach to reality. And even while Hook and Dewey were opening avenues away from Marxism, I could not help but think of the Bible as the most *important* of all books, containing ultimate if enigmatic truths that no mere philosopher or philosophy could encompass.

This issue of secular humanism has, for forty years now, been a matter on which Sidney and I have amiably agreed to disagree. He has, I think, been more puzzled than disconcerted by my obstinate refusal to find naturalism and humanism a sufficient philosophy of nature and/or life. ("Does Irving *really* believe in God?" he once inquired of my wife.) I, in turn, have concluded that there are many intelligent and thoughtful people, of whom Sidney is but one, who are "tone deaf" to certain dimensions of human experience, and that it is not particularly fruitful—though it can be a wit-sharpening exercise—to engage them in philosophical debate. Oddly enough, Sidney's very first publication, *The Metaphysics of Pragmatism,* did not so firmly exhibit his later philosophical stance; it is, in my opinion, his best purely philosophical work and should be more widely read and better known than it is. But that work pointed down a path not taken—repressed, one suspects, by the overwhelming personal influence of Dewey.

But all such intellectual tensions between Sidney and myself have remained on the margin during our joint involvement in over three decades of political debate and political controversy. Sidney's pragmatism would inevitably lead him to a certain indifference as to the more ultimate sources—or presumed sources—of people's political beliefs; and, in any case, pragmatism as a guide to political and social action, as distinct from philosophical contemplation, has an intellectual power that only a fanatic or a utopian would be immune to. So it was only rarely that I found myself uneasy in following Sidney's lead and guidance on the issues of the day.

And it was in bringing his extraordinary intellectual powers to bear on particular issues of social or political controversy that Sidney has been most effective as an educator, an intellectual torch-bearer. These days, one watches with a mixture of bemusement and bewilderment the efforts of academic philosophers to demonstrate their "relevance" by publishing articles on current social issues. How pointless and pathetic they appear when compared with the essays of Sidney over the years! The dominance of "analytical philosophy" in our university departments, with its imposition of the fact-value distinction on human affairs, with its insistence on "clarification through linguistic analysis," and with its further insistence that such clarification must lead all reasonable men to but one reasonable conclusion, has rendered the current crop of philosophers impotent in their efforts at intervention in the mundane affairs of the polity. Has any subscriber to *Philosophy and Public Affairs* ever actually experienced a change of mind or attitude as a consequence of reading an article in that journal? Indeed, does anyone who is concerned with social policy but is not an academic philosopher read that journal? Not even a John Rawls, the most influential of such philosophers, would find it possible to claim that his writings, which have stimulated an avalanche of academic criticism, exegesis, and emendation, have shaped nonacademic thinking about public affairs. On the contrary: it is not unjust to assert that, in its basic assumptions, his work merely reflects a current of nonacademic thinking about public affairs. It is more political theology (of a secular type, to be sure) than political philosophy.

In contrast, Sidney Hook's writings on such particular issues as civil liberties and nuclear disarmament have been widely read and discussed and have been accepted as serious, substantial contributions to public discourse. The reason does not, I believe, have much to do with the relative merits of philosophical pragmatism vis-à-vis the analytical mode of philosophizing—there are quite a few philosophical pragmatists, but only one Sidney Hook. (And in the area of education, where Sidney tends toward a Deweyian purism, his writings have had far fewer lasting echoes.) No, I would say that the secret of Sidney's intellectual power and authority as a social thinker is that, in addition to having a highly disciplined philosophical mind, he possesses a juristic cast of mind, a mind whose special skill—one may even say special pleasure—is precisely in relating the abstract concept to the particular case, and doing so in such a way as to respect the integrity of both the abstract and the particular.

I have thought that this nation of ours lost a great legal mind when Sidney decided to do graduate work in philosophy rather than go to law school. I find it impossible to doubt that he would have been the outstanding jurist of this century in the English-speaking world. Nor is it fanciful to think that he would have ended up as a justice of the Supreme Court, in which case his reputation would have been overshadowed only by John Marshall, if by anyone. For Sidney has always had a genius—that is not too strong a term—for seeing the larger implications inherent in any controversy over any specific issue of public policy and for converting those implications into explicit inferences. In so doing he has not only illuminated the case in hand but indirectly provided some enlightenment on a host of other, related issues.

This is the way juristic reasoning works when it is at its best. It is a rigorous art, not a science, which means it cannot be taught in a classroom, as analytic philosophy can, but can only be learned through a studious apprenticeship. I was one of thousands who served such an apprenticeship under Sidney, studying each of his essays as a lawyer or judge would (or should) study a masterly superior court decision.

In recent decades, of course, this kind of juristic analysis has decayed, to our significant loss. Jurisprudence itself has fallen into neglect, legal philosophy has degenerated into a species of bizarre scholasticism, judges proclaim rather than reason cogently, and political controversy has been drowned in partisan demagoguery. The kind of enlightenment—and this is the appropriate term—that Sidney provided to two generations of Americans is even harder to come by.

I think this situation may be about to change. Recently, in conversation with several young men and women of serious intellectual interests, I discovered that they have been reading Sidney Hook's essays and find them admirable, even exemplary. These young thinkers are not philosophical pragmatists—they all take religion seriously, finding it to be the only source of firm resistance to moral nihilism, and they pay less attention to the writings of John Dewey than they probably should. Moreover, they identify themselves as "conservative," though in varying degrees, and the fact that Sidney still defines himself as a "democratic socialist" they simply shrug off as a personal, forgivable idiosyncrasy. (One of them quipped to me that Sidney "is the best kind of socialist: an anti-socialist socialist.") But the fact remains that they are reading him, learning from him, in much the same way that I did forty years ago.

Once again, it seems, after too many years of neglect, Sidney is bringing into the social and political thinking of young people elements that are needed for a productive participation in the intellectual life of our democracy. The fact that he may not agree with them on many important matters is less significant than the fact that they find so much to agree with in him. The sign of a great teacher is not how much he manages to convey by his teaching but how much his students manage to assimilate by their learning. Sidney was such a great teacher for my own generation. He remains such a teacher for the 1980s.

PART II

Marxism, Socialism, and Communism

ANTONY G. N. FLEW

The Socialist Obsession

It is now nearly fifty years since the first and last publication of "that juvenile work," *Toward the Understanding of Karl Marx* (1933). It was, like Hume's *Treatise,* a brilliant, young man's book: Sidney's *Language, Truth and Logic,* you might say. It is not difficult to appreciate how it came to be written by such a person, in New York, in the years immediately after the trauma of the Wall Street crash, while the shining-eyed apparatniks of the New Deal were taking over Washington. Those were, after all, the days in and of which Rex Tugwell wrote:

> I have gathered my tools and my charts
> My plans are finished and practical
> I shall roll up my sleeves—make America over.[1]

What is puzzling is that the author of that first book, who has in the years between seen and seen through so much, should still be claiming to be, if no longer perhaps even a democratic socialist, then at least a social democrat. Why, in a world now having such abundant experience of practical socialism, a world in which so many peoples have for decades lived under total socialism, a world in which total socialism has always been, in practice, totalitarian, and in which the loss of liberty—as he has himself so often and so rightly insisted— has not even been compensated by great gains in prosperity, why, in the face of all this, has Sidney Hook not once and for always put away the socialist long- ings of his youth? Why has he not followed along the path taken by his own sometime comrade Max Eastman? Why has Hook not become, as have many, yet too few, a from-the-foundations-up reconstructed ex-Marxist, retaining only the knowledge of the main enemy of freedom, as the main enemy which it is?

35

I

Hook has, of course, addressed himself to these questions. Most appropriately, there was an exchange with Max Eastman in 1945, reprinted as Chapters 26-28 of Hook's *Political Power and Personal Freedom* (1959). There was in those days no question of urging that the word "socialism" be so redefined as to permit someone to continue bearing the socialist name while abandoning "belief in a planned collectivist economy" (*PPPF*, p. 397). Certainly in Britain, and I suspect everywhere else too, it darkens counsel to employ that word, or to pretend to employ it, in any sense in which the public and, in the main, presumably, state ownership and direction of "all the means of production, distribution and exchange" are not essential, and perhaps the sole essential.

The phrase quoted in the previous sentence is drawn from Clause IV of the Constitution of the Labour Party. This clause, insubstantially amended in 1959, has throughout my own political lifetime been printed on every party card as the statement of aims. Similar clauses are to be found in the constitutions of most of the largest and oldest labor unions, whose creature that party is. It is therefore quite wrong to assert, as so often is still asserted even by many paid to know better, that that party never was, or has only recently become, socialist.

By the way, it is surely of more than merely anecdotal interest to recall here that I had to press these points very hard indeed, when as a visiting professor at New York University in 1958 I first got to know Sidney Hook, in an effort to persuade him that, although of course some members were much more fervent and impatient than others, the Labour Party was then and always had been committed to total socialism. When Prime Minister James Callaghan denied this in 1976, he was, quite simply, committing the supposedly unpardonable offense of lying to the House of Commons: "As this party has always stood for a mixed economy and not a totally controlled economy, that must be the basis on which our economic policy proceeds."[2]

1. In 1945 Hook believed: that capitalism in Western Europe was finished; and that only collectivist economic planning could save us from "that chaos, hunger, and chronic unemployment" which are "the seedbed of totalitarianism" (*PPPF*, p. 398). With hindsight these beliefs may look unrealistic. For today even the most bigoted enemies of economic pluralism can scarcely ignore the lessons of the post-World War II track records: Federal as compared with Soviet Germany; soldier-socialist Burma as against always nonsocialist though usually military Thailand; the capitalist Chinese of Taiwan, Hong Kong, and Singapore in contrast with their Communist-ruled compatriots on the mainland; resurgent Japan stocking up against the USSR; and so on. Others, however, preserved the same complete confidence in the economic promise of socialism for much longer than Hook. Aneurin Bevan, for instance, was at the 1959 Labour Party Conference still insisting that "The

challenge is going to come from those nations which . . . are at long last being able to reap the material fruits of economic planning and public ownership."[3] In fact—as Bevan himself, unlike his biographer, would surely have recognized—the ever more formidable challenge now coming from "the world's first socialist country" is a challenge based upon the production and distribution, not of goods and services for peaceful consumption, but of military hardware.

For Hook in 1945, believing what he did then still believe, the problem was whether there could be a libertarian and democratic socialism. With a caution that must suggest already some hesitation, bearing in mind the wartime performances of the United Kingdom and the United States, and urging that overall planning does not have to involve total and monopolistic control in all areas without exception, he decides that it is at any rate possible: "Democracy may be lost in a planned society. If it is, its loss will not be an economic fatality but a moral failure, a failure of man to use his intelligence to liberate the great possibilities of plenty and freedom in a planned economy" (*PPPF*, p. 407).

It is obvious that Hook recognized the dangers, which in *The Revolution Betrayed* (New York: Pioneer, 1937) Trotsky summed up with characteristic violence: "In a country in which the sole employer is the State, opposition means death by slow starvation. The old principle, who does not work shall not eat, has been replaced by a new one: who does not obey shall not eat" (p. 76). Nevertheless, believing what he then did, both about those "great possibilities" and about the lack of any acceptable alternative, Hook's conclusion is that those risks, being after all only dangers rather than inevitabilities, have to be taken.

Max Eastman, in his rejoinder, points to the uncharacteristic lack of force in, and to the anti-climactic nature of, Hook's conclusions. It is indeed remarkable to find "our most brilliant debator" (*PPPF*, p. 408) maintaining only "that the case for a democratic Socialism, instructed by past errors and present dangers, is *stronger than for any other alternative*" and that there are some things "which make the abandonment by genuine democrats of a planned economy *seem a little premature*" (p. 409: Eastman's italics)! Eastman outlines the case for his own contention, that political pluralism can survive and flourish only on the basis of economic pluralism. The system of private ownership provides for many small powers, and for the multiplication both of possible points of initiative and of possible "safe houses" for all manner of eccentricity and dissent. But socialism concentrates all economic power into whatever hands hold political power, and socialism just will not marry with democracy: "The idea of running the whole economy of society by democratic process, or by a process that can be called representative and have the word mean anything, has been a fantasy all along" (ibid., p. 411).

Eastman is able to refer to the fuller development of this democratic and libertarian case for economic pluralism in F. A. Hayek's *The Road to Serfdom* (Chicago: Chicago University Press, 1945), which first appeared in America a few days after Hook's original paper. It is worth emphasizing that Eastman's thesis, like that of Hayek, refers to necessary rather than sufficient conditions: "We are asserting that *under a free economy political freedom is possible, under a state controlled economy it is impossible*" (*PPPF*, p. 413: italics in original). I regret to report that in offering what is presented as a reply to this thesis, both there and elsewhere, Hook mistakes it to be a token of the type historical materialism. Like so may others later, Hook misconstrues this claim to be the altogether different contention that a pluralist economic foundation guarantees, rather than makes possible, a pluralist "political superstructure." It is not surprising that he is able to make very short work of this straw man. (Compare also *Marx and the Marxists*, p. 128, and *Philosophy and Public Policy*, pp. 111 ff.)

I confess that I have myself never yet come across any reply to the Eastman-Hayek thesis, as actually put. Par for the course seems to be to offer the fully Marxist misrepresentation, and to rubbish this with some triumphantly sneering reference to Chile under Pinochet. Both the apparent lack of concern over this serious and impressively argued objection, and the expressions of support for Allende which so often accompany this wretched evasion, should raise doubts about the sincerity of democratic profession in such evasive socialist spokespersons.

Let us complete the present discussion of that 1945 exchange by noting that there are now many as-near-as-makes-no-matter fully socialist countries and that in none of these is there a legally functioning opposition party or anything like a free press. Can this really be a merely coincidental quirk of history? Certainly the rulers of these socialist countries are very sure that, in a favorite Soviet phrase, "it is no accident." In 1981, for instance, the Institute of Marxism-Leninism in Moscow, with its eyes most immediately upon Chile and France, sketched a program for achieving, through United Front or Broad Left tactics, irreversible Communist domination: "Having once acquired political power, the working class implements the liquidation of private ownership of the means of production . . . As a result, under socialism, there remains no ground for the existence of any parties counter-balancing the Communist Party."[4]

2. In 1955 in *Marx and the Marxists* Hook maintains that socialism presupposes democracy: that "democratic socialism" is, in effect, a tautological expression. Following Kautsky and Hilferding, and in their less Bolshevik moments even Rosa Luxemburg and Lenin, Hook maintains that the main message of Marx can be put in a single sentence: "The necessary and sufficient condition for the existence of the community of free and equal persons is the collective ownership and democratic control of the chief instruments of production" (*MM*, p. 16; and compare to pp. 55, 81, 103, 203, 210, and 242).

To this bold proposal we have to respond that, although many non-Marxist and some Marxist socialists have wanted to be both socialists and democrats, and although some of these have, like Hook himself, been democrats first and only secondarily socialists, precious few people either have used, or for the foreseeable future ever will succeed in using, the word "socialism" constantly and consistently in the way proposed here. Certainly Hook himself fails to observe his own stipulation. For before he is through with Part 1 of the present book he has slipped into distinguishing democratic from nondemocratic socialists: the former, he assures us, "are still in the vanguard of movements of social reform, but it is hard for them to distinguish where the socialist vanguard ends and the main body of nonsocialist public opinion begins" (ibid., p. 127).

Their troubles are intensified by a final revelation: "For all these reasons socialists conclude that what remains perennially valid in the ambiguous legacy of Marxism is the dedication to the scientific spirit and the democratic faith" (ibid., p. 130). Others, so little "terrified of the name 'socialism' " (ibid., p. 127) that they wish actually to defend and extend socialism, instead of merely preserving the word in some new and improved role, are apt to set off in the opposite direction. Having, under heavy controversial pressure, pretended that democracy is, and always has been, part of what they, and everybody else, meant by "socialism," these people, the moment such controversial pressure is eased, are then well content to relapse again into recognizing and recommending as socialist any country and only countries in which Clause IV is law; any country and only countries, that is, in which "all the means of production, distribution and exchange" are collectively owned and directed.

An appropriate example of this all too common evasive move is provided by Hook's and my sometime colleague Kai Nielsen. In an article written "In Defence of Radicalism" for *Question Seven* (London: Pemberton, 1974) Nielsen assures us that "by definition, a genuine socialist is not only committed to the principle of public ownership of the means of production, he is also, and equally, committed to workers' control and to a workers' democracy . . ." (*QS*, p. 63).

In that particular article it is no more than hinted that Nielsen has not in fact previously insisted, and does not in fact intend in future to insist, upon making democracy an equally essential part of the meaning of the word "socialism"; save perhaps in that factitious and disingenuous sense in which the Soviet Occupation Zone describes itself as the German Democractic Republic. In that article and at best Nielsen does remember to call the socialist countries only "quasi-socialist" (ibid., p. 59); although you do not have to be a weatherman to realize the way the wind is blowing, when someone writes— obviously with Hook among others in mind—that "such talk of freedom . . . on the lips of some cold war warriors . . . becomes an obscenity" (ibid., p. 54; and compare p. 64).

All is, however, made beyond any peradventure plain in abundant other publications. "On the Choice between Reform and Revolution," for instance, in *Philosophy and Political Action,* V. Held, K. Nielsen, and C. Parsons (eds.)

(New York and London: Oxford University Press, 1972), lists several sinner countries calling for socialist, and presumably revolutionary, transformation. This 1972 list—to no one's surprise—includes: the USA but not, of course, the USSR; West but not, of course, East Germany; Brazil and the Argentine but not, of course, Cuba; South but not, of course, North Vietnam; and so on.

3. In 1975 in *Revolution, Reform and Social Justice,* Hook appears to revert a little, yet not much, toward a more traditionally—and I would add more genuinely—socialist position. For while he still realizes that total socialism, "in the absence of deeply rooted and effectively operating democratic institutions, . . . may become the engine of a more terrible despotism than Marx ever conceived," Hook is only prepared to say that "it may not even be a *necessary* condition for the realization of the humanistic ideals of socialism. A mixed economy under plural forms of ownership . . . may achieve the best results with the fewest dangers" (*RRSJ,* p. 47: italics in original). Presumably he believes that nationalization has some sort of connection with such humanistic ideals. Nevertheless I cannot put my finger on any place where he tells us just what that connection is supposed to be.

There is not much else here which we need to notice in the present context. In a chapter on "The Rationale of Revolution" Hook makes one of his rare references to the crucial role of the enterpriser in wealth creation. It is made in connection with the expulsion or liquidation of such "anti-people and anti-socialist elements" by socialist power elites in would-be developing countries (ibid., p. 111). But this rare and perhaps reluctant tribute is balanced by the initial contemptuous mention of "an occasional splenetic outburst from the ideologues of 'pure' free enterprise" (ibid., p. 3: should I call "Touché"?) In a final chapter on "Human Rights and Social Justice" Hook becomes ready at last to abandon even the word "socialism": he is confident "that we can get greater agreement if we avoid large terms like "capitalism" and "socialism" and concentrate on a pragmatic approach to specific problems" (ibid., p. 284).

Again, while "Rethinking the Bolshevik October Revolution," Hook concedes that "in pure logic a complete collectivism is not incompatible with unlimited democracy . . ."; but he now puts heavy emphasis upon the near impossibility of any reconciliation in practice. (Has anyone, by the way, ever actually claimed such an impossibility "in pure logic"?) Since, however, concessions are being made I will not let the irenic occasion pass without suggesting that, so far from there being only no logical incompatibility, there is even "in pure logic" some one-way connection between common ownership and democracy. For how can an individual be said to have a share in an enterprise if he is altogether excluded from the control of that enterprise?

4. Several of the essays reissued in 1980 as *Philosophy and Public Policy* are relevant. "The Social Democratic Prospect," first printed in 1976, begins by deploring that socialism has too often been identified with socialism: "Unfortunately socialism has been identified too often . . . with collectivism or the nationalization of all means of production, distribution and exchange" (*PPP,*

p. 99). Such clearheaded directness is, Hook argues, unfortunate. For it has led some people, who are—like us—prepared both to face and to resist the realities of practical socialism as it is seen in the ever-extending lands of the Gulag, to a lamentable conclusion: that the only alternative open to those who love freedom is support of the free enterprise system . . ." (ibid., p. 100).

What is supposed to be so wrong in this alternative is never made clear. For, although he remains reluctant to confess that he positively wants a pluralist and largely private economy, Hook has at last become quite unwilling to accept the political risks or costs of one totally or even predominantly socialist. As always, he is not much interested in questions of comparative efficiency in wealth-creation and in meeting the wants of consumers. Although he will here allow that "an additional reason for preserving a private sector is that it can help provide greater incentives to productivity and innovation without which a minimum decent standard of living cannot be sustained . . ." (ibid., p. 115); it appears not to occur to him to ask himself, much less to tell us, why, if private sectors are indeed more efficient than public, we have to preserve the latter. In the end, Hook's latest yet not I trust final advice is not that we reject total or even partial socialism outright and forever, while un-Humpty Dumpty-like preserving the old word for its belatedly rejected referent, but that "we must recast the idea of socialism, whatever the terms used to designate the revision" (ibid., p. 114).

II

Elsewhere in the same book Hook asks and answers two rhetorical questions: "Who would be willing to die for capitalism? Certainly not the capitalists! Who would go to the barricades for a totally nationalized economy? Not even the Webbs" (ibid., p. 106). No indeed; no one will step forward as a volunteer martyr for capitalism. But quite a few—including Hook himself and even some capitalists—propose to fight if need be to the death in defense of those freedoms that predominantly pluralist and private economies alone make possible. More directly to the present point, and whatever the truth about the Webbs, Hook is plumb wrong to deny that there are any for whom a totally nationalized economy is if not the only then at any rate the supreme good. In fact there are many, and some very powerful. This is precisely the reason why it is so important to make a fully reasoned and decisive break with socialism.

1. Hook has, of course, in his own time and in his own way noticed the existence of such people, and opposed them. In the early sixties, for instance, he complained that "large numbers among the non-Communist left in England feel much more sympathetic to their 'fellow socialists' in the Kremlin and even in Peking than to their anti-Communist 'fellow-workers' in the American labor movement" (*RRSJ,* p. 14). Clearly he saw then that these twisted sympathies were a function of the socialist commitments of officials and activists in the corresponding British organizations; and, like President Coolidge with

sin, he was against it.

The situation today in Britain is far worse. Hook rightly commends "the consistent and principled struggle of the organized American labor movement, the AFL-CIO, against the denial of human rights anywhere in the world. The fact that it was George Meany who gave a public platform to Solzhenitsyn and Bukovsky and not Ford or Carter is of more than symbolic significance in the global struggle for human freedom" (*PPP,* p. 116). It is also of more than symbolic significance that, in the same year in which the AFL-CIO was honoring Solzhenitsyn, the General Council of the British Trades Union Congress entertained Alexander Shelepin, state-appointed boss of the Soviet arbeitsfront; and, as a former director of the KGB, Solzhenitsyn's goaler. Again, in these sad new times the Labour Party has taken to receiving at its Annual Conferences delegations from the ruling Communist parties of Eastern Europe. These men of the apparatus are welcomed as fellow-socialists and even, by some on some occasions, as fellow-democrats. Mr. Callaghan when Prime Minister went out of his way to grant a long interview to Boris Ponomarev, who had come specifically from the CPSU(B) on a party-to-party mission.

Hook proceeds to "a singularly eloquent example of a non-Communist socialist who to the end of his life pleaded for a united front . . . against the United States . . . the late G. D. H. Cole" (*RRSJ,* p. 14). It was Cole who, in 1941 when Chairman of the Fabian Society, wrote: "Much better be ruled by Stalin than by the restrictive and monopolistic cliques which dominate Western capitalism." Hook continues: "He admits without blinking the 'innumerable purges and liquidations,' 'the imprisonment and maltreatment of millions of citizens in the slave labour camps,' the extirpation of intellectual, cultural and political freedom . . .''; and so on and on. Thus for Cole, as increasingly for the TUC and the Labour Party, total socialism is the supreme value: if only everything is nationalized then anything can be forgiven. Hook sums it up by explaining Cole's general position, as well as his particular judgment that "the Russian and Chinese revolutions are the greatest achievements of the modern world," in terms of "his fetishism of 'the mode of production' " (ibid., p. 14).

2. It is unfortunate that Hook never spells out the implications of this fine and fitting phrase, a phrase so well epitomizing the position not only of Cole but of innumerable others. Had Hook done so he would have realized that for all these people socialism itself has become a value, and often the supreme if not the only value. They recommend, defend, and strive to extend socialism not because, or not primarily because, they believe it to be a suitable, or the one necessary, means to ends that are in their eyes good. Rather it is socialism as such, or at any rate the absence of any private ownership and direction of the means of production, that is for them good in itself. Once we are seized of this truth, we have to recognize that there is little profit in laboring to undermine the socialist faith in such people either by displaying evils accompanying

or consequent upon socialism in practice or by urging that various other ends cherished by some of them, too, can be best or only achieved without any socialist transformation. In the end, there is no escape from undertaking a task that can be indicated here but not begun—the task of establishing the legitimacy of a nonsocialist order.

It was, for instance, because she and her husband have rejected any non-socialist order that Jane Fonda refused to join Joan Baez in protesting the almost inconceivable horrors inflicted in Democratic Kampuchea by the victorious Khmer Rouge: "I never protest," she is said to have explained, "against anything done in a socialist country." Again, consider the conclusion of that leading Sovietologist Robert Conquest in *The Great Terror* (London: Macmillan, 1968): "For what it is worth, the evidence seems to be that Stalin really believed that the abolition of incomes from capital was the sole necessary principle of social morality, excusing any other action whatever." Conquest adds a judgment by Milovan Djilas: "All in all, Stalin was a monster who, while adhering to abstract, absolute and fundamentally utopian ideas, in practice had no criterion but success—and this meant violence, physical and spiritual extermination" (*GT,* p. 67).

Conquest's conclusion makes clear what those abstract and utopian ideas were. The heart of the matter lies in the labor theory of value, an intellectual scheme superfluous to and idle in *The Wealth of Nations*. It was without necessity left there by Adam Smith as a hostage to fortune. In terms of this scheme, so useless to Smith, Marx and other socialists have argued that private ownership of the means of production is always and essentially exploitative, since it is labor alone that contributes value to the product. It is then easy, albeit fallacious, to argue that this is the only sort of exploitation, or the only significant sort, that there either is or could be.

Anyone inclined to hail Wladislaw Gomulka's proclamation that "what is immutable in socialism can be reduced to the abolition of the exploitation of man by man" needs to be reminded of this Marxist fallacy. Hook, who was himself in 1957 tempted to put an optimistically generous interpretation upon this statement, also quoted from the same 1956 speech: "The best definition of the social contents inherent in the idea of socialism is contained in the definition that socialism is a social system that abolishes the exploitation and oppression of man by man" (*RRSJ,* p. 167). The promised de-Stalinization of that Spring in October was, alas, to prove to be no more substantial and longlasting than this supposed liberalization of the socialist ideal.

The same fundamental ideas, though usually in a form less crude and less cruel, are today misguiding most of those reluctant or more than reluctant to resist the advances of Soviet socialism—most notably the leaders of campaigns for further unilateral Western disarmament. But I draw my two final examples from somewhat earlier and more subtle sources. The first is Jean-Francois Revel's *Without Marx or Jesus* (London: Paladin, 1973). With the subtitle "The New American Revolution has Begun," Revel is in fact and with a splendid verve campaigning against the visceral pro-socialism and anti-Americanism of the French intelligentsia.

But though he sees close connections between these two gut reactions, and though he is in fact equally and rightly opposed to both, he can never bring himself to settle accounts with socialism above board and in the open, to reject not the referent only but the word also. Anything Revel is to support has at least to be called socialism. The result is a book in which a mass of good things are mashed up in conceptual confusion. In a curious and backhanded way he thus resembles those whom he reproaches for not backing Alain Poher against de Gaulle in 1969: "Most of the intellectuals with whom I discussed this problem evidenced great revulsion at the idea of supporting a candidate who was not an avowed socialist" (*WMJ,* p. 40). So of course Revel never confronts the challenge to the legitimacy of the whole business of hiring help to produce goods and services with an eye to profit.

The second final illustration is provided by Hugh Gaitskell, who as leader of the Labour Party tried at the 1959 Conference to secure the repeal of Clause IV. He failed; although it was in that same year that the German Social Democrats conceded to the triumphant market economy of Ludwig Erhard by jettisoning all their old Marxist baggage. In his speech there Gaitskell gave an unacknowledged quotation from Lenin's endorsement of his New Economic Policy. Gaitskell urged the party to content itself with imposing state monopoly on only "the commanding heights of the economy."

Yet it is by no means clear that he, any more than Lenin, was forthright in repudiating socialism. For only three years earlier, in a pamphlet on *Socialism and Nationalization* (London: Fabian Society, 1956), he had written: "The existence of unearned income is wrong in itself, no matter how it is distributed" (*SN,* p. 6). Three years later Anthony Crosland, a close friend and colleague, and the man offered by all our professional political commentators as the very model of the modern (nonsocialist) social democrat, wrote in *The Conservative Enemy* (London: Cape, 1962): "The object . . . is *generally* to increase the area of public ownership . . . It is sufficient to extend public investment in any direction; and it makes no difference how haphazardly the investment is scattered among different industries" (*CE,* pp. 47-48: italics in original). This passage, it appears, was overlooked by all those professional commentators; just as they failed to identify Gaitskell's quotation from Lenin—any more than that other, when Lord Hume as Foreign Secretary described refugees from Soviet Germany as "voting with their feet."

NOTES

1. On the same page of my scrapbook I find another less poetic expression of the appeal of the centrally planned economy to those who expect themselves to be among the central planners. This statement was made at the 1959 Conference of the Labour Party by Frank Cousins, general secretary of the world's largest labor monopoly, the Transport and General Workers' Union: "There are five or six million people who are socialists in embryo, waiting for us to go and harness

them to the power machine we want to drive."

2. See *Hansard* for May 3, 1976, and compare S. H. Beer, *British Politics in the Collectivist Age* (New York: Knopf, 1965).

3. See Michael Foot's *Aneurin Bevan* (New York: Atheneum, 1963), vol. 2, p. 646. Those familiar with the legislation introduced in 1975 by the author as Minister of Labour will be interested to contrast his earlier commendation of Bevan for repudiating tyrannical behavior by labor unions (vol. 1, p. 177).

In the present context all freedom fighters should be aware that this legislation vastly extended the closed shop, especially in the numerous industries already nationalized, and that some brave and principled persons were in fact dismissed by British railways, never to be employed in any such work again, for refusing to join the Transport Salaried Staffs Association, a union that requires recruits enrolling to sign a declaration of support for its socialist aims. Although some members of the Labour Party have since brought themselves to protest against similar demands recently made by the military junta in Poland, not one of their Members of Parliament dissented from that legislation or declared solidarity with these railwaymen victims of socialist persecution. This shameful charge holds just as true of all those who were later to defect to the Social Democrats.

4. All socialists claiming also to be democrats, and indeed all those whose socialism springs from any concern for the wishes and welfare of the people to be subjected to that system, should be much more concerned than in fact they seem to be about the unanimous agreement of the ruling elites in all the existing socialist countries that any substantial liberalization must result in triumph for the enemies of socialism. The most recent statement I have seen comes from an editorial in *Tribuna,* the weekly organ of the Central Committee of the Czech Communist Party: the introduction of "freedom and democracy . . . freedom of speech and the press for everybody . . . 'independent' labour unions and the like" could not but "create conditions for political pluralism and the destruction of the socialist system." (See *Reason* magazine for May 1981).

SEYMOUR MARTIN LIPSET

Socialism in America

The results of the 1980 elections in the United States point up anew a singular fact of American politics, that it is the only democratic industrialized nation in which not a single person representing an independent socialist or labor party holds elective office. This does not mean that Americans do not have the opportunity to vote for socialists. In the 1980 elections, candidates of a number of leftist parties were on the ballot in various states. These included the Socialist Labor Party, which has run presidential candidates since the late nineteenth century; the Socialist Party, a minuscule splinter of what was once a larger party using that name; the People's Party, a group calling themselves democratic socialists; the Socialist Workers Party (Trotskyist); and the Communist Party. None of these parties, however, polled as many as 100,000 votes nationally out of a total of close to 80 million. Among them they received less than one-quarter of one percent.

This sorry record of electoral support for socialism represents what is close to the lowest point in the more than a century-long series of attempts to build a socialist movement in the United States. The most successful such effort was that of the Socialist Party, which before World War I included the leaders of many trade unions, had 125,000 members, elected over 1,000 public officials, including mayors of a number of cities, state legislators, and two Congressmen, and whose perennial presidential candidate and leader, Eugene V. Debs, secured about 6 percent of the presidential vote in 1912.

This paper is a summary and codification of my research on the factors related to the weakness of socialism in the United States, to be reported in a forthcoming book on the subject. For a detailed earlier report see S. M. Lipset, "Why No Socialism in the United States?" in Seweryn Bialer and Sophia Sluzar, eds., *Sources of Contemporary Radicalism* (Boulder, Colo.: Westview Press, 1977), pp. 31–149, 346–363.

The Socialist Party declined after World War I, partly because of government attacks on it for its opposition to the war, but primarily because the Communists split the party, pulling out many left-wing members to form an affiliate of the Third International. The Socialists and Communists competed for support within the labor movement and among the general electorate for a number of decades afterward. The Great Depression of the 1930s produced gains for both. The Socialists, under Norman Thomas's leadership, won close to a million votes for President (2 percent) in 1932, while the Communists, though weaker electorally, were able to secure considerable strength in the growing labor movement of the late 1930s, particularly in the CIO.

Both parties, however, proved unable to use the Depression to build a viable radical movement. The Democratic Party administration, under President Franklin D. Roosevelt, supported a variety of welfare state and planning measures designed to help the underprivileged and the unemployed, and enacted legislation favorable to trade-union growth. Many socialists, and the Communist Party as a party, following the international anti-fascist Popular Front policy laid down by Stalin, supported Roosevelt for reelection in 1936. Norman Thomas's presidential vote fell to well under 200,000 that year.

Following World War II, neither party, nor various smaller splinter groups, were able to make much headway. The Communists suffered from government prosecution during the cold war era of the 1950s. The Socialist Party officially decided in the late 1950s to stop running candidates for office, on the grounds that the presidential system made it impossible electorally, and to cooperate with the trade unions in working for progressive major-party candidates, largely Democratic. Shortly thereafter, the party split into three groups, a tiny one that kept the name and still runs candidates, a right-wing faction, Social Democrats USA, and one with a more left tendency, the Democratic Socialists. The two latter groups worked within the Democratic Party and supported Jimmy Carter for President in 1976 and 1980. The Communists began running national candidates again in the 1970s, but they and the Trotskyists, who do the same, have had very little success.

The Sources of Weakness

The continued weakness of socialism in the United States has been a major embarrassment to Marxist theory, which assumes that the cultural superstructure, including political behavior, is a function of the underlying economic and technological structure. The class relationships inherent in capitalism as a social system should inevitably eventuate in a working class that would form a majority, come to political consciousness, and organize in a revolutionary socialist party. Logically it followed, as Marx put it in the Preface to *Capital:* "The country that is more developed industrially only shows, to the less developed, the image of its own future."[1] The most developed society should have the most advanced set of class and political relationships. Since the United States has been the most advanced industrial economy for close to a century, its political system, regarded as part of its superstructure, should be more appropriate to a technologically advanced society than are the systems of less developed societies. Until the Russian Revolution, a number of major Marxist theorists anticipated that, following the logic of historical materialism, the United States would be the first country in which socialists would come to power.[2]

Karl Marx and Friedrich Engels constantly looked for signs of class consciousness in the United States. Ironically, given the subsequent weakness of socialist and labor politics in the United States, Marx drew his conviction that the working class would inevitably develop class-conscious politics dedicated to the abolition of capitalism from his reading "the first story of an organized political party of labor in the world's history," the Workingmen's Party, which secured considerable votes in a number of American cities in the late 1820s and early 1830s.[3] Although the Party had disappeared by the mid-thirties, Marx and Engels, many decades later, were to emphasize to deprecators of American radicalism that the Americans "have had, since 1829, their own social democratic school."[4]

Yet, as we know, for more than a century and a half after the creation of the Workingmen's Party the United States has stood out among the industrial nations of the world in frustrating all efforts to create a mass socialist or labor party. This fact has occasioned a considerable literature by radical writers here and abroad, as well as by scholars seeking to explain "American exceptionalism," to use the curious term that emerged in debates on the matter in the Communist International in the 1920s.[5] These analyses cast a great deal of insight into the factors that determined the nature of American society, for ironically much of the discussion by socialists, including the observations of Marx and Engels themselves, stresses that the problem lies in the fact that, from sociological and political points of view, the United States was too progressive, too egalitarian, too open, and too democratic to generate massive radical or revolutionary movements on a scale comparable to those of Europe.[6]

The variety of specific explanations suggested for the failure of socialist parties in the United States fall into two categories. One involves emphases on societal variables; the other focuses on factors internal to the political system. While the two sets of hypotheses are of course not mutually exclusive, some have placed more of a stress on one dimension than on the other. The various hypotheses may be grouped under the following headings.

I. Societal Factors

1. America as a "New Society," the absence of a feudal tradition of class relations to structure politics along class lines.

2. Americanism as Surrogate Socialism or the Liberal Tradition as the predominant national one. This approach suggests that Americans see their society as egalitarian and democratic and have found no need for drastic changes to attain already existing objectives.

3. The emphasis in the value system on individualism and anti-statism supposedly derivative from the Protestant sectarian past, and revolutionary values, which imply support for decentralized radicalism, not a strong collectivist state. The syndicalist character of the U.S. labor movement has been related to this factor.

4. The impact of a steady rise in standards of living, particularly of the working class. The United States has been the wealthiest country in the developed world, at least since the post-Civil War period.

5. The considerable increase in the proportion of the per capita Gross National Product received by the less privileged sectors of the population in modern times, as compared to the pre-Civil War period. It is further contended by a number of economists that there has been a more or less continual upgrading of the lower levels from the 1930s through the 1970s. Various consumer goods, particularly education, have been more widely distributed in America than elsewhere.

6. Accompanying the growth in productivity, a shift to large-scale economic organization, and the spread of educational opportunities has been increased opportunities for upward mobility.

7. Recent research on mobility by historians and social scientists has documented the "remarkable volatility of the American working class" and reemphasized the propensity for geographic movement and the lack of stable community roots as factors operating to inhibit the formation of class consciousness.

8. The consequences of being a multi-ethnic and multi-racial immigrant society.

a. The impact of continued immigration in encouraging upward mobility by native-born whites. Census data indicate that from the second half of the nineteenth century to the 1930s, immigrants filled the lower-status, less-skilled, least well paid jobs, enabling the children of immigrants and third- and fourth-generation native-born to occupy more privileged positions. Since World War II, blacks, chicanos, Puerto Ricans, and new waves of immigrants have played the role once held by European immigrants. Hence beyond the factor of greater productivity is the advantage held by native whites.

b. Ethnic, religious, and racial differentiation has been held to have fragmented the working class and to have retarded the growth of class-conscious politics.

c. The fact that a very large proportion of the working class has been Catholic since the late nineteenth century is assumed to have weakened prospects for socialist strength, since the church worked actively to resist socialist appeals.

II. Political

1. The "gift of the suffrage." In the United States the "masses" attained suffrage prior to efforts to organize them into class-conscious parties. In Europe,

for the most part, socialist parties appealed to the workers for support before the vote was universal. Hence socialism grew in the struggle for electoral democracy. In the United States the voting franchise predated the party.

2. The constitutional and electoral system, which presses toward a two-party system in electing a president. It has been argued by many that a two-party system is almost mandated by the Constitution, that efforts at slowly building up third parties must fail. The introduction of the primary system of nomination is held to have strengthened this factor.

3. The flexibility of the two-party system to co-opt and/or respond to manifest evidence of pervasive discontent, often taking the form of mass movements and/or third parties. This flexibility often has involved a major party "stealing the thunder" of the radicals by adopting policies long advocated by socialists.

4. Movements, not parties, as the American response to social crises and to failures of the two major parties. The history of radicalism in the United States since the early nineteenth century has indicated a propensity for short-lived, often single-issue moralistic movements rather than institutionalized parties. To a considerable degree this propensity for moralistic social movements has been related to the "Protestant" character of the United States, i.e., the fact that this is the *only country* where the majority of inhabitants have adhered to the Protestant *sects,* Methodists, Baptists, and others, as distinct from churches, whose theology and practice relate to having been established state churches in Europe. The sects, directly or implicitly, have emphasized the obligation of the individual to be moral, to be responsible personally for sinful behavior. From this obligation has flowed the Protestant sectarian phenomenon of conscientious objection to war, the repeated presence in the United States from the War of 1812 to the Vietnam war of large anti-war movements, the anti-Catholic and Nativist crusades, the resistance to alcoholic beverages, and other moralistic drives relating to gambling, sex, and so on.

The parties almost invariably respond to the movements, thereby reducing social strains and the potential base for institutionalized radical parties.

5. Repression. Syndicalist, socialist, and communist movements have suffered from political repression, which broke up the continuity of radical protest.

Comparative Social Structure

Many of the efforts to demonstrate the validity of particular interpretations of American exceptionalism have been comparative, largely with Europe. The most influential one, that of the political theorist Louis Hartz, is historical and sociological. It places the United States in a category of overseas "fragment" societies formed in the Americas and Australasia by European settlers. Hartz's concept of the fragment refers to the fact that the groups that emigrated from European countries to settle abroad were only parts or fragments of the mother culture. These "new societies" developed very differently from the mother cultures since they did not embody the European "whole." Many important European strata, values, and institutions, usually those associated with the privileged classes, aristocracy, and monarchy, never reached them. Each left behind in Europe an ancient source of conservative ideology in the form of the traditional class-structure. Hence in British Canada, the United States, and Dutch South Africa particularly, liberal enlightenment doctrines could dominate. In Australia, created by a fragment of nineteenth-century Britain, radical principles carried by working-class immigrants could form the national tradition unhampered by the need to compromise with powerful Tory values and supporters. Latin America included some hierarchical aristocratic values, since most of the nations there were not fully settled societies. But, over time, the very absence of the traditional European right transmuted the liberal or radical doctrines into the conservative dogmas of the "fragment." It was impossible to build an ideological left in the liberal fragment cultures because there was no hereditary aristocracy against which to rebel and because the philosophical bases on which an ideological left might be founded were already institutionalized as part of the received liberal and radical tradition of the society.[7]

Some light on the relevance of this analysis for the explanation of socialist weakness may be cast by a precursor of the Hartz emphasis on the liberal tradition in the United States formulated by a British socialist, H. G. Wells, seventy years ago. In the context of discussing the weakness of socialism and class consciousness in the United States, Wells noted that the country not only lacked a strong socialist party, but failed to have a true conservative or Tory party as well.

H. G. Wells related the unique history and resultant class-structure of the United States to the absence of two such parties. As he presented the case, two major European classes, the subservient land-bound peasants and the aristocracy, were missing from the American social structure. The absence of the former implied no "servile tradition," while that of the latter meant that the sense of "state responsibility, which in the old European theory of society was supposed to give significance to the whole," was also missing. "The American community, one cannot too clearly insist, does not correspond to an entire European community at all, but only to the middle masses of it. . . . This community was, as it were, taken off its roots, clipped of its branches and brought hither. . . . Essentially America is a middle-class become a community and so its essential problems are the problems of a modern individualistic society, stark and clear, unhampered and unilluminated by any feudal tradition either at its crest or at its base."

The Fabian Wells essentially enunciated the theory of America as a liberal society in terms comparable to those put forth again a half-century later by Louis Hartz.

It is not difficult to show, for example, that the two great political parties in America represent only one English party, the middle-class Liberal party. . . .

There are no Tories to represent the feudal system and no Labor Party. . . . [T]he new world [was left] to the Whigs and Nonconformists and to those less constructive, less logical, more popular and liberating thinkers who became Radicals in England, and Jeffersonians and then Democrats in America. All Americans are, from the English point of view, Liberals of one sort or another. . . .

[My] chief argument . . . is that the Americans started almost clear of the medieval heritage, and developed in the utmost . . . the modern type of social organization. They took the economic conventions that were modern and progressive at the end of the eighteenth century and stamped them into the Constitution as if they meant to stamp them there for all time. . . . America is pure eighteenth century. . . .

The liberalism of the eighteenth century was essentially the rebellion of the modern industrial organization against the monarchical and aristocratic state, against hereditary privilege, against restrictions on bargains. Its spirit was essentially Anarchistic — the antithesis of Socialism. It was the anti-State.[8]

The argument that socialism is weak in the United States because the United States is the purest example of a non-European non-aristocratic society, that it is a pure bourgeois, pure liberal, born-modern society is of course not limited to the work of Louis Hartz and other contemporary analysts of the United States and Canada. One may find a variant of the thesis in the works of Marx, Engels, and Lenin, who saw the United States as the most modern, purely bourgeois culture and also as the most democratic one. As a result, however, they seemed to argue, as the American socialist theoretician Michael Harrington has noted, that one of the difficulties in building socialism in America was the fact that "America was too socialist for socialism."[9] Friedrich Engels, Marx's great collaborator, emphasized that socialism was weak in the United States "just *because* America is so purely bourgeois, so entirely without a feudal past and therefore proud of its purely bourgeois organization."[10] He noted: "It is . . . quite natural that in such a young country, which has never known feudalism and has grown up on a bourgeois basis from the first, bourgeois prejudices should also be so strongly rooted in the working class. Out of this very opposition to the mother country — which is still clothed in its feudal disguise — the American worker also imagines that the bourgeois regime has traditionally inherited something progressive and superior by nature and for all time a *non plus ultra*."[11]

The founding leader and theoretician of world communism, V. I. Lenin, also stressed the freedom and higher status of the workers in the United States. He described the country in 1908 as "in many respects the model and ideal of our bourgeois civilization. . . . [It has] no rival . . . [in] the extent of political freedom and the cultural level of the masses of the population."[12]

Writing in 1907, Lenin emphasized that the weakness of socialism in America stemmed from "the absence of any big, nation-wide *democratic* tasks facing the proletariat." Political freedom in America has produced "the complete subjection of the proletariat to bourgeois policy; the sectarian isolation of the [socialist] groups, . . . not the slightest success of the Socialists among the working masses in the elections, etc." American socialism was weak precisely because it was dealing with "the most firmly established democratic systems, which confront the proletariat with purely socialist tasks."[13] Or, to reverse Lenin's words, European socialism was much stronger because it could appeal to the workers for support, not on "purely socialist," but on democratic issues. As he noted, in Germany the Social Democrats were powerful because theirs was "a country where the bourgeois-democratic revolution was still incomplete, where 'military despotism, embellished with parliamentary forms' (Marx's expression in his *Critique of the Gotha Programme*) prevailed, and still prevails."[14]

Antonio Gramsci, perhaps the most important non-Russian theoretician of the Communist movement, following a logic similar to that of Wells and Hartz, also emphasized America's unique origins and resultant value-system as a source of its exceptional political and technological systems. Although a Marxist, Gramsci placed more emphasis on the causal role of values than on America's "so-called natural wealth" in producing a society that differed so much from Europe. As he explained the American situation, it was basically formed by "pioneers, protagonists of the political and religious struggles in England, defeated but not humiliated or laid low in their country of origin. They import in America . . . a certain stage of European historical evolution, which, then transplanted . . . into the virgin soil of America, continues to develop the forces implicit in its nature but with an incomparably more rapid rhythm than in Old Europe, where there exists a whole series of checks (moral, intellectual, political, economic, incorporated in specific sections of the population, relics of past regimes which refuse to die out)."[15]

Gramsci stressed that America's unique sociological background has resulted in a general value-system, a conception of life, which he called Americanism. It is pure rationalism uninhibited by the values of classes derived from feudalism. Americanism is not simply a way of life, it is an "ideology." Americans, regardless of class, emphasize the virtues of hard work by all, of the need to exploit nature.[16]

The conception suggested by Gramsci that Americanism represents a distinct ideological alternative to socialism, one that is accepted by American workers, has been independently elaborated by a number of socialist writers and social scientists in their efforts to explain the absence or weakness of socialism in America.

Herman Keyserling, a conservative German aristocrat, Leon Samson, an American socialist intellectual, Sidney Hook, socialist philosopher, Michael Harrington, leader of the Socialist Party, and American historian Carl Degler, in writings that span the period from 1929 to the present, have put forth or accepted the argument that socialism as a political movement is weak in the United States because the ideological content of Americanism is highly similar to socialism and that Americans believe they already have most of what it promises. As Harrington writes:

Americanism, the official ideology of the society, became a kind of "substitutive socialism." The European ruling classes . . . were open in their contempt for the proletariat. But in the United States equality, and even classlessness, the creation of wealth for all, and political liberty were extolled in the public schools. It is, of course, true that this was sincere verbiage which concealed an ugly reality, but nonetheless it had a profound impact upon the national consciousness. "The idea that everyone can be a capitalist," Samson wrote in a perceptive insight, "is an American concept of capitalism. It is a socialist concept of capitalism." And that, Marx had understood in . . . 1846, was why socialism would first appear in this country in a capitalist disguise. What he could not possibly anticipate was that this dialectical irony would still be in force over one hundred years later.

So it was America's receptivity to utopia, not its hostility, that was a major factor inhibiting the development of a socialist movement. The free gift of the ballot and the early emergence of working-class parties were portents of assimilation, not revolution. . . . [T]he country's image of itself contained so many socialist elements that one did not have to go to a separate movement opposed to the status quo in order to give vent to socialist emotions.[17]

Electoral Systems

In a recent discussion of the failure of socialism in the United States, the Canadian academic socialist Kenneth W. McNaught reiterated the argument that explanations emphasizing sociological and specific historical factors as reasons for the differences between the United States and Canada or Europe are incomplete. Rather, he would stress "the political consequences of the American Constitution and its evolution." As he argues in detail:

Why the Constitution is important should be apparent to any Canadian socialist. It does not permit the sharing of executive power by minority representation in the legislature and successive court interpretations have progressively reduced the significance of state powers. The resulting arguments on the Left in favour of single issue, pressure-group and extra-parliamentary methods has militated constantly against the permanent establishment of a democratic socialist party outside the "pluralistic" two-party system. . . . Yet anyone who has consulted left-or-centre Americans who say that if they had lived in Canada they would have voted CCF-NDP cannot miss the point that American socialism should long since have attacked more seriously the constitutional problems. Victor Berger showed, as early as 1910, that it is not impossible to get elected to Congress as a socialist if you have built a strong local machine. But what happens after election is governed by the rules of Congress and the "separation of powers." Even Woodrow Wilson understood (with his admiration of Burke and Bagehot) the need of party organization and responsibility of the executive to the legislature. This problem, which may seem at first to be academic and even arcane, has bedeviled American Leftists since they first started talking about socialism. . . . Yet when you talk to representative people on the Left you find almost to a man the belief that parliamentarism in the U.S. system will not work for democratic socialism (safe for boring from within the Democratic party). This seems a conundrum which should have been faced much more specifically in any discussion of why democratic socialism has failed in the United States.[18]

The thesis that constitutional factors have affected the failure of third parties in the United States, as evidenced by comparisons between it, Canada, or parliamentary countries in Europe, is a very old one. Friedrich Engels put it as number one on a list of those preventing the growth of a third workers' party, which he made up in 1893. As he stated, "the Constitution . . . causes any vote for any candidate not put up by one of the two governing parties to appear to be *lost*. And the American . . . wants to influence his state; he does not throw his vote away."[19]

The electoral factors undermining third parties were spelled out in detail in 1910 by Morris Hillquit, the Socialist Party leader, in the first major history of American socialism. Hillquit made the following observation about other parliamentary countries, such as Canada or Britain.

> The elections are by district and the ticket of each party is, as a rule, limited to one candidate for each district. Each electoral campaign is thus conducted on the merits of the given district, and is in no way dependent upon conditions in other districts. In an electoral district largely made up of radicals the voters may, there-fore, enter the contest with the expectation of victory regardless of the more con-servative sentiments in other districts or in the country at large. In the United States . . . the ticket handed to the voter . . . contains the names not only of candidates for the state legislature or congress, but also for all local and state officers and even for President of the United States. And since a new party rarely seems to have the chance or prospect of electing its candidate for governor of a state or president of the country, the voter is inclined in advance to consider its entire ticket as hopeless. The fear of "throwing away" the vote is thus a peculiar product of American politics, and it requires a voter of exceptional strength of conviction to overcome it.[20]

Following more than a half-century of electoral defeats, two leaders of the Socialist Party of the United States, Norman Thomas and Michael Harring-ton, also came to accept this explanation of the "general failure of 'third' parties." As Thomas put it in 1963, ". . . had we had a centralized parliamen-tary government rather than a federal presidential government, we should have had, under some name or other, a moderately strong socialist party." He placed particular emphasis on the fact that unlike the situation in countries with proportional representation or with single-member parliamentary district electoral systems, third-party supporters in the United States are always faced with the fact that they are casting a "wasted" vote that may help elect the major party candidate they most dislike.[21] Earlier, in 1938, Thomas recognized the weakness of the Socialist Party and suggested that socialists only hurt their cause by running independent candidates for president. By the fifties and sixties he had reluctantly come to the conclusion that the party's experience demonstrated the futility of third parties in America, a view that a majority of the Socialist Party came to accept by 1960.[22]

The alternative strategy suggested for American socialists and other radicals, given the difficulties that the Constitution and electoral systems placed in the way of third parties, has been to operate as a faction within one of the major coalition parties. The absence of any form of parliamentary party discipline and the primary system of nominating candidates clearly makes this possible.

This tactic was tried with considerable success by A. C. Townley, a leader of the Socialist Party in North Dakota. Believing that the American wheat-belt farmers were ready to accept Socialist policies, Townley formed the Non-partisan League in 1915. It called for a farmers' alliance "to grapple with organized 'big business' greed." The League's program proposed government ownership and control of various enterprises. Since Townley and his colleagues had determined that building a third party was very difficult if not impossible, they decided on the strategy of capturing the dominant farmer-based party in the region, and then the Republican Party, by entering a League slate in the primaries. In 1916, the first election contested by the League, it elected the governor and all of the state officials. After winning control of both of the houses of the legislature in 1918 it enacted a large part of its program into law: a state bank; a home-building association to lend money at low rates of interest; a graduated state income-tax distinguishing between earned and unearned income; a state hail insurance fund; a workman's compensation act that assessed employers for its support; the eight-hour day for working women; and regulation of working conditions in the mines.[23]

Many members of the Socialist Party thought that Townley had betrayed the movement, others openly supported him, seeing in the Non-partisan League a socialist organization. Townley's policies were defended in the Socialist Party's national newspaper by Arthur LeSeur, his legal advisor, and still a member of the party. "While the Non-partisan League in North Dakota is composed exclusively of farmers, the labor unions of the state have stood as one man with the League . . . [and] its program is composed of precisely the points included in the Socialist Party platform for the last six years."[24]

Organizing in the wheat area tributary to Minneapolis and St. Paul, the League was eventually able to enroll more than 200,000 members, although it never had the same electoral success in any other state. In South Dakota, the Republican Party adopted much of its program and set up a "state rural credit system, a state-owned coal mine, and a state cement plant," and promised that, if the North Dakota flour mill and packing plant were successful, South Dakota would adopt them as well.[25]

An offshoot of the Non-partisan League won power in Oklahoma in the early twenties, electing a governor and many legislators. It, too, was largely based on former members of the Socialist Party.

The strategy of building a Socialist faction that would contest the primaries of one of the old parties was followed with some success in the 1930s in the

West Coast states. Upton Sinclair, who had been active in the Socialist Party since the turn of the century, had run for governor of California in 1932, receiving 50,000 votes, and decided to try his luck within the Democratic Party. He formed an independent movement, End Poverty in California (EPIC), which ran a full slate in the Democratic primaries in 1934. Sinclair himself was nominated for governor and various other EPIC candidates won nomination for assorted posts in the United States Senate, the House of Representatives, and the state legislature. In the ensuing election Sinclair received close to 900,000 votes but was defeated by a campaign that was extremely well financed by an opposition fearful of his socialist program. However, the EPIC candidate for U.S. senator was elected.[26] In the neighboring states of Oregon and Washington, groups calling themselves the Cooperative Commonwealth Federation, the same name as that used by the Socialists in Canada, contested the Democratic primaries, again with a fair amount of success. A number of congressmen were elected as Democrats from the state of Washington representing the CCF. No comparable groups, however, were organized elsewhere, and these movements gradually disintegrated with the coming of World War II.

During the late 1930s, the Communist Party, under orders from Moscow to cooperate with all left-of-center elements to build an anti-Fascist Popular Front, worked within the Democratic Party. Earl Browder, the leader of the Communists at the time, has pointed out that, unlike his party, the Socialists refused to learn that they could participate as an organized group within the Democratic coalition and that they refused to learn any lesson "from the spectacular capture of the Democratic Party primary in 1934 by Upton Sinclair's EPIC Movement." Browder notes that as a result of the varying strategies of the two parties, the Socialist Party, which had been stronger than the Communists while both operated as third electoral parties, "lost ground steadily to them. By the middle of the thirties the positions of the two parties were reversed, the Communists had the upper hand in all circles that considered themselves left of the New Deal."[27]

Michael Harrington, Thomas's successor as leader of the Socialist Party, in discussing the success of the Communists in the 1930s and again during World War II, notes sadly that if the Socialists had only followed a similar policy they might have built the largest and most successful socialist movement in American history.[28]

The considerable strength the Communists built up within the labor movement and the Democratic Party following this policy was of course destroyed by its need to follow the changes of the international Communist line dictated by the Russians. Thus, in 1939, the Stalin-Hitler Pact isolated the party from much of the support of the membership that it had won from 1936 on. Again, in 1948, renewed hard-line tactics dictated by the emerging "cold war" broke the party's links to the Democrats revived during the war and forced many to choose between their influence in trade unions and the Democratic Party and their membership in or ties to the Communist Party.

The success of efforts by American radicals to build Socialist and Communist influence within one of the two party coalitions points to the fact that, in the United States with its coalition multifactional party structure, any estimate of the extent to which political tendencies comparable to those that exist in other countries requires examining the forces within the parties. In recent years a number of observers, Michael Harrington, David Shannon, and J. David Greenstone, have suggested that the welfare-planning state pro-labor politics adopted by the New Deal Democratic Party since the 1930s constitutes the American political equivalent to the Social Democratic and Labor parties of the British Commonwealth and northern Europe. As Shannon puts it:

> The British and Scandinavian political arms of labor pay homage to socialism in the abstract, but they in fact have put their main emphasis on welfare state features such as unemployment insurance, old-age pensions, and national health plans. American labor, with only a few exceptions, has failed to pay homage to socialism in the abstract, but it has in fact put a major political emphasis on gaining welfare state objectives. One can even make too much of the absence of an American labor party such as Great Britain's. . . . In the heavily industrialized states, particularly those with basic industries that the CIO unions organized in the 1930's and 1940's, such as Michigan, the Democratic Party's strongest element is organized labor.[29]

Labor historian J. David Greenstone has also emphasized the comparabilities, noting that, "in their support of the Democrats as a mass, pro-welfare state party, American trade unions have forged a political coalition with important — although hardly complete — structural and behavioral similarities to the Socialist Party–trade-union alliances of western Europe."[31]

Michael Harrington has described social democracy as America's "invisible mass movement."

> There is in the United States today a class political movement of workers which seeks to democratize many of the specific economic powers of capital but does not denounce capitalism itself. . . . And its impact upon the society is roughly analogous to that of the social democratic parties of Europe.[31]

He argues that, by identifying social democracy with the Socialist Party, observers have failed to notice that "the movement in this country followed the English, not the German pattern."[32] The turning point in the emergence of this movement was the alliance of the New Deal with labor, which in Richard Hofstadter's words, "gave the New Deal a social democratic tinge that has never been present in American reform movements."[33] Since the 1930s this alliance between labor and the Democrats has grown, the Democratic Party has become a firm supporter of state intervention and planning in economic affairs, and the AFL-CIO officially calls for government policies resembling those advocated by the Socialist Party that the AFL rejected earlier. Labor, through its political action committees, has "created a social democratic party, with its own apparatus and program, within the Democratic Party." George Meany, the president of the Federation, on a number of occasions accepted the description of the AFL's political program as "socialist."[34]

Harrington is careful to distinguish between social democracy, perceived as "an independent, class-based political movement with a far ranging program for the democratization of the economy and the society," and socialism, involving the elimination of private capitalism. As he sees it, a powerful social democracy now exists in America comparable to those in other industrialized countries, but not a socialist party, i.e., not a movement dedicated to the total transformation of the economic order.

In some of my earlier work I have made a somewhat similar argument to those of Shannon, Greenstone, and Harrington, adding the point that, since the 1940s, not only have the American labor movement and the Democratic Party behaved more like unions and social democratic parties in northern Europe and Australia, but that the latter have increasingly acted like the American organizations, placing more emphasis on serving the popular interest, on being multi-class parties seeking to extend the welfare state.[35]

It is clear that, however grandly we describe the social democratic force in American politics, it is much weaker than the left-oriented Social-Democratic, Labor, or Communist parties of Europe and Australasia. And, if we look at the United States' neighbor Canada, which is somewhat similar sociologically, we also find a relatively weak social democratic party.[36] Since its formation as the CCF in 1932, the CCF/NDP has contested 15 federal elections. Its percentages of the vote has varied from 8 to 19, with high points of 18–19 percent in 1965, 1972, 1979, and 1980. The CCF/NDP has always been considerably underrepresented in the House of Commons. In the last election, 19 percent of the vote gave it 11 percent of the seats.

After close to a half-century of campaigning, and with the endorsement and aid in recent years of the labor movement, the Canadian social democratic movement remains a weak third party. Currently, it does not hold office in any of the ten provinces. (Only the Labour Party in much less industrialized and highly religious Ireland is weaker than the NDP.) Canada still ranks with the United States at the bottom of the list in terms of support for leftist parties.

The two North American democracies are also low on other indicators of class consciousness and conflict. In every democratic country, except possibly France, the percentage of the nonagricultural labor force belonging to trade unions is much higher than in Canada and the United States. The approximate figures for Canada and the United States are 28 and 20 percent, respectively, compared with 48 percent for Britain, 38 percent for Germany, 58 percent for Denmark, 53 percent for Australia, and more than 65 percent each for Austria, Belgium, Israel, and Sweden. The low rates for the Latin countries, particularly France (23 percent) and Italy (33 percent), appear to be a result of a quite different format of unionism characterized by the existence of three or more politically backed competitive union centers that do not have an institutionalized contractual base. The issue must clearly be expanded beyond asking why socialism is less developed in North America than elsewhere, to why is the organized labor movement also so weak in the two most developed industrial economies?

A further indication of the low level of class consciousness and class-related conflict in North America may be found in studies of the correlates of voting behavior. In all democratic countries, left or liberal parties secure more support from less privileged, less educated, and working-class voters than the more conservative or bourgeois parties. But the correlations between class and voting are lower in the United States and Canada than in European countries and Australasia. Membership in trade unions is also less predictive of voting behavior in Anglo-America than on the European continent or in Australasia.

The evidence drawn from political history, from studies of voting behavior, and from patterns of trade union membership, all indicate that the underprivileged and the working class in the two predominantly English-speaking North American federal unions are less class conscious and less organized. Comparing the two with each other suggests that the varying constitutional and electoral systems provide protest and consensual politics in each, in different forms but with similar content. The fact that these nations remain so alike in their political and class relations indicates that what they have in common is more important than what differentiates them. Their relatively egalitarian status structures, achievement-oriented value-systems, relative affluence, absence of a European aristocratic or feudal past, history of political democracy prior to industrialization, all have operated to produce relatively cohesive systems that remain unreceptive to proposals for major structural change.[37] In other words, basically comparable structural conditions are decisive. As the MIT political scientist Walter Dean Burnham has emphasized: "No feudalism, no socialism: with these four words one can summarize the basic sociocultural realities that underlie American electoral politics in the industrial era. . . . There may well be much to support a theory of 'American exceptionalism,' a theory that emphasizes the uniqueness of the historical and cultural factors that have gone into the making of the United States."

Burnham goes on to note that the emphasis on "American exceptionalism" is reinforced by comparison with "its continental-sized pluralistic neighbor to the north." There, "CCF/NDP efforts to the contrary notwithstanding," may be found "two old and loosely articulated bourgeois parties that are hegemonic in the electoral system" resulting from the fact "that the historical, economic, geographical, and ethnocultural factors that have dominated American politics down to the present find their closest parallels in Canada."[38]

The evidence, as I judge it, in agreement with Burnham, indicates that Wells and Hartz are correct in their evaluation of the impact of the unique North American history and culture on the prospects for socialism and class solidarity. They are weak because the North American environment has not been supportive for ideological and class-oriented politics narrower than those offered by brokerage coalition parties.

NOTES

1. Karl Marx, *Capital,* vol. 1 (Moscow: Foreign Languages Publishing House, 1958), pp. 8–9.
2. See Lipset, "Why No Socialism . . .," pp. 49–50, for comments and references.
3. See Louis S. Feuer, *Marx and the Intellectuals* (Garden City, N.Y.: Doubleday–Anchor Books, 1969), pp. 198–207.
4. Karl Marx and Friedrich Engels, *The German Ideology* (New York: International Publishers, 1960), p. 123.
5. Theodore Draper, *American Communism and Soviet Russia* (New York: Viking, 1960), pp. 268–72.
6. Lipset, "Why No Socialism . . .," pp. 58–60.
7. Louis Hartz, *The Liberal Tradition in America* (New York: Harcourt, Brace and World, 1955). See also Louis Hartz, *The Founding of New Societies* (New York: Harcourt, Brace and World, 1964), pp. 69–122.
8. H. G. Wells, *The Future in America* (New York: Harper and Brothers, 1906), pp. 72–76.
9. Michael Harrington, *Socialism* (New York: Saturday Review Press, 1972), p. 118.
10. Karl Marx and Friedrich Engels, *Selected Correspondence, 1846–1895* (New York: International Publishers, 1942), p. 467.
11. Ibid., p. 501.
12. V. I. Lenin, *Capitalism and Agriculture in the United States of America* (New York: International Publishers, 1934), p. 1.
13. V. I. Lenin, "Preface to the Russian Translation of 'Letters by J. Ph. Becker, J. Dietzgen, F. Engels, K. Marx and Others to F. A. Sorge and Others'," in V. I. Lenin, *On Britain* (Moscow: Foreign Languages Publishing House, n.d.), p. 51.
14. Ibid., p. 61.
15. Antonio Gramsci, "The Intellectuals," in his *Selections from the Prison Notebooks* (New York: International Publishers, 1971), pp. 21–22.
16. Ibid., pp. 281, 285, 305.
17. Harrington, *Socialism,* p. 118 (emphases Harrington's).
18. Kenneth McNaught, "Dream Along With Me," *Canadian Forum,* 54 (October, 1975), pp. 34–35.
19. "Engels to Sorge," December 2, 1893, in Karl Marx and Friedrich Engels, *Letters to Americans* (New York: International Publishers, 1953), p. 258 (emphases in original).
20. Morris Hillquit, *History of Socialism in the United States* (New York and London: Funk and Wagnalls, 1910), pp. 359–60. The argument and best evidence for the thesis that the presidential system prevents a multi-party system may be in E. E. Schettschneider, *Party Government* (New York: Rinehart and Co., 1942), esp. pp. 65–98. See also S. M. Lipset, *The First New Nation: The United States in Historical and Comparative Perspective* (New York: W. W. Norton, 1963), pp. 294–95, 299–300.
21. Norman Thomas, *Socialism Re-examined* (New York: W. W. Norton, 1963), pp. 117–20, and *A Socialist's Faith* (New York: W. W. Norton, 1951), pp. 90–95.
22. Thomas, *Socialism Re-examined,* pp. 127–28, and *A Socialist's Faith,* pp. 252–255, and Harrington, *Socialism,* p. 262.
23. Herbert G. Gaston, *The Non-partisan League* (New York: Harcourt, Brace, and Co., 1920), pp. 285–87; Daniel Bell, *Marxian Socialism in the United States* (Princeton, N.J.: Princeton University Press, 1967), pp. 91–93.
24. Cited in Andrew A. Bruce, *The Non-partisan League* (New York: MacMillan, 1921), p. 56.
25. Benton H. Wilcox, "An Historical Definition of Northwestern Radicalism," *Mississippi Valley Historic Review,* 26 (December 1939), p. 391.

26. Oliver Carlson, *A Mirror for Californians* (Indianapolis: Bobbs-Merrill, 1941), pp. 291–302.

27. Earl Browder, "The American Communist Party in the Thirties," in Rita James Simon, ed., *As We Saw the Thirties* (Urbana: University of Illinois Press, 1967), pp. 237, 238.

28. Harrington, *Socialism,* pp. 262–63.

29. David A. Shannon, "Socialism and Labor," in C. Vann Woodward, ed., *The Comparative Approach to American History* (New York: Basic Books, 1968), p. 241.

30. J. David Greenstone, *Labor in American Politics* (New York: Alfred A. Knopf, 1969), p. 7.

31. Harrington, *Socialism,* p. 251.

32. Ibid., p. 255.

33. Richard Hofstadter, *The Age of Reform* (New York: Vintage Books, 1967), p. 308.

34. Harrington, *Socialism,* pp. 263–68.

35. S. M. Lipset, "Social Scientists View the Problem," in John H. M. Laslett and S. M. Lipset, eds., *Failure of a Dream? Essays in the History of American Socialism* (Garden City, N.Y.: Doubleday-Anchor Books, 1974), p. 40.

36. The Canadian social democratic party was known as the Cooperative Commonwealth Federation (CCF) from 1932–1961. Since then, it has called itself the New Democratic Party (NDP). See S. M. Lipset, "Radicalism in North America: A Comparative View of the Party Systems in Canada and the United States," in *Transactions of the Royal Society of Canada,* Series IV, 14 (1976), pp. 19–55.

37. For a discussion that seeks to apply some of these factors to an explanation of the different patterns of working-class politics in Europe and Australasia, see S. M. Lipset, "Radicalism or Reformism: The Sources of Working-Class Politics," *The American Political Science Review,* 77 (March 1983).

38. Walter Dean Burnham, "The United States: The Politics of Heterogeneity," in Richard Rose, ed., *Electoral Behavior* (New York: Free Press, 1974), pp. 718–19.

NATHAN GLAZER

The Death
of the Rosenbergs

In 1956, interest in and agitation over the fate of Julius and Ethel Rosenberg reached a new peak. They had been convicted for conspiracy to commit espionage to reveal the secrets of the atom bomb to the Soviet Union and had been executed in 1952. John Wexley had published a huge book, *The Judgment of Julius and Ethel Rosenberg* (Cameron and Kahn, 1955), arguing for their innocence. Major figures, among them Bertrand Russell, had been recruited in their defense. And Sidney Hook called me and urged me to write an article on the Rosenberg case to counter the huge tide of propaganda that argued that the United States was guilty of a judicial murder and that, as Bertrand Russell wrote, the FBI was guilty of "atrocities of whose techniques we have been made familiar in other police states such as Nazi Germany and Stalin's Russia."

Sidney Hook has been indefatigable in searching for the truth in disputed issues, in countering those who make arguments against the democratic process and who attempt to undermine it by insisting there is a corruption in it that makes it little better than, or indeed worse than, the politics and justice of totalitarian states. But even his energy has limits, and on many occasions he has recruited others to undertake tasks he could not. I was tapped because some years before, at another point of great agitation over the Rosenbergs, I had written a letter to the *New York Times* disputing a letter of Harold Urey's that asserted that on the basis of a reading of the trial transcript he found the Rosenbergs innocent. I had also just read the trial transcript. One could not remain unmoved by the fate of the Rosenbergs, young parents of two young children, insisting on their innocence and sentenced to die, and one wanted at least some assurance that the trial satisfactorily proved their responsibility for the acts for which they had been condemned. The trial transcript convinced me that they were guilty. Surprised that two readings, by two presumably open-minded people trying to make up their minds on the basis of the transcript, had come to such opposite conclusions, I wrote the *Times* to explain what had convinced me. The correspondence with Urey continued in private and petered out, and both of us were unmoved from our original positions.

I responded to Sidney Hook's urging that I examine the case again. It was now four years later, and the question was, What did the record show? The record was now much fuller. It included the mass of material that had been collected in order to argue for a new trial for Morton Sobell, who was in prison, the Wexley book, and other writings. Nothing it seemed had been brought up, despite the imaginative and widespread efforts of the attorneys for Morton Sobell, who was tried together with the Rosenbergs, that could convince judges a new trial was warranted, and there was nothing in the record that persuaded me that the original judgment that the Rosenbergs were guilty was in error. Indeed, there had been what was to me persuasive new evidence —the transcript of the trial of William Perl—of the existence of a spy ring of which the Rosenbergs were part, and which included other figures who had disappeared. I presented this evidence in a lengthy article that was published as a supplement to the *New Leader* on July 2, 1956. One could not be happy about the death sentence that had been imposed and carried out: and I raised some questions about it. About their guilt, I had no doubts, and assumed that in time more evidence would emerge that would convince all honest doubters.

It is now 26 years since that article was written. Many books have been written on the Rosenbergs.[1] Two important primary sources that were not available when I wrote in 1956 are now available—records of the deliberations of the Supreme Court and of the Atomic Energy Commission—and have been analyzed in scholarly articles.[2] Most important, a huge mass of documentation from the FBI and the Department of Justice on the government's role in the Rosenberg case has been released.[3]

One would think, after all this, that doubts as to the guilt or innocence of the Rosenbergs would have been stilled, that the mass of evidence would have weighed in on one side or the other. Strangely enough, it has not. Vast areas of potential evidence—about the role of various friends of the Rosenbergs who were believed to be members of their espionage ring by the FBI and who disappeared into Eastern Europe—remain as they were, absolutely dark. There is no smoking gun, on either side. Those of us who found the trial satisfactory, or as satisfactory as any trial can be when it is based on a thin trail of evidence, still find it so: Those who did not find it satisfactory then, continue to undermine it.[4]

However, the evidence that has emerged, in books, in documents from the Atomic Energy Commission, from the Supreme Court, and from the FBI and the Department of Justice, speaks with considerable force to another issue: Why were the Rosenbergs executed? And it raises troubling questions indeed about their execution. Why was a death sentence imposed, and why was it carried out, by the standards of American justice, with surprising speed? It can never be unimportant to ask why two people died, but this question raises another and larger question: Did they die because a hysteria prevailed in America in 1952 that demanded their deaths unjustly?

In 1956 all we know was that a single judge had pronounced the death sentence, for reasons he considered adequate; and there was no legal means of overturning it, nor were two presidents persuaded to grant clemency. And so the Rosenbergs died. But we now know that the death sentence was imposed by a judge who insisted on it, even when prosecutors and investigators were doubtful, who refused to bend on this, and who engaged in what seems distinctly odd and perhaps unjudicial behavior in his desire to sustain it and defend its rightness.

The investigators and prosecutors who have been so heavily charged with malfeasance by the defendants of the Rosenbergs always contemplated a lesser sentence for Ethel, and hardly anyone, apparently, aside from Judge Kaufman himself,[5] wanted the death sentence for her—we leave aside the question of whether their motive was to impose a sentence better suited to a lesser measure of guilt, or one designed to extract more information. Thus Carol Hurd Green, who has also consulted both the FBI files and, in particular, one collection of documents published by the National Committee to Reopen the Rosenberg Case, *The Kaufman Papers,* writes: "In April, FBI Director J. Edgar Hoover recommended a 30-year sentence for Ethel Rosenberg, because she was 'the mother of two small children' and 'would, in a sense, be presumed to be acting under the influence of her husband' (JR Headqtrs. file, vol. 19, no. 944). Assistant United States District Attorney Roy Cohn favored the death penalty, but noted: 'If Mrs. Rosenberg were sentenced to a prison term there was a possibility she would talk' (J. Edgar Hoover to D. M. Ladd, April 3, 1951, *Kaufman Papers*). But trial judge Irving Kaufman had already determined on the death sentence for both the Rosenbergs (memo, A. H. Belmont to D. M. Ladd, March 16, 1951, JR Headqtrs. file, vol. 17, no. 8940), and his decision remained."

What is of most interest is that the one party to the case who should have observed a judicial neutrality was the one who was strongest for the death penalty, seems to have determined on it before the end of the trial, and stuck to it despite every plea for some mitigation of the sentence. After all, by continuing to protest their innocence the Rosenbergs left open the possibility they indeed were innocent; there were two young children who would be left parentless; an alternative statute referring specifically to atomic secrets under which they might have been convicted did not call for the death penalty; the foreign country to whom they were transmitting information at the time was an ally; and so on. But none of this moved Judge Kaufman. Professor Vern Countryman of Harvard points out, on the basis of his reading of some of the FBI and Department of Justice documents, that Judge Kaufman "seems to have been in regular contact with the Justice Department prosecution staff, who were in turn passing information on to the FBI. . . . [T]wo days before sentencing, [Prosecutor] Roy Cohn told an FBI agent that Judge Kaufman 'personally favored' the death penalty for the Rosenbergs.'' Judge Kaufman seemed particularly concerned to defend his sentence and his role generally, and by means that strike me, without knowing more about proper judicial behavior—and strike Countryman, too, who does know—as distinctly odd. Thus, in February 1953, Kaufman expressed his concern to the FBI that the Supreme Court would not dispose of the case before its spring adjournment. On June 17, shortly before the Supreme Court's final action, he was passing information to the FBI that he had received from someone else about what Justice Douglas would do. He was again in touch with the FBI in 1957, concerned that Morton Sobell's motion for a new trial might succeed. He called the FBI on other occasions and, as late as 1975, to express concern to the FBI about a book on the Rosenbergs, a TV program, and an *Esquire* article.

No explanation of this behavior has been given by Judge Kaufman, who has gone on to a lengthy career on the Second Circuit Court of Appeals. Certainly one has reason to think that the Rosenbergs and Sobell would have received better treatment from another judge. Yet nothing that Judge Kaufman did, despite many reviews in the Second Circuit and the Supreme Court, was ever overthrown.[6] Under the circumstances, one must conclude that despite Judge Kaufman's behavior the outcome as to the jury's finding of guilt would not have been different. But one has very good reason to believe that the Rosenbergs would not have been given the death sentence at the hands of another judge, or that Ethel Rosenberg might have been spared.

A second aspect of the case, revealed more fully than before in the FBI papers, is the degree to which the threat of the death sentence was held over the Rosenbergs as a means to force them to confess. I make no suggestion that this was Judge Kaufman's intention: but given the sentences by Judge Kaufman, for his own reasons, the Department of Justice and the FBI exercised them cruelly to make the Rosenbergs talk.

This to my mind is not the function of a death sentence. It should be a sentence considered proper to a proved crime, and it may be seen as a deterrent to others to commit that crime—it is not to be used as a means to force self-condemnation from victims. Alas, the evidence is now clear that it was so used.

Radosh and Stern describe the final scene in Sing Sing prison, with FBI agents standing by to interrogate the Rosenbergs should, at any moment before their deaths, they indicate they had a different story to tell. At that point, the executions would be stopped. This is unsettling indeed. One of the earlier books on the Rosenbergs, it is true, had more or less said as much. Jonathan Root, in *The Betrayers,* had already described the strange arrangements to stop the executions if the Rosenbergs were willing to talk: United States Marshal William Carroll ''had the authority to stop the executions if either Rosenberg or his wife decided at the last minute to confess''

(p. 273). Stern and Radosh fill out the details.

I realize that reduced sentences are used as rewards to get potential witnesses, themselves involved in a crime, to testify. (And judges need not accept the deal, as Kaufman did not accept the government's recommendation of a lenient sentence for Greenglass.) But after the sentence has been imposed, and when that sentence is death, it would seem to me that it cannot be used as this one was to force confession and more information. It reminds one uneasily of the behavior of terrorists who hold hostages. The Rosenbergs, sentenced under law, and a law that held up through all appeals, in this sense were not hostages seized by outlaws, but they were treated, after the death sentence, much as hostages treat their victims when they demand demeaning self-degradation in return for not imposing death.

What legal redress was there against such behavior? I do not know. Ethel Rosenberg's attorney appealed to a judge regarding the conditions of confinement, when, as he argued, these conditions were made particularly harsh in an effort to break her. But Federal Judge Goddard ruled that "no evidence had been presented to show any attempt to 'break' the prisoner. . . . the transfer [to Sing Sing] was 'not unusual or cruel and inhuman within the meaning of the Eighth Amendment to the Constitution.' " Of course terrorists' hostages do not have this opportunity. But our judges' views as to what is cruel and unusual punishment have developed considerably in the thirty years since the Rosenberg case.

Whatever Judge Kaufman's behavior, whatever the treatment of the Rosenbergs as they awaited death, there was redress. And perhaps the most disheartening material that has yet emerged about the case is how the Supreme Court and the highest American officials—the president and the attorney general—responded to the efforts of the Rosenbergs' defenders to have their case reviewed by the Court on one ground or another. The story was not known before: The important article by Michael E. Parrish, "Cold War Justice: The Supreme Court and the Rosenbergs," in the *American Historical Review* for October 1977, has received much less attention than it deserves. If the Rosenberg judgment was to be modified, it had to be in the Supreme Court. It was not modified, for reasons that not only again remind us that the justices are human and can be petty but also now amaze us, because this reminder is given to us in a case in which life and death literally hung in the balance. Parrish's article is written principally from Justice Felix Frankfurter's papers, but also from the papers of Justice Harold Burton. "The refusal of the Supreme Court to review the Rosenbergs' convictions on at least seven occasions became for Justice Frankfurter one of the gravest moral crises in his lifetime. He wrote several public dissents at the time, but they pale by comparison with the bitterness he expressed privately" (p. 808).

In the first major appeal to the Court of Appeals for the Second Circuit, to a three-man court on which Jerome Frank (who opposed, as we know, the death sentences) sat, seven points were raised: That the Rosenbergs should have been tried under the safeguards that attach to trial for treason in the Constitution ("No person shall be convicted of Treason unless on the Testimony of two Witnesses to the same overt Act, or on Confession in Open Court"); that the death sentence was unconstitutionally "cruel and unusual punishment"; that the name of one witness (the photographer who testified on the last day of the trial that he had taken passport pictures of the Rosenbergs) was not provided to the defendants three days before trial, as required in the federal criminal code; that Judge Kaufman had exhibited hostility to the defendants; that the photographer committed "perjury," for he had seen the Rosenbergs in court the day before, but testified he had not seen them previously; that the prosecutor, by announcing the arrest of William Perl during the trial, possibly prejudiced the jury; and that the indictment, trial, and sentence should have been brought under the Atomic Energy Act of 1946, which, for atomic secrets, had superseded the older Espionage Act. The Circuit Court rejected these grounds for a new trial, but Judge Frank urged the Supreme Court to review the case to clarify some of these issues. The Supreme Court refused to hear the case on June 7, 1952, and again on November 8. Hugo Black wanted to review, Harold Burton wanted to review, Frankfurter wanted to review, but four votes were needed. William O. Douglas denied. Frankfurter wrote: "His 'deny' this time was unaccompanied by argument. But it was uttered with startling vehemence" (p. 817).

The Rosenberg lawyers tried to reopen the case with additional arguments before U.S. Court Judge Sylvester Ryan in December 1952, failed, appealed to the Circuit Court, failed again, appealed again to the Supreme Court. "On February 17, 1953, over the objection of government attorneys, the [Circuit Court] judges stayed the couple's execution until after the Supreme Court had acted on their petition to review [the Circuit Court's] decision. . . . Jerome Frank noted the argument put forth by the defense had merit, 'and for my part, I believe the Supreme Court should hear it.' Learned Hand, perhaps the second circuit's most cautious jurist, chastised the government for resisting the stay of execution. 'People don't dispose of lives,' he said, 'just because an attorney didn't make a point. . . .' " (p. 822).

Once again, on April 11, Justice Douglas refused to join those who wanted to review, now reduced to two (Black and Frankfurter). Frankfurter agonized over whether to write an extended dissent, finally decided not to, and Black and Frankfurter agreed they would simply append to the Court's order of a denial a note that they still thought the Court should review the case.

At this point Douglas wrote a memorandum, asserting he had changed his mind. He apparently expected now to join his two dissenting brethren. But then Frankfurter persuaded Justice Jackson to join the three, making four, enough for a hearing. The justices were discussing, on May 23, when the hearing might take place, when Douglas interrupted to say his memorandum was badly written, he didn't realize it would embarrass anyone, and he would withdraw it; at which point Jackson withdrew *his* vote. Thus having decided, after a number of refusals, to go with the minority and discovering to his surprise that he had now joined a group that had enough votes to require a hearing, Douglas threw a monkey wrench into the proceedings, and returned matters to where they had been before. Not everything in Parrish's meticulous account is clear, but his own conclusion is: "If Jackson's conduct did not exhibit the highest level of judicial integrity, Douglas's remains inexplicable in view of his later apparent interest in the case" (p. 826).

In June, the Rosenberg attorneys and various others desperately sought to find legal straws to stop the Rosenbergs' execution and on June 12 applied to Jackson for a stay only six days before the execution date. On June 13, Saturday, the Court met, with Jackson proposing that it hear oral arguments for a stay on Monday, June 15, its last day. Douglas once again was on the "no" side: He would not vote to hear arguments for a stay of execution only, but would vote to hear the case on the merits. But on this course Justice Burton was lost: "Burton, in other words, refused to grant a stay but would hear oral argument on the question. Douglas would grant a stay but dismissed the necessity for argument. Three justices—Black, Frankfurter, and Jackson— voted for either formula. Douglas's intransigence clearly doomed the application because, although both he and Burton insisted upon all or nothing, Burton asked for much less: a hearing on the application" (p. 832).

Once again, on Monday, June 15, the Court's last regular meeting day, with a writ of habeas corpus before the court, Douglas continued his strange behavior. Black and Frankfurter were again willing to hear the case. "To the latters' amazement, Douglas 'quite vehemently' sided with the majority. . . . By now, both Frankfurter and Jackson believed that Douglas had contradictory motives in the Rosenberg litigation. On the one hand, he worked to retain his image as a liberal tribune who, when necessary, fought alone on behalf of the oppressed. On the other, he thwarted collective efforts to review the case" (p. 833).

But two days after the Court had recessed, after having voted against three certiorari petitions, a recommendation by Jackson to hear oral arguments for a stay, and a plea of habeas corpus, Douglas jumped into the case and granted a stay on June 17, the day before the execution. Whatever the complexity of the motives that had guided his strange behavior, the Rosenbergs, it seemed, were now saved until the opening of the new term of the Supreme Court, when possibly the Court could act on one or another of the issues in American jurisprudence that so often prevent executions.

Now we must shift to other actors who ensured the Rosenbergs' execution. When Attorney General Brownell petitioned the Court to vacate Douglas's stay, Chief Justice Vinson recalled the vacationing justices. Finally, a variety of attorneys, both those who had steadily represented the Rosenbergs and those who had on their own entered the case, argued before the recalled Court on June 18, while the execution was held in abeyance. On June 19, the Court voted to vacate Justice Douglas's stay, the president refused again to grant clemency, and the Rosenbergs were executed in what seemed remarkable haste, while protests were carried on around the world.

Would it have mattered if the Court had held over consideration until the fall? The legal issues had been well canvassed, despite the haste at the end, and there was good reason to believe that the end would have been the same. The Circuit Court of Appeals for the Second Circuit was the only appellate court to review the case in some detail, and it found no ground to set aside the jury's verdict and Judge Kaufman's sentence. No really new issues were raised in all the subsequent appeals. Indeed, Justice Douglas's stay was granted on the grounds of the potential conflict between the penalty provisions of the Espionage Act of 1917, under which the Rosenbergs were tried, and the Atomic Energy Act of 1946. But the Second Circuit had already reviewed that claim and did not find merit in it. Would the Supreme Court have found differently? It is hard to think so; but had the Court held off the executions and reviewed the case it might yet have found some reason to prevent the execution of the Rosenbergs, and the case would then have lost much of the power it has since exercised on the American mind. The Rosenbergs alive could never have been the symbol that the Rosenbergs dead became.

Still one wonders at the haste, and presumably more detailed historical research would be necessary to understand it. It is hardly likely that those who were investigating the espionage wanted a hasty execution—as we know, they hoped still to learn more from the Rosenbergs; and while they lived, they might yet talk. One suspects that it was the worldwide protests more than anything else that persuaded Eisenhower and Brownell that to suspend the executions while more legal proceedings went on would be to betray weakness in the face of a cynical and determined enemy. The protests, to them, could only be the manipulated efforts of Communists and fellow-travelers to serve the interests of the Soviet Union and Communism, no matter how many distinguished, disinterested, liberal, and decent men had joined in them. The protests did combine in varying degree disapproval of and anger at the United States, pity for the Rosenbergs, support for the Soviet Union, opposition to the death sentence, and conviction that the United States was the new Nazi Germany and the FBI the new Gestapo. Some of this could only outrage President Eisenhower and Attorney General Brownell; some of it might move them. Unfortunately, all the interests came together in the protests, and it was not easy to disentangle one from the other. Undoubtedly a more effective, disinterested effort to save the Rosenbergs was inhibited by the fact that it would inevitably have become entangled in the movement the Communists and fellow-travelers had created and dominated.

Which brings us to our final considerations on the meaning of the Rosenberg case, indeed the meanings of the case. We have indicated what the case meant to American leaders at a time when they held it in their power to grant clemency or delay the executions. It was a battle in the cold war, one in which the United States had been successfully cast as an inhumane ogre, not only in the eyes of Communists and fellow-travelers, but in the eyes of many distinguished people who had no connection with Communism at all. But this view was overwhelmingly rejected in the United States: To the great majority of Americans, high and low, the Rosenberg case was a credit to the American investigative agencies and system of justice. The Rosenbergs had received their due and, at a time when the death sentence was handed out more frequently than it was in later decades, had received a sentence that most Americans considered just. Whatever we think of Judge Kaufman's decision today, the protest against it was for the most part limited to the left and radical fringe in American politics.

The matter has since become rather more complex—for both sides. Majority American opinion in time began to live with the fact that the monopoly of the atomic bomb had been lost, and would have been lost in time anyway due to the efforts of Soviet scientists and technologists. It hardly seems likely that the incredible situation in which we now live, in which two great powers have the capacity to incinerate each other and the earth, could have been avoided—perhaps it could have been delayed a few years if Klaus Fuchs and the Rosenbergs and the others engaged in atomic espionage had not existed. Espionage, most of us are now convinced, did not create the very dangerous world in which we live. Under the circumstances, the death sentences and the passions that helped determine it must seem excessive to most of us.

There is a second development that has shaped our view of the Rosenberg case: This is our changing conception generally of the 1950s. Was it an epoch of hysteria over atom spies, Communists, suppression of dissent, intimidation of unpopular opinion, an epoch in which many thousands of innocents lost their livelihoods, their reputations, some for a time their freedom, and two— in the end, strangely, only two—their lives? The defenders of the Rosenbergs have of course an interest in presenting the case in this context. To many of us, whether radical, or liberal, or even conservative, whether informed historians or not, that is only the simple truth, and this conception of the 1950s provides the proper context in which to see the case. It is one of the incidents in the period that our school histories now record as the epoch of McCarthyism.

There are problems with this approach, as we can see from the dispute that broke out over Lillian Hellman's book *Scoundrel Time,* which dealt not at all with espionage but only with McCarthyism per se, with the search for Communists, and how it harmed many people (Communists, first of all).[7] The problem with it is that it ignores a key question: How real was Communism? How real the variety of threats it posed? To the freedom of Western Europe? To the opportunity of many countries emerging from colonialism to develop free from a totalitarian dictatorship? To the cultural life of the Western World and its ability to free itself from illusions, from lies, indeed from a movement that represented tyranny and claimed to represent and defend freedom of mind and dissent? And, we might add, how real was espionage inspired by this movement, and how dangerous was it? When these issues are raised, the history of McCarthyism and the persecution of Communists can be seen in two strikingly different lights. From one perspective, McCarthyism was the extreme wing of a necessary defense of freedom, a defense that offered opportunity for political advancement to unscrupulous people, and in which there were excesses—but the defense was necessary. The unscrupulous in the end for the most part destroyed themselves, and American freedom and American liberties were scarcely harmed. And the conflict goes on.

The other perspective is strikingly different. In this perspective, America is always in danger, but only from itself. Its reserves of bigotry are enormous; its military power is a constant invitation to its leaders to support right-wing dictators and to engage in disastrous overseas adventures; its investigative agencies are corrupt; its system of justice serves government and the powerful; its liberties are constantly in danger. Communists really don't exist but are manufactured by the powers that be and by the mass media to suppress dissent and retain their own power. Such points of view are honestly held by many, but how convenient they have always been for those whose primary loyalties are to the Soviet Union and to Communism!

But this dichotomy has not remained stable, just as our horror at the idea of someone facilitating Russian possession of the atom bomb has not remained stable. In the latter case, our views as to the legitimacy of the death sentence must be affected by our present knowledge that it would have happened anyway, that American or Western exclusive possession of atomic arms could not have lasted long. Similarly, our view of the enormous danger posed by the international Communist movement has also for many of us been changed by events. Many people do maintain in 1982 the same attitude toward international Communism that they held in 1952. If this overwhelming menace to the liberties of free people is seen in 1982 as it was, by most Americans, in 1952, then perhaps we might end up with the same judgment as to the punishment due the Rosenbergs. But how cannot 30 years of history affect our view of the danger of Communism?

A number of elements contribute to this inevitable change of assessment. First, Communism is no longer one monolithic movement, directed from Moscow. Indeed, one of the gravest international conflicts separates the two great Communist powers—and one is treated almost as an ally by the United States.

Second, the American Communist Party, having been driven underground in the late 1940s and early 1950s, has never recovered its strength. Indeed, the great upsurge of radicalism of the later 1960s owed very little to Communism. Threats of liberty today can come from a variety of leftist movements and organizations. Soviet Russia does not stand as centrally as it once did as *the* threat to freedom. To the new radical movements of the late 1960s, the

Communists were the "old left"—archaic, clumsy, scarcely to be taken seriously. Certainly whatever their influence once was on American politics, labor, and culture, it was radically reduced in the 1950s, and has never increased again.

Third, we now realize (for a while we suppressed this knowledge, after the defeat of Nazi Germany) that there are other evils in the world besides Communism—for example, authoritarianism and militarism, often accompanied by the cruel destruction of opponents. Would we consider spying for Soviet Russia today worse than, for example, spying for a number of third-world rulers who might in their rage and fury against enemies be tempted to use an atomic bomb?

All this can be countered by arguing that Soviet Russia, as a military power, if not as an ideological threat, is a more serious opponent than it was in 1952. Quite true, but then it is also true, as I pointed out in beginning this reconsideration, that most of us would be incapable of judging the significance of even a great deal of effective spying. When the Russians and we both experiment with satellite stations, laser beams, missile-destroying missiles, missiles aimed from outer space, and the like, how could we ever again feel the same shock of betrayal and horror that so many felt at the time the Rosenbergs were tried?

Ironically, the weakened American Communists, who still of course play a role in the various lefts that succeeded the so-called "old left," still can take credit for one major element on the continuing agenda of the new lefts: That the Rosenbergs were unjustly tried, convicted, and executed, and thus stand as testimony to the injustice of American society. Nothing that has appeared since the Rosenbergs were executed, I would argue, has any bearing on the justice of their trial, and of their conviction. But much has bearing on the justice of their execution. And when we additionally take account of how the world has changed since 1952, who can defend that execution?

NOTES

1. Among them, Jonathan Root, *The Betrayers,* Coward McCann, 1963; Walter and Miriam Schneir, *Invitation to an Inquest,* Doubleday, 1965, (which I reviewed in the *New York Times Book Review,* September 5, 1965), 2nd ed., Penguin, 1973; Louis Nizer, *The Implosion Conspiracy,* Doubleday, 1973; Morton Sobell, *On Doing Time,* Scribner's, 1974; Robert and Michael Meeropol, *We Are Your Sons,* Houghton Mifflin, 1975.

2. Michael E. Parrish, "Cold War Justice: The Supreme Court and the Rosenbergs," *American Historical Review,* 82 (1977), 805-42; and Roger M. Anders, "The Rosenberg Case Revisited: The Greenglass Testimony and the Protection of Atomic Secrets," *American Historical Review,* 83 (1978), 388-400; and an exchange on this article in the *American Historical Review,* 84 (1979) 904-06.

3. There have been four articles that report on this documentation, all of which I have made use of: Allen Weinstein, "The Hiss and Rosenberg Files," *New Republic,* February 14, 1976; Vern Countryman, "Out, Damned Spot," *New Republic,* October 8, 1977, pp. 15-17; Carol Hurd Green, "Ethel Greenglass Rosenberg," in *Notable American Women: The Modern Period,* edited

by Barbara Sicherman and Carol Hurd Green, Harvard University Press, 1980, pp. 601-604; and Sol Stern and Ronald Radosh, "The Hidden Rosenberg Case," *New Republic,* June 23, 1979, pp. 13-26; and correspondence on this article, August 4 and 11, pp. 24-29, 47. Stern and Radosh promise a book, which has not yet appeared.

4. I analyze the "new evidence" as to guilt or innocence in a forthcoming essay, "The Rosenberg Case," of which this article will form a part, to appear in a volume edited by Roland Stromberg on American political trials which will be published by Henry Regnery in the spring of 1983.

5. Allen Weinstein, in his review of the first releases of FBI and Justice Department files ("The Hiss and Rosenberg Files," *New Republic,* February 14, 1976, pp. 20, 21), writes: The documents "suggest the degree to which the prosecutor's decision to ask for a death penalty in that trial emerged only after a period of heated bickering between the prosecutors (who initially opposed such a move) and the Atomic Energy Commission (which favored it and won out in the end). . . . A surprising revelation was that J. Edgar Hoover and other high government officials close to the case had recommended clemency for Ethel—but not Julius—Rosenberg."

6. Not as critical of Judge Kaufman is Michael E. Parrish, who has also studied the FBI records for his important article, "The Supreme Court and the Rosenbergs," op. cit., and reviews the material on the death sentence on p. 811, footnote 21. An FBI report in his account reveals that Judge Kaufman had consulted Jerome Frank of the Court of Appeals and District Judge Weinfeld. Frank was against the death penalty for any of the defendants, Weinfeld in favor of it for all.

7. See among others, my review, "An Answer to Lillian Hellman," in *Commentary,* June 1976, vol. 61, no. 6, pp. 36-39.

MARVIN ZIMMERMAN

Hooked on Freedom and Science

Sidney Hook is one of the outstanding advocates of freedom and scientific method as means for promoting the public good. At present, the Communists represent the biggest threat to freedom, and the religionists pose a serious challenge to scientific method. Of the two, the Communists are a greater danger to mankind, since freedom is more essential to human well-being.

In the following comments on current issues involving both freedom and scientific method, I have been influenced by the spirit and insights of Sidney Hook, whom I and countless others consider an embodiment of the Socratic quest for reason and morality.

The widespread influence of Communist domination and its continued advance over the past sixty years are incompatible with the survival of freedom. The Communists are a greater threat in power, range, durability, and technology than even the Fascists were fifty years ago. Their reliance on ideology and dogma (primarily Marxist-Leninist) as the basis for their beliefs is similar to the stance of religious fundamentalists and other religious adherents. Though the Communists pay lip-service to scientific method as their ultimate ideological basis, they are in practice dogmatic and overwhelmingly opposed to freedom and democracy. Religious fundamentalists' attitudes toward freedom and democracy tend to vary with the political climate in which they find themselves. However, their ultimate basis for beliefs are biblical and religious rather than empirical and scientific.

The Soviet Union is advancing toward military superiority and a first-strike capability that could result in the surrender and destruction of freedom. Since it is impossible to have adequate verification or reprisals for violation of strategic arms agreements, it is less risky to abstain from participating in treaties like SALT or the Helsinki Accords than to conclude formal arms agreements with the Communists. Agreements constitute a move toward ultimate suicide or surrender; abstention leads to continuation in the race for survival. Which is more likely to advance human life and freedom—appeasement or resistance, military inferiority or superiority? What do history and human nature teach us?

War, like death, may be inevitable, but firm resistance and military strength increase the chances of preventing war, or winning it, should it occur. Responses to the Fascists and Communists in recent history confirm this.

All too many liberals and socialists (Second International) have condoned the steady expansion of Communist influence and power. Ironically, they have been abetted, often unintentionally, by many religious forces throughout the world. The support of some of these groups for SALT agreements, detente, and policies of appeasement is based upon religious slogans and dogmas (love, brotherhood of man) with little regard for historical evidence of man's biological nature. In the quest for peace, these disparate groups appeal for a nuclear freeze, cuts in arms expenditures, and disarmament. Such pressures serve the aims of Communist military advantage and world domination, since the Communists are not subject to internal political lobbying.

In recent years the United Nations has been ineffective, indifferent, and partisan in response to the aggression, repression, and terrorism of the Communists and their allies. Furthermore its membership is predominantly undemocratic and negatively disposed toward the free world. How has the United Nations dealt with Hungary, Czechoslovakia, and more recently with Vietnam, Cambodia, Israel, Afghanistan, and Poland?

A plausible case can be made for the United States (and other democratic nations) to withdraw from the world body. All dialogues and discussions could be held, and agreements concluded, with any country or groups of countries in accord with our own interests without the involvement of the United Nations. In practice, this is precisely what has been occurring—witness the bilateral and multilateral military, economic, and political agreements participated in by the United States and other governments. Have the supporters of the UN found a new god to worship—another religious dogma?

Many are persuaded by wishful thinking found in traditional religion. Vague ideas like unity of mankind, brotherhood of man, world government, world law, God's kingdom on earth, and world socialism are illusory and unrealistic forms of dogma or rationalization.

Those devoted to humanity should favor human survival in the event of war or nuclear accident. Though military strength can discourage war, a strong civil defense would increase human survival if war occurs. It is ironic how little support one finds among the religious and the secular in the free world for fal out shelters and civilian defense. No doubt the former count on God, the latter on hope and wishful thinking. Both ignore reality and evidence. Apparently the major Communist nations, the Soviet Union and Mainland China, show more sense by maintaining massive defense shelters. As a consequence they increase their chances for survival and their threat to the free world.

We do not believe the Soviets are preparing for a first-strike attack merely because they have mass civilian defense programs. Yet, in the free world, some irrationally claim the reverse is true and therefore oppose civilian defense. Anything we do or fail to do might provoke the Soviets to engage in a first-strike attack. Our unwillingness to engage in civilian defense encourages them to expect success in a variety of military moves, including a first-strike attack.

In addition to the Communists, there are many other examples of threats to specific areas of freedom and the public good. Many arguments favoring government intervention in the economy are characterized by emotional, sentimental rhetoric. Taxes, regulation, and punitive actions by authority are supported even when unworkable, wasteful, and counterproductive. Some supporters of these measures, including liberals, socialists, and Marxists, use language characteristic of religion. Slogans like special interests, equality, fairness, have-nots, the poor, the hungry, love, and brotherhood are treated as self-evident. Sentiment becomes sufficient for government intervention and control. Objective empirical data is considered irrelevant or unnecessary.

There is strong evidence that countries with greater economic freedom have higher standards of living than those with greater government restrictions. That this has been historically so is ignored by ideologists who have their own political bibles and scriptures that they faithfully support (Marx, Lenin, Mao). However, the Communists have granted in practice what they repudiate in socialist theory. Communist governments frequently (though temporarily) remove economic restrictions on individuals to increase output and productivity.

The economically free tend to be politically free, whereas the economically restricted tend to be politically restricted as well. This is no mere statistical accident, since threats to one freedom (e.g., economic) endanger other freedoms (e.g., political).

However unclear the nature of man, historical evidence of corruptibility and concentration of power lends support to separation of power, majority rule, and a bill of rights. We tend to use the word "democratic" to refer to political freedom, including the Bill of Rights. Our defense of these freedoms against government interference depends on evidence that these liberties benefit humanity. *Economic* freedom and concomitant dangers of government restriction and abuse must be viewed within the same context of evidence. Support of economic freedom is no more a call for anarchy than is support of political freedom exemplified in the Bill of Rights. Taxation, subsidies, regulations, economic monopoly, control of prices, wages, profits, markets, confiscation of property, and much more have created enormous human suffering and stagnation. Government economic interference has also spilled over into the political, religious, educational, and private freedoms, with painful consequences. Fascist and Communist countries are good examples of harmful economic interference. Government intervention has been detrimental even for societies that maintain certain basic political freedoms.

Thus, protecting political freedom against coercive authority has a strong counterpart in the area of economic freedom. Granting even politically democratic government greater power over the economic sphere is as threatening to the public as power over the political sphere. If socialism is interpreted as a system in which government exercises significant control over the economy, then it becomes, in the language of F. A. Hayek, "the road to serfdom" and in the language of Orwell, "1984." The United States has moved in that direction and many parts of the world have surpassed it.

I contend that the evidence supports the view that democratic capitalism is more productive of human good than democratic socialism. This is in the tradition of David Hume, Edmund Burke, Adam Smith, Hayek, Milton Friedman, and many others. I use the terms "capitalism" and "socialism" to distinguish the extent to which government regulates, controls, and owns the economy of society.

Outside the economic sphere, cases of use, abuse, misuse, and nonuse of scientific evidence are pervasive. Let us challenge the biblical and scriptural approach to abortion, homosexuality, birth control, equality, and evolution. The difficulties here, including which bible, scriptures, and interpretations to accept, are endless and unresolvable. However, there are legitimate, empirical grounds for criticizing these beliefs.

Some pro-abortionists utilize invalid scientific arguments while some anti-abortionists use sound scientific analysis to establish their views. Indeed a good deal of the legal reasoning before the pro-abortionist 1973 Supreme Court decision (*Roe* v. *Wade*) was more scientific than that of the Supreme Court. The states had a dominant role prior to the Court decision. A few states used plausible scientific criteria, such as presence of brain activity, to determine the presence of human life. Thus they allowed abortion during the first few months of pregnancy. However, the 1973 Supreme Court decision extended to six months the period in which legal abortions could be conducted. To support their decision the justices invoked notions of viability that have little relevance to the scientific characteristics of human life. The dicta of viability is as incorrect as the biblical anti-abortionist view that human life begins at conception, without brain activity present.

One need not accept biblical or religious objections to homosexuality to recognize that the presence of homosexuals in the armed forces creates special difficulties and that they should not be lodged in the same private quarters with heterosexuals. Empirical studies indicate many complex psychological, biological, and cultural problems connected with homosexuality and other divergent life-styles. There are empirical grounds for encouraging monogamous and heterosexual life-styles, while realizing that there are limits to what can legally be proscribed. Biblical injunctions are of little use here.

One can recognize specious religious opposition to birth control and the inconsistence of opposing artificial birth-control while accepting natural methods. Nevertheless, mandatory birth-control (as in Communist China) and birth-control pills and devices have sometimes been used in ways detrimental to humans. In fact, the effects of birth control on sex attitudes, the family, divorce, pregnancy, promiscuity, venereal disease, and other health hazards are a mixed blessing.

Allocating different functions, roles, and rights for males and females sole-ly on a biblical or divine basis, thus implying unequal treatment of the sexes, has no scientific basis. Paradoxically there are also many unscientific and religious arguments in support of sexual equality. This is reflected in such phrases as "created equal," "equal in the sight of God," "endowed with in-alienable rights," "children of God," "brotherhood of man," "divine spark," "made in the image of God."

There are empirical grounds for treating males and females differently in order to aid society's advancement. Separation of the sexes can usually be justified in the military, prisons, schools, and police and fire departments. Equal treatment does serve the public interest in such situations as voting, holding political office, and equal pay for equal work.

Some people are treated differently and some equally on unscientific grounds. It is called unjust discrimination in the former case and unjust egalitarianism in the latter. Religious or sacred grounds for discrimination (e.g., divine right of rulers) and equality (e.g., all men are created equal) have no empirical support. Secular arguments for discrimination (e.g., racial theories) and equality (e.g., common humanity) lack strong scientific evidence. Neither religionists nor secularists have a monopoly on wisdom in this area.

Some secularists treat evolution as a static belief, not subject to doubt. This is contrary to the scientific principle of fallibility. It is similar in spirit to the dogmatism of religious infallibility and comparable to the unscientific biblical grounds the fundamentalists use to reject evolution. One cannot dismiss out of hand empirical questions or challenges made to the validity of evolution by biblical or fundamentalist adversaries. There are no infallible answers here any more than in the beliefs of Giordano Bruno, Nicholas Copernicus, Sir Isaac Newton, Albert Einstein, Fred Hoyle, or in the scientific concepts of gravita-tion, atoms, continuous creation, "big-bang," or "steady-state" theories. The history of changing beliefs, hypotheses, and theories in science should make us cautious, skeptical, and even humble. Ironically, biblical supporters, while pointing out gaps in evolutionary evidence, accept religious and scriptural claims contrary to overwhelming evidence, including evidence in support of evolution.

Let me end on a note on which I began. Sidney Hook has made a valid case for our making a case for whatever we believe in an atmosphere of freedom. Use of intelligence presupposes discovering the best evidence available, and this implies dedication to both freedom and scientific method.

DAVID S. LICHTENSTEIN

The Radical Intellectual and American Foreign Policy: The Vietnam Experience

I have the rather unique distinction among the contributors to this *Festschrift* of having been a student in the first class in philosophy that Sidney Hook taught at New York University. Although my recollection of Sidney's discourse on Plato and Santayana has faded over the years, I shall never forget the day this vivacious young teacher paused to tell the class about an Italian politico named Mussolini, who had the habit of pouring castor oil down the throats of his opponents. Compared to the gulags of Soviet totalitarianism later in this century, the indignities forced on his opponents by Mussolini turned out to be a mild form of oppression indeed. Nevertheless, Sidney's extracurricular remark caught my imagination, and at his suggestion I read Gaetano Salvemini's seminal book on Italian fascism.[1] Thus, at least one student in that first class was started on the road to a lifelong interest in social and political philosophy. More important was the seed that was planted by a teacher who conveyed through his writing and lecturing an undying hostility to totalitarianism in all its forms, its gulags, and its contempt for humanity.

It is not fortuitous, therefore, to find Sidney Hook writing devastating critiques a half-century later about Lillian Hellman, Alger Hiss, and Kenneth Galbraith.[2] For the role of the radical intellectual in American culture has turned out to be the Achilles heel of democratic societies in the worldwide battle against totalitarianism. The "red decade" of Eugene Lyons has faded into history. Overt communist penetration of trade unions, governments, and teaching is but a memory. The challenge that faces democratic societies today is far more insidious and pervasive, since it comes from within our own intellectual elite.

In a brilliant essay in *Foreign Affairs* (July 1967), Irving Kristol pointed out that the American intellectual class actually has an interest in thwarting the adoption of any kind of responsible and coherent foreign policy by the United States. The United States, he indicated, has been projected into the responsibilities of a great power unavoidably, and as such it must have social equilibrium at home if it is to act effectively in the world.

But, he concluded, for any great-power policy to work effectively, it needs intellectual and moral guidance. "But the intellectual community en masse, disaffected from established power even as it tries to establish a power base of its own, feels no such sense of responsibility. It denounces, it mocks, it vilifies—and even if one were to concede that its fierce indignation was justified by extraordinary ineptitude in high places, the fact remains that its activity is singularly unhelpful." Here is a new class that is "alienated" from the established order—and Kristol offers as a reason for such alienation the belief of the intellectual class that this order has not conceded to it sufficient power and recognition.

How valid is this analysis? As a description of the gradual erosion of public support for an effective anti-communist foreign policy, for which erosion radical intellectuals are largely responsible, Kristol's analysis shows considerable insight. That a whole new intellectual class has emerged as a result of "the explosive growth, in these past decades of higher education in the United States" is undoubtedly correct. But having perceptively located the source of our current malaise, which amounts to a profound cultural and spiritual crisis ranging far beyond foreign policy, Kristol falters in developing an explanatory hypothesis to account for the behavior of the radical intellectual in the specific area of American foreign policy.

Kristol states that it is among American intellectuals that the isolationist ideal is experiencing its final convulsive agony. This misconceives the nature of the problem, since intellectuals were not isolationist with respect to the war against fascism; quite the contrary. Kristol is much closer to the truth when he indicates that intellectuals will "do nothing to strengthen the position of their antagonist." The significant question to determine is whom the intellectual considers to be his antagonist, and why foreign policy has become the crucial arena in which the confrontation between the intellectual and his "antagonist" is being fought out. There are, of course, other arenas of struggle where domestic problems have been inflamed to the point of emotional intensity, but there can be no doubt that American global responsibility, and particularly the recent role of the United States in Southeast Asia, launched almost the entire intellectual community into a hysterical all-out assault on any foreign policy predicated on the assumption that revolutionary communism constitutes a danger to the national interest. Why the intellectuals responded with such passion and determination to the Vietnam war is in a sense the burden of this inquiry.

The avalanche of literature assailing the merits of United States intervention in Vietnam is enormous. Highly placed officials in both the Kennedy and Johnson administrations rushed into print to deny that they had anything to do with recommending any increase in U.S. military power in Vietnam. What was the motivating force that drove the intellectual into such a passionate hatred of our involvement in Vietnam? What particular stake did he have in the outcome of U.S. intervention?

That the radical intellectual has such a stake was adumbrated by Senator Fulbright, who had difficulty restraining the intensity of his feeling. On April 4, 1971, he stated that the international pushers of anti-communism are no better than the international pushers of dope. In his book, *The Arrogance of Power,* he asserts that

> communism, for all its distortions in practice and for all the crimes committed in its name, is a doctrine of social justice and a product of Western civilization, philosophically rooted in humanitarian protest against the injustices of nineteenth-century capitalism. [p. 80]

> The point that I wish to make is not that communism is not a harsh and, to us, a repugnant system of organizing society, but that its doctrine has redeeming tenets of humanitarianism; that the worst thing about it is not its philosophy but its fanaticism; that history suggests the probability of an abatement of revolutionary fervor; that in practice fanaticism *has* abated in a number of countries, including the Soviet Union; that some countries are probably better off under communist rule than they were under preceding regimes; that some people may even want to live under communism; that in general the United States has more to gain from the success of nationalism than from the destruction of communism. [p. 81]

Mr. Fulbright's naiveté is reminiscent of Sidney and of Beatrice Webb. Recently, Sidney Hook, in an otherwise devastating critique of Kenneth Galbraith's foreign policy, maintained that Galbraith is ignorant of "the theory and practice of communism."[3] I have serious reservations about excusing Mr. Galbraith's foreign policy recommendations on the grounds of his "ignorance" of the practice of communism. There is a substantial difference between failure of perception and being "ignorant."[4]

Unfortunately, Mr. Fulbright occupied a critical position as chairman of the Senate Foreign Relations Committee during the Vietnam war. Fulbright employed the committee as a forum for launching attacks against the moral basis of American intervention in Southeast Asia. His denial that any vital interest of the United States involvement in Vietnam was grounded on an interpretation of American foreign policy that was characteristic of a dominant group of American intellectuals. In *Arrogance and Power,* he wrote:

> Why are Americans fighting in Viet Nam? For much the same reason, I think, that we intervened militarily in Guatemala in 1954, in Cuba in 1961, and in the Dominican Republic in 1965. In Asia as in Latin America we have given our opposition to communism priority over our sympathy for nationalism because we have regarded communism as a kind of absolute evil, as a totally pernicious doctrine which deprives the people subjected to it of freedom, dignity, happiness and the hope of ever acquiring them. I think that this view of communism is implicit in much of American foreign policy; I think it is the principal reason for our

involvement in Viet Nam and for the emergence of an "Asian Doctrine" under which the United States is moving toward the role of policeman for all of Southeast Asia. [p. 106]

The crime of the North Vietnamese that makes them America's enemy is that they are communists, practitioners of a philosophy we regard as evil. [p. 107]

The occasion for this potentially massive American involvement in Asia is of course the war in Vietnam, but its genesis is the priority of anti-communism over sympathy for nationalism in American policy and the terrible difficulties we encounter when confronted with a communist party which is also an indigenous nationalist party. [p. 111]

As the agony of frustration built up during 1965–1968 and more American troops were committed to the war, academic intellectuals (Hans Morgenthau, Edwin Reischauer, Arthur Schlesinger, Robert Tucker of John Hopkins) mounted a furious assault on the moral basis of American intervention. Their basic fear was that the war might arouse public passion and turn American foreign policy into an "anti-communist crusade." As Norman Podhoretz points out, engaging in an anti-communist crusade would, they warned, bring back all the horrors of McCarthyism.[5] That they might suffer the moral condemnation of future generations for having betrayed the national interest was of little moment compared to their own status and prestige. Academic intellectuals were committed to "revolutionary forces" in the so-called underdeveloped areas who presumably represented the true aspirations of peasants formerly under the yoke of "feudal regimes." Only one barrier remained in their campaign to seduce public opinion and to demonstrate that Ho Chi Minh and other revolutionary leaders represented indigenous nationalist movements. That barrier was a pushover for the verbal skills of academic writers who launched the concept of "polycentrism" as an irrefutable reply to those who maintained that communist-led guerrillas were trained and supplied, and their strategy orchestrated, by the Soviet Union.[6] There is a dreadful fear on the part of radical intellectuals that if the American people were alerted to the coordination and support by the Soviet Union of so-called national liberation movements in Latin America and Africa, they might be aroused to a sustained anti-communist foreign policy. Such resistance to further communist aggression might be accompanied by an emotional public reaction that would demand accountability for the consequences of the ideas and policies of the intellectuals who were responsible for assailing the moral basis of U.S. intervention in Indochina, the tragedy of the boat people, and advocating the myth that the Indochina communists were true nationalists whose victory would bring reconstruction and reconciliation.[7]

A question may be presented as to whether an account of *la trahison des clercs* during the Vietnam war is of more than historic interest. I submit that the betrayal of the national interest by the intelligentsia during that period was to have momentous consequences. For one consequence, the loss of the war was the impetus for Kissinger's détente policy.[8] Second, as Carl Gershman points out in *Commentary,* July 1980, the "old Establishment," whose central policy rested on containment, was demoralized by its shattering failure in Vietnam. The vacillation and failure of American policy to develop a global strategy can be directly traced to the loss of Vietnam. The ultimate denouement was the implementation of McGovern's foreign policy under Carter. Again, as Gershman very incisively points out, while writers like George Kennan, Zbignew Brzezinski, and Stanley Hoffman differed in the emphasis they gave to various issues, such differences were much less important than their agreement that containment was no longer a valid policy for the United States. This attitude was not merely the result of the demoralization of the old establishment resulting from the Vietnam debacle, but was the logical conclusion of the premises articulated by Morgenthau, Galbraith, and Schlesinger during the war.

In the midst of that war, when the support of public opinion was indispensable to the effective action, academic intellectuals provided the rationalization for surrender to communist aggression. Thus Galbraith, in a widely circulated pamphlet, "How to Get Out of Vietnam," argued that "we are in a conflict not alone with the Communists but with a strong sense of Vietnamese nationalism. If so, a further and massive conclusion follows. It is that we are in a war that we cannot win, and, even more important, one should not wish to win." He says further that "it was the centrally guided, conspiratorial aspect of communism by which we felt threatened and by which we felt Southeast Asia to be threatened. . . . Since we took this decision the whole foundation on which it rested has collapsed. Relations between China and the Soviets have been ruptured. . . . If the ultimate direction of the war is in Vietnam, we are concerned, in short, with national communism. Instead of the original enemy, we face one that elsewhere we not only tolerate but encourage." Galbraith further states, "Now we see that we oppose not a Soviet- or Chinese-dominated imperialism but an indigenously motivated nationalism led by Communists or in which Communists have a dominant role. This being so, the goal of restoring Saigon authority in all the country becomes (and here I choose my words deliberately) quite ridiculous. The people do not want such 'liberation.' "

The same line was pursued by Hans Morgenthau in a revealing chapter in his book *In Defense of the National Interest*:

> If those who refer to Communism as the real issue have primarily the revolutions in Asia in mind, they speak of something fundamentally different. While the Communist revolution could not have succeeded and will not succeed in any European country without the intervention of the Red Army, the revolutionary situation in Asia has developed independently of Russian Communism, and would exist in some form, owing to the triumph of Western moral ideas and the decline of Western power, even if Bolshevism had never been heard of. The revolutions in Europe are phony revolutions, the revolutions in Asia are genuine ones. While opposition to revolution in Europe is a particular aspect of the defense of

the West against Russian imperialism, opposition to revolution in Asia is counter revolution in Metternich's sense, resistance to change on behalf of an obsolescent status quo, doomed to failure from the outset. The issue of revolution in Asia is fundamentally different from that in Europe; it is not to oppose revolution as a creature and instrument of Russian imperialism but to support its national and social objectives while at the same time and by that very support preventing it from becoming an instrument of Russian imperialism. The clamor for consistency in dealing with the different revolutions sailing under the flag of Communism is the result of that confusion which does not see that the real issue is Russian imperialism, and Communist revolution only in so far as it is an instrument of that imperialism. [p. 79]

In his book *A New Foreign Policy for the United States,* Morgenthau deplores the fact that "the anti-Communist crusade has become both the moral principle of contemporary globalism and the rationale of our world-wide foreign policy." He further indicates that "it is our fear of Communism that forces us into an anti-revolutionary stance" (p. 28). In a paper delivered to the American Political Science Association at the 1968 annual meeting, he stated:

. . . we have tended to take the Communist postulates and prophecies at their face value and in consequence have been unable to divorce our political judgments from the assumption of the monolithic, conspiratorial character of Communism. Thus we have been unable to judge Vietnamese Communism on its national merits, as an indigenous phenomenon due to the peculiar circumstances of time and place. Instead, Vietnamese Communism has appeared to us as a special instance of a general phenomenon which is not by accident the same regardless of time and place. For it has been created by a worldwide conspiracy whose headquarters are assumed to be in Moscow or Peking or both and whose aim is to communize the world. In this view, what happens in Vietnam is just an episode in that world-wide struggle between Communism and the "free world" and consequently the outcome of the Vietnamese War has worldwide significance.

Our final exponent of the "new isolationism"[9] is a distinguished professor of international politics at Johns Hopkins University, Robert W. Tucker. His writings on the Near East in *Commentary* have attracted wide attention. Although Tucker maintains an aura of scholarly objectivity by purporting to present different points of view, i.e., the "radical view," the "liberal realist," and the "prevailing liberal critique," it is apparent from a comparison of his books that his loyalty is dedicated to the so-called "liberal critique" of U.S. foreign policy. Perhaps the clearest presentation of his position is found in the chapter he contributed to *Retreat from Empire*:

In the prevailing liberal critique, it was the very success of early containment policy that paved the way for a diplomacy culminating in the disaster of Vietnam. For this, when taken together with the momentum generated by the cold war itself, helped reinvigorate an outlook that had never been abandoned. The quintessential expression of this outlook was, of course, the Truman Doctrine, with its unlimited and indiscriminate commitment, its sense of universal crisis, and its messianic hope of redeeming history. The gradual triumph of the Truman Doctrine in policy describes the essential course of American diplomacy over the following two decades. What began as a policy largely limited to Europe, directed primarily against the expansion of Soviet power, and designed to restore a balance of power, ended as a policy unlimited in geographic scope, directed primarily against communism itself and designed to preserve a global status quo bearing little, if any, relation to the balance of power.[10]

Here again appears the main theme initiated by Morgenthau; i.e., our intervention in Southeast Asia was counterrevolutionary. Vietnam, according to this view, was a legacy of the cold war and represented "an indiscriminate commitment to intervene anywhere and everywhere against revolutionary change."[11] Like a swelling chorus, academic intellectuals rose to challenge the idea that communist revolution in the third world constituted a threat to the vital interests of the United States. Raising the banner of polycentrism, they defied all empirical evidence that so-called national liberation fronts, whether led by Ho Chi Minh or Castro or the Sandinista guerrillas of Nicaragua, are dedicated to the destruction of free societies, share the same ideology, and would rapidly vanish as a revolutionary force without the military and economic assistance, coordination, and training by the Soviet Union. The guns and ammunition that killed American soldiers in Vietnam were supplied by the Soviet Union—a small matter that seems to have been overlooked by the advocates of polycentrism. The use of Cuban mercenaries by the Soviet Union as cannon fodder in Angola should give the authors of maudlin sentiments about the "true aspirations" of the peasants in Africa and Asia some food for thought.

And now we can turn to the question originally posed: Why is the intellectual so bitterly opposed to U.S. intervention in "wars of national liberalism" or to intervention against a potential Castro-type takeover in Latin America? Why has the intellectual so insistently urged upon the American public that world communism has been fragmented and no longer constitutes a threat to our security, thereby undermining the will of the American people to resist totalitarian communism? The answer is partially foreshadowed by Irving Kristol in his reference to the new intellectual class. Their moral authority achieved its first certification during the early days of the New Deal, when the intellectual was called upon as the expert to staff and advise the bureaus of government engaged in the transition toward a welfare capitalism essential to any modern industrial society sensitive to the hazards of unemployment, old age, and economic insecurity. The prestige of the intellectual became identified with his dedication to "liberal and progressive" programs. The war against fascism coincided with the intellectual's natural interest in establishing his identification with any battle against reactionary ideology or "rightist" totalitarianism. The subsequent McCarthy era (so-called) was a traumatic experience for intellectuals, since the charges of the senator threatened to associate the entire class of intellectuals with responsibility for the infiltration of communists into high places in government. However, it turned out, ironically, that the ultimate result was a substantial victory for intellectuals, not merely because of the political demise of their bête noir, but because they were able to implant in the American consciousness the widespread conviction following the McCarthy episode that anti-communism is indecent, uncivilized, and, indeed, likely to emerge without warning as a form of disease from any and all "right-wing" elements.

It would take nothing short of a volume to describe the subsequent developments in the meteoric rise in status and prerogative of the intellectual—through the civil rights movement; then as the definitive authority on presidential commissions (Scranton Commission, Kerner Commission, and so on); the emergence of journalists and newscasters as a *soi-disant* intellectual elite controlling the newscasting of the powerful mass media. (See Moynihan, "The Presidency and the Press," *Commentary,* March 1971.)

But our interest is primarily foreign policy, and that is where Kristol's idea of intellectual confrontation with government is significant. It is no coincidence that foreign policy is the crucial area in which the intellectual is determined to fight it out. For the control and direction of American foreign policy is essential to the survival of the intellectual's power and prestige. An American foreign policy that assumes a grave danger to the U.S. interest from an international communist movement is predicated on the grounds that the Soviet Union is committed to the ultimate destruction of the free world and that peaceful coexistence is a delusion. Such a policy would have no room for the radical intellectual in any position of influence or power. From the standpoint of the intellectual, a "hawklike" American foreign policy would spell the doom of everything he holds dear in life, including his self-interest as a dominant elite, as well as his dream of revolutionary change in underdeveloped areas still subject to what he considers "feudal" or "reactionary" regimes.

An example of one crisis in foreign policy may serve to illustrate the way in which the intellectual becomes involved in the struggle for power and influence. A fascinating book by Mario Lazo, *Dagger in the Heart,* relates the amazing story of how Arthur Schlesinger, Chester Bowles, Richard Goodwin, and Adlai Stevenson, abetted by Bobby Kennedy, manipulated Jack Kennedy and fought off the Joint Chiefs of Staff in order to sabotage any successful invasion of Cuba that would have toppled Castro from power. It was indeed a battle between the radical intellectuals and the anti-communist military and the CIA, supported by Dean Acheson (curiously) and C. Douglas Dillon. Some astonishing facts come to light, such as that Adlai Stevenson proposed that the United States abandon the great naval base at Guantanamo Bay and consider offering to remove its bases in Turkey in exchange for the removal of the Soviet missiles from Cuba, and that Robert McNamara was opposed to any United States attempt to liberate Cuba.

The radical intellectuals achieved power, prestige, and influence in the

Kennedy Administration. When he was assassinated, they lost their patron and their influence in molding American foreign policy. In rage, they turned against Lyndon Johnson and, through their domination of the mass media and university publications, they succeeded in forcing the abdication of one of the toughest characters ever to hold power in the White House. The radical intellectuals would accept nothing short of full presidential surrender to their views on Vietnam and other issues of foreign policy. Richard Nixon escaped the murderous onslaught of the mass media during his presidential campaign only because they turned their fire on Humphrey in a vicious display of revenge for not yielding to their demands for immediate surrender in Vietnam. Johnson bought a respite only by total cessation of bombing in North Vietnam. He paid the price they demanded.

There is only one way in a mass democratic society for a president to purchase immunity against the radical intellectuals (Fulbright, Galbraith, Schlesinger, Roger Hilsman, et al.), and that is to arouse the American people and ask their support for a firm policy of resistance to any further subversion of the free world by Communism. Johnson's failure to arouse a sense of urgency on the part of the people cost him anguish, bitterness, and, finally, abdication. Johnson thought he could appease the intellectuals and the academic community by fighting a half-hearted war. He achieved no immunity despite the concessions he made in restraining the military; and the gradual erosion of public support for the war in Vietnam was more the result of fighting with one hand tied behind our backs, and the failure to arouse the American people to the dangers we face, than to any inherent impossibility of winning or the lack of patriotism and willingness on the part of the vast majority of Americans to see it through once they were aroused. The fact that the government gave up on the war long before the people did was recognized by Seymour M. Lipset, writing in *Foreign Affairs,* April 1971:

> However, surveys showed that the majority of students supported the war until 1968. Not until June of that year did a Gallup Poll indicate that the proportion of students who thought America had made a mistake in becoming involved in Vietnam had reached 50 percent. At that time the same view was taken by 48 percent of the general public but by only 38 percent of the entire youth group from 21 to 30 years of age. This difference within the younger population was to continue in succeeding years.
>
> The perception that the Vietnam war was a mistake grew greatly following the dramatic communist Tet offensive in February, the cessation of the bombing of North Vietnam at the end of March 1968, and the beginning of negotiations in Paris in May 1968. In effect, once the U.S. government had given up the goal of defeating the communists on the battlefield, it became impossible to prevent a steady erosion of support for the war, particularly, though obviously far from exclusively, on the campus.

It was the radical intellectual class, in and out of government, that demanded a U.S. withdrawal from Vietnam. However, since our purpose is not to debate the merits of American policy as such, but rather to explore the psychological and social motivation of the intellectual, we must attempt, finally, to draw the implications from what a humorless social scientist might call "the data." Raymond Aron, in *Opium of the Intellectuals,* suggests that the American intellectuals of today are in search of enemies. History has moved with astonishing speed since Aron penned that line, since not only has the intellectual found his enemies, but he is engaged in mortal combat for supremacy. The confrontation between the intellectuals and the conservative forces (in the most generic sense) of American culture have reached a degree of intensity unprecedented in American history. The control of the mass media by intellectuals has offered them one of the most powerful weapons available in a democratic society to seduce public opinion. As Daniel Moynihan perceptively points out, "The press grows more and more influenced by attitudes genuinely hostile to American society and American government." In a fluid society that has had no well-defined elite since the days of Jefferson, Monroe, and Madison, the intellectual has pre-empted the role of establishing the standards of "respectability" for acceptance in educated circles and the values worthy of pursuit by its more enlightened citizens.

At a time when our nation is required to meet resolutely the global challenge — internally and externally — of a clever and ruthless international enemy, the radical intellectuals in government and mass media are doing all in their power to weaken the defenses of the country. As Hugh Seton-Watson, the British historian, points out in the periodical *Problems of Communism,* January 1970: "in varying degrees in all Western countries, the political class appears to have lost its nerve. If the paralysis of political will which we see in the West progresses to the point where Western nations cannot govern or defend themselves, then the narrow-minded semi-barbarous but disciplined and resolute Soviet leaders will have the world at their feet."

It may be that no democratic society can survive the experiment of allowing an alienated intellectual elite to determine its values, poison the channels of public opinion, and cow into submission its normal political leaders. Absent the threat of a barbarous totalitarianism keenly aware of the crumbling power of democracies, the worst that could happen in the foreseeable future, as a result of radical assault on traditional values, would be a drift toward anarchy and the ultimate breakdown of modern industrial society. But, tragically, the free world has little time available to recapture confidence in its moral values. Outside the crumbling barriers of Western civilization the leaders of the Communist empire lie in wait, with infinite patience and considerable cunning, and with vast populations under their total control. Driven by ideological passion to destroy the last bastions of freedom and democracy, the totalitarians may yet succeed in overrunning what remains of a civilization critically weakened by its own radical intellectual class.

NOTES

1. It was some ten years later that Sidney called my attention to Max Eastman's path-breaking

article in *Harper's,* "The End of Socialism in the Soviet Union." At about the same time, Sidney wrote "Reflections on the Russian Revolution," *Southern Review* 4, no. 3 (1939), which constituted a profound analysis of Soviet totalitarianism. Whatever their differences in interpretation of Marxist philosophy, Sidney Hook and Max Eastman were the first American intellectuals to sound the tocsin about the true nature of the Bolshevik revolution.

2. "Lillian Hellman," *Encounter,* February 1977; "The Case of Alger Hiss, *Encounter,* August 1978; "On John Kenneth Galbraith," *American Spectator,* October 1981.

3. Sidney Hook, *Political Power and Personal Freedom* (New York: Macmillan, 1962).

4. Hook wrote:

It is an elementary truth of the psychology of perception that what a man sees depends often upon his beliefs and expectations. The stronger the beliefs the more they function like a priori notions whose validity is beyond the tests of experience. Hopes can be so all-consuming that they affect even the range and quality of feeling. The consequence is that the shocks of reality, in terms of which the natural pragmatism of the human mind experiences actuality, lose their educational office. To say that a man is seized and transformed by an abstraction is a metaphor but it expresses the empirical fact that an idea-system, instead of functioning as a guide to conduct, can operate in such a way to transform habits, feelings, and perceptions of the individual to a point where marked changes of personality are noticeable. [p. 175]

5. "The Future Danger," *Commentary,* April 1981, p. 45.

6. To bring the career of "polycentrism" up to date: on February 24, 1981, the *New York Times* published the text of a State Department White Paper on communist support of Salvadoran rebels. The report presents overwhelming evidence of the clandestine military support given by the Soviet Union, Cuba, and their communist allies to Marxist-Leninist guerrillas now fighting to overthrow the established government of El Salvador. As the White Paper states:

The evidence, drawn from captured guerrilla documents and war materiel and corroborated by intelligence reports, underscores the central role played by Cuba and other Communist countries beginning in 1979 in the political unification, military direction and arming of insurgent forces in El Salvador.

The situation in El Salvador presents a strikingly familiar case of Soviet, Cuban and other Communist military involvement in a politically troubled third world country.

By providing arms, training and direction to a local insurgency and by supporting it with a global propaganda campaign, the Communists have intensified and widened the conflict, greatly increased the suffering of the Salvadoran people and deceived much of the world about the true nature of the revolution.

Their objective in El Salvador as elsewhere is to bring about—at little cost to themselves—the overthrow of the established government and the imposition of a Communist regime in defiance of the will of the Salvadoran people.

7. For an account of a contemporary assault by the intelligentsia on Podhoretz for his temerity in suggesting that there was a moral basis for U.S. intervention in Vietnam, see Arnold Beichman's article in the *National Review,* September 3, 1982.

8. Admiral Elmo Zumwalt, in his book *On Watch,* describes a conversation with Kissinger in 1979:

Kissinger feels that the U.S. has passed its historic high point like so many earlier civilizations. He believes the U.S. is on a downhill course and cannot be roused by political challenge. He states that his job is to persuade the Russians to give us the best deal we can get, recognizing that the historical forces favor them. He says that he realizes that in the light of history he will be recognized as one of those who negotiated terms favorable to the Soviets, but that the American people have only themselves to blame because they lack the stamina to stay the course against the Russians, who are Sparta to our Athens.

9. Not isolationist with respect to a war against fascism, or indeed even to the protection of Europe from Communist aggression, but "isolationist" with respect to the "periphery," i.e., communist revolutions in the third world.

10. *Retreat from Empire: The First Nixon Administration,* ed. by Robert Osgood et al. (Baltimore: Johns Hopkins University Press, 1973), p. 40.

11. Tucker, in his book *The Radical Left and American Policy,* states:

To the liberalist-realist critic, contemporary globalism, the gradual universalization of the Truman Doctrine in the realm of policy, is the very antithesis of the early policy of containment, with its focus on Europe and its principal objective of restoring a balance of power. With its indiscriminate commitment to intervene anywhere and everywhere against revolutionary change, globalism substitutes sentiment and ideology for interest, imaginary fears for what were in an earlier period well-grounded fears. It reflects a view of the world that is profoundly at odds with the reality of a pluralistic world, that has resulted in the over-commitment of the nation's resources, and that if not abandoned must betray the American purpose both abroad and at home.

Cf. Tucker, "America and the World," *Commentary,* March 1977, and my critique in *Commentary,* July 1977, p. 14.

PART III

Education

DAVID SIDORSKY

On Liberalism and
Liberal Education

Sidney Hook extended the heritage of John Dewey's pragmatism in traditional philosophical fields like metaphysics, epistemology, and ethics. This activity reflected in many ways the common task of a philosophical generation that found its pragmatic theses deeply challenged by logical positivism, linguistic analysis, phenomenology, and existentialism. Yet one important part of Hook's distinctive role in the development of Deweyan pragmatism was his assertion with special force and his elaboration of the Deweyan concern with the relevance of philosophy for education and of the demand upon a philosophy that it probe itself by its significance for educational ideals, theory, and practice.

Hook's articulation of those theses took a variety of forms ranging from the question of the secular or religious foundations of moral education to educational planning, including the analysis of the options of elective or core curricula. There was an inevitably shifting topical agenda in this part of Hook's *oeuvre,* including the examination of progressive education in the 1930s, the assumptions of the "great books" curriculum in the 1940s, the legitimacy and limits of educational dissent in the 1950s, the politicization of the university in the 1960s, the meaning of academic integrity in the 1970s, among others. Yet one enduring basis of this agenda for Hook is his exploration of the nature of liberalism and of its implications for education.

There are three interpretations of liberalism that have special relevance to the characterization of liberal education. These interpretations sometimes reinforce each other, but they also generate elements of tension and conflict.

Liberalism may be conceived, first, as the application of rational and critical methods to the institutions of government and of society. It follows, then, that liberal education is construed in a general sense as a training in rational methods of inquiry and in their use for the understanding and reconstruction of social institutions. In a second conception of liberalism, in which its continuity with secular humanism is crucial, liberal education involves an initiation into the values and accomplishments of the humanistic cultural tradition from Homer to the present. A third sense of liberalism stresses its connection with the value of liberty. In a conflict of values among security, fraternity, equality, or liberty, liberalism asserts the priority of liberty. Liberal education, on this view, requires the articulation of that priority in educational contexts ranging from the importance of freedom of choice in the construction of curriculum to the significance of individual self-expression in the education process.

My examination of the relationship between liberalism and liberal education takes its point of departure from the identification of these three kinds of liberalism. The strategy of that examination is to consider three kinds of criticism of liberalism and to apply them in turn to each conception of liberalism.

One familiar type of criticism of liberalism argues from the social genesis of liberal doctrines to their validity. In this criticism, liberalism is to be understood as an "ideology" in the sense that its doctrines embody an expression of class interests. They are to be judged by reference to the legitimacy of those interests and the harm or benefit the satisfaction of those interests would generate. A second kind of criticism examines the explicit arguments that justify the values or methods assumed in the assertion of liberalism. Third, since there are competing interpretations of liberalism, each of those interpretations can be assessed by its critical confrontation with the others.

I. Rational Liberalism and Liberal Education

The first conception of liberalism is that it is primarily a commitment to a method of criticism. Liberals are involved in the skeptical analysis of all inherited social institutions and cultural traditions with a view toward their reconstruction in the light of reason or experience. Liberals have differed in their stress on the rationalist or empirical aspects of their critical methodology. Broadly speaking, Continental liberalism, appealing to Descartes or to Kant, required the assertion of such criteria as consistency and rational justification in the analysis of social or political institutions; while British liberalism, appealing to Locke or Mill, required the assertion of experience or empirical utility as tests of the adequacy of inherited institutions. For Americans in the twentieth century, John Dewey and several of his students, including Sidney Hook and Ernest Nagel, formulated methodological liberalism almost paradigmatically. They articulated explicitly a definition of liberalism in terms of the willingness and confidence to apply scientific method to the investigation and reform of all major social institutions.

Despite the diverse national origins of these variant versions of liberal doctrine, the claim is that a universal perspective derives from a commitment to the primacy of method. The assumption is that it is always possible and desirable to adopt a critical point of view toward the prevalent tradition in any country or time and to investigate the wisdom of institutional reform.

On this view, liberal education is, above all, an education in the methods and techniques of critical inquiry. In stereotypical simplification, the premodern educational institution is perceived as the workshop where master trains apprentice in the tradition, or as the classroom where the text, divine or true, is exegetically interpreted. In contrast, the liberal image would require the colloquium where colleagues challenge proffered opinion, or the research group that is directed to discovering new truths. A parallel set of stereotypes confronts the ideal of the educated man as learned in the tradition with the model of the cultural critic or experimental investigator. The appeal to these images does not adequately report the historical facts, but it does indicate the values of methodological liberalism in their application to education. I believe that the connection between liberalism and liberal education emerges more clearly in the course of our analysis of each of the interpretations of liberalism from the critical perspectives I have proposed.

1. *The Ideology of Liberalism: Class and "Critical Conformism."* The familiar ideological criticism of liberalism is that its genesis is in the ascendancy to economic and political power of the middle classes of Western Europe and America. The force of this genetic argument is that liberalism is not to be debated on its merits but to be exhibited in its function or role. Liberalism was the instrumentality for criticizing the values and institutions of medieval Europe or feudal societies. As an ideology it served to reinforce middle-class values or assumptions and is not capable of a self-reflective examination of those values and assumptions. Its appeal to scientific objectivity in the analysis of social institutions is fraudulent and therefore inhibits more appropriate institutional or ideological criticism of bourgeois culture.

For many years, radical theorists, whether of the school of Marx or of Veblen, held a virtual monopoly on the charge that a university is implicitly an institution that serves class interests. More recently, conservative thinkers like Irving Kristol and Robert Bartley have advanced a significant interpretation of the "class" analysis. They have reexamined the empirical aspects of the claim, that is, the evidence of the class bias among the groups that dominate or govern the university, and have concluded that the university, or more correctly a major proportion of the liberal arts faculties in the university establishment, form part of the "New Class." The New Class comprises also those working professionals of the media and those exponents of the institutions of the counterculture who are identifiable by their consistent antagonism to the institutions of American industrial capitalism and to the "bedrock" values of middle-class American society.

In an argument that partially parallels the Marxist criticism, they argue that the liberal university may pay lip service to objectivity or value neutrality but that its implicit and pervasive bias, manifested in its faculty power-structure and in its empirical educational process, marks it as an institution supportive of the interests of the New Class.

These arguments raise interesting and important empirical issues for investigation of the actual practices of contemporary universities in educational

policies, faculty recruitment, and classroom performance. Without here going
into the empirical merits of these claims, the theoretical issue is whether a commitment to methodological criticism is bound by class interests of one kind or
another, or is capable of universalism and objectivity. The "New Class" thesis
provides some evidence that universities have been able to develop individuals
who are capable of criticism of major historical vested interests of society. The
same logic would suggest that the safeguards on freedom of inquiry developed
in the university might lead to critical examination of the doctrines and views
that may be fashionable or regnant within the universities.

The critics of liberalism have also drawn attention to what they see as a
caricature of methodological liberalism: the emergence of a "critical conformism," that is, articulate and seemingly individually reasoned reiterations of
convergent, fashionable opinion. There are diverse reasons for the phenomenon of convergence of attitudes in the university community. To the degree to
which there is an element of difference between the present situation and historic experience the new importance of the media suggests one reason for this
difference. The assumption that an education in critical method would represent a continuous criticism and reformulation of inherited doctrine was formulated in a society in which the mass media had not yet developed to their present
state. University education now operates in a society in which the media are
important educators on social and political questions.

Entirely apart from any imputation of partisanship or bias, the mass media
have the unavoidable problem of transposing the complexity of a real situation
into a very brief, readily understandable interpretation that can attract interest.
Consequently, that transposition requires a simplified version of the situation
that has dramatic impact. Those transpositions of reality that are too subtle or
complex, that are too tentative or lacking in drama, fail to gain a hearing in the
competition for media space and time. Those transpositions of events that succeed in imprinting themselves upon the mass media then become the definitive record of the event. Having achieved a basis in public acceptance, they are consequently reiterated and repeated with variations in all the other recording media.

The result of this process is that events become what is the accepted report
of events. In the greatly enlarged palimpsest of complex reality that is now
available to the communications net of our society, social reality is the selective recording of isolated segments of that reality. Certainly, as liberal faith in
critical intelligence asserts, it is possible for skeptical and independent scholars
to probe any particular record and to confirm or refute that record on the basis
of evidence. Yet within the academic lifetime of a generation of students, the
flow of social reality is the sequence of interpretations that are "in," or that
make up the trendy record. The very definition of the issues in terms of which
critical scholarship on social and political questions is to function as a correc-
tive is first fixed by the media. The university community as an involved group
that is not insulated or isolated from involvement in the public arena may well
be in the forefront of those who reflect media trends and interpretations.

Fashion has always had a place in the academy as well as in the marketplace. Yet it would seem to have gained pervasiveness, particularly in the interpretation of political, social, and economic events, precisely when methodological liberalism reasserts its confidence in critical interpretation of these events. In that sense, the phenomenon of critical conformism provides a striking challenge to the liberal's confidence in critical methodology and in the possibilities of social scientific understanding.

2. *Progress and Scientific Method.* Turning to the more direct criticism of liberalism, there are two themes of special importance. The first relates to the value assumptions of liberalism and the second to its methodological assumptions. The value assumption is that of progress; the methodological assumption, that there is a single scientific method.

Faith in the possibilities of progress or human perfectibility was often closely connected with the application of rational or empirical social criticism. Descartes had expressed this hope most dramatically when he argued that the development of the true rules of logical method that could be applied to extended things, that is, to human bodies, would lead to the control of illness and might eventually do away with "la facheuse habitude de mourir."

The model for the American liberalism of John Dewey was explicitly derived from Charles Peirce's interpretation of science. For Peirce, scientific method always mediated among conflicting hypotheses by testing their experimental consequences. The method guaranteed that successively emergent hypotheses would be better than their predecessors, since each new hypothesis had to successfully account for all past evidence and to more adequately predict the course of future experience. In that sense, science is necessarily progressive and perfectible, since tomorrow's acceptable hypothesis is, by methodological guarantee, more warranted than yesterday's.

A contrary example, once advanced in a volume on medieval science by the medieval historian C. H. Haskins, may suggest the plausibility of Peirce's version of scientific method. Haskins pointed out that medieval chemistry believed in the theoretical possibility of a transmutation of elements, that nineteenth-century chemistry denied that theoretical possibility, and that twentieth-century chemistry has refuted its immediate predecessor and returned to the medieval view of the matter. On Haskins's view, the shift of scientific opinion, like so many other shifts of opinion, is not necessarily progressive or convergent but reflects other changes of cultural climate. Yet despite the analogy between atomic physics and alchemy on the possibility of transmutation of elements, it would seem to make better sense to point out how nineteenth-century science progressed beyond medieval science and has, in turn, been correctly displaced by more recent views. There are much more systemic difficulties with Peirce's formulation, as Quine has shown in his criticism of the analogy to mathematical convergence to a limit and as Kuhn has argued on the basis of studies in the history of science. Yet the operation of science as model for the progressive character of inquiry has been one of the primary motivations for educational reform.

The difficulty with the use of scientific progress as a model for social progress, which Dewey advocated, however, goes beyond the question of the adequacy of the Peircean interpretation of science. There are areas of human
activity where the conception of progress is inappropriate. The sense in which
there may or may not be progress in art has been much debated in the literature. There is an obvious sense in which the history of art or of literature
denies the perfectibility or cumulativeness of a progressive series. An example
of many, chosen because there is a certain geographical locus for an extended
time series, is that neither Goya nor Picasso, in their many superb paintings of
their chosen subject, the bull, did not surpass the achievement of prehistoric
depictions of that animal at Altamira. The idea of progress seems inappropriate
in any review of the series of works.

So if we concede a model of progress in scientific inquiry and yet reject the
idea of progress in a series of artistic works, the critical question of locating
the meaning of progress in the changing of social institutions is intentionally
left open. Since liberalism advocates the reconstruction of social institutions
on the basis of evidence and experiment, it has argued that social reform incorporates the progressive character of scientific inquiry. Yet social change often
seems regressive. And even when amelioration is apparent, one set of social
problems may be seen to have been replaced by another.

Even more directly the methodological issue is raised as to whether there is
a single scientific method. Dewey championed the view that there was such a
method. Its application to society might upset the conservative, as "it put some
portion of a stable world in peril"; yet that application bore with it the progressive hope that "frail goods be secured, secure goods be extended, and that pre-
carious promise of good which haunts experienced things be more liberally fulfilled." For Dewey, the fundamental crisis of our society was caused by a gap
between social readiness to adopt scientific method in the control of natural
phenomena and unwillingness to adopt scientific method in the areas of social
experimentation and control. Dewey's demonstration that there was a single
scientific method available in both the natural sciences and the social sciences
was schematic and general. It did not rest on the empirical record of the social
sciences as much as on their promise. More generally, it was supported by the
commitment to philosophical naturalism that demonstrated the legitimacy and
possibility of social-science inquiry. Certainly it may be true that people learn
from experience in all fields of endeavor and should seek to imaginatively
invent testable explanatory hypotheses for both natural and social phenomena. Such attitudes toward both kinds of events do not, however, show that
there are methods available in politics, or international relations, or education
that are progressive as are those of physics or chemistry. Yet this assumption
was significant in many ways for the liberal approach to educational theory
and practice during the past fifty years.

3. *Rational Liberalism and Tradition.* From the point of view of both its
partisans and its critics, liberalism has usually been understood as a "secondary"

culture (a conception that accords well with the interpretation of liberalism as a methodological commitment). The primary institutions and formative traditions of a society — its family structure, legal system, religious practices, ethnic or national loyalties — have not been the product of liberal culture. Liberal ideas and attitudes have reformed some of these primary institutions, particularly since the Enlightenment, to a marked degree. Liberalism is accordingly characterized by its functions as gadfly, critic, reformer within a context of primary institutions but not as the dominant substrate of society. This function of liberalism as a minority opinion in confrontation with the more fixed views of the conventional majority lends itself to distortion in situations of high volatility or rapid social change, for then there is no established or dominant framework against which liberal criticism serves as reforming agent.

This reading of the secondary character of liberalism has generated recurrent criticisms of liberalism in post-revolutionary periods, a criticism first formulated by Benjamin Constant in the period between the French Revolution and the consolidation of Bonapartism. Constant believed that liberalism, which had correctly criticized the despotism of the *Ancien Regime,* would, in the aftermath of the Revolution, result in a new, militant, populist despotism even more powerful than the old. Similar sentiments have since been expressed by critics who see Weimar as prelude to Nazism, or Kerensky's Russia as paving the way for totalitarian Communism. This view of the historical process can generate controversy far beyond the scope of the present discussion. The relevant thesis for analysis in this context is the need for a reexamination of the attitudes and values of liberalism in the light of unanticipated consequences of liberal criticism of the status quo, namely, its replacement by totalitarian or authoritarian despotism rather than by the envisaged liberal democracies.

With the lessening of liberal confidence in the progressive replacement of inadequate social institutions by better ones comes a much greater stress on the substantive values implicit in the liberal tradition and a corresponding shift away from a future-oriented conception of education toward a reevaluation of the past as a source of values.

II. Humanistic Liberalism and Liberal Education

There are significant connections between liberal education, in the sense of a classical or humanistic education, and the evolution of liberalism. The idea of liberal education as an education in the classics antedated the rise of political liberalism and preceded the formulation of a self-conscious rationalist methodology. The concern of humanist educators that all texts, secular or sacred, be exposed to dispassionate critical analysis so that they may be enriched by scholarship contributed to the secular character of modern liberalism. Yet illiberalism was not defined exclusively in terms of religious dogmatism, but by reference to the factors that abort the discussion of ideas, values, and texts generated by Western civilization. So, various forms of absolutism, including ideological extremism of totalitarianism or mindless involvement with the action and passions of the moment, have emerged as inimical to the traditions of scholarship. On this view, the connection between the nature of liberalism and of liberal education is found in the commitment to rational and continuous inquiry about the values of human civilization.

There has been a broad measure of agreement as to what such a commitment involves in terms of the curriculum of a classical education. It requires the study of the culture of Greece and Rome as well as the classics of the national "high" or literary culture. The assumption is that these works express fundamental aspects of human nature; they provide an irreplaceable avenue into the understanding of man and the evaluation of his actions. The further assumption is that a chain of tradition especially binds students brought up in the Western languages and societies with the formulation and expression of human values in the Western tradition. Whatever additional training or stimulation men and women may need or use—in arts or crafts, in professional or vocational skills, in the habits of contemporary institutions or in the understanding of other cultures—there is an irreducible minimum requirement of participation, at some level of literacy and comprehension, in the chain of that tradition.

Claims on behalf of the classical curriculum often refer to two virtues: first, training in rigorous thought and clarity of expression and, second, an education in values. The significance of the first claim is its connection with the thesis that this training in rigor is transferable in some way to other fields of endeavor. The mastery of the skills required for the critical reading of texts, the parsing of sentences, and the writing of analytical expositions should be reflected in an enhanced ability to weigh evidence and to make prudent decisions. The second claim is even more challenging. Since the values asserted or explored in the diverse works of the humanities curriculum are complex and dissonant, the collectivity of these works can never be used to indoctrinate the student with a particular set of values. Yet a student who has read *Macbeth* or *Faust* must be more sensitive to the corruptive potential of power; and one who has studied Plato or Swift, more alert to the risks of utopianism. After his initiation into the empathic probing of values in such literary masterworks, his own response to moral responsibility, in whatever area, will be changed to some degree for the better. These are not small claims. Much can and has been written about them, but the framework I have selected for critical investigation of liberalism will serve to delimit the relevant aspects of the issue.

1. *The Ideological Criticism: "Elitism" and "Humanist Barbarians."* The criticism of liberalism as an ideology does not invoke an examination of the merits of these two theses regarding the transferrability of intellectual training or the residual benefits of initiation into the enduring issues in the discussion of values. Rather, the argument relates to the ways in which the social genesis of this educational program determines its function. In simple terms, it is asserted that the educational system was designed to technically train and to

reinforce the loyalties of the civil servants and managers of the capitalist state and industrial corporation. It also provides a leisure-class activity for a segment of the upper classes. Just as "class" was the reductive term for methodological liberalism, so "elite" becomes the categorizing phrase for liberal classical education.

Debates in this area have long been choreographed with move and countermove well laid out. Their rehearsal can indicate the range of issues that this debate opens. The most general argument for a humanistic tradition is its powerful impetus for egalitarianism in any society, since it exhibits so dramatically how virtues and vices, suffering and nobility, can be ascribed to individuals independent of their race, class, sex, wealth, or power. Focused more specifically on the practices of liberal education, the point is that discrimination among students is solely on the basis of mastery of an intellectual tradition, to the exclusion of such "elitist" and inegalitarian criteria, whether of social class, economic wealth, or political power. The historical record shows that many who advanced in society on the basis of their intellectual achievements had their origins in the lower classes of the society.

Several responses to these arguments, though equally familiar, are still challenging. The actual operation of the classical educational system, it is charged, does not stress the egalitarian message of the humanist tradition but becomes caught up with the demonstration of the scholarly guild's ability to interpret the finer points of a masterwork. The guild therefore characteristically removes itself and its scholarship from involvement with the great majority of persons, and fosters a divisive inegalitarianism. It is further claimed that literary skills require background preparation in the schools, the lack of which has effectively excluded the extremely poor and the socially disadvantaged from achieving mastery. Since the educational system serves as a screening mechanism, classical education, in placing special stress upon verbal skills, as Professor Higgins pointed out to Eliza Doolittle, has effectively closed access by working-class persons to positions of power and responsibility.

The counters to these arguments suggest that even if classical education might at times have been used in this way, it remains egalitarian in its insistence upon relevant reasons for any criterion that would discriminate among persons. It is elitist only in the legitimate sense that it recognizes the appropriateness of intellectual hierarchy where intellectual performance is relevant. It has therefore served as a paradigm for the demand that careers be open to talents.

Over the past decade some of these arguments have generated much social passion. To the degree to which the disagreement is amenable to rational resolution, it seems to depend on two principal issues. First, whether the egalitarian ideal is to be interpreted as specifying discrimination for relevant reasons only, or whether it is viewed as requiring a greater measure, even a proportional ratio, of social participation by all groups in all aspects of society. Second, the disagreement hinges on factual or policy assessment about differing means for achieving egalitarianism. For some, a priority route to the goal is universal access to higher education, while others believe there are more practicable means for realizing a greater measure of social equality and that a stress on access to the institutions of higher education is counterproductive. To a degree, however, the division reflects a fundamental divergence of value on the question of how much weight society should assign to the preservation of humanistic education.

Some who criticize liberal education on the grounds of its elitism press a different argument. They hold that there are "humanist barbarians," that is, persons initiated or learned in the cultural masterworks of the West whose actions contradict the fundamental values implicit in that tradition. In the trauma of twentieth-century European history, for example, masters of the classical tradition are found on both sides of the great divide in moral values.

Yet such difficulties with moral education are not new. There have never been guarantees of the consequences of any educational system and no malpractice insurance has ever been offered. After all, Plato suggested that virtue can not be taught on the ground that Pericles did not succeed in transmitting political virtue to his own children. Nevertheless, too much should not be conceded from the evidence that humanistic education does not immunize its students against succumbing to some virulent form of barbarism. The relationship between educational institutions and their moral consequences is too remote to permit any firm conclusions. The existence of "humanist barbarians" is a cautionary guard against the illusion that there can be a formal education for morality. It is not necessary to conclude that an education in the skills and substance of the humanist tradition is not justified by its intellectual and moral results.

2. *Literary Method, Science, and Pluralism.* On the first conception of liberalism reviewed in this essay, liberalism was a method of continuous reconstruction of inherited social institutions through the application of scientific method with a view to progress. On the second conception of liberalism, the focus shifts, because of the centrality of liberal education for that conception, to a stress upon the critical interpretation and appreciation of the works of the past that have enduring value. The first assumes the possibility of convergence to the values of the future; the second, the possibility of convergence upon the relevant values of the past.

The method of understanding of the past is literary in that it involves the cultivation of a literary sensibility in the interpretation of the great works of preceding generations. In a conference on curricular topics organized by Sidney Hook, Charles Issawi pointed out that the curriculum represented the works of man, of God, and of the devil. The humanities were the products of great men. Through the devil's alleged invention of avarice, lust, envy, and other vices, he has also created the subject matter of economics, political science, and history. The works of God, however, were the "furniture of earth and the choir of the heavens"—subjects for the natural sciences. In our time, even though God is in hiding or eclipse, the investigation of nature through the sciences has led to techniques far more complex than common sense and an interpretive mechanism that differs from literary or historical sensibility.

The heightened significance of scientific achievements for understanding aspects of the world has confronted humanistic education with a new situation. Some evidence of the tension and irresolution that still obtains in the new situation is exhibited in the many discussions of the ways natural sciences can be taught in the liberal arts colleges.

One strategy has been to study the records of the results of science as though they were great works of literature. Both are approached as cultural artifacts of their times. The curriculum of St. John's College at Annapolis, for example, seems to suggest that it is possible to study Sophocles or Euclid, Newton or Hume, Clerk-Maxwell or Mill as if these were all great books of different literary genres. Yet this suggestion, when carried out, misses the point that the past is irrelevant for science in a way in which it is not for literature. In contrast to this approach, most scientific curricula are governed by a desire to avoid the historical presentation in favor of training in the state-of-the-science.

Another humanistic approach to science has been to teach it as the product of the processes of creative imagination of gifted individuals. Just as the environment of Mozart affected his music, for example, so the background of Planck presumably had a role in generating quantum theory. Again, contrary to this approach, most scientists prefer to ignore the historical or psychological interpretation of scientific creativity in favor of the best presentation of scientific theory.

Still others have sought to teach science in humanistic curricula through an examination of the scientific issues relevant to current decision-making, from air pollution to space travel. Whatever the merits of this approach in training for citizenship, it does not seem to involve the student in an understanding of the sciences.

In confronting the gap between humanistic education and scientific education, there has been a tendency toward separate institutional development: the liberal arts college for the humanist and the institute of technology for the scientist. Attempts to reduce this gap may result in no more than an act of cultural piety. In scientific institutes, there is the nod of obeisance to the sources of one's culture in the humanities before turning to the serious work of mastering scientific method. On the other hand, many liberal arts colleges have abandoned the attempt to provide humanists with the degree of literacy required for understanding science.

The gap between the humanities and the sciences is significant for understanding the predicament of liberal education. Liberal education as humanistic education derived its self-confidence and sense of mission from its belief that what it taught was central for development of the educated person. Yet, in contemporary society, since the humanists do not employ the technical languages and methods of the sciences that interpret the world, they risk becoming peripheral.

The humanist response has sometimes been to stress that humanities are also technical fields that involve rigorous initiation into the techniques of the discipline. Thus, the polarization into what has been described as "the two cultures"—that is, two disciplines inaccessible to each other—becomes manifest. Yet the recognition of the increasing number of ways in which science shapes our perception, both of facts and of values, poses an important problem to any traditional idea of liberal education. It is an obstacle to any effort to reassert the centrality of the classical humanities for liberal education.

The greater place of science in the modern world has not been the only reason for the displacement of Western literary tradition from its position of centrality in liberal education. The heightened awareness of the cultures of the non-Western civilizations has also suggested that traditional humanistic education is parochial. If the study of the Western classics is an avenue for the understanding of human experience and the analysis of issues of universal import, then the study of the classics of another civilization also serves as such an avenue. The traditional presupposition was that the chain that binds us to Greece and Rome was part of our own past. Isaiah Berlin reports how Herder, in asserting the values of self-discovery and self-expression, exclaimed, "We are not Greeks, we are not Romans." Perhaps German educators of the nineteenth century believed that it was valuable to identify Greece as a model for German education, just as some British educators of that period saw Rome as an expression of their civic ideal. Yet these choices represented conscious selection from the past. In the phrase used by pragmatists, experience was what was taken, not what was given. The availability of different cultures for exploration, whose place in the curriculum depends on our interests, values, and attitudes, thus confronts the classical liberal education with a more pluralistic interpretation of the idea of freedom.

3. *Liberal Education and Freedom.* If the cultural tradition to be taught is open to selection, then the "givens" of the classical curriculum are transformed by the possibility of freedom of choice. Several considerations enter into the exercise of this freedom. There may be a valuable perspective on our society to be gained by an effort to master the literature of a non-Western civilization. Further, this freedom of choice, once recognized, has not been restricted to non-Western culture. It also generates selection of other cultural traditions of the West as proper objects of study for liberal education: folk culture, pop culture, middle-brow culture, and, perhaps most dramatically, in America the ethnic subcultures of our society. It is an empirical issue whether study of these works can develop the same qualities of literary expression or sensitivity to human values as study of the classics apparently has done. Some proponents of their introduction argue that they can, while others shift the grounds for introducing these works into the curriculum. On their view, these cultural traditions may be studied as part of the student's search for identity, or as a

vehicle for his self-expression. The assumption is that a liberal education may legitimately provide an opportunity for an exploration of identity or for self-expression. In ascribing a unique past tradition to the present, it is charged that classical education has proscribed the search for individual authenticity. Permitting selection of the culture to be studied therefore involves more than a rhetorical skirmish between classicists and scholars, on the one hand, and modernists and consciousness-raisers, on the other. It changes the rationale for liberal education. The idea of liberal education as an initiation into the Western tradition has now been confronted with a conception of liberalism that places its weight upon individual freedom of choice and upon maximizing such freedom.

III. The Priority of Liberty and Liberal Education

The third conception of liberalism defines liberalism in terms of the priority of the value of liberty when this value is in conflict with other values, such as security, equality, or growth. Both the liberalism of John Stuart Mill and that of John Dewey or Sidney Hook comprised a priority value of freedom, including the most extensive exercise of individual liberties compatible with other fundamental values. The disagreement between Mill and the pragmatists reflected, to a considerable degree, a difference on the relationship between the individual and his society or culture. In these background interpretations, decisions as to what part of social or cultural institutional reality is to be accepted as a "given" and what is to be identified as a "taken" and open to individual preference have obvious significance for the curriculum.

To cite an extreme example, it would seem to be difficult to raise children in a neutral language like symbolic logic so that they can have an unprejudiced and autonomous choice among languages at maturity. To greater or lesser degree, differing cultures have assumed that sexual orientation, religious affiliation, nationality or ethnic identification, vocational choice or class membership are either given or taken. In the one case education becomes an initiation into the social inheritance, while in the other it becomes a preparation for exercising intelligent choice among competing hypotheses.

Most modern interpretations of liberalism as maximizing liberty are couched in individualistic terms. This is so both in the liberalism of Mill, with his sense of self-regarding actions, as well as in Kant, with his stress on autonomy or self-determination. The value of self-determinism is augmented by the related value of self-expression or even, in Herder's phrase, by the "wish to create the self."

The educational impact of this idea has affected educational issues that range from introducing an elective curriculum into the colleges to how severely standard forms of English ought, in the teaching of English in the public schools, to be imposed on variants. Even on these libertarian assumptions, however, traditional standards or the classical curriculum can still be justified. The justification requires that they are chosen, or that they are legitimate ingredients in the formation of the mature self that would rationally be chosen by autonomous persons. Of course, by the same argument, they can be criticized as representing a heteronomous intellectual authority illegitimately imposed upon the development of the individual self. The criterion for deciding what is a liberal education is, on this view, derived from the priority value of maximizing liberty.

1. *Developmentalism and "Vacant Freedom."* Liberalism interpreted as maximization of liberty has also been criticized in ideological terms, though not as systematically as the two preceding interpretations. Critics point to the close connection of this interpretation of liberalism with nationalist ideologies of the nineteenth century that promoted the various movements for national self-determination: German, Czech, Greek, Italian, and others. According to this argument from genesis, the stress on self-determinism arises when people who have achieved awareness of latent possibilities of self-realization are frustrated in the achievement of their self-determination. Stable or mature national cultures, in contrast, do not assert the possibilities of national self-realization but focus on the values that are being realized.

Similarly, a developed person is not excessively concerned with discovery of the self or with creation of the self but with "the other." Thus, the self, on this account, is developed in the solving of real problems, or the transformations of situations, or in acting with those for whom consideration is due. Santayana, a severe critic of the coherence of liberalism, abusively termed the concern with the possibilities of self-development in the absence of an awareness of concrete goals for which freedom is prerequisite as "vacant freedom." He contrasted it with "vital liberty," where freedom is used for realizing goals or ends. This ideological criticism, when applied to the area of education, suggests that there is distortion in a stress on the free choice provided by the curriculum rather than on the values that can be realized through the exercise of choice.

2. *Justifications of Liberty and Limits on Absolute Liberty.* The priority of liberty over other, conflicting values is not self-evident but requires justification. That justification is seldom the intrinsic worth of the act of exercising freedom. Further, the kind of justification that is advanced does not imply that we should achieve the most extensive liberty possible in every situation. Liberty is usually justified because the denial of liberty leads to abuse, to the denial or the deprivation of other values. A person who has lost his freedom suffers consequences in many areas of his life: in security, equality, growth, and so on.

On the level of individual freedom, persons whose security and life are threatened may decide to accept a lesser degree of freedom, as those who chose periods of indentured servitude over starvation have done in many societies. Such choice is not irrational and there are many contexts where limitations of liberty for the sake of other values would be the most rational decision. Like any other value, freedom is justified by its fruits in choice among competing values. It cannot be assigned an absolute priority without reference to those fruits or to other values.

There is, however, a special justification for freedom as a presupposition for methods of inquiry. Thus, freedom of inquiry raises a special problem for the absolute priority of freedom. Presumably, as John Stuart Mill argued, we would not be justified in making choices among values if we did not have freedom to investigate all the alternative possibilities. To that degree, there is a methodological priority for freedom. On this view, freedom, unlike other values, cannot be abridged, since it provides us with the necessary condition for making decisions among values in conflict. Yet even this argument does not require freedom of inquiry in every context. A society may decide not to investigate certain questions (in areas like genetic research) because of reasonable concern with the social consequences of experimentation. This is true even if further investigation of the question might be able to show that some of the basis for the original decision was in error. To hold otherwise would be to give freedom an absolute weight in the cluster of values. This would render it immune from the test of consequences and, paradoxically, make a decision in favor of freedom not be the outcome of rational inquiry.

There is some clarification of this complex issue if we shift to an educational context. The virtue of having students freely construct or select their own curriculum is that they often construct a curriculum better suited to their needs and talents. Even if we discovered that they consistently chose a curriculum inadequate to their own needs and desires, we might still prize the freedom of individual choice sufficiently not to change to a less elective system. But we could not, on grounds of freedom, ever exclude completely the conclusion that free choice should be limited. In most cases, we value educational freedom both because it leads to growth and because the denial of choice opens the door to abuse.

This point is made in caricatures of the model of liberal education as self-expression or free choice in, for example, Randall Jarrell's *Pictures from an Institution* and Mary McCarthy's *Groves of Academe*. Their satires suggest that the value of self-expression is significant only when there is a self that is concerned with realizing some value other than self-expression and, further, that there is an important human value in the awareness of the "obdurate other." This criticism does not deny the liberating role that introduction of some form of elective system had in the reform of American education, or that the recognition of student autonomy was important in reforming many authoritarian schools and many rigid curricula. It does point to the risk of construing liberal education as a period of "extended adolescence," where random choice is exercised because the self is liberated from the authority of its past, while choice is not yet directed, since responsibility has not been assumed for the consequences of choice. Yet despite the faults of progressive education, the virtues in a liberal education aimed at the identification of latent or potential interests that have not yet been realized, or at the effort to discover and express the self, deserve recognition.

The relevant philosophical point is that the value of autonomy cannot be absolute without reference to the plural values that an ideal of liberalism comprises. A Kantian educator could, I believe, require students to learn Newtonian physics or Euclidean geometry while preserving their autonomy, since each rational person, unknown to himself, legislated for himself the laws of physics and geometry. Those of us who are not Kantian may still mandate physics or geometry, but we must then recognize that we value these studies on grounds other than the assertion of student autonomy.

3. *Freedom of Choice and Tradition.* There has been a reciprocal process in the presentation of these three interpretations of liberalism. The justification of liberalism as the most extensive liberty can lead us back, in part, to the first view that the value of liberty is connected with methods of inquiry. This is so because the justification of liberty, as we have seen, often rests on the significance of freedom as a condition for decision making and on the consequences of applying free inquiry to social institutions. Similarly, concern with maximizing liberty is informed by the possibility that, to be free, the self also must adjust to the environmental constraints. In so doing, a free self may require an initiation into an appreciation of the usable tradition and funded values of social and cultural inheritance. To that degree, the three variants of liberalism involve elements of circularity.

The legitimate and required reciprocity, symbiosis, and integration among different strands of liberalism and different interpretations of liberal education call for continuing investigation and criticism. In the present essay, a methodological liberalism was confronted by the humanist emphasis on the substantive values of the tradition. This humanist version, in turn, was then faced with the liberal concern with autonomy and self-expression. And autonomy, in turn, requires a recognition of the historical or biological factors that make possible self-determination as well as a recognition of the role of rational and empirical methods of decision making in the development of individual values.

As Sidney Hook's own lifelong effort to clarify the diverse varieties of liberalism testifies, liberal thought in the United States has moved away in significant measure from the landmark positions that I have reviewed. The divergence between these traditions of liberalism and the kind of "ritualistic liberalism," to use Hook's phrase, that is characterized by a turning away from the commitment to critical reflection of the relationship between ends and means and that is prepared to assert a false symmetry between the imperfections of democracy and the normative institution of totalitarianism has widened during the past two decades. Sidney Hook's response to this development was not to abandon the battlefield of liberalism to those who do not value critical intelligence and free inquiry but to insist on dialogical confrontation. In doing so, he deepened and clarified the analysis of liberalism while becoming a paradigm of moral courage.

EDWARD SHILS

Academic Freedom and Academic Obligations

With Some Thoughts on Departmental Autonomy, Permanent Tenure, and the Academic Appointment of Revolutionaries

A free society is one in which members of the society are free to act intellectually, economically, socially, and politically without restraints or restrictions, within the Constitution, within the law, and within some very general institutional conventions or moral rules. Constitution, law, and conventions are restrictions on the freedom of individuals and corporate bodies, but they are also the condition of the freedom of individuals and corporate bodies. A free society is one in which there is freedom of association for political ends, i.e., to gain positions of authority within the state and to influence the decisions of the state. This entails participation in competitive elections to representative legislative bodies. A free society is one in which there is freedom to form organizations to act corporately, to compete with similar bodies for the custom and support of whatever section of the populace it addresses. In a free society, individuals are free to seek, singly or in collaboration, particular goals such as self-enrichment and the enhancement of status or power, and to do so by the persuasion of others through reasonable argument and through influencing their conduct by payments for the procuring of their performance of legitimate actions. These goals include the attainment of the possession of truth by research and study and the disclosure of the intellectual results of such activity.

In a free society, governmental actions toward individuals must be in accordance with law; the law must be substantively as well as procedurally restrictive of government.

113

A free society is one in which autonomous corporate bodies perform many functions for the citizenry. The right of these corporate bodies to autonomy has precedence over governmental desires and demands, just as individual freedom does, with the limits indicated. They do not, however, have unqualified precedence. The benefit of the doubt is to be given corporate bodies and individuals, but there are limits to the application of this rule. A free society is one in which the prerogatives taken to itself by the state on the grounds of "overriding government interest" or, as it used to be called, *raison d'etat* is rarely used and only in cases of genuine emergency.

A free society has a legitimate place for government. A free society includes among its conventions a respect for government and authority more generally. This respect for authority is not uncritical submission. A critical attitude toward authority is not the same as antinomianism.

Traditionally the limit on the freedom of action of individuals and corporate bodies has been the point at which specifiable injury is done to specifiable individuals. So it has been at least in theory. Injuries to institutions that are not monetarily assessable have not been thought to be fit objects of restraint. I propose a change in this theory in a way that seems to me more realistic, or more prudent. The limit should not be located at the point of specifiable injury to other individuals, including specifiable infringements on the freedom of other individuals. It seems to me that the traditional point of limitation on the freedom of individuals disregards the dependence of individual and corporate freedom on the institutional setting on which the continuation of freedom depends, and it also disregards the intention to do damage. It is not possible for the freedom of individuals and corporate action to persist if individuals do not restrain themselves and if corporate bodies and government do not restrain themselves. It has often been pointed out that freedom carries with it obligations, that rights carry with them duties. One of the obligations of freedom is respect for the institutional setting that makes that freedom possible. By respect I do not mean ceremonial deference, nor do I mean lip-service. I mean consideration to avoid injury to the institution that provides the necessary condition for freedom. I wish to narrow the range of individual freedom by prohibiting actions intentionally injurious to institutional arrangements and traditions that are necessary for the maintenance of individual and corporate freedom.

I know that this is a very difficult role to formulate with precision or to apply with complete confidence in its fairness, because the assessment of damage to an institution is extremely difficult to conduct with any precision. It introduces a very ambiguous standard for the restriction of the freedom of individuals and corporate groups. It does so in principle at least. Sometimes it is assessable with some specificity but sometimes not so specifically. Yet the issue is a real one: Should individuals or groups be permitted to act in ways that will damage the opportunities for free action in the future? Should they be permitted to act in ways that are injurious to the effective functioning of the institution, as long as the institution itself has acted within the limits imposed by the law and by the appropriate conventions?

This is a difficult matter. For one thing, it assumes that one can determine the injury that an institution is likely to suffer and that one can confidently connect an injury to an injurious action. There are situations in which the injury and the relationship between injury and the injurious action can be fairly clearly determined; there are certainly others where it is not so clearly determinable. The general argument I am putting forth here with respect to academic freedom is not new, but it has not frequently been asserted because it appears to be inconsistent with the traditions of individualistic liberalism and partly because collectivistic liberals have thought that it would strike against extremists with whom they were sympathetic.

I

My concern here is with freedom in universities in liberal democratic societies. Academic freedom has a multiplicity of meanings. One of these, the one most commonly invoked in the United States, refers to the freedom of university — and college — teachers to enjoy the freedom of speech and action that other citizens are constitutionally, legally, and conventionally empowered to exercise. These include the freedom to organize for the purposes of promotion of particular, legitimate ends and to speak and to write in public on behalf of those ends and to take the legitimate actions deemed necessary to promote those ends. Such freedom of expression of belief and freedom of action are available to all citizens in liberal democratic societies in principle, and it is therefore right that it should be available to academics.

There have been numerous occasions in the history of American higher education on which it has not been available to academics. In these situations when academics availed themselves of the freedom that other citizens had and which were constitutionally, legally, and conventionally assured to them, sanctions were exercised against them by the authorities within their own institutions. When Edward Ross spoke in public against the importation of Chinese "coolie" laborers into the United States, what he was doing was perfectly in accordance with the Constitution and the laws of the United States and the state of California. When Scott Nearing wrote and spoke in public on behalf of legislation to protect female and juvenile workers, he was doing what any citizen was constitutionally and legally entitled to do; and he was doing it under circumstances in which it was legitimate for him to do it, namely, in speaking on behalf of such legislation before legitimate assemblies and writing in publications that were legally admitted.

The matter of circumstances is important. A right to action in freedom might be guaranteed by the Constitution, or laws promulgated in fulfillment of the Constitution, but the citizen is not free to practice it under all circumstances.

An individual enjoys the right of freedom of propagation of his religious beliefs, but he does not enjoy that right in the residence of another individual who has not invited him to do so. A worker in a factory or on a ship or in a mine or in an office is not free during the stipulated and agreed hours of work to conduct propaganda or to carry on organizational activity on behalf of a political party or association to which he is devoted. An office worker who is responsible for maintaining certain records or conducting correspondence with customers of the firm is not entitled to the freedom of disregarding during "office-hours" the maintenance of the records with which he is entrusted, nor is he entitled to the freedom of including, in the envelopes in which the business letters to customers are sent, leaflets making representations on behalf of his political party or association. A civil engineer who was sued for the construction of a bridge that collapsed as a result of faulty design could not properly adduce in self-protection the statement that, during the hours in which he was being paid to design the bridge, he was delivering speeches on behalf of his political party. Sometimes, these matters are difficult to disentangle, but they are in principle quite clear. Freedom of action is appropriate in some circumstances and not in others.

II

So much for the freedom of academics as citizens. This promulgation of the freedom of academics as citizens postulates a distinction between political activity and academic activity, just as there is a distinction between accounting and political activity, between coal mining and political activity, and between bridge-building and political activity. Academic activities are teaching and research and the maintenance of the academic institution in which teaching and research takes place. The activities comprised in "the maintenance of the academic institution" include the making of appointments of new members of academic staff, such as promotion and discontinuance, making decisions about syllabuses and courses of study, constructing, administering, reading and assessing examinations, supervising dissertations, and so on.

These various academic activities are not the same as political activities, although there are, inevitably, some overlaps at certain points between them and political activities. For example, the social sciences that deal with contemporary societies are bound to present factual images of various processes and sectors of societies, which, having the same subject-matter as the factual images presented by political parties or groups in their campaigns and programs, will either conform with or diverge from those of the political parties or groups in question. Therefore it might be said that the knowledge, such as it is, that social scientists put into their writings or teaching affirms or denies the assertions made by political parties about the same subject-matters. Nevertheless, the distinction between political activities and academic activities is a valid one. This being the case, there is an academic freedom that is more central to the life of the mind than the freedom of academics as citizens. This academic freedom is different from the freedom of academics to do whatever they wish, whenever they wish, wherever they wish, and in any way they wish. The latter is in fact the view of academic freedom held by some academics, but it is a self-indulgent and wrong view, seeking unjustifiable privileges.

Academic freedom is the freedom of academics to do academic activities without let or hindrance. Academic activities are concerned with truth about serious matters. If nothing is serious and if no truths can be ascertained and asserted, then academic activity is an occupation in which certain persons accept payments, titles, and audiences that they can manipulate and deceive; it is an arrangement that enables them, for reasonable remuneration and with more leisure than most other employed persons enjoy, to amuse or otherwise busy themselves as a way of passing the time under relatively agreeable physical conditions. Academics are committed by their acceptance of an academic appointment to acknowledge that their task is to teach and to seek the scientific or scholarly truth in their respective subjects to the best of their abilities.

Academic activities, being different from practical activities, even though the results of these academic activities can affect practical activities, have their own object; that object is the truth as well as it can be attained by scientific and scholarly procedures within their respective scientific and scholarly traditions. It is undeniable that many activities have been carried on in universities and colleges that are fairly remote from the concern with scientific and scholarly truth, for example, the purchase of bedding for dormitories or cereals and bread for meals in student refectories, the administration of health services for teachers and students, and the maintenance of the grounds of the university campus. These are all practical activities; they are subservient to the concern for scientific and scholarly truth and for the understanding of great works of the traditions of humanistic studies on the part of students and teachers. It must also be recognized that both students and teachers are human, and certain allowances must be made for that! The students should be provided with a place or places to live and places where they can have parties, dances, and balls and where they can play games, and the members of the teaching staff should be provided with places where they can have lunch and play billiards or chess or bridge. At least it is good if such amenities can be provided, although they are certainly outside the boundary of academic activities proper and away from the central object of academic activities, which is the understanding of great works and the ascertainment or discernment of scientific and scholarly truths. They are not essential.

The valued object or end of academic activities is knowledge, knowledge or understanding for its own sake and for subsequent incorporation into practical activities. A practical activity is oriented to bringing about a particular change in a particular series of events — or preventing a change that would otherwise occur; or it is oriented to changing the behavior of a class or classes of objects — or preventing a change that would otherwise occur. An academic activity is oriented toward acquiring and transmitting knowledge—observation, assessment, interpretation, and understanding. Even when the universities train young persons for practical professions, the training they offer is for those professions that require a large amount of knowledge that can be acquired only by disciplined, supervised study and research. It is beyond their jurisdiction to provide certification for the practice of professions to which such knowledge is not essential.

It is a contradiction in terms to speak of research whose conclusions are determined by external authority. External authority might prescribe the task or problem, but for it to impose or require certain conclusions is to render the conclusion valueless. The conclusion must be arrived at by a person who knows how to apply the criteria appropriate to the intellectual activity and who decides that the conclusion is sustained by evidence and reasons that he believes valid. Of course, the conclusion arrived at might be wrong, but its wrongness has to be decided on the basis of criteria of intellectual validity, and that means by persons capable of applying those criteria. The same conditions obtain in teaching. A teacher can of course expound views with which he disagrees, while pretending to his students that he does agree with them. Such a teacher must know that he is serving his students poorly, and the students are in fact being cheated because they are being taught things that their teacher, who has studied the matter, believes to be untrue. At universities, teachers are expected to know the subjects that they teach and hence to be capable of discriminating truth from falsehood. In totalitarian states, where rulers care less for truth than for submissiveness, the authorities may decree that a certain interpretation be taught and a teacher might indeed teach it without believing in its truth (or he may be indifferent to its truth or falsity). But in liberal democratic societies, where true knowledge is thought to be superior to false knowledge or error, universities are not usually expected to be and certainly should not be institutions concerned to make political propaganda on behalf of governments. A teacher guided by the best work in his field of study and teaching should be better qualified to pass judgment on what is correct than a person who has not studied the subject. He therefore should be free in the decision as to what is closest to the truth among competing hypotheses. This assumes, however, that he will live up to his side of the bargain.

Academic freedom is the freedom to do academic things, to apply the criteria of truthfulness that are appropriate to academic activity, i.e., teaching and research and the maintenance of the institution. The third activity—the maintenance of the academic institution—that should come under the protection of academic freedom is a necessary condition for the continuation of teaching and research at the highest level possible, given the available talents and resources.

III

Since the withdrawal of the churches from their campaign against the "higher criticism" of the Bible, external interference with strictly academic matters in universities has become relatvely rare in liberal democratic societies. In Great Britain, W. Robertson Smith and Benjamin Jowett were the object of charges of disrespect for orthodox doctrine; in France, Renan was dismissed from his post at the Collège de France for his account of the character and status of Jesus Christ. There are still minor fundamentalist denominational colleges that insist on conformity with a view of the Bible that is contrary to the view developed by great German scholars in the nineteenth century and then disseminated throughout the Western world of learning. In the physical sciences and the biological sciences there have been practically no incidents of restriction of academic freedom once evolutionary ideas found wide acceptance. (The recent scare about recombinant DNA is quite a new thing; so are some of the intrusions of the Department of Health and Human Services regarding the study of human subjects.)

The compulsory teaching of the view of human origins contained in Genesis is not significant as far as universities are concerned, although its imposition in colleges governed by fundamentalist denominations has occurred and is an infringement of the academic freedom of qualified teachers who do not regard the fundamentalist view as true.

The situation of academic freedom has perhaps been different in the social sciences. The standards of achievement being less easily enunciated and applied than they are in the natural sciences, there being less consensus about what is true and what is false, and because the social sciences touch on matters of contemporary contention, there has been a little more intrusion in these subjects. History and political science were subjects on which distrust fell in the First World War. The trustees of Columbia University instructed Charles Beard to tell his colleagues that they would not tolerate "teachings likely to inculcate disrespect for American institutions." In this period of intrusion by trustees, which ran up to the Second World War, little distinction was made by the trustees or by their academic opponents between teaching and research within the university and public declarations of political — that is, partisan — attitudes. The failure of the antagonists to make that distinction does not demonstrate that such a distinction is invalid or superfluous. (To insist on this distinction does not mean that it is more reasonable to restrict the freedom of academics as citizens than it is to restrict academic freedom as the freedom to do academic things within the university.)

The failure to make the distinction obscures several important facts: one is that the freedom of teaching and research have been much less frequently the objects of restriction than were sanctions against university teachers for speech, writing, and associations outside the university. In making this distinction, I must emphasize that I regard the latter as utterly deplorable. Reductions on the civil freedom of academics outside the university were degrading to the academic profession through making them subject to the usually baseless apprehensiveness of trustees; they were also unjust in that they made academics subject to restrictions in public expression to which editors, polilticians, businessmen, trade union leaders, bohemians, and agitators belonging to minor political sects were not subject. (Of course, sometimes the latter were subject to unnecessary restrictions also.)

My interest in this paper is not in the civil freedom of academics. Although it has sporadically suffered many restrictions in the past, it is not a serious problem at present. Trustees, presidents, and deans either are wiser and less excitable than they used to be or they are more indifferent or they are themselves collectivistic liberals; whatever the cause, trustees, who were the chief agents of restrictions on the civil freedom of academics, intervene less frequently than they used to do not so many years ago. Furthermore, presidents of universities are now both less subject to anxiety about the political views of their trustees and less imperious than they used to be in dealing with their teaching staffs; they are less powerful and either more sympathetic with collectivistic liberalism and socialism than they used to be or more anxious to avoid being called reactionary. In any case, instances of the types of infringement on the civil freedom of academics such as occurred between 1890 and the 1950s have become very rare.

It is more important at present to bring to the fore academic freedom proper — that is, the freedom to do academic things — and to consider how it is to be supported.

IV

Let me say at the beginning that academic freedom in the universities is not the freedom to do nonacademic things in the university. Some years ago, a distinguished young scientist, now, fortunately for Chicago, at Harvard, sent a circular letter to his colleagues urging them to use their offices or laboratories to serve as asyla for persons who were evading military conscription and who were being pursued by the Federal Bureau of Investigation. This was to "test the university's attachment to academic freedom." I replied that the rooms of the universities were given to members of the staff for academic purposes and to flout and frustrate the government was not an academic purpose. I suggested that he should use his home, which would be a more convenient place for his wards to stay in. Naturally, there was no reply to this counterproposal.

I see no reason why a teacher may not hold a meeting for advancing a particular legitimate political cause in his university room as long as it is quiet and causes no distracting commotions, but he cannot claim this as a right to be protected by the invocation of the rule or principle of academic freedom. It is the arrogation of a privilege attendant on having the perquisite of an office. It would be no infringement on academic freedom if a university were to insist that members who wish to participate in that favorite form of academic political activity — namely, affixing their names to "open letters" — must not attach to their signature the name of their university. The impropriety of the citation of the signatory's university is already being grasped by some persons since it is now common to insert — perhaps hypocritically — a note to the effect that "university affiliation is only for identification." This is hypocrisy, since the organizers know very well that without the reference to the "institutional affiliation," their little-known or unknown signatories would carry no weight at all with readers. These are, however, very trivial activities. Their performance is not protected by the right of academic freedom. These are in fact slight transgressions of academic obligations; they are the exploitation of appointment in a university for political purposes whose objectives lie outside the university. But since they are very trivial infringements of the obligations of academics and are in conformity with the civil rights of academics to perform political actions outside the university, I pass them over without anything more than slight disapproval.

The inability to do academic things well or the unwillingness to do them is not protected by the right of academic freedom. Actions that are injurious to the institution's performance of its academic functions should not be protected by the right to academic freedom.

Among the actions that an academic might perform and which in fact were frequently performed in the past two decades, and which are not to be protected by the right of academic freedom, are the following: attempts to persuade students to absent themselves from classes or to interfere with university administration with the intention to embarrass or disrupt the conduct of political agitation in academic class, and the organization and incitation of students and teachers to obstruct the university's performance of the functions of teaching, research, and institutional maintenance. There are many others.

It is no infringement on academic freedom if a person is penalized by dismissal or the withholding of promotion or the refusal of permanent tenure if he is demonstrably guilty of the performance of such actions. It is no more an infringement of academic freedom to use sanctions against persons performing such actions than it is an infringement of academic freedom to dismiss or otherwise penalize a teacher who appears very frequently in his classes in a state of alcoholic intoxication so severe as to prevent him from speaking coherently or remaining awake or standing upright, or, for other reasons, is frequently absent from his classes. It is not an infringement of academic freedom to exercise the sanction of dismissal or suspension against a teacher who is demonstrated to have cheated in his research or who does only very poor research filled with careless and easily avoidable mistakes.

V

The refusal or discontinuance of an appointment is no more evidence of an infringement on academic freedom than is the refusal of promotion or permanence of tenure. Incumbency of an academic post for a certain number of years may or may not be a good qualification for granting permanent tenure to the incumbent, but it is certainly not an infringement of academic freedom unless it is reasonably demonstrated that the decision is a sanction for the assertion, in the classroom or a report on research, of beliefs honestly held and based on knowledge of the tradition of the subject both in its substance and in its rules.

It is unfortunate that "permanent tenure" and academic freedom have become intertwined and confused with each other. Logically, academic freedom and permanent tenure have nothing whatsoever to do with each other. Permanent — or indefinite tenure — should be awarded on ground of superior quality of teaching or research, or both, and a reasonable level of academic citizenship. These are the obligations that an academic undertakes when he accepts an appointment. Why should the appointment continue if he ceases to observe that obligation? The institution of permanent tenure is, however, a protection of the individual from infringement on his academic freedom just as it is a protection for the academic's exercise of his right as a citizen; it protects those freedoms from infringement by preventing the authorities of the institution from threatening the dismissal of the teacher who exercises his right to speak the truth as he sees it in his classes and in his writings and to act civilly.

This is the main reason why the concern with permanent tenure became so prominent in the activities of the American Association of University Professors. A university teacher who has an assurance of permanence of tenure is safe against any conspiracy of his colleagues to eject him from the university; he is protected against jealousy of colleagues who disapprove of him because he is too successful in his research or teaching or because he is obnoxious to them for temperamental reasons or on political grounds; he is immune from the efforts of trustees or higher administrative authorities in the university to eject him from his post because they disapprove of his political activity. He is free to do whatever he wishes and he is free not to do anything, including conscientious teaching and research. Permanent tenure also protects the individual against the sanction of discontinuance of his appointment for insufficient conscientiousness in teaching, indolence, slovenliness, incompetence or commonplaceness in research, and severe deficiency or subversion of the performance of the obligations of academic citizenship.

It is difficult to determine with complete precision whether an individual is a good teacher, because it is not easy to observe his teaching; it is also not easy to assess its effectiveness, even if it has been observed. It is easier to assess the merit of achievements in research, because the works in which his research is reported can be read in publicly available journals, books, and monographs, although disagreements about their merits are possible, even with good will on all sides.

The performance of the obligation of academic citizenship can be observed more easily than can be teaching, since departures from it are sometimes made with the intention of gaining the largest possible amount of publicity. Those actions that are departures from academic citizenship but are carried on in the course of classroom teaching are more difficult to observe. Their reprehensibility is not diminished by the difficulty of discerning them reliably.

Even in disciplines that are relatively free from political content, it is not always possible to make explicit the criteria of achievement and to apply them in a way that compels agreement from all who judge a piece of work or a body of work. The more the subject-matter of a discipline overlaps with beliefs about things that are in political or moral controversy, the more difficult it is to arrive at an intellectually well-founded consensus. The social sciences are especially susceptible to such difficulties. Nevertheless it is possible in the social sciences with goodwill and scrupulousness to distinguish work of high quality. The estimation of achievement in teaching also is not an arbitrary affair there either.

The task of assessing the intellectual quality of performance in teaching and research can be carried out if those charged with it are careful in studying the documents before them and watch over their own political and temperamental predilections. It is not easy but it certainly can be done. If it is not possible to do this, then every academic institution except the very worst is in danger of intellectual deterioration.

It has become difficult to discuss academic obligations and academic freedom in the United States without discussing permanent tenure, because in the United States the mode of argument of the American Association of University Professors has linked them and not wholly without justification. Under the conditions of politicization in American universities it has also become difficult to discuss promotions, retentions, and permanence of tenure without claims of infringement of academic freedom being brought into the discussion.

The proclivity of the American Association of University Professors to think of permanent tenure primarily with regard of academic freedom — usually the civil freedom of academics — is understandable. The Association came into existence after about a quarter of a century of scattered and intermittent incidents of infringement on the civil freedom of academics. The infringement usually took the form of such sanctions as dismissals or denials of promotion. It was unreasonable for the Association to think that the best way to protect the civil freedom of the academic was to deprive the administrative authorities of the institution of their power to damage the university teacher's career by dismissal or blocking of promotion in rank or salary, or both.

In consequence of this, permanent tenure has become a feature of the academic career about which academics are extraordinarily sensitive. At a time when the academic sense of obligation to his own academic institution is disregarded or derided and when the faintness of that sense of obligation is approved of much more than in the past, academics insist more than ever on the obligation of their universities to them. The chief of these obligations of the university to the individual academic is the assurance of the permanence of his appointment.

Yet permanent tenure should not be regarded as a sacred cow that is not to be criticized or modified; although, if modified, it ceases to be permanent tenure. I myself would modify the terms of academic appointment so that the granting of permanent tenure, if it is granted, would be granted conditionally on the maintenance of a standard of intellectual quality and conscientiousness in teaching, research, and academic citizenship.

VI

Over the past three decades, there have been several interesting discussions of permanent tenure in the academic profession. It has, for example, been pointed out that there are professions that do not have permanent tenure and that academics have claim on permanent tenure because of its traditionality. It has also been argued that academics who have permanent tenure can relapse safely into indolence and neglect of duty. It has further been argued that academics would be more productive if they knew that their reappointment—or the continuation in their existing appointments—required that they be more active in research and more diligent in teaching.

In favor of permanent tenure is the major argument, already mentioned, that it protects the academic in the free exercise of his rights as a citizen.

There are additional arguments in favor of permanent tenure, as well as the argument that it is an arrangement that protects the intellectual and civil freedom of the academic. It is said that it reduces the anxiety of academics and renders it easier for them to apply their minds, without distraction, to their tasks in teaching and research. It is also said that it is the condition of assuring institutional loyalty because that attitude takes a long time to develop and because it can be formed only where the academic trusts his academic colleagues and the administrators or his institution.

All these arguments on both sides are reasonable, although it should be said that the quality of research that is done only because the research worker is afraid of the loss of his appointment or his retention in the same rank is not likely to be very good. There is already too much undistinguished research being done, research that few scientists read and which contributes little or nothing to the growth of important knowledge. The research done at the point of a gun and not because of a strong desire to gain a better understanding would most likely be undistinguished. The intellectual world would be at least as well off if much of the research being done nowadays were not done. If, however, the danger of dismissal or of remaining at the same rank caused teachers to apply themselves more assiduously to improve the quality of their teaching by widening and deciphering their study of the literature of their subjects or by devoting more attention to helping students intellectually, that would certainly be a beneficial consequence of the modification of the present mode of permanent appointment.

Of all the arguments advanced for permanent tenure the strongest is that it protects the political freedom of the academic. It is a negative argument; it assures no positive consequences, only the prevention of negative ones. Still it is not to be disregarded, but it should not be accepted as conclusive if the conditions that it guards against are not as they are averred.

The argument was developed at a time when university presidents were more domineering in their actions toward their academic staff than they have since become and when trustees were also more intrusive into the affairs of the universities they governed. Academic freedom was conceived entirely as the civil freedom of the academic, and that was the particular freedom that was at stake.

The prevailing mood in the United States until the Great Depression of the 1930s was individualistically liberal and very hostile toward collectivism; there was, however, a strong current of collectivistic liberalism in the social sciences in the universities and to a lesser extent in the humanities; this led to intermittent conflicts of presidents and boards of trustees with particular academics who were active outside the university as socialists. (Communists were very rare in universities during the period in question.) The collectivistic liberal academics were on the weaker side in this conflict and they were therefore sometimes victims of the sanction of dismissal, which could have been forestalled if the victims had been contractually assured of permanent tenure in their academic appointments.

The dangers of infringement on the civil and intellectual freedom of academics at the hands of administrators and trustees do exist. Nevertheless, it must be recognized that the danger from these sources has greatly diminished over the past quarter of a century. Those who would maintain or even reinforce the institution of permanent tenure persist in the traditional argument for permanent tenure and the movement of the Moral Majority as the grounds for their position. This seems to be a rather feeble argument. That is why some of the critics of permanent tenure think that it should be eliminated. This does not seem to me to be wholly persuasive, because the present ascendancy of collectivistic liberalism might weaken and academics would again be faced with abrogation of their rights as citizens.

There is another reason for the retention of the practice of appointments in permanent tenure more compelling in my view. If every academic had to be reviewed every five years by his colleagues, there would be a particular excitation in every department. Every year there would be one or several committees sitting to decide whether certain colleagues should be given another appointment for five years. This would breed much insecurity and it would generate much "log-rolling." This would mean that reappointments would either become almost perfunctory—in which case permanent tenure might just as well be retained—or that the problems of reappointment would be taken seriously, and then every person called upon to participate in the decision would have to spend a lot of time reading all the works of his colleagues, pondering on them and then troubling his mind about which side of the line he would support. In the latter alternative, there would be much commotion and distraction from teaching and research in universities where there is already too much distraction.

Thus there are fairly good arguments for retaining permanent tenure in its present form. There is, however, another danger to universities that appointments on permanent tenure do not avert and indeed make more threatening to the well-being of universities.

This danger is the failure of academic citizenship. Fifty years ago academic citizenship was not as important as it is now, because universities in the United States had at that time long been conducted as tyrannies or oligarchies. The half-century then approaching its end was an age in which academics tended to be deferential to authority and were generally moderate in their political outlook insofar as they were interested in politics; no less important was the imperiousness of university presidents, who with deans and permanent heads of departments made practically all the decisions in the universities. They worked closely with the board of trustees and excluded the mass of the teaching staff almost entirely from the conduct of the universities. The great changes over the past fifty years have been due to the devolution of authority in the universities from presidents and boards of trustees to departments and individual academics. Junior members as well as professors have shared in the devolved authority.

Academic citizenship always had some place, even if only a small one, in universities because authority could never be completely concentrated in the hands of the tyrant or oligarchs. The nature of teaching and research requires freedom, which can never be completely set aside by decisions by authorities external to the actions and situation of teaching and research. Thus there was always a place in universities for some freedom of action in teaching and research and hence a place for obligations to be fulfilled without coercion. With the changes in the distribution of authority, the place has become very much larger. Academics have become even more important in the conduct of their universities; they have become especially influential in the making of academic appointments.

This period of redistribution has also been a time of rapid expansion of academic staffs and also of unprecedented "self-financing." It has also been a time in which academics have become more interested in politics and politically more active in the ways in which academics do politics, namely, demonstrative and agitational politics outside the conventional framework of major political parties. It has also been a time when the distinction between intellectual activity and political activity, between cognitive propositions and political beliefs, have been obscured or denied.

As a result of these developments, there has been an extension of the range of freedom of academics within universities. Greater freedom has meant also greater freedom to infringe on obligations. The role of members of the academic staffs in encouraging the disruption of the universities by students in the second half of the 1960s and early 1970s illustrates this defection of the academics.

The subsequent elevation of political criteria in appointment is another illustration of this exploitation of academic freedom and failure to meet academic obligations. Symbolic of the entire development was the transformation of the American Association of University Professors into a trade union. From having been an association for protecting the civil rights of academics through the institution of permanent tenure, it has become an association whose main aim is the guarantee of permanent tenure regardless of any but the most minimal academic qualifications.

VII

The derelictions from academic obligation include not only the gross interferences with the functioning of the university and the gross negligence of proper intellectual standards in teaching and research. They also include appointive actions that bring about the intellectual deterioration of whole departments. This active, even if not intentional, furtherance of the intellectual deterioration of departments is a consequence of dereliction from academic obligation in the sense that it is a result of negligence or positive misconduct in appointment.

Appointments on political grounds, or on sexual or ethnical grounds, are infrequencies. Negligence, complacency, jealousy of superiority, and comfort in mediocrity are just as inimical to universities as the intimidation of academics by nonacademics inhibiting the academics' search for and promulgation of truths about the various objects of academic teaching, study, and research. It is a dereliction from academic obligations and it is unjustifiable to claim that such decisions in matters of appointment are a proper exercise of academic freedom. The harassment of colleagues, either because they refuse to join a trade union or because they are members of a trade union, is an infringement of academic obligations and cannot be accorded the protection afforded to the exercise of academic freedom. It is neglect of the duties of academic citizenship to be content to appoint on a permanent basis persons of qualities below the standard appropriate to the university as a whole, given the resources available and the attractive power of the institution. There is no reason why this kind of conduct in a university should come under the guarantee of academic freedom. Repeated appointment and promotion of poor scholars and teachers or of politically sympathetic persons is not a privilege that should enjoy the protection of academic freedom. The sanctions for such action need not be the same as for cheating in research, misconduct in teaching, or disruption of the university. Nevertheless, the self-government of a department is placed in question by such negligence. Its suspension should be considered.

To deal with these actions of defective academic citizenship as well as with serious neglect of teaching duties, I would like to recommend certain changes in the existing system of guarantees of internal academic freedom. These changes might be regarded as restrictions of academic freedom; they are indeed intended to be restrictions of the freedom to act inimically to the university's interests as an intellectual institution. The most important recommendation is that the institution of permanent tenure be revised but not discarded totally. A second recommendation is closely related to the first; it is that the convention of departmental autonomy in making or proposing appointments be qualified.

I shall deal first with the latter. Departmental autonomy in appointment should certainly not be abolished, but it should be withdrawn or qualified in the case of departments that have by recurrent actions allowed themselves to deteriorate and done nothing to improve their quality.

Departmental autonomy in the fixing of syllabuses and courses of study and departmental power in nominating and recommending candidates for appointment and promotion and for discontinuance have the same justification as has academic freedom in teaching and research. In all these cases, legislators, trustees, newspaper editors, civil servants, and representatives of civic organizations, whatever merits they might have in their own spheres, are not qualified to decide on what scientific and scholarly beliefs are true, or what particular views about the particular subjects studied by scientists and scholars should be taught to students in university classrooms. Nor are they qualified to decide who among the candidates for a particular academic candidacy is the best one.

The fact, however, that academics are best qualified to render judgment on academic matters does not mean that academics always act up to the level of the obligations which their qualifications confer on them.

The modification of departmental autonomy that I propose is that "weak" departments that have weakened themselves by a succession of weak appointments should be deprived of the right to propose appointments by their own appointive bodies, whether it is the entire department or the senior members of the department or a committee of members of the department. Appointive bodies for such "weak" departments should include persons from adjacent disciplines from the same university and from the same discipline in other universities. The "external" members should not be chosen for the appointive body on the recommendation of the members of the "weak" department; they should be chosen by deans or the heads of adjacent departments that have maintained a higher standard in their own appointments and in their own intellectual achievements.

This proposal has drawbacks too. The external members from adjacent departments might not know enough about the subject; the external members of the same discipline in other universities might be indifferent. It is also invidious to the department and administrators who might be reluctant to take any action that would embarrass longstanding members of the university, amiable persons with whom they sit at lunch and whom they entertain in their homes. They will have to face accusations of infringement on academic freedom, discrimination, ignorance, and so on. These are obstacles to the occasional suspension of departmental autonomy in matters of appointment, but they do not make it any the less necessary.

There are very good reasons for retaining the institutions of departmental autonomy and of permanent tenure, because they both recognize the fundamental need for freedom in teaching and research. The principle is the right one, but it does not always work well and it should be modified when it is not working well.

Departmental autonomy is a relatively new phenomenon; permanence of tenure reaches much further back into the past as a perquisite of priestly ordination and of appointment to the civil service.

As a perquisite of the academic profession in the United States, it is of uncertain age. What is certain is that it became an issue in the second decade of the present century, when it was already well established in German and British universities. (Its history in France might be as long as it is in Germany, at least in the highest ranks.) In the early decades of the present century in the American academic world, many individuals enjoyed it *de facto* and it then became conventional for senior teachers after long service in their universities and colleges. The explicit establishment of permanent tenure as a condition for continued appointment on the academic staff of a university after one or several fairly brief probationary periods is largely a phenomenon of the second third of the present century. Before that time, many eminent academics served continuously for many years until retirement without contractual assurance of permanent tenure. Since the Second World War, explicit permanence of appointment at the rank of associate professorship or full professorship after probationary terms has become common in the United States; in the same period, the length of appointment at lower ranks has been shortened so that it has had to terminate after a specified number of years in either promotion to the next higher grade or in discontinuance. The aim has been to shorten the terms of limited appointments and to reduce the number of times an appointment at a junior grade could be extended. The trend has been toward greater selectiveness and then permanence. The number of renewals of short-term appointments has been sharply reduced in many universities where recurrent reappointments for terms of a single year had been allowed to go on for as long as about a decade or a decade and a half; that recurrence has come to be regarded as constituting a presumptive right to permanence of tenure.

Permanence of tenure has invariably meant continuance until the contractually or legally set date of retirement or superannuation. Its establishment in the United States has been regarded as a meritorious achievement. It has been regarded as an enhancement of the status of the academic profession. It has in fact been a check on the arrogance and arbitrariness of academic administrators and heads of departments and it has removed a common source of grievance.

Yet no sooner had permanent tenure become nearly universal throughout the universities and colleges of the United States than it came under criticism in Great Britain. Some of the criticism derived from the fact that it places academic budgets under an excessively inflexible strain. It has burdened university budgets with a disproportion of teachers on higher salaries. Permanence of appointment has left universities with little flexibility or room for new appointments in many countries.

In the discussion of permanent tenure in the United States, there has never been any claim on the part of university teachers and their spokesmen that all academics, even at the very beginning of their careers, should be appointed with the assurance of permanence. A period of probation at the beginning seems to be accepted. Universities in the United States have varied in their practices regarding the length of the probationary period but what is regarded as progress in the past half century is the placing of a determinate limit on the length of the probationary period after which it has become illegal to discontinue the appointment of a university teacher. The shortening of the probationary period or the period of short-term appointment has reduced the capacity of universities to diminish the burden on their budgets when income and numbers of students have diminished. An unduly large proportion of a teaching staff on permanent appointment has also restricted the opportunities for entry of younger aspirants for academic careers.

There are more marginal arguments regarding the worthwhileness of permanent tenure to be added to those which have already been mentioned. The arguments for permanent tenure go back well into the present century. The arguments against it are mainly of recent origin.

My own view is that appointment on permanent tenure should continue but with a modification that makes it presumptive rather than assured. I would replace permanent tenure by tenure of indefinite duration. Tenure of indefinite duration should be a presumptive permanence of tenure, conditional on meeting a reasonable standard of exertion and achievement in each of the three categories of academic activity. Appointment on tenure of indefinite duration should mean that appointment is not periodically reviewed; it should mean that an appointment can be reviewed and revised. This would mean that unless there were grounds for declaring that an appointment of indefinite duration should be reviewed, there would be a presumption of continuous appointment.

It is invidious at present to be reviewed for permanent tenure instead of being promoted automatically. It will be somewhat more invidious to be reviewed when one is on an appointment of indefinite duration, because such reviews would be undertaken when there are grounds for opening the question of the desirability of continuing the appointment of the person in question. The invidiousness is regrettable but I think that it is a burden that has to be borne.

Procedures would have to be developed to govern the initiation of a review of a person on appointment of indefinite duration and to govern the conduct of the review to assure the quality of the evidence it assembles, the justice of its determination, and the sanctions it proposes or decides on. Decisions to institute such reviews should be cautiously made, but caution should not be so great that such reviews are never conducted. If the latter becomes the case, the entire scheme will fall into desuetude.

It will be very difficult to work out the right arrangements for such reviews. It will be even more difficult to obtain the acceptance of such a scheme, because academics with unqualified permanent tenure will not eagerly accept an arrangement that abridges their privilege; presidents and boards of trustees will lack the courage to argue for it and the first universities to introduce it will be at a disadvantage in recruiting new staff in competition with universities that continue to provide unqualified permanent tenure.

It will also be said by others who will oppose the scheme that to institute such an arrangement will breed divisiveness in the universities, which are already afflicted with divisiveness. It will, it is likely to be said, lead to witch-hunts as pretexts for excluding distasteful colleagues. It will cause much turbulence. It will lead to anonymous denunciations; it will lead to paying off scores on old grievances; it will make moral lepers out of the persons reviewed. Many other objections can be raised and by no means unreasonably. Such a scheme is susceptible to being abused, but so is the institution of unqualified permanent tenure, which has certainly been abused. Furthermore, even with permanent tenure full and associate professors have often been instigators of turbulence and divisiveness. Permanence of tenure has not automatically made professors into solicitous custodians of the good order and intellectual merit of their universities.

Something must be said about each of these objections. But, before doing so, I wish to say that I think that there is something seriously amiss in the teaching staffs of quite a number of American universities today, particularly in the social sciences and to some extent in the humanities. There is a lot of self-indulgent arbitrariness and much neglect of academic obligations. The universities of the United States may become infected by politics. Indolence, cynicism, and politicization are certainly not universal in American universities but they are too widespread, especially in certain groups of disciplines. The universities have not become this way through accident. They have reached this condition largely through a combination of negligence and design. The unsatisfactory condition is partly the result of a determined, although undoubtedly not nationally concerted, campaign by political radicals to establish themselves in the university and to bring their fellow-believers into their departments. It is also partly a result of misguidedly liberal good intentions and of cowardice and intellectual indifference of other members of the departments in question. Sometimes a desire to embrace anything that can be called an "innovation," or a fear of being called "reactionary" or "obsolete" has contributed to bringing about this condition. Sometimes it has been simply the indifference to criteria of intellectual quality that has led the universities into this condition or helped them to stay there.

Indifference to intellectual quality, enthusiasm about fashions, and the determination of political radicals to bring more of their own into teaching staffs are noticeable in English, philosophy, political science, sociology, and anthropology departments. Insofar as there is no conflict in these departments and no "divisiveness" it is because the more traditional academics who are not radicals or fashion-mongers have resigned themselves to the situation out of pessimism or fatigue or out of fear of being castigated as reactionaries, philistines, elitists, and whatnot. Those who declare the fear that "divisiveness" would result from qualifying permanent tenure are the ones who are benefiting from the peace that the appeasers have given them. Progressive, collectivistic liberals resist the appointment of those they call "reactionaries" on the grounds that "old wounds would be reopened," but they themselves inflicted those wounds in the first place.

Regarding the "witch-hunt": The fact that there were never any witches among those persecuted by witch-hunters does not mean that there are not lots of American academics today who are taking advantage of the loose ideas of academic freedom to introduce into the interior of the university the agitation that their civil freedom permits them to conduct outside the university. They do so to promote what they think are their political interests. They exploit their permanence of tenure for such purposes; they neglect their obligations by giving their students less of intellectual value than they are entitled to have.

The possibility that the introduction of qualified permanent tenure or tenure of indefinite duration would stir up turbulence and division within the university should be taken into account. I think that the danger would not be great. The radicals on the teaching staff of universities do not have a great deal of support from students nowadays, although initially they gained their present positions as a result of the readiness of their seniors to placate radical students. I think that the turbulence would not be great because in many respects the reforms that I am recommending will be to the advantage of students, although students can frequently be misled into agitation by teachers who flatter their prejudices.

The changes I am recommending would not be drastic changes. Permanence of tenure would remain, and so would departmental autonomy; but they would be somewhat restricted. The existing arrangements would only be qualified and conditional; the qualifications would come into play only as conditions warrant. It could also be stipulated that no review of the tenure of a university teacher could take into account his external political activities. This would protect the freedom of university teachers to exercise the legitimate freedom of citizens in public places outside the university. Reviews of appointments of indefinite duration would be explicitly restricted to considerations of the academic's achievements in the fulfillment of the obligations in teaching, research, and academic citizenship.

VIII

This leads into a difficult, but separate, question. I will devote a few pages to it. Should persons who declare themselves to be or who can be plainly seen to be enemies of the constitutional order be appointed to university posts? One may draw an analogy with governmental appointments: If the enmity to the constitutional order is only a matter of belief and not of action, and if the beliefs are legally entitled to be held, then there can be no objection to appointment to posts in which no civil harm can be done, such as custodianship of museums, dentists in a health service, toll collectors on highways, and a host of other employments in which there can be no influence on the state of public order or on relations with foreign powers. The enemy of the constitutional order may well hold a post as a teacher of zoology or entomology or biochemistry or statistics or mathematics or astrophysics or Sanskrit or classical archaeology or other subjects that do not offer any opportunity for subversive action or for the moral and political manipulation of students' belief about society.

Where a person has in writing repeatedly and unambiguously declared himself to be determined to destroy the existing order of society by unconstitutional means and to replace it by something that is a fundamental negation of the existing constitutional order, the decision in the matter of appointment of such a person should be dependent on *(a)* whether he is an outstanding teacher who does not introduce political propaganda into his teaching, *(b)* whether he is an outstanding scholar or scientist, and *(c)* whether he is a faithful academic citizen. The first and third categories would have to be scrutinized with great care; the second should also be examined with the same care given to that category in the appointment of other scholars in the same field, but that is relatively easy to do since the evidence is publicly accessible.

Persons who have committed themselves, even if only in writing, to the subversion of the existing constitutional order have no grounds for seeking remedies under an order whose legitimacy they deny. Their commitment to a conception of the world that declares the principle of academic freedom to be a deception because academic freedom cannot exist and their commitment to an ideal society that would obliterate academic freedom and all other freedom as well—except for the freedom of the heads of a dictatorial party—make it hypocritical for them to claim the protection of a rule that they themselves declare invalid. In other words, they rule out their protection by the principle of academic freedom.

Nevertheless, the fact that they are hypocritical and self-contradictory does not release us from our obligations to act in accordance with our own principles and the facts of the case. My own view is that if the person in question is an outstanding scientist or scholar who, despite his own denials of the principles, accepts in fact the standards of validity that obtain in scientific and scholarly communities and if he is a good academic citizen and if he refrains from political propaganda in the university, he should be as seriously considered for academic appointment as any person who is not a revolutionary. Nonetheless, for candidates having those political commitments it is incumbent on appointive committees to scrutinize with even greater than usual care their adherence to the academic ethos in the three categories repeatedly referred to here.

Academic freedom is one freedom, in a larger, more comprehensive structure or pattern of freedom, that is complicated by the fact that the freedom of academic activity, like the freedom of religious activity, is an orientation toward symbolic or ideal objects. In other words, academic activities are oriented toward symbolic configurations about the world; so are revolutionary political activities. Revolutionary political activities—of the "right" as well as the "left," if one likes such a distinction—are doctrines about the ideal and about the existent. Political doctrines have a closer resemblance to the analytical theories that academic intellectual activities are concerned with. For this reason, it is not easy in the humanities and the social sciences to separate the political from the intellectual. It is difficult to know whether a given theoretical belief about society or man and his works is a product of serious intellectual study or whether it is a product of a commitment to a revolutionary or any other political ideal and doctrine to which the individual theoretical beliefs have been bent. In other words, the commitment of a candidate to a point of view and program that is inimical to the existing constitutional order but which the existing constitutional order allows to be propagated in present-day society is a signal for caution beyond the usual caution with which all candidates are to be treated, but it is not an unqualified imperative for exclusion.

IX

The freedom to do academic things presupposes a certain degree of corporate self-government of universities. This academic freedom and university autonomy are integral elements in a pluralistic, partially consensual society. This pluralistic, partially consensual society is, under conditions of modern life, also a liberal democratic society with representative institutions, rule of law, freedom of the ownership and use of private property, and freedom of the press, association, assembly, petition, and representation.

The liberal conception of society allots different functions to different institutional spheres in accordance with the various legitimate ends of human activities. These spheres are not completely independent of each other but the incompleteness of their autonomy is fully compatible with a far-reaching autonomy. The function of the sphere of higher education is the cultivation, acquisition, and transmission of knowledge at advanced levels. Why should universities be autonomous and why should the sphere of higher education be autonomous, to the extent that the autonomy of any institution or institutional sphere is possible in society? The answer, at least in a first approximation, is simple: no one can look after knowledge except one who knows it, who cares for it, and who knows the way to conduct the institutions through which it moves.

This principle of autonomy extends also to departments and to individual academics in universities—or to faculties and chairs in the old European arrangements. Each is the appropriate bearer of the responsibility for free and autonomous action in its and his sphere of competence. This applies equally to the university as a whole.

This conception of the autonomous university in a pluralistic, liberal democratic society presupposes the separability of science and scholarship from political activity. But complete separation is impossible and undesirable. This is the justification for the political freedom of academics outside the university. But this does not diminish the absolute importance of knowledge and its autonomous pursuit. That is why the freedom to do academic things is integral to the university. It must be freedom from the intrusion of politics from the outside and from the inside. The current theory of academic freedom emphasizes immunity to political domination from outside the university. I wish to emphasize the necessary immunity of the university from political domination from the inside. The highest good of the university should lie in its preoccupation with the maintenance, improvement, and transmission of knowledge.

The arguments for university autonomy, departmental autonomy in the making of academic appointments, and the freedom and obligation of the individual university teacher all belong together. The justification for all of them is their contribution to methodical gathering of new knowledge and disciplined interpretation and transmission of already acquired knowledge. Permanence of tenure is not justifiable primarily on the ground that it assures the civil freedom of the academic. That might be a good justification insofar as the academic is a citizen as well as an academic. But we should also ask whether permanent tenure is an equally good assurance of the performance of academic obligations by the individual academic. The answer to this question is also affirmative but with more qualifications. It does not always work effectively. Arrangements that guarantee the civil freedom of the academic are not necessarily also the guarantees of the performances of academic or intellectual tasks. The same may be said about departmental autonomy, especially in matters of appointment. It is generally a protection from the intrusion of irrelevant, i.e., nonintellectual, nonacademic, criteria of selection of prospective members and retention and promotion of the academic staff of the university. Departmental autonomy is justified by its protection of academic appointments—and other academic activities—from all informed intrusions by presidents, trustees, deans, and any other unqualified persons. This assumes that the members of a department, a committee made up of members of a department will not introduce or apply unintellectual, nonacademic criteria in the selection of new members or in the retention and promotion of existing members. But it does not always happen that way. Sometimes the academics in a department who can do what no one else can do in applying the appropriate criteria of intellectual quality—including quality in research and quality in teaching—do not do so. They might fail to do so out of prizing political standpoints more than they prize intellectual merits, or they might prize qualities of personal congeniality or of an inclination to work in a particular scientific or scholarly subfield or problem more than they prize higher intellectual quality in some other parts of the departmental jurisdiction, or they might simply be indifferent to or intellectually incapable of forming a judgment of the scientific or scholarly achievements or promise of a candidate. Whatever the causes, they are in default. As a result, the performance of the function that justifies departmental autonomy is being neglected.

The question is whether departmental autonomy is of such intrinsic merit that, even if it results in damage to the university as an intellectual institution, it should be allowed to go on without any restrictions. My answer is that it should not be allowed to do so.

X

Universities have existed in aristocratic republics, small princely states, constitutional monarchies, in empires that are partially constitutional, like the German and Austro-Hungarian monarchies, and in liberal democracies. They have not fared well in totalitarian states, which is only to be expected since totalitarian states do not admit that any constituent institutions should be free to devote themselves mainly to their own values or ideals. The absolutist monarchies of eighteenth-century Europe and what remained of them in the constitutional pattern that dominated Europe in the nineteenth century were willing to allow a certain measure of autonomy to universities in their respective realms. In the latter part of the nineteenth century, under regimes that were de facto pluralistic, universities thrived, as they did in liberal democratic republics like the United States, Canada, and Australia in the twentieth century.

A university without autonomy in the pursuit of the ideal of truth in teaching and training and research could not be a university. To be a university presupposes the separability of the intellectual activities from political activities. That is why the autonomy of universities and the academic freedom of individuals is necessary and hence justified.

The assertion that intellectual activities are invariably and exclusively political is nonsensical and self-contradictory; it is incompatible with the functioning of a university; it renders meaningless the autonomy of universities and the academic freedom of individual academics unless the intention is to create and maintain a politically privileged elite who are supported to conduct political activities while not admitting that they are doing so. Those persons who deny that political activities are different from intellectual activities, and really mean their denial, cannot with any degree of consistency concern themselves seriously with intellectual things; and they cannot consistently affirm any loyalty to the university as an institution. They would be unable to fulfill their obligations as academic citizens and could not take their research seriously if they really acted in accordance with their asserted beliefs that all ostensibly intellectual activities are really political activities. Their teaching would, if they were consistent, be political discourse aimed at winning their pupils to support a practical political party or group or "movement." Such persons are in principle not qualified to be members of universities; if they mean what they say and, more important, really act as they say, then they should not be appointed to posts in universities and, if they have already been appointed, they should not be continued. But human beings are inconsistent and they often assert principles and doctrines to which they do not adhere in their own intellectual work of teaching and research. It is a glaring deficiency of an academic to assert a political and epistemological doctrine, and then flatly contradict that doctrine in his own teaching and research and academic conduct. Nevertheless, there are persons like that and sometimes they are even very excellent scholars or scientists and very fine teachers whose performance belies their principles; that must be borne in mind by appointive bodies. Human beings are sometimes better than they say. But not always; often they are just as bad and sometimes even worse.

This is only one of the numerous difficulties in the decisions as to who is entitled to the assurance and protection of academic freedom. Fundamentally, however, the problem of deciding whether to confer an appointment of indefinite duration to a person who is wholly innocent of any asseverations about the supremacy and all-pervasiveness of politics, and the problem of whether to reconsider the tenure of a person whose research is extremely deficient and whose teaching is intellectually weak and unstudious, and the problem whether to suspend or qualify all of the appointive powers of a particular department all come down to the same problem. That problem is the intellectual one of deciding about whether the person or persons in question are meeting their academic obligations in teaching, research, and academic citizenship. The first is difficult to discern, the third is vague, only the second is fairly clear. And even if all three could be discerned with equal clarity and reliability, how is mediocrity and even failure in one to be measured against incontestable excellence in one or both of the others. It is no easy matter but the responsibility cannot be abdicated. Alongside of that, the problem of the political freedom of the academic offers relatively little moral or intellectual difficulty.

PAUL SEABURY

A Free University
in a Free Society

This paper addresses a problem much on the minds of scholars, university administrators, parents, and politicians during the recent decade. In writing it I fear that some of you may turn away from the topic with—if not boredom—at least distaste at having again to endure another disquisition on a troublesome, long-argued, familiar issue. The topic is that of the free university in a free society. My treatment of it considers the university in American society.

In tumultuous times, such as American universities experienced in the 1960s, our understanding of issues becomes dangerously oversimplified. Confrontations encourage simplistic depictions of what is at stake and caricatures of rights and wrongs, of what is just and unjust, and so forth. When this happens, we must not overlook the seriousness of the issues. A crisis can bare fundamental truths that are taken for granted in normal times. I remember an occasion (during the first major campus disruption at Berkeley in the mid-1960s) when, confused as to what was going on, I took off to read Ortega y Gasset's famous little book, *The Mission of the University,* which that civilized Spaniard wrote in the early 1930s. Naively, I thought that reading it would help me understand what was going on around me, at Berkeley, in a very different context. I was disappointed; the chief issues Ortega addressed in this book did not seem to apply to our university situation in the mid-1960s. Ortega raised the question: How can Spain recover from the cultural degeneration that had made it a backward part of European civilization? The university, he argued, could be the agency of recovery, a locale of national renaissance. But this required fundamental reform, to rescue it from its archaicisms. Rehumanization required Spanish higher education to assist in the revitalization of the country. How, I then asked myself, could this appeal to Spanish patriots enlighten our American situation?

By the mid-1960s (that is, before campus explosions occurred) American higher education had become the exemplar to the world of how *best* a society could devote great public resources to the enrichment of higher culture and the arts, and to the education of its young people in ways that heretofore had seemed almost inconceivable. No other nation in the world then could match (even on a per capita basis) the immense resources that Americans had agreed to invest in its colleges and universities. Foreign educators were swarming all over American universities trying to find the secret of this American success story. Thousands of Ph.D.'s were being produced every year, in growing numbers. American names dominated each new list of Nobel prize-winners. The educator's dream—every qualified young person would get a college education—neared fulfillment. State legislatures and the Congress were appropriating vast funds to make this possible. Then this—this revolution! I do not intend here to give a disquisition on the causes of the student revolt of the 1960s. A Spanish philosopher, whose Delphic entrails I consulted that troubled afternoon, had little to tell me. From then on, I became an autodidact, trying to figure everything out for myself.

Ortega was perfectly correct: what he was saying was that the vitality of a national culture depended upon the vitality of its higher parts. Moorish civilization, which brought learning to the Iberian peninsula, did this before it was expelled. The recovery of German civilization in the nineteenth century entailed the growth of universities in the Humboldt form. Napoleonic educational reforms made possible the fusion of the arts and sciences in Paris and elsewhere. While the case cannot be made that the advances in knowledge that Europe then experienced were chiefly due to the renaissance of its universities, these universities—and those of America as well—were expected to be *national* centers of learning, respected for what they accomplished in advancing all sorts of knowledge and no longer regarded as ivory towers. The esteem in which a professor came to be held in the Western world was not confined to scholarly circles but was generalized within a confident middle-class public.

While the character of American higher education in the twentieth century was much more diffuse than the European—being spread among many private and public, religious and secular, institutions—nevertheless the momentum of growth in excellence chiefly was due to state and state-supported universities *infused with public purposes.* If a principal public purpose turned out to be the education of larger parts of the nation's youth, this goal—not to be seen in the traditional aims of university life—displayed the egalitarian thrust of a democratic society, where parents wished a gift to be bestowed on their children: the prospect of a better life than they themselves enjoyed. De Tocqueville, that extraordinary prophet of the influence of American democracy on the world, would scarcely have been surprised had he lived to see how swiftly this American aspiration spread to other countries, especially after the Second World War. The effects of this can be seen in the almost ubiquitous thrust, in Europe, Asia, Latin America, and elsewhere, toward what we now call mass higher education.

We have also seen some bizarre consequences of the application of this worthy principle, both in our own country and abroad, where the pressure of vast numbers of students upon a finite store of resources results in deliquescence and in a lowering of the quality of instruction and learning. The idea that higher education is a right and not a rare privilege now is so widely accepted that only some catastrophe could reverse popular attitudes about it. For better or for worse, it is something that we accept, even as it takes its toll of the commonsensical notion that at any one time there are only so many people who can truly profit from, and add to, the store and quality of knowledge that a university contains. A university—as we should know at least from the terrible Chinese cultural revolution—can be destroyed when its purposes are reduced to the single one of striving for a truly egalitarian society.

Safe to say, this large tendency, one that became most pronounced in America during the 1960s, provided the cause and the energies that gave rise to other university problems of the time.

In theory, we best can appreciate the varieties of derangements possible in the relationship between a free university and a free society in those rare occasions when no one of many possible crises thunders so loudly as to drown out all other possibilities. Unfortunately, history is no kinder to universities than it is to anyone else—our challenges and difficulties come sequentially; each has its own special character. We cannot expect to meet them unless we have some inner conviction as to the essential nature of our vocation.

In the 1960s the derangement arose from *within* the university due to violent student uprisings that threatened in many instances to transform our universities either into ruins of their former selves or into intensely ideological action centers and enclaves similar to many Latin American universities. One wit at the time, in commenting on the threats posed to academic freedom by this sudden irrational wave, made the point that defenders of academic freedom had made the same mistake that the British defenders of Singapore had made before the Japanese conquered: they and we had our guns pointed in the wrong direction; we had never expected the attack on academic freedom to come from *within!*

In the 1970s, after that war was over, if not actually won, the threat then came from the *outside,* and the issue posed was that of massive federal intervention in the internal operations of universities. Few scholars genuinely concerned, in the sixties, with academic freedom as it should ideally be defined would have raised the flag of "university autonomy" so vigorously had they been aware of where this conceivably might lead—to an internal ideological tyranny sheltered, by barricades, from a free society. But in the seventies, when *that* crisis had passed and a new one appeared in the form of vast, comprehensive federal programs forced upon universities for "social purposes," the flag of autonomy was dusted off and raised on our ramparts to flap defiantly at government bureaucrats. Now that *that* era's wave seems also to have crested and receded, we should be a bit wiser: the possible sources of derangement within the university and between it and the outside world are such that no institutional principle, such as autonomy, can be raised to an absolute one, the way many irresponsible journalists today wrap themselves in the sacred vestments of the First Amendment.

I argue that today the difficulties we experience arise from within and without the university both, and simultaneously, and that if American colleges and universities are to recover their academic excellence we will need all the help we can get, from inside and outside both, and that perhaps what is most needed is the recovery of vigorous academic leadership at the top, which can also draw upon moral support within their faculties and from the outside community and government as well.

As the remarks above suggest, there long have been two puristic vantage points from which the American university has been perceived: one, with a long history, which, revering higher education, has seen it as a condition for the general improvement of society in all its parts, and in particular has viewed access to it as a goal of public, and private, policy. It has viewed the university as a benign servant of a democratic society, to which society can turn to help solve the problems that, in any given period, are deemed of importance. Many great state universities in America owe their existence to land-grant acts of the 1860s; yet a principal motive of the architects of the Morrill Act was to establish colleges for the improvement of *agriculture*—a good idea certainly, but hardly one that should be deemed the central purpose of a well-rounded university.

Time and again American universities have been called on to serve national or social purposes and have responded. In 1945, for instance, when the so-called GI Bill became law, universities with enthusiasm opened their doors to huge numbers of ex-servicemen as reward for their wartime sacrifices in much the same way that veterans of past wars were given land to till and horses to till it. In wartime our universities have responded to drafts of their most distinguished scientists and scholars; the OSS in World War II was staffed at the top by Ivy League scholars; the late Allen Dulles of the subsequent CIA wanted the architects of that postwar espionage agency's headquarters done up in Princeton Gothic! Yet the most enduring social claim on universities is that which comes from parents who have dreamed (or come to expect) that their children can go to college. This sincere and eager aspiration entails considerable expense out of pocket, at least for the American middle class; they want the best that money can buy. Finally, I point out that the atomic bomb, which gave us Hiroshima and total victory in the Pacific War in 1945, was the creation of drafted professors, working under the shadow and encouragement of that great mathematical genius Albert Einstein. From our historical knowledge, and personal memory, universities in peace and in war are called on to serve social purposes.

The other equally noble and puristic vantage point sees the university as a corporation of scholars exclusively committed to the advancement of knowledge and truth in the investigation of the ever complex realities of nature and man. I should add that *this* conception of the university and its proper role has a much longer history than that of the "socially responsible university" I have described. It originates in the medieval world of scholarship, long before the rise of the nation-state. The central merit of it is that it has handed down to us a tradition of the essential unity of knowledge—a conceptual framework that great nineteenth-century scholars and reformers like von Humboldt subsequently secularized. According to the purest of such advocates, this "learning corporation" and the branches of knowledge that it contains should be preserved and improved chiefly by its own corporate members—learned, credentialed scholars and scientists; standards of merit and excellence should be upheld and improved by those of the university itself. In particular, as some of these have recently insisted, policies governing student admissions criteria and the hiring and promotion of faculty ought to be set and maintained by the scholarly community, who are best qualified to identify merit and excellence since they are most familiar with the state of knowledge. Because of the powerful demands from outside the university in recent years for more egalitarian admissions policies and for hiring based upon race and sex criteria, such scholars have feared the debasement and decline of university standards with a subsequent atrophying of the university; they have amassed considerable evidence to prove their case.

All this is so familiar to you that I need only flag it as an issue that has been one of passionate disagreement within universities and between universities and outside pressures. We have by no means seen the end of it. There are now those in California today who recently nearly succeeded in having the University of California divest itself of Scholastic Aptitude Tests as means of distinguishing talent among university applicants—this simply on grounds that the effects of such means is to discriminate on grounds of race.

The use of the threat of withdrawal of government funds for non-compliance with government regulations has had the effect, within universities, of punishing the innocent even when no charges have been established as to who is guilty. But these stories are too familiar to bother going on with.

The point about this purist viewpoint is that in its extreme formulation it *denies* that the university has any business engaging in the solving of social problems and that its exclusive task is that of the pursuit of Truth; its concern with such matters of learning can be dissipated by attempts to fulfill "social tasks." The core of the university consists in the physical, biological, and social sciences and philosophy. Unless these four key elements dominate the citadel of learning, an institution of higher (or, as some egalitarians would say, "post-secondary") education is not a university. It is the very nature of these combinations of knowledge that they dictate the agenda of the institution, for students and faculty alike. All else is peripheral.

I submit that this question, or dispute, will not and cannot disappear or be resolved as long as free universities and free societies continue to exist. There could of course be a "third way," often suggested by some economists, which I note in passing. Universities in a certain sense *could* be free, or freer, from such outside interventions while performing valued tasks were they to be run on free-market principles. Then what was demanded would be that which was offered for sale; as demand changed, so would supply; and supply in turn would seek to create its own demand, as so often happens in the market. Universities would make their own decisions and also a profit. But this solution, advanced by some libertarians, is no solution to the dilemma at all. Free enterprise is not what the university is about. A university that allowed supply-demand criteria to govern decisions as to what was to be studied and taught would betray itself, even if it achieved autonomy and prospered financially from doing so. Supply-demand theory, sensitive as it is to the consumer's wish, is entirely indifferent to the necessary, enduring components of knowledge that constitute the legacy of our civilization. To succumb to the whims of a market well could result, for instance, in Mozart succumbing to the Grateful Dead.

As I said, this dispute will not and cannot disappear or be resolved as long as free societies and free universities continue to exist. Those universities of the sort that even have come close to approximating the ideal that the advocates of autonomy defend are after all ultimately accountable to someone; they are not sovereign states. They are accountable to others who pay for them. In this era of big everything—big government, big recipients, big appropriation—we now experience a very timely debate over autonomy versus accountability. The debate by no means is confined to higher education. It is a serious one indeed, particularly when we know that the future probably will not contain a cornucopia of resources more abundant. As Ortega himself wrote in his *Mission of the University,* which I referred to earlier, that mission must respond to "the atmosphere of national culture in which it is immersed." It cannot succeed unless it does so. It is not a *Ding an Sich.*

I was reminded of the ubiquitousness of this matter of autonomy and accountability when reading an editorial in the *Wall Street Journal.* It told of a sudden raid on an Indian-run food-distribution warehouse in South Dakota by federal officials who appropriated the contents and the task of allocating these goods to needy Indians. The story went on to explain that such programs had been set up some years ago after Indian spokesmen had protested that federal food-stamp programs really would not alleviate the misery of the Indian poor, who in any event were too cash-poor to buy the stamps in the first place. Language barriers and lack of transportation to supermarkets intensified their deprivation. In consequence, the task of food distribution in this instance permissively was devolved upon tribal organizations. But this new arrangement was no solution: tribal managers diverted the food arbitrarily, mismanaging their trust—some got little or none, others too much. When the tribal authorities' license to distribute was withdrawn, the managers protested the invasion of the autonomy of their land and the attack on their customs. As the *Wall Street Journal* observed, laconically, "Projects like the commodities program are hard to administer under the best of circumstances. They are more difficult still if you are a tribal official standing between government demands for accountability and the . . . sometimes disorganized facts of tribal life."

There are facts of tribal life among scholars too. I would submit that now, as the recent problems of student radicalism and excessive government regulation have disappeared or become less pressing, our attention should concentrate on inner and outer derangements of a very different kind. I would like to itemize what I see as the principal ones.

First, the recent profound shift of emphasis in many universities to professional programs and away from those core disciplines I have referred to. This emphasis of course is to be seen in the surge of enrollments, particularly in programs such as business administration.

Second, the collapse in many universities of a coherent liberal arts program in colleges of letters and science, with the consequent subinfeudation of curriculum in the hands of specialized departments. When the authority of college programs capitulated in the late 1960s to student demands for greater freedom in choosing their programs, one odd and unintended consequence of this was to shift the principal locus of academic requirements and programs to departments. Another consequence of this subinfeudation is to be seen in the abandonment of foreign language requirements, cheating a whole generation of students of skills that would unlock otherwise inaccessible treasures of knowledge. My department (political science) at Berkeley today is for all intents and purposes a sizable college and is run as such. Symbolic of this (and this may not be true at some other universities) commencement ceremonies at Berkeley now are exclusively conducted by departments, depriving students of even a ceremonial sense of collegiality, of having been at a *university,* rubbing shoulders (if not minds) with scholars and students in an atmosphere of the liberal arts.

Third, the debasement of the grading system. It now takes an extraordinary concentration of will on the part of a student to actually fail a course. A slight exertion of the mind, in many courses, suffices to earn a B grade. For most, a low B is seen as a deprivation of civil liberties. At some universities, such as Stanford, the majority of grades given by professors are in the high B− to A level. Some call this grade inflation, but they have it all wrong: monetary inflation does not equalize prices, for there is no ceiling. In grade transcripts, A is the ceiling; when grades float upward to that ceiling, they stop. The phenomenon I describe is grade *equalization.* I do not wish to philosophize much about this sorry process, save to note that the chief victims are students who genuinely have achieved excellence, and have little to show for their effort. Merit has been dissolved in egalitarianism. Honors mean little. In many universities grade-point averages—used, for instance, by Phi Beta Kappa chapters when deciding to honor true scholars—no longer are even *approximate* indicators of what a student has achieved. Transcripts are thus of less and less value to future employers, professional and academic graduate programs, and to the truly educated student. This has not come about by reason of a deliberate decision. But it has occurred, and the chief victim of it has been the idea of excellence. The perpetrator has been the faculty. There are nuances: such is the corruption in *some* degree programs within universities that a departmental reputation for soft grading is sometimes used deliberately to entice students into an otherwise unattractive departmental major, thus to strengthen a department claim on university resources.

Fourth, as I mentioned before, we have the attack upon objective admissions standards—focused in some states upon objective tests such as the SAT (Scholastic Aptitude Test). This is a not unimportant problem; high schools too have experienced grade equalization; how are university admissions officers to know what applicants know, how qualified, or even literate, they are, unless there is some objective evidence of accomplishment? The argument has been that of professional "minority advocates," and it goes as follows: the tests must be biased since in the administration of them certain minorities—blacks, chicanos, and so forth—do not on average score as high as other minorities. (Today, we are all minorities.) Thus the all too familiar attack upon merit, on the basis of a demand for equality of *results,* once more penalizes truly talented and accomplished students. In the Board of Regents of the University of California the pressure to abandon the SAT came recently to be supported by a near majority of its members; a few more regential appointments by our governor and this pressure could have succeeded.

Some academic purists claim that a university (when you get down to brass tacks) is its faculty. A great university is one that has an excellent collection of fine scholars. This is a half-truth. A combination of fine scholars with average or poor students not only demoralizes the scholars but sets in motion a tendency for them to disappear into their studies. Furthermore, insofar as universities realistically seek to serve increasing numbers of "deprived" students, the temptation is to lower expectations of undergraduate student performance and thus to accentuate the processes of egalitarianism that I noted earlier. In the worst instances, university programs must concentrate on remedial education —doing the work that high schools are supposed to do.

The items above suggest a very different perspective on the relationship between universities and society than are most talked about today. For taken together they raise a new question of accountability: to the extent that universities' academic programs and standards are diluted, are they cheating the public as well as their own students? On this kind of question, put this way, there should be absolutely no conflict of interest between the university and society. The public *should* want the university to be institutionally strong and academically excellent. And that of course is what the university wants too. If university programs are cheapened, for any reason, it is not only the university that is cheated, but also the public.

Today, when attention is concentrated upon the "crisis of public schools," we may forget that deterioration in secondary education sooner or later (usually sooner) is reflected in higher education. One constructive role that universities could play in this difficult situation is one that they have played in the past: setting and enforcing high performance standards and requirements for entering or applying students, universities could enhance the morale of high school teachers and administrators genuinely concerned to prepare their students for advanced work. High schools and high school administrators after all have been quite sensitive to universities' standards; when such standards deteriorate in tandem with those of public secondary schools, this will be noticed; so will their improvement. If, in the attempt to meliorate the condition of "deprived' students, the content of education is reduced, everyone is cheated. This already has happened.

When I read Ortego y Gasset's *Mission of the University* that day some years ago, one of his diagnoses of the university-society relationship that then struck me as irrelevant to my quest for enlightenment was his sad recital of the low state of Spanish culture and the consequent loss of national and individual self-respect. "My purpose," he said, "is to make clear to you what constitutes [the] fundamental ailment of Spain and the Spaniard, which I call slovenliness. . . . Slovenliness . . . grows accustomed to its own presence; it finds itself pleasantly comfortable, and tends to spread and perpetuate itself." In his view, this aspect of the deterioration of his culture was worse even than crime: "Crime is something violent and terrible, and in this regard, respectable." To him, the recovery of Spain entailed the recovery of form: "The opposite of slovenliness is *to be in form.*"

> You people well know the tremendous difference there is between an athlete when he is *in form,* and the same man when he is out of form.

But, he continued:

> [A] group does not acquire . . . form unless it has disciplined itself, and continues to discipline itself; unless it sees with perfect clarity what it proposes to do.

In the mid-sixties, I passed over these references to Ortega's afflicted national culture. Now I do not. They need to be taken seriously by Americans, and also by those concerned with the role of knowledge *in our own culture.* As I realize now, Ortega was perfectly correct on one major point; no university can survive as such—in striving to represent its ideal—unless it recognizes and upholds its central tasks. When outside influences strengthen these tasks, so much the better; when they intrude to deflect the university's mission to peripheral activities, the university and society suffer together. Here, there is no contradiction between a free society and a free university. Jefferson himself was absolutely on the right track when, in his correspondence with John Adams, he sought to reconcile the claims of democracy and the claims of knowledge.

For what he anticipated in America, as higher education enlarged and recruited from ranks in society, was the emergence of an "aristocracy of talent." A free university in a free society should not be ashamed to reaffirm that meritocratic yet democratic principle as our goal.

STEVEN M. CAHN

A Sculptor in Snow

Professor Sidney Hook, one of the most influential classroom teachers of his generation, once wrote: "Teaching is an art and like all arts it can be learned with varying degrees of proficiency. . . . An enormous amount of time can be saved by familiarizing oneself with teaching devices and techniques. . . . There are some things that are best learned *not* on the job."[1] In this brief essay I seek to elucidate some of those pedagogical insights that I believe Professor Hook would commend to all those who face the rigorous challenges inherent in teaching.

I begin with the fundamental principle that a teacher is responsible to both students and subject matter. Sacrificing either one for the other amounts to failure.

To see the practical implications of this principle, consider the simple case of teaching a friend how to play chess. You start by explaining the different possible moves of the various pieces, and soon your friend assures you he has grasped these basic maneuvers. Suppose then, after stressing the importance of strong openings, you proceed to demonstrate your favorite, the slashing King's Gambit. Knights, bishops, and pawns whiz back and forth over the board, accompanied by your running commentary on the strengths and weaknesses of such variations as the Cunningham Gambit, the Kieseritzky Gambit, and the ever-dangerous Falkbeer Counter Gambit. At last, you complete this detailed analysis and look up proudly, awaiting your friend's approval. He stares at the board, shakes his head, and finally remarks, "I guess I'll stick to checkers. I like it better when all the pieces move the same way."

What is the problem? Your presentation of the King's Gambit may have been flawless, but while concentrating on the details of the subvariations, you have overlooked your friend's confusion as he tried to keep in mind such fundamentals as how pawns can move and where knights can jump. A good instructor anticipates such difficulties, realizing how tenuous a beginning student's claim to understanding may be. Lacking this insight, you might succeed as a chess analyst but not as a chess teacher.

Assume, however, that in an effort to sustain your friend's involvement, you do not warn him about the complexities of opening theory but merely advise that he attack quickly with his queen. You regale him with anecdotes of your triumphs over weak players who fell into such elementary traps as the Fool's Mate. Your friend supposes he has mastered a surefire strategy and, full of confidence and enthusiasm, marches to the nearest chess club. There he soon encounters some intermediate players who deftly parry his premature assaults and laughingly defeat him with ease.

What went wrong this time? Unless your friend eventually realizes the inadequacy of the preparation you provided and possesses the dedication to study the technical materials you suggested he bypass, he will again and again be beaten badly, quickly grow discouraged, and perhaps give up the game altogether. He may, nevertheless, have thoroughly enjoyed his lessons with you. If so, you succeeded as an entertainer but, again, not as a teacher.

Anyone who thinks teaching is easy has never stood in front of a class of thirty restless teen-agers and tried to arouse and maintain their interest while simultaneously attempting to communicate a subject's complexities. In such circumstances individuals quickly become aware that not everyone cares who they are or what they have to say.

Of course the mechanics of sheer drill backed by the pressures of reward and punishment will normally result in some learning. But if the attention of students is engaged only by gold stars or raps on the knuckles, the removal of these reinforcements may well be accompanied by loss of interest. Students will thus have failed to acquire that most important of qualities, the desire to continue learning. Persons whose educations end when they leave school are doomed to spend much of their lives in ignorance. Good teaching, therefore, is not merely the transmission of information and skills, but the encouragement of zest for further study.

Sheer gusto, however, is not sufficient. If it were, teachers could succeed merely by going along with the whims of their students. If the students wanted to learn history but not economics, instructors could teach history and not economics. If students found most history boring but were fascinated by the history of the American cowboy, instructors could teach that history and nothing else. If students wanted to see cowboy movies but not read any books about the West, instructors could turn their classrooms into movie houses. And if students wanted just to picnic in the park, instructors could make themselves useful cooking the hamburgers.

The interests of students, however, may not match either their own needs or the needs of a democratic society whose welfare depends in great part on the understanding and capability of its citizens. Teachers, therefore, have the responsibility to lead their students to master appropriate subject matter without misrepresenting or diluting it, yet at the same time arousing appreciation for it. How can they achieve this result?

Since teaching is a creative endeavor, there are no infallible guides to success. Good instruction, however, typically involves four elements: motivation, organization, clarification, and generalization. Let me consider each in turn.

As to motivation, I have found it useful to distinguish two types of teachers: Those who pull the subject matter behind them and those who push the subject matter in front of them. The former use their own personalities to attract students and then try to transfer the students' interest from the instructor to the subject. The latter minimize their own personalities and seek to interest students directly in the material itself.

Those who pull the subject behind them usually have little difficulty in arousing enthusiasm, but their characteristic pitfall is the failure to redirect student interest away from themselves and toward their subject matter. As Professor Hook has noted, a teacher "must be friendly without becoming a friend, although he may pave the way for later friendship, for friendship is a mark of preference and expresses itself in indulgence, favors, and distinctions that unconsciously find an invidious form. . . . A teacher who becomes 'just one of the boys,' who courts popularity, who builds up personal loyalty in exchange for indulgent treatment, has missed his vocation. He should leave the classroom for professional politics."[2]

But this is not to say that teachers who pull the subject behind them cannot be superb instructors. Indeed, if they succeed in involving students as much in the material as in the instructors' own manners, they can exert an enormously beneficial influence on an extraordinary number, for such teachers invariably attract many devoted admirers who will follow wherever such instructors lead, even down the rugged road of learning.

On the other hand, those who push the subject in front of them need have no worry about misdirecting a student's interest. Their worry is whether such interest will be aroused at all. In many cases they must overcome the necessarily abstract quality of their subjects and make apparent the connections between the seemingly esoteric material and their students' own sphere of experience. Perhaps the most reliable tool for doing so, and one instructors need to master, is the use of well-chosen examples that relate to the purposes or passions of the students. The subject itself thus becomes their personal concern.

But whatever the particular approach of their instructors, students should be led to appreciate the subject not merely as a means but as an end, something of intrinsic worth to be enjoyed on its own account. Their lives will thereby be enriched and the material rendered more vivid and even more useful when serving some purpose beyond itself.

Teachers who fail to convey the significance of what they are discussing can see their own inadequacy reflected in the eyes of their apathetic students. Obtaining a sound education is difficult enough for a person interested in the work; for one who is bored the process is intolerable.

A motivated student is ready to learn, but a teacher must be organized enough to take advantage of this situation. Admittedly, inflexibility can hinder an instructor from making the most of opportunities that arise spontaneously in the course of discussion, but a rambling presentation may well dissipate initial enthusiasm. What is too often forgotten is that lack of planning usually leads to stream-of-consciousness instruction, resulting in the sort of class that meanders idly from one topic to another, amounting to nothing more than an hour of aimless talk.

Each day before setting foot in the classroom, teachers should decide exactly what they intend to accomplish during a particular session and precisely what they expect their students to know by the time the period ends. In Professor Hook's words, "the bane of much . . . teaching is improvisation."[3] A teacher's obligation is to guide students, and to guide requires a sense of where one is headed. If the teacher does not know, then everyone is lost.

Careful organization, however, must be complemented by an equal concern for clarification. Otherwise, even the most highly structured course of study may prove incomprehensible to the uninitiated.

Since academic subjects tend toward complexity, classrooms are often rife with confusion. But good teachers foresee this problem and substantially reduce it by making every effort to be as clear as possible. They use concrete cases to exemplify abstract concepts, and, realizing that individuals differ in how they arrive at an understanding of particular ideas, good instructors take pains to explain fundamental principles in a variety of ways.

Of course not every train of thought can be rendered in very simple terms. A book entitled *Kant Made Easy* is surely the work of a charlatan or a fool. Effective teachers, therefore, must be shrewd judges of both the difficulty of their materials and the ability of their students.

Why do some instructors seem to make so little effort to express themselves clearly? Many do not realize that good teachers direct their remarks not only at the best student, or at the top ten percent of the class, or even at the majority; instead, good teachers speak so that virtually all their listeners can follow. These teachers realize that when more than one or two students complain they are lost, many others, whether they themselves realize it or not, are also in need of help.

Having now discussed motivation, organization, and clarification, I turn to the fourth element of good instruction: generalization. Because a thorough knowledge of any subject matter depends upon a firm grasp of its details, the tendency of many instructors is to emphasize analysis at the expense of synthesis. But to master a subject requires awareness of its connections to related areas of inquiry. Details are necessary to understanding, but they are not sufficient. Also required is perspective, and that can be achieved only by viewing specific information within a broad framework.

I still vividly recall my high-school history teacher who insisted that we memorize the dates, locations, and names of the commanding generals for every major battle of the Civil War. Only in my college years when I heard a series of enthralling lectures on the causes, strategies, and results of that war did I come to understand and share my earlier teacher's fascination with the events of that period.[4]

A student should not be allowed to become lost in minutiae. For, although generalizations without details are hollow, details without generalizations are barren.

I have thus far been considering the components of good teaching, but great teaching involves yet another element. Great teachers not only motivate their students, organize the class, clarify their material, and provide illuminating generalizations; in addition, they project a vision of excellence.

Even after considerable study, it is not easy to distinguish what is adequate from what is excellent. How many of us, observing two physicians, would know which was merely competent and which superb? How many of us, reading a history of Europe, would realize whether the account was exceptional or just satisfactory? Recognizing such distinctions depends upon an awareness of critical subtleties, and each great teacher in distinctive and in inimitable ways leads students to acquire and prize such insight.

Professor Hook has written that a teacher is "a sculptor in snow" who leaves behind "no permanent monument."[5] But through the vision of excellence Professor Hook has projected to so many thousands of students, he has himself constructed a monument to the ideals of great teaching. It stands as a permanent reminder of the noble and mighty aims to which all teachers can aspire.

NOTES

1. Sidney Hook, *Education for Modern Man: A New Perspective* (New York: Alfred A. Knopf, 1963), p. 217.

2. Ibid., pp. 230-31.

3. Ibid., p. 226.

4. The college instructor who so inspired me was Professor James P. Shenton of Columbia College.

5. Hook, p. 235.

PART IV

Issues in Ethics, Humanism and Human Nature

PAUL KURTZ

The Ethics of
Secular Humanism

I

Sidney Hook is undoubtedly the outstanding secular humanist philosopher in America today, and one of the most influential in the twentieth century. Humanism has come under heavy and unremitting attack of late, particularly by so-called right-wing fundamentalist critics. It is being blamed for most of the evils of the contemporary world. Especially singled out for criticism is Hook's conviction that secular humanism can provide a meaningful ethical alternative to the moral doctrines of traditional religions. Unfortunately, there is little understanding by its opponents of the nature of secular humanism or of its basic ethical position.

Humanism is one of the most pervasive intellectual movements in the modern world. Although it has deep roots in the history of human civilization, its critics often simply identify it with "modernism"—especially in so far as it expresses an interest in improving the human condition, using science and technology for the betterment of humanity, and judging social and political institutions by whether or not they recognize and respect basic human liberties and rights. Authors representing widely differing points of view profess belief in these humanistic ideals. Who will admit to being anti-human or opposed to a humanitarian concern for humankind? Not Christians or Marxists, liberals or conservatives, libertarians or radicals. Like democracy and socialism, humanism has thus come to mean all things to all men.

Secular humanism, however, has been singled out for special attack by conservative religious critics—and they are legion. Secular humanism is often compared with *religious* (theistic) humanism. Literally, *secular* refers to "worldly" or "temporal" values in contrast to the "spiritual" or "sacred."

Secularists believe in the separation of church and state and in protecting various public institutions of society from religious intrusions. According to theistic critics, secular humanism expresses a nontheistic, agnostic, or atheistic view of the universe and man's place within it. This they maintain is not only false, but immoral. They attribute the moral defects and excesses of contemporary life to the influence of secular humanism.

Curiously, these critics insist that, though secular humanism is non- or anti-religious, it is nevertheless a religion. They refer to Supreme Court decisions that accord to secular humanists the same rights granted to believers.[1] If one agrees with Paul Tillich that religion expresses one's ultimate concern, or with John Dewey that religion is an expression of one's highest ideals, then perhaps this argument is not without some merit. It all depends of course on one's definition of religion. Hook earlier objected to the attempted naturalistic redefinition of "God" (such as Dewey's) because he considered it to be an unethical misuse of terms. Perhaps he was prophetic; for the linguistic chickens have come home to roost.

The critics of secular humanism now seek to define "religion" by arbitrary fiat, so that virtually everything is religious, including the nonreligious. Like Humpty Dumpty, up is down and down is up, or whatever else one chooses to make them. The effort to redefine secular humanism does have important political consequences. For, if these critics are correct, then our democratic institutions, and especially the public schools, are dominated by the "religion of secular humanism"—in so far as the schools teach evolution, comparative social-science courses, moral education, and other secular subjects. And this is allegedly a violation of the establishment clause of the First Amendment. Some secular humanists have no doubt helped to confuse the issue by agreeing that their beliefs function religiously; they did so in order to gain the constitutional immunities and protections afforded to theistic religions. The basic fallacy in the argument of fundamentalist critics is that of the undistributed middle; for instance, although secular humanists support courses in science, literature, and philosophy, so do many others, but this does not make these others secular humanists. What is being taught is not secular humanism per se, but an enriched educational curriculum developed for the modern world.

The question that I wish to raise in this paper, however, is on a more fundamental level than the current debate being waged in America. I ask: Can, or indeed ought, there be a secular morality not grounded in theistic religion? This question is a central one for the contemporary world, and it has been basic to Sidney Hook's philosophical position. For Sidney Hook has consistently argued for a naturalistic ethics without religious foundations. Indeed, Hook's definition of humanism means precisely that ethics is autonomous: "Humanism," he says, "is the view that morals are autonomous and independent of religious belief, that they are relevant to truths about nature and human nature, truths that rest on scientific evidence."[2]

II

Our world is witness to a number of revolutionary forces at work. First, there has been an apparent decline of some forms of traditional religious beliefs. How widespread and genuine it is, is open to debate. Second, developments of science and technology have transformed the face of the globe, raising standards of living and improving health and longevity; new forms of communications and mobility have uprooted human beings from their traditional localities and enlarged their horizons. Third, there has been an enormous advance in literacy, education, and cultural opportunities. Fourth, liberal and radical political movements have extended the ideals of freedom, equality, and justice for all, and the concept of human rights is gaining prominence throughout the world. Fifth, a world culture is emerging that transcends national boundaries, and this has scientific, moral, cultural, and economic dimensions.

Regrettably, the world is still a place of competing ideological, ethnic, racial, national, and religious isms. Many of these are based upon ancient tribal myths and loyalties. The question emerges as to whether moral values and principles can be developed that are global in character and appropriate to the post-modern technological age. In particular, what do we do with historic religious faiths that persist and are rooted in our nomadic or rural past. Judaism, Christianity, and Mohammedanism have their sources in the Old Testament and in prophetic and revelational traditions outdated by the modern outlook. Other religions have ancient, prescientific origins—Hinduism, Confucianism, Buddhism. Should one religion finally prevail, will a new mythological cult then emerge to take its place? Or can a secular and scientific humanism provide an authentic basis for a new moral order?

We have seen brutal secular ideologies emerge in the twentieth century that give pause to any easy optimism. Fascism was a secular movement, but it was anti-humanistic. It did not have a clearly defined philosophy and engendered intense racial and national hatreds. Marxism is both secular and humanistic (in the sense that it is nontheistic) and is concerned with universal values and social justice, but it is based on class conflict and is prepared to adopt violent means to achieve its utopian vision. The development of Marxist ideology is perhaps the most dramatic intellectual event of this century; it is still unresolved whether Marxism can overcome a dogmatic state ideology imposed from above and develop freedom and democracy.

Today, many varieties of secularism and humanism compete with traditional religion. The only kind that I would defend—and Sidney Hook has taken the lead in pointing the way—is *democratic* secular humanism, i.e., that which encourages pluralistic values and the ideals of freedom.

I shall provide a minimal working definition of secular humanism. This definition is both descriptive and normative. Secular humanism, I submit, involves at least three characteristics: (1) an outlook, (2) a method of inquiry, and (3) a set of values.

(1) Modern secular humanism has been influenced most by the development of science. This naturalistic view of the universe holds that nature is intelligible to human reason and explainable in terms of causal laws. The human species has evolved by natural processes; it is not separate and distinct from them. Secular humanism is dubious of any effort to divide nature into two realms or to read in a supernatural, occult, or noumenal reality. At the very least, it will suspend judgment until such time as evidence for claims about the transcendent can be responsibly examined and verified. Appeals to alleged revelations as the basis of religious truth are highly questionable.

(2) Secular humanism is committed to the scientific method of inquiry. Broadly conceived this is the hypothetico-deductive method, in which hypotheses are introduced, deductively elaborated, and experimentally tested, directly or indirectly, by the evidence. The scientific method is not an esoteric art open only to a narrow coterie of experts. Nor does it lay down fixed rules of investigation. Rather, it is continuous with ordinary common sense and critical intelligence, and it involves the controlled use of the methods of inquiry that are successful in other areas of life as well. Knowledge claims are tentative; even verified hypotheses may be later modified in the light of new evidence or more comprehensive explanations. Thus the scientific method entails some degree of skepticism about claims to ultimate truth. Secular humanism is receptive to a wide range of human experiences, including art, morality, poetry, and feeling. But it is unwilling to declare any belief to be validated by private, intuitive, mystical, or subjective appeals, until, that is, they can pass the test of intersubjective confirmation.

(3) Secular humanism expresses a set of values. Some consider this aspect to be its differentiating characteristic. These values have deep roots within Western philosophical, literary, and scientific tradition; they are the pagan virtues of Greece and Rome, rediscovered during the Renaissance and the Enlightenment and coming to fruition during the modern period.

III

What are the essential features of the ethics of secular humanism? The basic premise is that moral values are relative to human experience or human nature and need not be derived from any theological or metaphysical foundations. Implicit in this is the idea that ethics (like science) is an autonomous field of inquiry. For the Greek philosophers the good life was achievable on earth; and the task of reason was to discover the conditions that enable us to realize happiness. There has been some controversy in the history of ethics as to whether happiness primarily involves hedonic pleasure or rather the satisfaction of our basic needs, creative actualization, and growth. A whole line of philosophers, from Aristotle down through Spinoza, Mill, Dewey, Hook, and others, have agreed that ethical choices, at least in part, are amenable to reflective wisdom.

One should deliberate before making one's choices. Value judgments are based upon various criteria: means-end analysis, an estimate of the costs of our actions, and the relevance of various proposals in view of their consequences in concrete situations.

There is some disagreement about whether the main test of moral norms should be teleological or deontological—i.e., should we judge moral rules by whether they fulfill our long-range ends or by whether (following Kant) they have some independent status. I submit that we need to take into account both sets of data: values and moral principles. The former refer to the things we consider good, cherish, and hold dear; the latter, to our conceptions of right and wrong. Moral principles are prima facie general rules. They denote the moral decencies—such as truth-telling, promise-keeping, sincerity, trust, benevolence, altruism, fair play, and so on. These principles provide the basic rules of the game for social intercourse. They are deeply embedded in our social life and are based in part upon empirical generalizations about how to live together effectively. As such, they cannot be easily violated without negative consequences. They are based upon reason but supported by our passionate commitments to our sense of justice. Our values and principles undergo some revision and evolution, particularly as societies interact and change.

One point that should not be overlooked is the fact that, although the traditional religious literature expresses moral insights, it is not adequate to the present situation; it is based upon an earlier level of the moral development of mankind. Sidney Hook has persuasively argued that: *(a)* Given the fatherhood of God, any number of moral injunctions may follow: belief in the sanctity of monogamy or the permissibility of polygamy, differing views of the appropriateness of divorce and abortion, contrasting conceptions of pacifism, etc. Jerry Falwell, the Ayatollah Khomeini, Menachem Begin, and the Reverend William Sloane Coffin all claim to believe in God, but they draw different moral and political conclusions from their commitments. *(b)* Moral obligation need not depend upon divine sanction. Indeed, to do something because of God's commandments is hardly moral, but tends to impede the development of a mature moral consciousness. It was morally wrong for Abraham to sacrifice his son Isaac, but not because God eventually commanded him not to do so. Plato observed, in the *Euthyphro:* Something is not good because the gods say so, but if they say so it is because it is good.

A whole series of modern critics—Nietzsche, Marx, Freud, Hook, and others—have shown that religion may seek to censor truth, repress individuality, oppose progress, exacerbate human impotence, and offer solace instead of encouraging the effort needed to ameliorate the human condition. "No deity will save us; we must save ourselves," says *Humanist Manifesto II.* We are responsible for our own destiny; we cannot look outside for succor or salvation.

The two key humanist virtues are knowledge and courage, as opposed to ignorance and dependence. Humanistic ethics focuses on human freedom. It encourages individual growth and development. It focuses on the need for control of our destiny, a willingness to take responsibility for our plans and projects, to enter into the world not merely to understand or adore it but to bend it to suit our will. It emphasizes independence and audacity. Prometheus is the "patron saint" of humanism because he challenged the gods, stealing fire and endowing man with the arts of civilization. Life has no meaning per se. It presents us with possibilities and opportunities. The meaning of life grows out of what we discover in our own mortal existence; it emerges in our acts of free choice. Man is a being that exists for himself. In some measure he is able to define his own reality. He is in a process of becoming. The salient virtue here is autonomy. Concomitant with this, however, is the recognition that no man can live in total isolation; we are social animals. Among the most enduring of human goods are those that we share with others. Most of our projects involve other persons. Self-interest is not the totality of a person's life. Some form of altruism is essential to our very being. Thus a concern for equality and justice emerges. One may say that one of the main contributions of our religious traditions is the ideal of the brotherhood of man—not because God commands it, but because moral reflection recognizes that we have responsibilities to other human beings. Each individual is to count as equal in dignity and value, as an end in himself, and is entitled to moral consideration. This is the basis of our conception of human rights.

The conflict between self-interest and the social good provides the classic moral paradox. Perhaps there are no ultimate solutions for some of the dilemmas that we encounter in life. Only reflective decision can best weigh competing values and principles and balance the appeal of self-interest with the needs and demands of others. Although there are some guidelines, what we do depends in the last analysis upon reflective inquiry in the situations we encounter.

Now, I have said that contemporary secular humanism emphasizes the democratic ethic. It recognizes that moral truth is often the product of give and take among competing conceptions of the good life. Thus we should tolerate the rights of all individuals—so long as they do not harm others—though we may disapprove of their moral values. And we reserve the right to educate and modify their tastes and conceptions by persuasion. This suggests that we use the method of peaceful negotiation, rather than force or compulsion, to adjudicate differences and that we attempt to reach compromise by expanding our knowledge and discovery of moral truths.

Sidney Hook's own definition of humanism is that it is primarily ethical. He states: "An ethical humanist today is one who relies on the arts of intelligence to defend, enlarge, and enhance the areas of human freedom in the world. Ethical humanists may differ from each other, but they respect those with whom they disagree. They are not fanatics of virtue. They recognize that good conflicts with good, right with right, and sometimes the good with the right. To these conflicts they bring the only value that is also the judge of its own efficacy and limitation—human intelligence.''[3]

IV

Two major objections have been raised against the ethics of secular humanism: (1) Critics allege that a naturalistic ethics of freedom leads to promiscuity and the breakdown of moral order. Unfortunately, some humanists have simply identified humanism with personal liberation, meaning the inviolability of private choice and the near sanctity of the immediacy of enjoyment. But the fact that ethical values are relative to human experiences does not mean that they are "subjectivistic" or immune to objective criticism. The fact that reflective choice is situational does not mean that "anything goes." However, secular humanists need to emphasize that moral education is essential to their conception of the good society; liberty without virtue can have highly undesirable consequences. All education is in a sense moral; thus we have an obligation to nourish moral character in the young. This includes an appreciation for temperance, prudence, excellence, and the development of sensitivity to the needs of others. To tolerate different life-styles is an implicit value of an open democratic and pluralistic society. But it need not imply permissiveness, nor the view that all life-styles are equivalent in dignity and worth; nor should it mean that they are beyond criticism or modification. The basic task of humanistic morality is to cultivate virtues in the young, to educate and elevate taste, and to develop the skills of cognitive moral inquiry. Today, as in the past, the front line for moral reform is in the public schools. If we fail in that venture, then humanistic morality will face a losing battle.

(2) Will a purely secular morality, devoid of divine sanction, provide a sufficient ground for obligation? Are religious institutions with their symbols of majesty and awe a necessary support for moral conduct? Perhaps they are for many individuals. But it is equally apparent that countless individuals have led lives of nobility and excellence without a concomitant belief in divine salvation. Moreover, the existence of religious beliefs and traditions is no guarantee of morality. To act because of fear of retribution or to gain reward is hardly moral. Religion in this sense is the enemy of mature moral behavior. The question of whether duty and responsibility will remain if God is removed is often asked of the secular humanist. If religious institutions no longer are to play this supportive role, others need to take their place—the family, the school, the economy, the legal system—in order to develop civic virtues and cultivate moral decencies. This means also that there may need to be some support systems for human beings replacing those vacated by religion: stronger ties with family (in one form or another), some ceremonial rites of passage (birth, puberty, marriage, retirement, and death), and some emotional and dramatic expression of our virtues, values, principles, and ideals.

From the end of the nineteenth century to the middle of the twentieth, most scientific thinkers expected religion to gradually disappear. With increased literacy and education and the decline of poverty and disease, at least in the affluent countries, intellectuals confidently predicted the displacement of religion by the development of a new morality as man outgrew the infancy of the race. That this has not occurred is a cause for dismay and concern.

Now, presumably, one can be an ethical humanist and not hold a scientific world-view, but it is much more difficult to be a humanist if one has a theistic or magical view of the universe. Thus there is the conviction that ethical humanism in some way depends upon the scientific method. If this is the case, my work with the Committee for the Scientific Investigation of Claims of the Paranormal (which was founded in 1976 to examine pseudoscientific claims) has convinced me that there is little reason to be confident that theistic or magical thinking will diminish and that the ethics of secular humanism will take its place.

There are many reasons for my skepticism. For one, religion is not simply a question of belief. Although there are periods of upheaval in which old religions die and new ones emerge and are spread by conversion, most individuals are born into a religious tradition. One's religion is more a question of ethnicity and kinship, of blood and nationality, than one of conscious choice. Religions persist, especially where there are strong traditions against intermarriage and concerning the rearing of children. We are living through a period when many of the traditional religions are being challenged. Today individuals are wrenched from the locality and ethnicity of their roots; they experience a mixing of many influences. Hence there is a greater possibility of free choice of religion. Moreover, wide sectors of the population have the benefit of comparative history, scientific knowledge, and philosophical skepticism. Why is it that evangelical, literalist, and fundamentalist religions seem to be growing rather than the liberal and humanistic ones? Why does creationism still vie with evolution for adherents? Why do bizarre cults of unreason thrive? Why is it that new forms of folk-religion fixated on the paranormal seem to be gaining ground?

What is so troubling is the fact that the strangest beliefs will find dedicated supporters. This is the age of believing the unbelievable: "scientific creationism," Scientology, the Unification Church, Yoga, Zen, Transcendental Meditation, tarot reading, seances, levitation, witchcraft, astrology, and psychic superstitions are flourishing. Why do people accept beliefs for which there is little or no evidence or evidence to the contrary?

One reason that can be given is that the public is not exposed to critical dissenting scientific data. They simply lack the negative information. Skeptical debunking has not had equal time with supernatural belief. This applies as much to traditional religious beliefs that are surely in need of critical analysis as it does to the newer paranormal cults. If people were to receive such criticism, would they abandon their overbeliefs? One would hope so. Yet two recent studies have jarred my confidence that this will easily happen.

Western Europe shows a marked decline in formal religious identification. Unbelief is widespread in Great Britain. In the United States, studies indicate that only 56 percent of the population are formal members of religious bodies. Many others, of course, are nominal members. What happens to those who are disaffiliated? Do they become free thinkers, imbued with the scientific spirit of humanistic ideals? A recent study by W. S. Bainbridge and Rodney Stark at the University of Washington in Seattle shows that those who claim to believe in the newer cults tend to be those with no religious affiliation as well as mainline Protestants and Catholics.[4] According to a 1977 Gallup poll, some 34 percent of American adults claim to be "born again" or identify with conservative Christianity. It is this group that Bainbridge and Stark find most resistant to the newer paranormal and occult claims. It is those who break away from traditional and conventional religions who are surprisingly sympathetic to such claims. Far from being resistant to superstitions, they tend to adopt new ones. This does not deny that there has been a growth in religious skepticism in recent decades, but this apparently still involves only a small minority of the population.

A second series of studies, by psychologists Barry Singer and Victor Benassi, also provided disturbing results.[5] Singer and Benassi introduced students in introductory psychology classes to "Craig," a person dressed in a long purple robe and sporting a medallion. In two of the classes, the instructors introduced Craig—still outside the classroom—as a performer who claimed to have psychic powers; the instructors did not express their own belief or disbelief. In two other classes, he was introduced as a magician who would present a magic act. The instructors did not know the purpose of the experiment, nor did Craig; and Craig was not aware of the differering introductions. His act consisted of various "psychiclike" magic tricks: he bent a metal rod seemingly by psychokinesis; he "read" numbers from a concealed notebook while blindfolded; he transferred ashes from the back of a student's hand to her palm, etc. They were simple tricks that any amateur magician could perform.

Singer and Benassi were surprised to find that in both the "magic" and the "psychic" classes about two-thirds of the students reported that they thought the performer was a "psychic." Only a few students seemed to believe the instructor's description of Craig as a magician in the two classes where he was introduced as such.

Psychic beliefs were not only prevalent; they were strong and loaded with emotion. In the "psychic" demonstrations, many of the students expressed fright and emotional disturbance. Most expressed awe and amazement. Some behavior was extreme. A number of students covered their questionnaires with exorcism terms and exhortations against the devil. By the time Craig was halfway through the "bending" chant, the class was in an excited state. "Students sat rigidly in their chairs, eyes glazed and mouths open, chanting together. When the rod bent, they gasped and murmured. After class was dismissed, they typically still sat in their chairs, staring vacantly or shaking their heads, or rushed excitedly up to Craig asking how they could develop such powers.'' Craig's performance had produced an extraordinarily powerful behavioral effect. "If Craig had asked the students at the end of his performance to tear off their clothes, throw him their money, and start a new cult," Singer and Benassi said, "some would have responded enthusiastically. . . . We did not imagine that having someone dress in a choir robe and do elementary-school magic tricks would produce such fright."

Singer and Benassi continued the experiment in other classes. They changed their introduction to stress that they were presenting a magician, that he was going to do magic tricks, and that he *did not* have psychic abilities. This description did succeed in reducing psychic belief slightly, but never below 50 percent. This was the most salient result of the test, they said. At no time in the experiment did the magician himself say that he was a psychic or make a psychic claim. Singer and Benassi have concluded that people will stubbornly maintain a belief about someone's psychic powers no matter what evidence to the contrary is provided.

It is a mistake to think that these results apply only to the university where this experiment was carried out. Upwards of 80 percent of students in colleges and universities in all areas of the country accept various forms of paranormal magic as true. Moreover, similar tests have since been conducted at UCLA and Ohio State University with the same results. Singer and Benassi conclude: "We believe that our results, bizarre as they may be, are of wide generality and that the psychological processes we have tentatively identified as being involved in supporting psychic beliefs are present and active in the general population."

It may be that these students had not been exposed long or extensively enough to criticism of psychic magic and that, if they had been, they would not have been so easily swept away. Nevertheless, the prima facie results are disturbing, because they show how difficult it is to develop the secular and scientific outlook. Moreover, we are today surrounded by a larger cultural milieu in which psychic phenomena are often accepted as true.

V

The research described above sheds some light on the issues we have been addressing. It is important because it does not deal with traditional religions, but with the formation of new ones, where we have control groups in a sense. Traditional morality has had a theological basis. Whether it is the Ten Commandments, the Sermon on the Mount, or the Koran, magical revelations are offered as a basis for moral injunctions. That ethics need not be so based is the conclusion of the history of ethical and philosophical inquiry. How many human beings are able to separate morality from religion? Can there be an autonomous ethics?

This leads to a number of further questions about whether the scientific enlightenment and increased levels of education will advance the cause of secular humanism. First, are gullibility and self-deception very deep in human nature? Is there a native tendency to accept beliefs without evidence? Are there limits to scientific objectivity? Does the will to believe enter in? How effective can education be in developing rationality and skepticism? Scientists who are competent in their own fields often do not carry the scientific attitude to other areas, such as politics, morality, and religion.

Second, how deep-seated is magical thinking? Is there an enduring fascination with the unknown? Does the lure of the mysterious entice human interest? Is man an imaginative animal, forever hankering after the transcendental? For many, the myths surrounding Moses, Jesus, and Mohammed have been supplanted by UFOs from outer space manned by semi-divine creatures capable of ESP. Science fiction has, for them, become Holy Writ; and it seems to be performing functions similar to that of traditional theistic religion. Does the morality of the future need to be dressed in prophetic garb to be effective? What about the role of charismatic figures in transforming morality and awakening commitment and faith? Perhaps, where Marxism has succeeded as a secular alternative to classical theism, it does so because there is a messianic and millennial message. And so we may ask, Will secular humanism need a new mythology, and will this betray its very nature? How can we develop a reasonable yet inspiring secular morality? How can we re-awaken enchantment with its ideals?

Third, will a secular morality succeed in satisfying man's existential quest? Perhaps this is the most troublesome question. Humanistic ethics focuses on the development of self-reliant individuals willing to accept responsibility for their own destiny, capable of freedom, autonomy, and rationality and willing to live with uncertainty and ambiguity. But it may be that this is a moral ideal appropriate to only a limited number of *Ubermenschen,* to use Nietzsche's word. It demands courage and fortitude, will and perseverance. But some people are weak and timid, fearful of life and its challenges and especially weighed down by its burdens. The *Ubermensch* is alive with a sense of the opportunities that life presents; he expresses the strenuous mood. He does not wish simply to fulfill human nature, but to exceed it in a creative will to power. But the average man or woman, in many cases, seeks solace and peace, tranquility and quietude; he or she may wish to get through life with the least hassle. This is an escape not only from reason but from freedom as well, and this failure of nerve may be a perennial feature of the human condition.

Daniel Bell, in his controversial essay, "The Return of the Sacred," published in his recent book, *The Winding Passage,* argues that the sacred can never be dispensed with entirely.[6] This is so, he says, agreeing with Kierkegaard, because of the tragic dimensions of human life. How would a secular morality deal with existential despair, the awesome reality of human finitude and death? Bell thinks that the secular city that we seek to construct and improve ultimately provides a limited vision. Lurking in the background is always the quest for eternity as a solution to our existential predicament. He maintains that the traditional forms of religion, though they are not literally true, provide some consolation for the weeping soul. He thinks that tradition gives firmer moorings for our longings and some psychic stability in an otherwise transient sea. It may be that the fascination with the paranormal, the speculative leaps to the edges of the universe and to the possibilities of other dimensions of reality that I have described, satisfy this desire for there to be something more.

I do not have a simple answer to the questions I have posed. I do not have a sense of the tragic myself, or surely not an exaggerated one—nor does Sidney Hook. The secular humanist looks upon life as a challenging scene; problems are to be solved, not moaned about. Although we strive to fulfill life and avoid death, at some point we must accept it as a natural fact. Perhaps for some of us life has been too good and we owe the universe some suffering. Perhaps these differences in attitude have a biochemical or genetic source; or perhaps it is a matter of different personality types looking at the world through different lenses. Nevertheless there are large numbers of individuals who crave something more in the universe. For them the underlying function of religion seems to be eschatological. Unable to face death and nonbeing for themselves and their loved ones, they create fantasy worlds of wish-fulfillment. Will they continue to need to do so in the future? Philosophers of a pragmatic and humanistic bent have denied any such necessity. But in the last analysis, these are problems for empirical research, not philosophical speculation.

There are a number of further questions that need answering: *(a)* Why do human beings believe the way they do? What is the role of cognition in the formation of both beliefs and values? *(b)* Why does the fascination with magical thinking persist in this age of science? Is it again due to some psychological hunger? *(c)* To what extent are all individuals capable of autonomous rational choice, self-reliance, and independence?

I would hope that psychologists and behavioral scientists would give us some help in resolving these questions. We need to know more about human nature, its limits and possibilities. Until we have such knowledge, we should be wary about venturing predictions about the extent to which a secular morality is possible and what forms it may take. The present worldwide growth of paranormal and fundamentalist beliefs may only be a throwback to a prescientific mode of thinking. Perhaps it is the last gasp of a dying culture, to be replaced by a scientific and secular moral order. Or is it the harbinger of a future civilization based on a new myth, and are secular humanists only anomalistic oddities?

My own guess is that both cultures will continue to exist side by side, but we have no guarantee that secular humanism will make appreciable and lasting headway in the foreseeable future. Perhaps the best we can do is to provide some criticism of the excesses of religious fanaticism and offer alternative humanistic options for those who seek them. Perhaps the most we can hope for is that we may moderate and liberalize intolerant moralities and seek to develop mutual respect and tolerance as moral principles necessary in a pluralistic world.

In any case, the defense of the secular-humanist outlook is an ongoing task and we can thank Sidney Hook for his heroic contributions to the cause. If our optimism in the post-Dewey age has been shaken, this does not deny the continuing need to define and defend the ethics of secular humanism, a philosophy dedicated to the furtherance of the ideals of human freedom and critical intelligence.

NOTES

1. Especially in *Torcaso* v. *Watkins* (1961), where the Supreme Court ruled that Torcaso could be exempt from an oath declaring religious belief in God when being sworn in as a justice of the peace. Justice Black, in a footnote, said that secular humanism could function as a religion for some persons.

2. "An Interview with Sidney Hook at Eighty," *Free Inquiry* (Fall 1982): 4-10.

3. "The Snare of Definitions," in *The Humanist Alternative,* ed. by Paul Kurtz (Buffalo: Prometheus Books, 1973), p. 34.

4. William Sims Bainbridge and Rodney Stark, "Superstitions Old and New," *Skeptical Inquirer* (Summer 1980): 18-31.

5. Barry Singer and Victor Benassi, "Fooling Some of the People All of the Time," *Skeptical Inquirer* (Winter 1980-81): 7-24.

6. Daniel Bell, *The Winding Passage* (Cambridge, Mass.: ABT Books, 1980).

JOHN BUNZEL

Rescuing Equality

All men are born equal. The tough job is to outgrow it.
                                            —Anonymous

For more than two hundred years, irrepressible and powerful forces in American life have been attempting to overcome long-standing injustices and to deepen and strengthen democratic processes set in motion when this republic was founded. The history of those sometimes peaceful and sometimes convulsive changes was made in the interest of transforming our democratic principles into realities and as an expression of our passionate belief in democracy.

It is not something we passively endorse as a nation. Rather it is the touchstone of our national identity. It is because democracy has been such a central theme in our existence, shaping each of us individually and, in turn, being shaped by our emerging collective will, that it is important for us constantly to be in touch with ourselves and our heritage. We need to remind ourselves that our nation has had a good record, perhaps even a uniquely good record, in the cumulative and fundamentally orderly transformation of the lives of most of its citizens. Nor should we forget that this astonishing transformation has taken place in one of the most complex and humanly diverse industrial cultures in the world. For all of its divisions and bitternesses, our society has remained humane, open, and responsive to an amazing array of human needs.

It is true that things are far from perfect. It is also true that some take inordinate pleasure in their naive or even malicious discovery of this lack of perfection. But since no perfect society has ever existed (and seems unlikely to emerge), we would do well to reject such complaints. They breed a spirit not of pragmatic reasonableness and open resolution of the infinite problems of mankind, but rather of the polarizing, angry, and totalistic apocalypse. Distinctions become blurred; the familiar truths recede; our certainties become

171

transient before our eyes. Words and slogans become our tyrannical masters rather than the instruments to fulfill our basic goals.

In recent years we have had more than our national share of being victimized by language. Correcting that inflamed vision has always been the task of education, just as it has always been the special task of political inquiry to replace flabby and unexamined ideas with rigorous alternatives. An unthinking tyranny of terms characteristically takes the known and the respected and converts it into its antithesis. That, for example, has been the recent history of the once-respected term "relevance." As invoked in its recent polemical heyday, the term bullies the opposition instead of persuading it. It generates puzzles and irreconcilable dichotomies. Who, after all, wants to be known as an *opponent* of relevance? Doesn't opposing relevance make one an exponent of *irrelevance?*

Happily, the dismal shallowness of the corrupted usage of this particular term has by now been widely recognized. But in losing its virtue by becoming an embarrassing cliche, "relevance" has pretty much been lost to respectable discourse. It is a sad loss because we need every word we have in our continuous struggle to overcome or adjust to an intransigent natural and human world. This is why we are required continuously to undertake the arduous task of reclamation.

The present rescue mission centers around the word "equality." Properly understood, it has long been at the center of the American creed. But in the course of our recent national struggles it has produced much well-intentioned moralizing and confusion, with the result that some of the typical uses of equality cry out for clarification.

Are Not All Men Created Equal?

It is a familiar charge by now that the institutions of society thwart the principle professed in the Declaration of Independence that all men are created equal by supporting a system of rewards that perpetuates inequality. After all, everyone is aware that our society is riddled with expressions of inequality. Smith is admitted to Harvard while Jones can only enter Oshkosh Business College. Gloria, who is an honors student at Radcliffe, aspires to be our first female president, while Griselda, who has been attending Hohokus Community College, does not aspire beyond being a beautician. Jasper is in the top one percent of the national college entrance exams and is offered a fellowship at MIT, while Clarence scores in the bottom one percent and is advised to become a day laborer.

These illustrations are only the merest beginning of an infinity of inequalities impossible to catalogue. Some people are strong, some are weak; some are old, some are young; some are happy, others are melancholy; some are decent while others are swine. Some live to see their children flower and prosper while other parents may watch their children struggle against pernicious and fatal diseases. And some will wonder why or how these and other inequalities in the distribution of the world's goods and benefits can be tolerated by a democratic and moral society. Clearly there is no single way to confront such a formidable set of questions and perplexities.

The problem is made especially difficult by the lack of a definition of equality that has general acceptance either in the history of political thought and practice or in moral and social philosophy. For some, equality may mean guarantees by the state that despite any individual differences, the outcome of each of our encounters with fate will somehow be made uniform or "equal." For others, equality may require that all productive property be held in common or even that some ultimate civil authority must enforce prohibitions against the possession of any private property in order to assure equality. Or one could insist that equality means the absence of all distinctions of authority —e.g., orchestras should not have "dictators" called conductors and, perhaps, students and secretaries of university departments should have equal votes in the hiring of faculty. These illustrations are not fictions composed merely to serve as convenient straw arguments. They have all been advocated not only in the distant past but in the debates of the last ten years or so about the proper educational and social policies for America.

The single most famous American formulation of the problem of equality occurs at the opening of the Declaration of Independence: "We hold these truths to be self-evident—that all men are created equal; that they are endowed by their Creator with certain inalienable rights . . ." Is it, in fact, self-evident that this formulation is true? In the experience of each of us, we see beyond a doubt not the evidence of equality, but rather the reverse. Has anyone known two or more people to be equal in endurance, intelligence, sensitivity, moral stature, future possibilities, conviction, and so on? Nor is it possible somehow to obscure this omnipresent knowledge of inequality by arguing that each of us is equal at birth but somehow is made unequal by the factors that condition our development. Which of us has seen two babies equal in health, voice projection, motoric movement, physical dimensions, and the like? Does the Declaration of Independence somehow require us either to refuse to recognize these differences or to commit ourselves to overcoming them through the power of the state?

The second clause from the Declaration of Independence may seem equally perplexing and wrong-headed. What is inalienable about the rights we are alleged to possess? Have there not always been people—from the time of the emergence of man or from the time of the founding of the republic—who have had their rights taken away from them? In what sense, then, are they inalienable?

Suppose it is postulated that the authors of the Declaration meant that men are equal *only with reference to their rights,* the only form of equality that is actually mentioned in this passage. If we think of this possibility, we may immediately conclude that the assertion that "all men are created equal" does not require us to believe that they are equal in all their attributes. The evidence of our gross senses has not misled us. Some men are short and others are tall. Some have flexible joints and agile fingers and can brilliantly perform Mozart sonatas, while others have hands that move swiftly about the business of metal sculpture. Some are bald while others must tie their luxuriant locks in braids. Thus men may be—indeed *they are*—unequal in this or that attribute of their being. But regardless of these differences, the Declaration asserts that they are still equal with reference to their worth as men.

This brings us somewhat closer to a working definition of equality. It allows us to see that the equality of citizens in the United States does not in any way require us to assume what R. H. Tawney called an "equality of personal gifts." By definition, all citizens of a democracy are political equals and by virtue of that equality each is endowed not with the same skills and abilities, but with the same rights. *These* are the rights that are postulated as inalienable. Citizen Abraham Brody has these rights not because he is Jewish, brown-eyed, and five feet seven inches tall, but because he is a person and shares his humanness with other persons. It is *that* attribute of his being—his humanness—that makes him the equal of any other man, even one who is six feet four, has blue eyes, and is a Protestant. The Declaration of Independence is correct: these rights cannot be alienated while Brody remains a man.

Of course a tyrannical government or the Ku Klux Klan may prevent Brody or any other man from acting on his rights. (Government tyranny may also not be so direct and outspoken. It may even be impelled by high motives.) But that mistaken act of tyranny does not diminish Brody's inalienable right to equality. He *can* be prevented from acting on these rights, in which case he can expect the full support of the courts. But these rights cannot be taken from him. In short, the Declaration of Independence asserts the moral claim that by virtue of being human all men as individuals have rights that are inalienable.

Is Equality a Supreme End in Itself?

Some advocates of equality argue that, since "all men are created equal," and since equality is the central value of our society, equality must be assured at all costs for everyone. This argument is frequently made with particular force in support of those ethnic and racial minorities that have long been the hapless and persecuted victims of bigotry or poverty. In some senses of the word *equality,* it is proper and just that such an argument *should* be made. But left in this unqualified form, it provides too easy a temptation to insist on the supremacy of a single word at the expense of understanding what that word presupposes. Taken too literally, it can too readily be reduced to mere polemical bombast intended not to enlighten and liberate but rather to obscure and browbeat.

Just as the term *racist* is sometimes used by racists consciously or unconsciously to denounce or frighten their opposition into compliance and self-castigation, so too the term *equality* can be used by non- (or anti-) equalitarians to intimidate the advocates of democratic equality. For example, it is one thing to say that "yellow power is beautiful"; it is something else again to say that "yellow power is *more* beautiful." It is one thing to say that "white is beautiful"; it is another to say that white is superior to black. It is part of the tragedy of much of the current struggle for ethnic dignity and self-confidence that movements that begin with "we are beautiful" find themselves caught in a mounting spiral of auto-intoxication that ends with a fevered ethnicity. From there it is a small step to the assertion that "we are *more* beautiful than all the rest." Thus it is one thing to say that equality for blacks is necessary; it is another to say that equality for blacks requires the remedial imposition of quotas that can only have the consequence of discriminating against others.

The liberal tradition of equality in America is presently undergoing a major transformation. Accompanying a growing disenchantment with the liberal values of merit, opportunity, and achievement is a shift in emphasis from universalistic rights for all as individuals to particularistic ones for the group. Put simply, individual rights are surrendering to group rights in the demand for equal rights. We are moving from eliminating discrimination wherever it exists to guaranteeing representation of groups. Instead of equal access for all individuals, we now talk of special rights and proportional representation for particular groups.

The fact is that long-standing notions of equality are under serious challenge by absolute equalitarians. They want the federal government to play a new and vigorous role in making all of us equal not only in opportunity but in actual results. Thus, going to school, they say, may well provide everyone an equal opportunity and yet still not guarantee that those who go will receive equal rewards and benefits. To borrow an example from the world of sports, school provides us a hunting license and it trains us to shoot. But that is not enough. The new equalitarians want the hunters "to come back with equal amounts of bear." They would simply divide the bears shot among all the hunters. As Harvard's demographer Nathan Keyfitz puts it, "Whatever the sport, we are not merely to go into the game with no handicap, but we are all to emerge with the same score."

These equalitarians claim that justice requires equality not at the beginning of a race (to shift the sport) but at the end. They want the minority or female "runner" to be given more than equal treatment with the white, male runner. As Professor Howard Sherain has suggested, they want the scorekeeper to ensure that the minority and female runners win a certain percentage of the races.

It is the worst form of condescension, as every self-respecting woman and member of a minority group would be the first to agree. It is also a strange definition of equality. It carries with it the principle that in order to make some people equal we must use the authority of the state to make others unequal.

But how much of an advance is that over the injustices of the past?

Advocates of absolute equalitarianism pummel the meaning of equality into a form that is no longer recognizable. Setting aside a complex range of elusive ambiguities—e.g., are they advocating equality of human rights, income, psychological well-being, happiness, political freedom, and so on?—we are immediately faced with the problem that in their hands equality seems to exist in isolation, untempered by a sense of its connections with other values. Their definition of equality is stated in so undifferentiated a form that we are, in effect, forced to embrace a mere slogan or a utopian ideal rather than a political principle that can be made part of our lives and coordinated with other cherished beliefs. Like every other human value, equality does not have any meaning in a vacuum. Either it can be related to other democratic values or it becomes a kind of verbal whirlpool into which all other values are drawn, only to be destroyed. After all, can one be an advocate of equality while also being an enemy of fair play, even-handedness, and the sanctity of freedom of the individual? Can reasonable men advocate a definition of equality that requires them to subordinate these other values in the interest of achieving equality? What sort of equality would it be? Are we prepared to say that we want to use the full weight of our moral sanction to enforce equality without regard for the consequences?

There was a time not too many years ago when freedom and equality were almost always looked upon as "two virtues" standing together rather than in conflict with each other. Many of those who once thought this to be true are no longer so sure. They now believe it is closer to the truth to say that the real problem today is the noticeable and important differences. An Israeli socialist made a perceptive observation when he said recently that those nations that have put freedom ahead of equality have ended up doing better by equality than those which have accepted the reverse priority.

The change for these thoughtful observers is that over the years they have discovered they care as much for freedom as they do for equality. They cannot be satisfied with a social calculus that is blind to the fact that equality is not an absolute and should be inseparable from evaluating each person according to his or her merits, from fair play and the like.[1] They have come to appreciate what England's Professor John P. Plamenatz noted when he said that "equality of opportunity in a free society differs from equality of opportunity in a society which is merely equalitarian."

This does not mean that equality is valued less. It simply means that, unlike the pure egalitarian for whom there is no more powerful argument than the argument of equality itself, there are many people who do not view equality as the only goal of a democratic society. Equality derives its meaning as well as its limits from the larger system of democratic values to which it belongs.

"The fallacies of the new egalitarianism," says Professor Charles Frankel, "come largely from having ripped the notion of equality loose from its context. The result is to turn it into a principle vagrant and homeless, and identifiable in fact only if a quasi-theological context is unconsciously imported." Frankel calls it "redemptive egalitarianism."

There are also other considerations that make equality easier said than done. Plamenatz and others have pointed out that complete equality can only be attained in the simplest society, which is why Rousseau, who cared so much for equality, preferred the life of the small community. But in the large and complex society of modern industrialism there is differentiation of roles and statuses—in a word, hierarchy. And with hierarchy come many kinds of inequalities. The question is, What kinds of inequality are consistent with equality of opportunity?

Just as some inequalities preclude equality of opportunity, said Plamenatz, so others make it possible. Men are not unequal because they have different rights. The rights attached to a job or occupation are enjoyed only by those engaged in it, but the others who do not have these rights are not inferior to them. Men are not unequal when their rights differ—that they must always do —"but when the rights that all men must have if they are to be free are enjoyed only by some, or by some more securely than by others." Plamenatz summarizes his argument this way:

> What does it matter to a man that other men should have greater power or wealth than he has, provided he has as much freedom as society can afford to give him, if it is also to give freedom to others? Power and wealth are means to freedom. No one doubts that no man's power and wealth should be allowed to diminish the freedom of others. But it does not follow that persons who are unequal in power or wealth are unequal in freedom. The relations between power and freedom are subtle and difficult to define. Some kinds of inequality are fatal to freedom, others are conditions of it. The equality that really matters is equality of freedom, or in other words, equality of opportunity.

Can Some Groups (in a Good Cause) Be Made More Equal Than Others?

There is a compelling need today to examine a philosophy of "group-think," which is committed—perhaps unwittingly—to the belief that it is legitimate to give rights to some groups that are denied to other groups. Most of us are accustomed to confronting such a view when it is expressed by, say, the White Citizens' Councils of Mississippi. On these occasions, those of us who are friends of equality find no difficulty in expressing our indignation and unalterable opposition. But the problem becomes more complicated when such a view is espoused by some equalitarians who argue that there are certain rights reserved for certain racial groups.

In American society rights are held by individuals and are nowhere held in any restrictive or exclusive sense by racial groups per se. It is, quite properly, illegal and immoral in our society for Caucasians, for example, to have rights that blacks do not have, or for Chinese-Americans to be prevented from exercising political rights *because* they are Chinese-Americans while white Irish-Americans are allowed to exercise those very same rights. Such differences would mean that one racial or national group was less equal than the other. The attempt to do away with discrimination by disadvantaging some groups—either groups that have allegedly perpetrated discrimination against others or groups that are known to be innocent—ought to be regarded as illegal and unjust.

White people cannot legally be punished as a group any more than black people can. But that is precisely the sort of injustice that has occurred when, say, an academic department in a university lets it be known that it intends to hire only women or persons from certain minority groups. Among other things, such selective racial or sexual exclusion might require us to believe that all members of the group were equally guilty of discrimination against women or minorities and therefore were equally deserving of being punished. But could all white people—because they are white—be equally guilty of discrimination?

Even if we were to grant—and we should not—that there is such a thing as group rights in this sense, such a view of the guilt of all white people or of all males is patently absurd because it would require us to adopt some sort of mystical or racist view of a group's collective guilt. It is virtually self-evident that at least *some* members of a group who become the victim of reverse discrimination *must* be innocent. It therefore follows that groups that are the presumed victims of discrimination cannot be offered preferential treatment at the expense of other groups. Such an act would result in creating a new cycle of injustice by making these other groups the victims of discrimination without reference to the guilt or innocence of individuals. This kind of discriminatory strategy could survive only at the expense of continuously finding new sacrificial group-victims that could be used not as ends in themselves—the only basis of a just social order—but rather as the means to the achievement of some perhaps remote social end.

A related issue is the problem of how one can hold one's contemporaries accountable for wrongs committed by members of previous generations.[2] Some commentators seem to believe that it is proper and moral for white people to be "temporarily" disadvantaged by various quota arrangements in order to correct ancient wrongs. It is as if such an argument alleged that white people should submit to discrimination *because* they are white rather than because they are guilty. They could, of course *be* guilty of discrimination; but if that is the case, they should be punished as individuals—as the law quite properly provides—rather than as members of a group. In any event, isn't it clear that there is no moral or legal warrant to use discrimination as a suitable remedy or social punishment to overcome inequality? Further, even if some white *employers* are guilty of discrimination against minorities or women, should we punish them by enforcing quota programs that deprive white *applicants* of an equal opportunity to compete for jobs? After all, the applicants have not been proved guilty of anything. Should the employers, who in our hypothetical case are demonstrably guilty, be encouraged to suppose they can somehow atone for their guilt by punishing the innocent? Such a social policy would compound our national confusion, since it not only results in discriminating against the innocent but it also allows the guilty to escape. It so muddies the waters of accountability that a wrong may be convincingly enough perpetrated as to appear to be right. Such a theory of group guilt may provide ample opportunities for vengeance, but it does not contribute very much to a defensible theory of distributive justice.

An attempt to overcome discrimination by resorting to quotas is not a remedy for righting injustice. It is simply a way of changing the target of injustice so that one group suffers rather than another. If a certain number of people enter heretofore inaccessible areas of employment by virtue of a group quota who would not have entered on the basis of an individual merit system, it is precisely to that degree that such a social policy invalidates itself as self-contradictory and unjust. Each instance of such advancement constitutes the imposition of a standard of group identity that assesses the merits of people by their group affiliation rather than as individuals.

It is often overlooked that the injustice of discrimination is, by definition, an injustice suffered because someone has not been treated according to a universal standard. Some arbitrary or incidental aspect of their identity—their accent, their height, the way they choose to comb their hair, their color, etc.— has become the basis of judgments about them rather than a standard of merit that applies equally to everyone. But it is only with reference to such a general standard of merit that one can conclude that discrimination or injustice has occurred. If such a merit standard had never been articulated, the entire attempt to discover the existence of injustice could never have taken place.

Traditional opposition to quotas rests on the conviction that they are devices that single out certain people for special persecution or for special advantages. For example, a quota might establish that only three Jewish applicants will be admitted to a law school, medical school, social club, executive appointment, or whatever. The effect of such a constraint is to say that Jews will not be considered by a general standard applicable to all. This amounts to a violation of an individual's right to be free from discrimination or preferential treatment because of his religious beliefs, his color, or his ancestry. In short, he has become the victim of a category crime. His individuality has been superseded or reduced so that, in effect, he is no longer a person but is rather the occupant of a category.

We are presented with a paradox. We are confronted by the advocates of quotas with the contradictory injunction that we should abandon the merit principle despite the fact that the very discovery of discrimination rests on the principle of merit.

Is Statistical Underrepresentation Prima Facie
Evidence of Inequality?

Some equalitarians continue to make a seemingly powerful argument that is frequently reduced to a simple formula—namely, that statistical evidence of disproportionately low employment of minorities or women is and must be prima facie evidence of discrimination. Such a view is often complicated by the fact that there is no general agreement about the appropriate base point against which to measure this supposed discrimination. Sometimes the base point is presumed to be the nation, the state, the region, the city, or some other official or unofficial geographical entity. Obviously, it is likely to make a considerable difference whether a state like North Dakota, where black people total 1 percent of the population, is required to construct its public institutions so that they are 1 percent black, or whether they should construct their institutions to reflect the fact that blacks are 14 percent of the population of the United States.

Consider a university analogue. Should a department of biology at Yale University contain minorities proportionate to the number of minorities in New Haven, Connecticut, the Connecticut Valley, New England, or the United States in order to assure equality? Or should the proportion of minorities hired by the department of biology be proportionate only to the number of minorities with Ph.D.'s in biology that live within the limits of the continental United States? Still another version of this problem is revealed in trying to determine what sort of statistical evidence is required of a university to demonstrate that it is not engaged in discrimination or the willful perpetuation of inequality. Should we require that each department or cluster of departments demonstrate statistical evidence of the employment of a proportionate number of minorities, or should we require that the employment figures for the entire university reveal the retention of a requisite number of women and minorities?

These are all complications attendant to monitoring or assessing the existence of what is often called discrimination or inequality. They are likely to arise because it may already have been concluded that statistical underrepresentation of minorities is in fact prima facie evidence of unequal treatment. But is that the case? What possible meanings can be attributed to "equality" in such a context of analysis? Do we really mean to argue that because Jews constitute 3 percent of the total population of the country that they should be represented in that proportion in the police force of Oshkosh or Chicago, in the class of executives in the $50,000-$100,000 bracket, or among professors of physical education, political science, and English literature? Clearly they are underrepresented in all of these categories. But does that prove there is discrimination or that they have been treated unequally? It becomes additionally implausible if we continue to ask such questions about the proportions of Samoans who are insurance salesmen, Eskimos who are mechanics, and so on.

Those who argue that statistical underrepresentation is the equivalent of discrimination or inequality conveniently overlook two things:

1. The issue is not representation as in the political representation process. We do not want to hire Jewish professors of physics because they can represent Jewish physics. That is what the Germans did when they insisted on a German physics. We do not want a black professor of economics to be a representative of black economics. After all, there are many different ways of being black. How can we be such wholesale reductivists as to suppose that appointing a black person to teach Chaucer means that he or she now represents black people? A black person represents himself or herself and, one would hope, does not try to perpetuate a black view of Chaucer, since there is none.

2. There have always been differences of values, orientation, taste, expectation, and the like among the varied groups that compose this or any other nation. Many cruel perversions of our political life have exacerbated these differences, sometimes making them into heavy burdens or vicious stereotypes that have barred the way of some minorities to advancement. We need to continue and indeed to deepen our moral resistance and legal opposition to such betrayals of the principle that all men are created equal.

But to do this effectively we must have a clear mind about what is to be concluded from our observations of the real world. The fact is that many of the differences that have influenced a disproportionate number of Italians to become opera singers, Armenians to become truck farmers, or Jews to become doctors, college professors, and novelists express prima facie evidence not of unequal treatment but rather of the vitality of democracy. These specialized choices are derived from deep allegiances to group loyalties, religious ties, sentimental attachments, cherished traditions, and ethnic identification. It is not necessary to believe that every aspect of these choices has been free of constraint in order to defend them as expressions of democracy. Such a view would be perfectionistic and unrealistic. It is only important to understand that the alternative to such choices—a system of quotas that would assure proportionality—is an infinitely greater source of constraints on our freedom.

We also need to remember something else. Past discrimination (and we should, of course, concede that there is still considerable discrimination in the present) has a perseverative effect so that, even in the absence of active discrimination, past victims and their descendants may be disadvantaged. The country must commit itself to overcome this inheritance, surely one of the shameful parts of our history. But we do not overcome discrimination by assuming that disproportionality means conscious discrimination, always and everywhere. An exclusive focus on overcoming discrimination, including past discrimination, often fights symptoms rather than causes. The more urgent need is to help the victims of discrimination overcome the disabilities of poverty, a bad family situation, and the like. In the area of education, for example, we need to rescue good young minds before they become dulled and ill-equipped to go on to college. We need to mass our remedial efforts in the form of state and national search programs at the high-school level where talented young people—blacks, Chicanos, poor whites—which is to say all of the disadvantaged who otherwise get locked into a lifetime of inequality—can be found and helped. This country would be willing to pay for an educational program that would benefit the victims of discrimination who are unpardonably handicapped. We engage in *that* fight not by forcing other people into giving them special privileges but by providing all of the handicapped with real and tangible assistance. That is what affirmative action should be all about.

The problem with quotas and mathematical formulas and proportionality is that they are likely to reduce the incentive for genuine reform. The inequalities that quotas or fixed percentages or group ratios are presumed to diminish originate in widely dispersed areas of our social and political life. Quotas may too readily provide a disincentive to transform these areas since they will encourage many people to believe that discrimination can be and is being dealt with by relatively mechanical means. Some may argue that quotas are in fact not only the way to abolish discrimination but that the ends of quotas, i.e., the outputs, will themselves provide evidence that discrimination is being contained or defeated. After all, such an argument might run, if quotas are successfully enforced, the employment statistics will reveal that discrimination no longer exists. In the presence of such arguments we are perilously close to the never-never land of the murderer who has killed his parents and now asks for the compassion of the court because he is an orphan.

Can One Believe in Equality Without Lowering Standards Until There Are None?

As already suggested, in a free society there will always be tension between the ideal of equality and the liberal values of individual merit and achievement. One of the problems with the public debate about equality today is that in the hands of many doctrinaire equalitarians it has been heralded as a single Truth handed down from on high. But the rule of Harvard Law Professor Paul Freund is preferable: "When you perceive a truth, look for the balancing truth."

Thus it is not enough to ask if one is in favor of equality. The important question is what kind of equality, how much, in what areas, for what reasons, and at what cost? Framed in this way, it becomes quickly clear that the concept of equality must be viewed in relation to other competing and legitimate values. The challenge is to balance one's obligations. One of the major challenges facing our colleges and universities today is how they will adapt themselves to a society that is redefining itself. There are some basic principles in conflict with each other that must be accommodated. For example, higher education must deepen its commitment to the principle of equal access, but it must not diminish its determination to maintain high standards. In the words of Dr. Edward Levi when he was president of the University of Chicago, "We need to reach more minds without deserting the mind."

Many dogmatic equalitarians regularly charge that anyone who defends the university as a meritocracy is an "elitist" and, by extension, an anti-democrat. This argument deserves to be met head-on. A university is not organized on the principle of "one person, one vote," which is why it is not a political democracy. Its essential role is not to represent the people or to govern. Nor is it an egalitarian political institution. The relationship between students and faculty is not inherently equal. As Professor Daniel Bell has said, "The university is dedicated to the authority of scholarship and learning and to the transmission of knowledge from those who are competent to those who are capable." That is the essential mission of the university.

Bell's point is that many of the questions about equality and inequality have little to do with the issue of meritocracy, if, as he says, "we define the meritocracy as those who have an *earned* status or have achieved positions of rational authority by competence." There cannot be complete democratization in the entire range of human activities. It makes no sense, he points out, to insist on a "democracy of judgment" in the arts for the simple reason that you cannot determine by popular vote which painting or novel or violin concerto is better than another. In science and scholarship, achievement is measured and ranked on the basis of accomplishment—and, he adds, a university had better remain a meritocracy "if a degree of culture is to prevail."

The serious concern about the increasing difficulty to maintain excellence and quality in higher education can be expressed in still another way. Perhaps the major apprehension about the move to collective bargaining in our colleges and universities is that the special thrust of equalitarianism where unionization is established is likely to have a leveling effect on the application of professional standards to faculty review and performance. Will it be harder to reward excellence and quality in individual accomplishment as demands are made to spread the benefits more equally among all members of the faculty? Will meritorious performance and scholarly achievement become less important in individual tenure and promotion decisions than length of service and other generalized but less discriminating standards of competence? Unionization tends to place a lesser value on qualitative distinctions in individual performance and favors instead such standards as seniority, leading to the flattening out of individual differences. In short, when it comes to high academic standards, the unions would discount individual promise and achievement in favor of equity for the group.

The impact of collective bargaining on higher education puts in sharp focus the collectivist outlook and equalitarian norms firmly fixed in unionization. There is good reason to worry that an unrestrained equalitarianism will tend to deteriorate into a monotonous level of uniform, self-perpetuating mediocrity and undistinguished equality. We need to keep in mind that colleges and universities are and should be in the business of making discriminating judgments. It is one reason why some institutions have excelled and others are only ordinary. One would like to purchase equity for our campuses, but (to borrow a phrase) "at a price less than excellence."

One can go further. This country should not try to purchase equality at the cost of quality, unless we wish to become a nation of followers without leaders. It has been said that we seek the "highest mean level in the world," but it is also true that the pace of progress is set "not by the mean but by the best." There is nothing in the vocabulary of equality that suggests we should be satisfied with achieving the "highest level of mediocrity" in the world.

There are other paradoxes of equality. For example, those who have spent years in the classrooms believe in equal consideration of students. But they also know that good teachers must treat their students differently. The fact is that the principle of equality, if taken too literally, will not lead to social justice because, as Sidney Hook has pointed out, the notions of equality and human welfare are both involved. Should the poor have to pay the same percentage of their income in taxes as the rich? That would prelude another kind of equality, an equality of obligations and burdens.

It is no surprise that equality is tied to the question of justice. But surely, someone will say, justice requires that everyone be treated equally. The response is that, if one values freedom and diversity and individualization, one will acknowledge that justice also consists in treating people differently.

It was said at the outset that we have too often been victimized by words and slogans. Justice is no exception. In the name of justice we have been told by many equalitarians today that the way to make up for past discrimination against women and minorities is to discriminate against others now. It is a mischievous argument. The equalitarian values of most Americans lead them to believe that as a nation our goal should be to eliminate all kinds of discrimination. Put simply, they believe that in a democratic society an individual's worth has a higher moral claim than his color, his sex, or his origins.

We need to remind ourselves, especially at a time when some people seem intent on dividing us all into special groupings based on race or sex or ethnic background, that there is no such thing as black justice or brown justice or female justice. There is only Justice. Justice wears her blindfold that she may recognize no favorites, but she holds a scale in which merit is weighed.

Can Equality Depend upon "Mere Reason"?

In recent years one particular question has frequently emerged in various forms. Sometimes it is asked in good faith. At other times it is stated more as an accusation than as a question. In one form or another it deals with the problem of whether—or, perhaps, how—everything we have asserted thus far about the nature of equality can be true, but still somehow be false. Can it be possible that our feelings represent a higher truth than the truth of cold reason and logic? In discussing equality, this argument goes, aren't we dealing with the deep feelings and fundamental aspirations of human beings? Can we expect millions of people to be concerned with the complex collection of cross-cutting obligations and the logical constraints that invariably accompany a thoughtful attempt to make equality a reality? Isn't it inevitable (and just) that those who have been denied what is rightfully theirs will no longer wait docilely in tidy lines while rational arrangements are made to redistribute the world's goods? Aren't we obliged to conclude that reason and logic cannot know everything? In short, do we dare oppose the revolution of feelings that now demands immediate recognition? On what grounds can we refrain from instantaneously granting equality to all?

It is undoubtedly true that in the convoluted affairs of men there are occasions when our feelings, to paraphrase Rousseau, can have "reasons which the mind cannot know"—or at least the mind cannot know them metaphorically speaking. Presumably it cannot know them in precisely the same way and with the desired simultaneity, intensity, and drama. Unfortunately, this formula does not tell us when it should be applied—that is, it does not tell us self-evidently whether these "reasons" are defensible or not. Nor does it tell us when our feelings ought to have primacy. Certainly it would be absurd to argue, as the early romantics did during the storm and stress period in late-eighteenth-century Germany, that the "yearnings of our heart" are *always* right. In modern politics, at any rate, it has been clear from the work of J. L. Talmon and others that such romantic views about the superiority of feelings have been disastrous.

We may easily suppose that people's feelings about a variety of matters differ widely. The same may be true of reasons of the mind: they, too, will vary widely from person to person. But surely it is evident that, in matters of critical importance to the republic, the consensus required for social and public policy can be more readily reached by recourse to reason than to feelings. The very question we are considering here is a case in point. Can we settle the social meaning of equality in a democracy by turning to feelings alone? Can we take some plebiscite of the heart in defiance of the mind and still expect an outcome consistent with the principles of democracy? Furthermore, how does the heart cast its vote in the absence of the mind?

Advocates of emotive uses of equality sometimes may find special gratifications in recognizing both the purity of their own motives and the immediate and untrammeled nature of their responses to perplexities about the meaning of equality. Sometimes those who prize the heart more than the head believe that feeling is more pure and therefore closer to the inner authentic man. They disdain the delay that accompanies thought, analysis, and calculation. However, equality is a problem that transcends the merely personal. There is no problem of equality in a world composed only of individual separate wills. None of us lives in such a world, which is why we must reject the notion that our personal satisfactions can be self-contained and self-justifying. In considering the meaning of equality we are required to examine it at a level that reaches beyond our personal gratification. Our good motives are not at issue. What is at issue is desirable social outcomes and an authoritative consensus.

Finally, those who turn to feelings rather than the mind are invariably those who believe that social problems can be solved if men will only rearrange their feelings and respond to the direct yearnings of their true natures. That true nature, of course, is symbolized by what men feel rather than by what they think. Volumes have been written in recent years in defense of such a simplistic view of the human dilemma. We have been told that equality is at hand (along with the millennium) if only Consciousness III will be permitted to flower—or that all men will be equal when the revolution of feeling has made polymorphous perversity a universal condition of man. New versions of such incantations to transcendence continue to blossom despite the fact that they denigrate the contingent nature of democratic institutions. They imply or argue directly that anything is within our grasp. They see politics as providing millennarian solutions.

Against such sirens, de Tocqueville's philosophy of democracy and equality should be counterposed. De Tocqueville perceived in his *Democracy in America* that equality could more readily be pursued than grasped, and he understood the character of the chaos that could arise from the unbridled pursuit of the unreachable. He saw that in America

> the means for everybody to rise to the level of everybody else . . . are constantly proving inadequate in the hands of those using them . . . Democratic institutions awaken and flatter the passions for equality without ever being able to satisfy it entirely. This complete equality is always slipping through the people's fingers at the moment they think to grasp it, fleeing . . . in an eternal flight; the people grow heated in search of this blessing, all the more precious because it is near enough to be seen but too far off to be tasted.

NOTES

1. Of course an absolute equalitarian would insist that his point of view was put forward in the interest of fair play and justice. Everyone, after all, wants to be seen as an advocate of virtue. But it is never enough merely to declare one's good intentions or to invoke the right words. Just as scoundrels can pretend to be patriots by wrapping themselves in the flag to escape criticism, so certain equalitarians can pretend to be advocates of fair play by dealing fast and loose with democracy. The test is not in the mere invocation of certain honorific words. Rather it is in the logic that governs their use and in the assessment of the consequences entailed in their application to the problems of society.

2. In his excellent book, *Affirmative Action Discrimination: Ethnic Inequality and Public Policy* (New York: Basic Books, 1976), Professor Nathan Glazer addresses this question directly: "Compensation for the past is an insidious principle. It can be extended indefinitely and make for endless trouble. Who is to determine what is proper compensation for the American Indian, the black, the Mexican-American, the Chinese or Japanese American? When it is established that the full status of equality is extended to every individual, regardless of race, color or national origin, and that special opportunity is also available to any individual on the basis of individual need,

again regardless of race, color or national origin, one has done all that justice and equity call for and that is consistent with a harmonious multigroup society.''

MARVIN KOHL

Is Human Life Itself a Value?

Few philosophers have defended the "quality of life" point of view with greater tenacity and courage than Sidney Hook. Long before it became fashionable to defend the right to suicide, Hook argued that death is often our friend and that, under certain circumstances, choosing to end our own life "would be a legitimate means to attain our ends, often a praiseworthy means, and sometimes even an obligatory means. . . ."[1] Similarly, Hook has been a great champion of the intelligent resistance to tyranny. He has vigorously defended the right (if not the obligation) to resist tyranny, even if that resistance results in a threat to our own life.[2] The great enemy is the fear of death, because it is tantamount to the fear of living well if there should be any resistance, even moderate resistance, to doing so. For history and the long sweep of human experience has demonstrated that, when mere survival becomes a fetish, not only is the good life with its higher forms of excellence sacrificed, but meaningful life as well.

In other words, the melioristic pragmatist maintains that it is not life as bare subsistence, but the good life, that is the object of intellectual endeavor.

> Paradoxical as it may sound, life itself is not a value. What gives life value is not its mere existence but its quality. Whoever proclaims that life is worth living under any circumstances has already written for himself an epitaph of infamy. For there is no principle or human being he will not betray; there is no indignity he will not suffer or compound.[3]

Thus for the pragmatist, life is important only as the condition and opportunity for the good life, and he prefers not to live at all if he must live under certain circumstances.

All these points are important and most are well taken. Extreme vitalists and "quantity of lifers" are largely mistaken. Contrary to what they suggest, the fear of death and the conviction that life is worth living under any circumstances is not conducive to, or even supportive of, a meaningful or a good life. To tell the poor, the needy, or the oppressed that they should be content with whatever they may have as long as they can live is not merely worship of the status quo but a mockery of the ideal of excellence and the very notion of human dignity.

The vitalist and his like are also mistaken as to the nature of this value. Life is not an absolute value. Even Albert Schweitzer was willing to kill certain life forms in order to save others. And Gandhi, the patron saint of twentieth-century pacifism, a man who abhorred almost all forms of killing, writes:

I see there is an instinctive horror of killing beings under any circumstances whatever. . . . [But] should my child be attacked with rabies and there was no helpful remedy to relieve his agony, I should consider it my duty to take his life.[4]

We may define morality differently, but no matter what our conception of the good is, if we do not corrupt or destroy the notion of friendship and the notion of a lesser evil, death is often found to be a friend or, at least, the lesser of two evils.

Nor is it true, once we escape from the self-serving metaphysical fiat, from the presupposition that all being must somehow be good, that unhappy existence is always better than death because life, even at its worst, is always better than nonexistence.[5] Notice my objection is not to the claim that men generally prefer existence to nonexistence but rather to the claim that they *always do so* or that they *always ought to do so*. For the evidence indicates that human beings generally prefer life to death. So that if the mode be an empirical one, it is difficult to see how one can honor truth, and when confronted with the claim, proceed to deny that most humans, by their very actions, show they prefer some of the most meager (but not meaningless) forms of human existence—lives of endless toil and hardship, slavery or near slavery, and even great mental or physical disability—to that of death.

The other large area of agreement concerns the value of intelligent resistance. Hook correctly insists that a rational and high-minded being may prefer resistance to surrender, even death to a life of complete and utter degradation. That mere survival is not to be made a fetish. That

No man can win freedom unless he conquers his fear of death. No nation can preserve its freedom unless it is willing to risk destruction in its defense. . . . [That] the free society from Pericles to the present has survived because it has valued some thing more than survival, because of its vision of human excellence, dignity and joy has made some kinds of life unworthy of man.[6]

Yet for all the vitality and great power of Hook's position something is wrong. It is well not to overestimate the value of life. But it is not well to underestimate its value or to argue in a manner as to give the impression that only life at its fullest or near fullest is worth living. And it does not seem right to say that only the good life is worth living and that life itself is not of value.

Following Dewey and Hook, I shall say that in empirical fact the measure of value a person attaches to a given end is not what he *says* about its preciousness but the care he devotes to obtaining and using the *means* without which it cannot be attained or adequately protected.[7] Thus, to value an object is to be disposed to actively behave in such a way as to achieve, sustain, or enhance the welfare of that object. Now it would take us far afield to discuss the question of the good and the truth of the form of ideal utilitarianism I wish to support, viz., the marriage of a plurality of ideals, including open ideals, with the pluck and will to achieve and defend them. What is relevant, however, is to note that there are advantages to not equating goodness with value, as Dewey and Hook appear to do. Briefly stated, what are the advantages of not identifying goodness with value, as value is here defined? First and foremost, it enables us to intelligently discuss those objects that may not be presently valued. Second, it allows us to account for mistakes in valuation, such as when something is initially judged to be of value but then it is discovered that the benefits are meager and the costs are irrationally high. And finally it enables us to avoid the Charybdis of a rigid Aristotelianism, the notion of a predetermined limited number of ends inherently arranged in a rigidly fixed order of increasing comprehensiveness and finality, *and* the Scylla of an empty behaviorism.

The following seems to be true. First, human beings, by their actions, do generally value life. They do generally strive to defeat, or at least postpone, death. Perhaps they ought not. Perhaps they should only value the good life. But that is a different question. The question before us is whether life itself is of value and not whether it ought to be of value.

Second, since human life as a normal biological fact is of value, it is not fully accurate to say that human life itself is not of value. Strictly speaking, what is generally not of value is not life itself, but irrevocably meaningless existence. What is generally not of value is a life so irretrievably blasted by accident, malady, or birth so as not to warrant rational hope.

The third point relates to the claim that only the good life is worth living. Philosophers, following Aristotle, are generally intoxicated with the idea of the good life. They repeatedly claim that it is not life itself that is worth living, but only the good life. They tend to forget that, for Aristotle, the good life presupposes a fairly high and relatively rare level of human achievement. They also seem to forget that if Aristotle's doctrine of the good life is strictly adhered to, and if the injunction be true, then it follows that the lives of most human beings are not worth living.

Surely something is amiss here. Failure to achieve the good life does not, in itself, result in degradation and obloquy. Perhaps the achievement of a full life is an important end. But a life that is not full is not necessarily empty. And a life that is neither fully nor richly meaningful is not meaningless. Fortunately for most human beings, there are various levels of meaningful life between bare subsistence and the good life. Although they may not be of intrinsic value, they are typically found to be sufficient to sustain the souls of most men and are, therefore, of value.

NOTES

1. Sidney Hook, "The Ethics of Suicide," *International Journal of Ethics,* 37 (1927), 178. Reprinted in *Beneficent Euthanasia,* ed. by Marvin Kohl (Buffalo: Prometheus Books, 1975), pp. 57-69.

2. Sidney Hook, *Pragmatism and the Tragic Sense of Life* (New York: Basic Books, 1974), p. 12. For similar statements, also see ibid., p. 53, and "The Ethics of Suicide," op. cit., p. 186.

3. Sidney Hook, "A Foreign Policy for Freedom and Survival," *Political Power and Personal Freedom* (New York: Criterion Books, 1959), p. 426.

4. Mahatma Gandhi, *Young India,* Nov. 18, 1926, quoted in *The Essential Gandhi,* ed. by Louis Fischer (New York: Vintage Books, 1962), p. 216.

5. St. Augustine, *The Problem of Free Choice* (Westminster, Md.: The Newman Press, and London: Longmans, Green, 1955), bk. 3, pp. 158-64.

6. Sidney Hook, *Political Power and Personal Freedom,* p. 445.

7. Cf. John Dewey, *Theory of Valuation* (Chicago: University of Chicago Press, 1939), p. 27.

ERNEST NAGEL

Freedom and Civilization

There is a common assumption that human beings possess various "rights" as inalienable possessions simply because they are human. Theories of natural or human rights have been advocated by major thinkers in Western countries; those theories have a long and complex history and have played important roles in the struggle for various specific freedoms and immunities. In my judgment, however, attempts to validate or justify claims to various individual freedoms by appealing to some version of the doctrine of inherent and inalienable human rights have not been successful in the past, are unlikely to be successful in the future, and are therefore ill-advised. The burden of this brief paper is indeed that justifications, *via* that doctrine, of proposed social ideals or objectives, whether these be personal liberties or more "positive" benefits (such as medical care or employment), do not provide a sound or even a plausible basis for adopting them.

In my view the notion that there are universally valid natural or human rights does not stand up under scrutiny. I will give only two of my reasons for skepticism. In the first place, advances in science have made clear that the philosophical assumptions on which most—and perhaps all—theories of natural or human rights rest are at best extremely dubious. For the claim that men have natural rights, or that a specific type of action is a human right, is based in one way or another on the assumption that the claim is self-evidently true or that our reason apprehends it as correct—an assumption that was stated explicitly in the American Declaration of Independence. This assumption seemed quite plausible at one time, since it was essentially like the belief, accepted as sound for centuries, that the axioms of Euclidean geometry or of Newton's first law of motion can be established as correct by an appeal to their self-evidence and to purely "rational" considerations. This manner of justifying claims concerning what is to be included in the class of alleged human

This paper is adapted from a talk at the International Conference in Honor of Andrei Sakharov held at Rockefeller University, New York City, on May 2, 1981.

rights provides no way of settling disputes when people differ, as they frequently do, in their judgments of self-evidence; and in consequence, there is no limit to the number and variety of liberties and benefits that might be counted as human rights. But more damaging to the doctrine of natural rights was the construction (or "discovery") of alternative systems of geometry and mechanics (and eventually of other branches of mathematics and physics), each of them as internally consistent as the traditional systems were assumed to be. For these constructions showed once and for all that the alleged self-evidence of the basic premises of a system could not be taken as a mark of their truth. It became no less dubious to regard the supposed self-evidence of assumptions in political and moral inquiries as a sufficient ground for accepting those assumptions as warranted.

I come to a second reason for dissatisfaction with the doctrine of natural rights. The doctrine has helped to break up the cake of ancient custom and to emancipate men from oppressive restrictions on their behavior; but it has also been used to place limits on what a society might do to improve the fortunes of its members. For proposals to change certain features of the social and economic order in the interest of greater well-being of the poor and underprivileged were often believed by other and more influential members of society to be violations of *their own* inviolable human rights and were therefore bitterly resisted. Accordingly, the doctrine of natural rights has not always been an instrument of human liberation; and during a number of periods of history it has been a major obstacle to human betterment. But a theory which can be used to justify a social policy as well as its contrary is not a reliable instrument for evaluating proposed social changes.

For these reasons, among others, the assumption that men are natively endowed with various human rights seems to me an unsatisfactory basis for justifying claims to any specific freedoms or benefits. Such a justification requires the establishment of two theses: the first is that there are indeed human rights, and the other is that the specific immunity or benefit in question *is* such a right. However, neither of them has yet been supported by considerations that carry general conviction; and in my opinion, proposed justifications of claims to freedoms and benefits *via* a theory of inherent human rights are bound to remain indecisive and controversial.

The criticisms of the doctrine of natural rights that I have outlined are quite familiar, and they have been effective in undermining its one-time plausibility. But despite the difficulties to which those criticisms call attention, the doctrine has been repeatedly revived during the present century, sometimes in response to the barbarities committed by totalitarian societies of our day. In this revival the notion of what is a human right has been often considerably extended to cover much more than was denoted traditionally by the phrase "human right" — for example, to include such matters as receiving proper nourishment and higher education. In my opinion, however, the revival has not been accompanied by a better grounding for the doctrine of human rights than it has received in earlier centuries.

Let me add that I am aware of the fact that some contemporary thinkers profess a conception of human rights according to which those rights are not created by society, but have a "variable content" and are not absolute or imprescriptible. However, they have not made clear just what is connoted by the term *right* when an alleged right is not a social product, how the claim that there are such human rights is established, or how conflicting claims concerning them are to be resolved. There are also writers who reject most if not all the traditional meanings of the phrase *human rights* but who nevertheless insist on retaining the *language* of human rights. They *reinterpret* the phrase to signify morally justified *proposals* to continue certain social policies, or to adopt specified social policies if they are not already in existence, in order to satisfy some alleged human needs. However, to assign this sense to the phrase is to fill old bottles with wine not described by their familiar labels. The suggested reinterpretation is comparable to retaining the *word* "God" but using it in a manner incompatible with long-entrenched connotations of the term. I must confess that I see little merit in either maneuver.

I am therefore unable to subscribe to the doctrine of human rights as a way of justifying various individual liberties and positive privileges demanded by individuals. The *sole* justification, stated in general terms, I have been able to find for maintaining or extending individual human freedoms consists of the evaluation of the *consequences for human beings* that result from the existence of those freedoms. My defense of those freedoms is therefore utilitarian in a broad sense—perhaps consequentialist would be a better description of my position—but does not involve the assumption that the measure of utility is the pleasure produced or would likely be produced. Moreover, although my defense is in important respects like the one John Stuart Mill gave for various human liberties, it is unlike the latter in that I do not believe a set of personal liberties can be circumscribed that are inviolable and cannot rightly be limited or taken away by society under any circumstances. Finally, my justification is empirical and tentative: for the consequences of any proposed social change cannot be ascertained a priori, and statements about what those consequences are or are likely to be may have to be revised—either because of some error or oversight in reporting what those consequences are, or because unforeseen and unobserved modifications of the social fabric may nullify the expected consequences of deliberately instituted changes. My argument for a society in which the people generally possess a variety of personal freedoms is that in societies in which reliable knowledge of nature's ways, as well as of the ways of human beings, is indispensable for satisfying the needs and aspirations of the people, freedom to inquire and to engage in critical evaluation of the conduct and outcome of inquiry is a condition for acquiring such knowledge.

A large quantity of factual data, obtained from comparative studies of societies of both the past and the present, supports this contention. I shall discuss here only one serious objection to my thesis. It has frequently been noted that the natural sciences have often flourished in societies in which freedom of speech and other individual liberties did not exist for their citizens in general but were at best available only to a small minority. It has been concluded from this that those freedoms are not essential for a thriving science. However, two points should be noted. In the first place, while various branches of natural science have indeed advanced in societies in which freedom of speech was severely restricted, there is compelling evidence to show that *on matters related to their inquiries* scientists were in fact at liberty to communicate their views to other students of the subject. But there is also considerable evidence to show that in societies in which scientists lacked such freedom — as was the case in the Soviet Union during the Lysenko period in genetics — their disciplines rapidly deteriorated. It seems that Soviet authorities have learned the value of freedom in pursuing inquiries in the natural sciences.

The second point to be noted is that though freedom of inquiry in the natural sciences is quite compatible with the absence of such freedom in the study of political, economic, and social questions, there is evidence to support the claim that when the latter is the case the attainment of reliable knowledge in those domains is seriously hampered. Accordingly, on the assumption that a society should augment its knowledge of matters that are potentially significant for increasing the material and spiritual welfare of its members, the case for freedom of inquiry and all that goes with it seems to me fairly well established as being a *necessary* though not a sufficient condition for the acquisition of reliable knowledge.

I do not believe that, if the word *civilization* is used as anthropologists tend to use it — in a morally neutral way, so that it has no honorific associations — the idea of civilized society can be equated with the existence of institutionalized individual freedoms. On the other hand, *if* a major objective of civilized societies is postulated to be the realization of the potentialities of their citizens and the enrichment thereby of their satisfactions, and *if* that objective is best attained through the systematic application of reliable knowledge, the maintenance and the extension of individual freedoms are indispensable for realizing a central aim of those societies. Those freedoms are both the instruments for achieving a high civilization and evidence of its existence.

ERNEST VAN DEN HAAG

Natural Law

I have never formally studied with Sidney Hook, yet I have learned from him as much as any student can hope to learn from his teacher. Perhaps I should say Sidney Hook has taught me as much as any teacher can; he should not be held responsible for what I learned, and above all, for what I did not learn.

I met Sidney when I had barely started to shed the left utopian blinkers I arrived with in New York. Sidney (abetted by our mutual friend Abba Lerner) greatly hastened the process by acquainting me with facts and ideas to which I had turned a blind eye. My improved vision I owe to him. I shall never forget Sidney's sensitive understanding and warmth that did so much to foster the delicate psychological and intellectual process. We remained friends and I have continued to learn from Sidney, though still not necessarily what he sought to teach me. I became a conservative in culture and politics, whereas Sidney remained a socialist. His heart is even more generous than his mind.

Readers will discern Sidney's influence, which so suffuses the following essay that I have not been able to track it down instance by instance. I am delighted to acknowledge it, though, lacking *mens rea,* Sidney is not responsible for anything I wrote.

I   History

Nature as Power

Many eminent scholars have investigated the history of "natural law" and of its offspring, "natural rights." I intend merely to sketch a rough background for the argument to follow and do not expect to make a contribution to the historiography of these ideas.

Custom arises from history, tradition, and function. In early times, especially,

much of what had been customary for a long time was regarded as "natural."
It is this pseudo-derivation that originally may have given rise to the notion of
"natural law." Explicitly legislated positive law, when it came into existence,
was thought to articulate, apply, extend, and help enforce nature's law, where
nature neglected to do so. If inconsistent with what was regarded as "natural
law," i.e., ancient custom, positive law was thought incorrect, and invalid.[1]

To allow the law of nature (and finally of its God) to be broken by the
impious with impunity was thought to risk provoking nature's own sanctions
(or divine wrath), which might harm the whole community that included an
unpunished wrongdoer.[2] Thus it was believed that legal punishment of offenders against natural law, whether they offended knowingly or not, would be
preemptive; and by punishing solely the actual offenders, legal punishment
would be economical as well.[3]

Nature as Moral Law Giver

Neither custom nor the law of nature originally had a distinctly moral content.
Both were observed (in both senses) because they were believed to be backed
by natural (later supernatural) power, itself scarcely distinguished from morality. When morality became differentiated from natural power, "natural law"
acquired two different senses: (1) description of observed regularities, and
(2) prescription for human conduct. Unlike the former, the latter was vindicated by morality itself, by God, and by positive law as well.

Ever since "natural law" acquired these two meanings, philosophers have
tried to explore the link between them. Their views have ranged widely. Some
find identity between the two senses of natural law, or a relationship in which
natural law is a necessary and/or sufficient cause of moral law and totally
determines it. Others find a loose limitation of the moral dimension, or some
influence on it, by the natural law, or find that at least some moral rules are
determined by nature. Still others, such as the Platonic Protagoras, or David
Hume, find no prescriptive determination of moral rules by natural law, or by
human nature. They believe that nature at most determines the limits, the setting, of moral problems by limiting possible human action, since "ought"
implies "can," or, as the jurists have it, *ultra posse nemo obligatur*. But "can"
does not imply "should." Nature only determines what we can do, not what we
ought to do: individuals and societies must make their own moral rules to narrow the wide range of possibilities nature presents us with, to decide how,
whether, or which of the possibilities it offers should be used. Only the impossible is "unnatural"—and we obviously need not bother about it. The same
range of opinion is found whether natural laws or natural rights are at issue.

Purpose

Men often have conscious purposes even in their spontaneous actions.[4] We
incline to ascribe purposes to others as well. Finally we tend to explain observed

regularities in nature by attributing purposes to it. Thus we projectively tend to impute motives and designs to the effects and correlations we actually observe. If the things observed are nonrational, or inanimate, purpose may be ascribed to anthropomorphic spirits thought to animate them; or things are thought to be designed in order to fulfill inherent purposes. Ultimately everything may be believed to be part of a design imputed to nature, or to its creator, just as our own creations usually are designed for some purpose. Anthropomorphic projection thus leads us to conflate function and purpose so that effects are seen as telic or dystelic, conforming to natural law (purpose) or not, and rarely as merely ecbatic. Telic behavior, behavior according to natural law, is thought to be nature's command, which we are bound to obey, lest nature be offended and we be offenders.

Universality

That much is held in common by religions ranging from animism to secular humanism. Although there are numerous variations on the tune, there is a common belief that the moral rules stemming from natural law are nonarbitrary, invariable, binding, and universal. They are ordained, or, at least, justified by some prescriptive authority, nature, God, or reason itself, and not impelled merely by the individual or collective interest or will.[5] Moral rules are thought to be in the nature of things so that the rules could not be different and correct. Natural law philosophers differ on whether reason merely discovers, or endogenously produces, natural moral laws and, in the former case, on whether the moral laws are due to an exogenous creator. But this difference becomes relevant only once prescriptive natural law is accepted.

From Antiquity to the Twentieth Century

Zeno of Citium is commonly believed to have first articulated the notion of natural law in the mandatory prescriptive sense. His Stoic followers came near to identifying natural law and reason. The Roman lawyers inherited the idea, found explicitly in Cicero. Natural law was summarized by Domitius Ulpianus: *honeste vive; neminem laede; suum cuique tribue*: do not cheat; do not harm anyone gratuitously; do not take from another (or, do give to each) what he is entitled to.[6]

The notion of natural law was taken over from the Romans by the church fathers and schoolmen. Thomas Aquinas held that natural law binds all persons, since it is recognized by the light of reason alone, in contrast to divine law, which binds only the faithful to whom it has been revealed. To this day proponents of natural rights, such as Alan Gewirth and Ronald Dworkin, think these rights are morally binding on all, inherent in things, and recognized by *recta ratio*, usually their own. In modern times various pseudonyms for natural law or natural rights are used (such as moral rights or human rights) but their true identity, although obscured, is scarcely disguised.

In the seventeenth century, most of the explicitly metaphysical and teleological baggage of natural law began to be thrown overboard. Yet the conflation of the descriptive with the prescriptive remained. The changes made by Hugo Grotius, or John Locke, seem largely cosmetic. Despite a brave and immensely productive try, I do not think that even Immanuel Kant managed to overcome the hurdles to which David Hume had drawn attention, although he perhaps most radically replaced nature with inherent and a priori reason, its categories and imperatives.[7]

Attempts to derive morality and rights from nature have not ceased. The moral norms attributed to nature vary, but the difficulties of derivation remain. Natural law as moral mandate continues to be conflated with necessary conditions (observed regularities) of human and social existence.

Thus H. L. A. Hart's half-hearted attempt to establish "The Minimum Content of Natural Law" would be beside the point, had it succeeded, since Hart merely undertook to point out the rules he thought indispensable to social living, without explaining why these rules ought to (not do or may) become prescriptions and why the prescriptions ought to be accepted as morally binding.[8]

Indispensability of means surely cannot be equated with moral obligation unless the end they serve is shown to be morally obligatory. If correct, Hart's view that "there are certain rules of conduct which any social organization must contain if it is to be viable" does not show why these rules are *eo ipso* morally binding. Would social survival be morally obligatory if it required morally repugnant means such as cannibalism? Why is the rational interest in survival, if it exists, a morally binding natural law at all? From Hart's reasoning a moral obligation to eat, or to bear children, could be inferred, indeed an obligation to engage in any human behavior needed for social survival. (In Kantian terms Hart, at most, states hypothetical imperatives where categorical ones are wanted; their alleged universality is contingent as well.)

As Ronald Dworkin points out in *Taking Rights Seriously,*[9] John Rawls too implies natural rights, if not natural law, although his method of discovering them obscures the implication. Rawls derives his rules of justice from people's (presumed) choices in an experimental situation. But he does not explain why these choices should be morally binding or even why they reflect "justice."[10] His insistence that the choices are rational does not help, since his risk-aversive rationality is not the only one available. However, Rawls contends that the choices dictated by reason lead to justice, as a moral concept, rather than to viability, wherefore they are at least morally relevant, as Hart's are not.

Robert Nozick's notion of justice is an extended gloss on Ulpian's *suum cuique tribue* although he might as well have taken his cue from John Locke's "The law of nature . . . obliges everyone; and reason . . . teaches . . . that no one ought to harm another in his life, health, liberty or possessions." One would not want to disagree with any of these rules. It is their meaning, their derivation, and their epistemological status that is the problem. The trouble with Nozick, in particular, is that the validity of title to possessions, and of the obligation to regard it as morally binding, can be readily questioned by redistributionists, unless one holds strong opinions on nature's title granting authority, and on its presumed use of it. Nozick apparently does, although he is not telling why.[11]

II Some Characteristics

Natural Rights

Rights always being creatures of law, natural rights are the offspring of natural law. Natural rights are thought to express the nature of our human nature, more perhaps than that of the universe, but also the will of nature or of nature's God, or to be inherent in universal reason and morality; they are thought to obligate us more than positive law can on these grounds, though how much more is controversial. Legitimate or not, natural rights proved highly philoprogenitive, endowing us, and lately it seems other creatures as well, with indefinite "human" or "moral rights" — to whatever we need or want — which positive law is supposed to accommodate and not to override. Usually little is said about how, and at whose expense, society is to accommodate the steadily proliferating human rights. We are not told either why society is bereft of a natural right to override the natural rights of individuals, although early natural law theories insisted on no less even before Hobbes.

Whereas natural law often was used to justify the existing order against individual dissenters, natural rights came to be used largely by individuals against the community and its ruler. To paraphrase Leo Strauss, "natural law" suggests the duties of individuals, the claims of the whole, of society (or of morality) against the parts, whereas "natural rights" suggest the claims of the parts against the whole, of individuals against society. Moreover, law, including natural law, tells what one must or must not do; whereas rights, including natural rights, tell what one may do and what *others* must or must not do. Natural rights gained currency as individualism did. Different origins of natural law and of natural rights were duly discovered. But this matter will not be pursued here.

Reason, Natural Law, and Natural Rights

Hugo Grotius said clearly, as William of Ockham[12] did before him, that "the law of nature is a dictate of reason," and "unchangeable . . . so that God . . . cannot cause that that which is intrinsically evil be not evil,"[13] i.e., Grotius thought natural laws to be objective, universal, intrinsic, and unchanging, as he thought the laws of mathematics to be. They are not the dictates of God, but of reason (which God endowed us with). Cicero[14] thought that "right reason" which is a "true law" is "unchangeable and eternal, binding at all times on all men."[15]

Natural rights are alleged to have as objective a source as natural law does. They are rights derived from human nature and independent of, prior to, positive (legislated) law, which ought to articulate them and which according to Ronald Dworkin[16] may be superseded by natural rights where it is inconsistent with them. "Moral rights" do not seem to differ much from "natural rights," at least in Dworkin or Gewirth. Both derive from our nature and are more authoritative than the will of legislators. Both can be demonstrated to be correct by reason and are therefore binding on all rational beings. Both are deontological and differ from consequentialist calculations, or axioms derived merely from intuition. There is no doubt in the mind of proponents of natural rights that "all men," in Jefferson's phrase, "are endowed by their creator with certain inalienable rights," which are universal ("all men") and independent of positive law ("inalienable").

Duties and Rights

Natural rights imply at least one duty: everyone must respect them and refrain from interfering with them. Duties are not necessarily reciprocal. Humans may have the moral duty to refrain from gratuitous cruelty[17] to animals, but animals have no duty not to be cruel to humans. Therefore, they have no rights either. For only members of a class that can recognize the rights of others by *recta ratio* (and respect them at least potentially) can have rights.[18] Thus rights holders may have duties also to those who do not have rights. Duties, then, do not always create rights for those toward whom they are held, although duties imply the right of duty bearers to act in accordance with them. Rights in turn impose at least the duty of noninterference on all those who can reason. Thus, there are no rights without duties (of others), although there are duties without rights of others.

It is sometimes argued that not all rights impose duties. A prisoner of war is said to have a right to escape, but his guards obviously do not have a duty not to interfere. However, this does not refute my contention that there are no rights without duties of others.

1. Fellow prisoners, rather than guards, have a duty not to interfere with the escape. Thus the right of the prisoners implies a duty of noninterference by some others, though not by guards. More important, guards and prisoners owe allegiance to different governments. Their government imposes the duty on prisoners to try to escape. Their "right" is but a recognition by others of the duty the prisoners owe their government. (Criminal prisoners have no such duty and no such right.) In turn, the government that employs them imposes the duty not to let the prisoners escape on the guards, wherefrom flows their

right to interfere with the rights of the prisoners. If each wants to respect the other's allegiance and the rights and duties flowing therefrom, each must concede the other's right to respectively escape and hinder escapes — but neither need act according to the right of the other which depends entirely on the other's allegiance. With respect to escape, each side is bound by its own allegiance.

2. The situation would be different if both guards and prisoners had endorsed a universal right to escape (or a universal duty not to). In that case the guards would have a duty not to guard (or prisoners not to escape). But the guards only recognize — as do the prisoners — that the prisoners' government imposes the duty to escape and the guards' government the duty to guard. Both may regard their duties and rights as legitimate and despite the conflict, they are not inconsistent, if we assume that allegiances to different sovereigns are legitimate. That assumption is made by international law.[19]

Imprescriptibility

The notion of universal and eternal natural law and of rights based on reason and on nature is unclear in a number of ways. For instance, there is little agreement on how imprescriptible natural rights are. Thus Ronald Dworkin writes: "Bentham thought that the idea of moral rights was 'nonsense on stilts.'"[20] Since Bentham actually wrote: "natural rights is simple nonsense: natural and imprescriptible rights rhetorical nonsense — nonsense upon stilts" it follows that Dworkin identifies his "moral rights" with Bentham's "natural and imprescriptible rights." But, although Dworkin's "moral rights" are but a trendy pseudonym for natural rights, he qualifies their imprescriptibility by writing, "the government may override [a] right when necessary to protect the rights of others, or to prevent a catastrophe, or even to obtain a clear and major public benefit" (p. 191). (The latter only "if the right in question [is] not fundamental.") Thus, according to Bentham, Dworkin's view is "nonsense" but not "upon stilts," contrary to what Dworkin suspects.

Yet, Dworkin also writes that a right cannot be overridden merely because overriding it "is likely to produce overall a benefit to the community" (p. 192). These qualifications do not help clarify the status of moral rights; indeed they leave the strength, even the meaning, of "moral right" vague. Dworkin's own, "if someone has a right to something then it is wrong for the government to deny it to him even though it would be in the general interest to do so" (p. 169), sounds good but does not help.[21] Wherever anyone's right, that entitles him to anything, comes from, it would always be wrong to impinge on it without good reason. That much is implied in the definition of "right" and is independent of any qualification of the right as legal, moral, natural, or whatever. The positive law stipulates reasons sufficient to override the rights it grants on occasion. Dworkin's theory simply tells us that the reasons for overriding his "fundamental" moral rights must be important. But how important? What kind of reasons? The mumblings about preventing a catastrophe or obtaining "a clear and major public benefit" imply no more than that some community interests sometimes have precedence over some individual moral (a.k.a. natural) rights. Since the attempt to make the individual's interest in his life, liberty, or whatever, into an absolute imprescriptible right must fail, as Dworkin himself implies, we are left with an interest normally to be protected by the community as a right and sometimes to be sacrificed to its interests or rights. This is where we would be under all conceivable circumstances as long as legal rights or even interests of any kind are recognized. Dworkin may have outsmarted himself here; which wasn't that hard after all.

III   The Basic Difficulty

Necessary Conditions and Moral Imperatives

The notion of natural law as moral prescription arises from an identification, or conflation, or, sometimes, from a confusion, of conditions deemed necessary for human or social existence with moral prescriptions for it. While for some philosophers these conditions are *sine qua non* indispensable to human existence, for others they need only be distinctive of the human species; or of a desirable existence; or, in a more or less unavoidable way, inherent in human nature. The conditions, or at least the prescriptions derived from them, may also be ascribed to "reason." The epistemological status of natural, moral, or human rights is quite similar.

Now, there are indeed some universally indispensable conditions for human existence (such as the presence of oxygen); and for social existence; and, not least, for appealing or civilized existence. Some of these conditions are inherent in the nature of nature, or in our own nature, as we know it, at least to a large degree.[22] Some are environmental; and some refer to our own conduct.

But, from a correct observation, such as 'if we defy the law of gravitation, or do not eat food, or stay permanently drunk, we will not survive long,' a moral, as distinguished from a prudential, conclusion cannot be drawn. Moral conclusions require moral premises.[23] Here the moral premise, if any, seems to be: *vivere necesse est,* i.e., we have a moral obligation to preserve ourselves by following (descriptive) natural law. Nature somehow is vested with moral authority and assumed to use it to command us to survive. Yet its power cannot give nature moral authority. Power, including natural power, only yields prudential, not moral, norms. Nor does nature evince a desire for our survival or extinction. Nature neither desires nor prescribes. It only makes things possible. If nature did have desires or purposes, it still would lack the authority to obligate us. I cannot see how any moral norm can be imputed to it, or to any alleged factual condition.

If we do desire to survive, and require certain conditions, would the survival and the conditions necessary to it become morally obligatory so as to bind us all? Only if the desire to survive is morally obligatory more than a shared interest. But neither nature nor reason can make it so.[24] To be sure, if we want to associate fruitfully with one another, such dicta such as, e.g., (1) *pacta sunt servanda,* and (2) *neminem laede,* must be observed. But for entirely prudential reasons.

1. Promises, by definition, declare actual intentions and contract obligations about the future. If we refuse to promise we refuse to commit ourselves to the future. If we do not intend to act as promised, we make pseudo-promises (which become incredible).[25] If promises are not made, or kept, we suffer inconveniences that promise making and keeping avoid. Yet the morality of promise keeping does not follow from this prudential consideration, unless we add that that which makes life easier is morally good and therefore binding or is prescribed by nature, and therefore binding. There is no warrant for this addition.[26]

Finally, one may contend that the moral and the prudential are identical. Consequentialists certainly can do so. So can those who believe that there are no moral rights, or norms, not reducible to interests; and that interests are not morally binding unless we (not nature) first have made them so; and that they are epistemologically arbitrary, i.e., that they could be different. However, proponents of natural law cannot argue that the prudential and the moral are identical unless natural law is emptied of customary and, indeed, of any distinctive meaning.

2. People could not associate unless they feel reasonably secure in their lives. Hence only those associations continue where some degree of security is provided. Which makes *neminem laede* desirable, but not a moral precept derived from nature; rather a common interest.

Whether one says 'the human condition prescribes what is necessary, or helpful, to human (or social) existence' or prefers to say 'nature presents us with conditions for human or social survival' is a matter of indifference if we are aware that we are considering prudential matters. Yet we are reluctant to accept as much. We long to hear a voice telling us that our moral decision are inspired, even dictated, by moral rules and standards that transcend our interests and are prior to and independent of them. The wish to hear this voice, the voice of the father, must not be confused with its fulfillment.[27]

God

Some find the ultimate source of moral authority in God, directly, or through some quality, such as reason, He endowed us with. But belief in a superhuman authority would not help in our discussion for two reasons. First, belief in God requires faith. But our discussion is confined to argument independent of faith, which, by definition, is not ultimately proved by, or subject to, argument.[28] Incidentally, if we rely on faith, why should it not be available for the moral standards themselves? However, if moral standards are to be validated by faith, we foreclose the very discussion we are engaged in: we need not ask whether there is anything—such as natural law—other than faith, on which moral norms can be shown to be based.

Second, faith in God merely postpones meeting the problems of the kind we are concerned with. God may transcend these problems psychologically, but not philosophically. God may directly or indirectly dictate binding moral norms; but the existence of God, however much one believes in Him, poses questions about His authority, our submission to His will, and His morality. Faith in God does not answer these questions without a second *saltus fidei,* required to achieve faith in the sufficiency of the *mysterium tremendum.* Attractive and admirable as these leaps are, they do not answer, but merely supersede, or dismiss philosophical questions. The philosophical rule is that the Gordian knot is not to be cut. It must be unraveled.

Reason

The attempt to demonstrate that reason validates moral norms, or requires the granting of moral rights, often universalizes some necessary condition of human action, which, from a necessary good, is then promoted to become a generic right. Since it is necessary to him, the agent claims that the good ought not to be interfered with by others. They must be granted the same right; and, presto, we have a human right granted by nature and reason. Alan Gewirth elaborates at great and often instructive lengths on this.[29] But a natural or necessary condition of human agency, such as the one which, according to Gewirth, we are required to grant as a universal right, on pain of inconsistency, does not become a human right even when implicitly needed and claimed by everyone. A universally shared interest does not, *ipso facto,* become a morally binding right.

There is no reason why a person who has not received Professor Gewirth's instruction should claim that his interest, however indispensable, is a right and universalize it. If he did there is no reason why his claim makes what he claims a right. But he may be satisfied anyway to promote what he wants or must want as a shared interest that is not morally binding. He may also perceive his interest as conflicting with that of others. He may wish to interfere with their interest and may not grant them the right that according to Gewirth he must grant. Would such an agent's actions be incoherent? No, only the propositions Gewirth has put in his mouth would become inconsistent. The agent may actually see his interest in conflict with similar interests of others.[30] Gewirth insists on representing these interests in propositions, which, if the interests conflict, become inconsistent. He thereupon expects the agents to act so that he can represent the actions by a set of consistent propositions. An unreasonable demand: the actors have no reason to accept Gewirth's propositions and to transform their interests into rights. If they do protect their interests by granting rights in positive law, they do so for prudential reasons and are not required to do so by logic or morality. It is not necessary in the individual interest of agents to grant to everyone the right to be free from interference with his freedom.

Even if the agents followed Gewirth, he would have persuaded them, at most, to recognize a universally shared prudential interest in noninterference; not to grant, or claim, a morally binding right.[31] Propositional formulations of interests cannot transform them into human rights.

Kant

Before Kant, the main role of reason was to discover nature's prescriptions. After Kant, reason itself often does the prescribing. Reason is thought of as part of human nature, inherent, permanent, universal, and objective. So therefore are its prescriptions. However, Kantian prescriptions usually are less eudaemonistic than Aristotelian or Thomistic prescriptions, since Kant defined moral virtue largely as the motive for restraining one's nonmoral desires. In this definition of morality, Kant was seconded by Hume before and by Freud afterwards. Post-Kantian prescriptions once more tend to become eudaemonistic.

Kant's attempt to rest morality on reason alone deserves more comment than I can give it in a paper on natural law. Kant's "reason" does not suppose a prescriptive natural law.[32] Nor does he identify prudential interests with rights. Kant identifies the moral and the rational. The categorical imperative is a dictate of neither nature nor prudence but of rationality. However, I do not believe that universalizability can take the place that natural law had to vacate; nor indeed does it constitute a meaningful moral rule, except in a heuristic sense.

The categorical imperative, *qua* categorical, has no content and ceases to be categorical when it is given a content. It tells us not to do what we would not universalize. To begin with, this is a very unrestrictive restriction — after all, different people might universalize different rules. To wit: Abortion should (not) be permitted, prisoners of war should (not) be killed, murderers should (not) be executed, the rich should (not) be compelled to support the poor, etc.[33] We are given no criteria to choose among universalized preferences.

More important, the requirement of universalizability only appears to rule out anything. Actually, nothing is ruled out. I may defend murder by saying, "Anybody being named Ernest van den Haag may, or even should, kill everybody with a different name," a universal maxim. This may sound frivolous. But for "being named Ernest van den Haag" one can readily substitute "being German," "being poor" or any other characteristic.

I suspect that one could stipulate some restriction to the Kantian rule to prevent such use, but I don't know any that would satisfy the Kantian criterion of being derived from rationality and required by it. Thus the Kantian imperative does not really discriminate between the morally permissible and the forbidden. But it was a brave and enormously productive try — possibly the only one that came near justifying, though not producing, a cognitivist ethic.[34]

IV   Contents and Effects

A Historical Note

So far I have been concerned with the derivation of natural law and with its epistemological status. Let me turn now to its content and ask: (1) Would natural law be a safer basis for desiderata, such as liberty, than the alternatives? (2) Are there predictable social differences dependent on whether or not one accepts natural law as the basis for positive law and for human rights? (I assume a reasonably traditional content of natural law.)

In the past, moral authority came from God, through Scripture, interpreted by churches. As the link with the superhuman became weaker and churches were separated from the state, a more secular moral authority was found in natural law. It was known and accepted before, but it was newly stressed, because it seemed to be the only moral authority left. Religious believers as well as nonbelievers feared living in a society shorn of perceived objective moral authority. They feared that positive law would rule supreme and be dissociated from any morality prior to it. The positive law itself might not be morally binding but only prudentially so. Malevolent tyrants or mobs might be in charge of making positive laws. There would be no appeal against it and no restraint on it. Bereft of divine guidance and of natural law, society might return to some of the cruelties attributed to pre-Christian Roman emperors.

Whether justified or not, fear or need cannot logically produce or validate natural law, or the objective moral authority craved. Needs, however dire, unfortunately do not produce whatever is needed.[35] But the assumption of such a need legitimizes the question we must turn to: Is the absence of natural law as calamitous as assumed by its proponents? Are the social consequences of the absence as undesirable as alleged? This is an empirical question.

Surely the presence of natural law, even when it was generally recognized as moral authority, throughout the middle ages and up to the nineteenth century, cannot be said to have done much for individual freedom. Natural law did not protect liberty from the tyranny of rulers, or of revolutionaries, even when both recognized it. The Roman Catholic church did. So did the medieval rulers. So did the Reformation. So did the French revolution. Individual freedom did not gain from this recognition.

Now, defenders of natural law may suggest that the versions that led to, or justified, undesirable actions were incorrect. Quite possibly they were and natural law cannot be blamed. One may also suggest that, in the instances at issue, correct natural law, although known, was violated. If we grant the cogency of these defenses we are still confronted with the fact that the general acceptance and philosophical justification of natural law did not prevent the undesirable events that its defenders now tell us natural law, and natural law alone, can prevent.

In more recent times, the totalitarian dictatorship of the Nazis and the continuing totalitarian dictatorship of the communists were not, and are not, based on what proponents of natural law often call "relativism." Both dictatorships were and are based on what Sir Karl Popper calls essentialism—a view indicating that there are inherent values that are morally binding and objective and demonstrated. The Nazis found these inherent values largely in pseudobiological speculations. Marxists find these values in pseudohistorical speculations. The Nazis felt they were commanded by biology, to which they ascribed final moral authority, to do what they did. The Marxists feel charged by history, to which they ascribe final moral authority, to suppress individual freedom and to commit the outrages they still commit.[36]

Thus objective value structures, firmly believed in, need not be helpful to individual freedom. To be sure, the objective value structure of natural law is quite different from the Nazi or communist system. Nonetheless, belief in natural law did not vouchsafe individual freedom either. At times it served to defend freedom, at other times to help suppress it. Its social effects are not predictable. They cannot be, for the actual content of natural law is discovered by reason to be different in each historical period, tradition merely accompanying reason as an *obligato*.

Benefits

This is not to deny the psychological benefits belief in natural law, or any objective morality, may bestow. However, they are philosophically irrelevant; and the social effects seem unpredictable. Still I believe that it is unlikely to be socially advantageous to teach that morality is but a matter of taste, nor has this ever been done until now.

There have been major civilizations with considerable achievement but without belief in objective value systems recognized or justified by philosophers. In the contemporary world there are moral persons who do not believe in a cognitivist system of ethics, and there are immoral persons (by commonly accepted standards) who do.

Belief in the worthwhileness of an end—be it playing tennis, making movies, writing novels, exploring physics, winning wars, or bringing up children—a belief that is needed for achievement, seems but questionably linked to the presence (or absence) of the convictions of philosophers and intellectuals about objectively demonstrable values. Nor can the behavior of nations and individuals be shown to be determined by the presence or absence or diffusion of such doctrines.

The link between the psychology of achievement—or on the other hand of hedonism in the demoralizing sense—and belief in cognitivist ethics intellectually held has not been sufficiently explored. Thus the link between morality, morale, or demoralization, and the intellectual justification of moral standards of conduct remains obscure. Still it is entirely possible that we may now live on the capital of the past. Whatever may be said about non- or pre-Christian societies may not be true for a post-Christian one, which may have become too individualistic to produce a shared value consensus.

Under the circumstances, we may be well advised to keep what belief there is left in objective values if only for prudential reasons of great psychological and social import — though of no philosophical relevance. Certainly the institutions that cultivate such beliefs should not be weakened by the government.[37]

Alternatives

1. *Relativism.* Proponents of natural law are most disturbed by the presumed effects of nondeontological alternatives such as "relativism," "utilitarianism," and "consequentialism." The meaning of most of these alternatives, as it appears to believers in natural law, is not altogether clear. Still, let me try.

I am not a "relativist." I believe that the distance between New York and Los Angeles is greater than the distance between New York and Chicago — a relative statement that I can demonstrate to be true. I also feel, though I cannot demonstrate it, that some values are better than others — also a relative statement. Surely "relativism" must mean more than acceptance of these statements; but I am not sure what it does mean.[38] Do relativists believe that values are always subjective, never in any sense objective? If so, I don't know why they would. If values cannot be objectively demonstrated; if they follow from undemonstrable axioms, values still may be objective. From nondemonstrability only nondemonstrability follows, not that that which cannot be demonstrated is not objective even though it cannot be shown to be. That which can be demonstrated exists; it does not follow that that which cannot be demonstrated does not.[39]

Do relativists believe that the values of any culture are as good as those of any other? Or that there cannot be any intercultural values? Or comparisons? If they believe that the superiority of any value, or culture, over any other cannot be demonstrated, they imply that the equality of the two cannot be demonstrated either. Intercultural equality itself may be promoted to function as a metaphysical axiom. But it would be as undemonstrable as intercultural inequality and considerably less reasonable. If we lack intercultural measurement we do not know whether any culture is equal to any other. But the alleged impossibility of intercultural comparisons is, at best, an odd anthropological proposition of no philosophical relevance. Philosophies can be compared, and values, whether or not demonstrated as true, can be compared and preferred, even if the preference cannot be easily demonstrated to be correct.[40]

2. *Utilitarianism.* I am not a utilitarian, because I do not believe that the principle of utility, or the maximization of aggregate happiness, however distributed, is, or ought to be, the only principle of human action; nor that this principle is inherent in us, and/or somehow morally binding. Yet all of us are utilitarians up to a point. We differ only on where that point is. (See sections V and VI.)

As for governments, I am more interested in liberty, freedom from interference in the pursuit of my ends, than in any government attempt to help me succeed in that pursuit by restricting my freedom to pursue by the means I choose, or my freedom to select ends. Utilitarians, however, are interested in liberty only if it enhances, or coincides, with happiness, which it need not do.[41]

As an analytical proposition, the principle of utility seems unhelpful by simply defining action as that which attempts to maximize happiness. As an empirical proposition, it seems wrong until it becomes analytical once more. Incidentally, what actually makes individuals happy usually is the achievement, or, better, progress toward the achievement, of their ends whether known or unknown to them.[42] However, once they go beyond biological minima, ends are largely determined by ideas prevalent in the society in which we live. Wherefore the principle of happiness maximization, by telling us that society should have as its end the maximization of the happiness of individuals, can scarcely help us decide what ends society should adopt. Ends are not biologically determined, but, where it matters, they are socially determined. The end of "happiness," were it accepted, would not help to determine them.

Even if we had solved all of the problems alluded to, even if we knew what it means to maximize happiness (surely not a homogeneous quantity readily aggregated), utilitarians, crypto-analytical propositions aside, have not demonstrated that we must. Where does the moral obligation to maximize happiness come from? Surely it cannot come from the alleged fact that we try to.

3. *Consequentialism.* Consequentialism to me means to give up, or suspend, the invention of objective or inherent natural moral laws and rights, and to confine oneself to understanding and relating long- and short-term interests.

I am aware that consequentialism can take us only part of the way and does not help us much to make decisions in many situations. Consequentialism does not tell us how to evaluate the consequences it views as decisive. In practice, consequentialists usually are utilitarians, or crypto-utilitarians. But I'm not ready to commit myself to any general principle beyond consequentialism, because I do not know how to justify it.[43]

Consequentialists believe that interests thought to be important, as a matter of prudence and protection, may be made into positive rights and laws. Positive rights and laws may be suspended, or changed ad hoc, in the light of consequences found desirable. The practical effects of consequentialism may, I believe, come into conflict with some of our prima facie moral intuitions, as well as with natural law and rights theories.[44] The time has come to consider these conflicts.

V   Antinomies

Should We Be Unjust to Individuals?

Conflicts arise if we take seriously the view of some philosophers that private citizens, let alone courts of law, can never be justified in being unjust to individuals. Thus Charles Fried writes "we must do no wrong," even if we could reduce suffering thereby, or prevent greater wrongdoing by others.[45] Ronald Dworkin too asserts the moral priority of individual rights over social interests.[46] These views follow Kant and are shared by most deontologists.

To assert the right or even the moral duty to be unjust to individuals in certain circumstances, as I shall do, one must believe the known consequences of an act, or of an omission, or of a rule, more decisive than the intrinsic moral quality, or justice, of the act *in se*. I share utilitarian views sufficiently to be willing, in some situations, to sacrifice what is right, or just, to the maximization of the good, or to the minimization of wrongs. I thus reject the notion of indefeasible rights.[47]

The Positive Law

The positive law sides with Professor Fried and the Kantians, although not altogether consistently. Thus, the law allows everyone to keep what he's entitled to, however great the need of other persons. There are some exceptions, mainly when the perceived need is communal: we have eminent domain and redistributive tax powers. But no one may be compelled to give his food, let alone his blood, to another person to whom he is not obligated by specific law or contract, even if he could do so without much inconvenience, whereas the individual in need might die without. It may be that transfusions, or transplants, are still so new that the law has not quite caught up with the possibilities opened by science. On the other hand, I shall argue (VI) that every person ought to continue to be entitled to his own body, including his blood, and that no one else should be entitled to any part of it — but not as a matter of moral right or principle. Rather, because it would be awkward to have third parties determine when somebody must part with one of his healthy organs to be given to someone who needs it more.

There is no obligation in positive law to protect others from harm not caused by oneself, even by making comparatively minor sacrifices, unless one voluntarily assumed a duty to do so (a policeman does) or that obligation has been specifically imposed by law (it is imposed on a soldier). At most, one has the duty to warn of danger. The law is far from consistent, however. While I am not legally obligated to give my food or blood to anyone in dire need of it, even though I have plenty, I may be drafted and obligated to give my life for my country.

The legal never exhausts the moral. Surely there are circumstances in which, although there is no legal obligation, there is a felt moral obligation to part with some of one's property, if one recognizes almost any set of moral axioms.[48] I shall suggest as well that there are situations in which, for the sake of others, or of the community, private citizens, or courts, are morally justified to use individuals unjustly or, for that matter, illegally.[49] Let me present some cases before arguing them.

The Dilemma

1. A mob insists on lynching an innocent person, and threatens to kill those who protect him, or other innocents, unless he is handed over. Should he be handed to the mob to save more than one innocent life?

2. A tyrant decides to shoot a hundred innocent prisoners. However, he is willing to spare ninety if a bystander will shoot ten; or, if the bystander will shoot ten innocent persons not among the prisoners; or, finally, if ten innocents (among the prisoners or not) are executed upon being convicted by judges of capital crimes they did not commit.

The lynching case is familiar; the case of the tyrant and of the judges is similar to occurrences in Nazi-occupied Europe. To yield to the tyrant (or to the mob) is unjust to the individuals sacrificed. Can that injustice, that overriding of the basic interests of the individuals concerned, be justified? Let me dispose first of some irrelevant but influential points.

Irrelevant Matters

Authorities who yield to threats and order, or allow, the killing of innocents to save others may be motivated by indifference to those to be killed rather than by concern for those to be saved. Or, commanders may fear that they would suffer personally if they defy the threats of mobs or of tyrants; and commanders or judges may hope to gain personally if they yield. Thus, authorities may act out of selfishness, cowardice, or ambition, and not out of concern for the welfare of others. Perhaps that is why commanders who yield to monstrous demands are usually vilified—however many lives they may save; whereas those who defy such demands become heroes—although their defiance may have cost more lives than it saved. However, the rightness of actions, not the goodness of actors, is at issue here. The character and motives of the actors, however blame- or praise-worthy, are not relevant to the rightness of their actions. The question to be answered is: How should we program a computer if it were to make the decision?

Another point looms large in the psychology of decision-makers, although of doubtful relevance to the rightness or wrongness of their decision. If one actively participates in wrongdoing one appears and feels as an accomplice, even if one participates only to prevent greater wrongs by others. One feels guilty if one surrenders a prisoner to a mob, and more guilty if one actually kills innocents—even if fewer innocents are killed because the prisoner was surrendered to the mob, even if a hundred innocents are spared because one personally killed ten. It is psychologically easier to wash one's hands of the matter, to pretend not to know, or at least not to be responsible for the effects of one's refusal.[50] However, anxiety about personal guilt does not justify refusal to do a wrong if doing the wrong would reduce the total wrong done by others. One's wish to avoid involvement and the ensuing anxiety is scarcely a moral argument.

Legally there is no obligation to shoot the ten—on the contrary, to do so does carry legal risks. There is a legal obligation to protect the prisoner, but it is not absolute. The legal answers obviously do not meet the moral problem. (The law does not envisage the problem.) However, the difference between omission and commission, which is so important in legal reasoning, cannot be altogether irrelevant: morally, too, omissions are properly regarded as less culpable than commissions. Failure to reduce harm by charitable contributions cannot weigh as heavily in the moral balance as would actively producing the same harm.[51] The failure is not intended to produce the harm it does not avoid. One is more responsible for what one does intentionally than for the incidental effects of what one fails to do, even if the harmful effects of incidental omission be greater than those of intentional commission. Yet a deliberate failure to save a hundred persons, at the expense of ten, and of one's own participation in wrongdoing, requires a moral justification: surely one's failure to save a hundred by killing ten is not as wrong as a tyrant's active killing of a hundred. Is it wrong at all? Is the killing of the ten a moral duty?

Prudential Matters

Before further examining the dilemma at issue, consider some prudential reasons for refusing to do a wrong, an injustice to individuals, when it seems to avoid greater harm to others. Often conflated, or even confused, with moral reasons, prudential reasons are certainly relevant to any decision. But they are logically independent of the moral reasoning on which I want to focus—although that moral reasoning may ultimately derive from prudential reasoning of a different, less contingent kind.[52] Here are some prudential justifications of defiance.

1. If defied, the threats of a lynch mob, or of a tyrant, may not be carried out. This prospect by itself may justify taking the risk of defiance, depending on the probability one assigns to the threats being carried out. Thus one may opt for prudential defiance, even if, were it certain that the unjust threat will be carried out, one would comply with the demands made.

2. Yielding to wrongful demands of mobs or tyrants may set a demoralizing precedent. Over a period of time that precedent may cost more lives than were saved when it was set. Wrongful demands and yielding to them may be encouraged, or the community may become demoralized by having yielded to them.[53] This too is a prudential reason for not yielding—one that is readily, but wrongly, conflated with moral reasons.

3. Defying an unjust demand may inspire a more altruistic and noble attitude in the community than caving in would. Defiance may produce a higher degree of social solidarity and long-term benefits that might more than offset the net loss of life caused by the defiance. Valid or not, this too is a prudential argument. A strictly moral argument for defiance along Kantian, or, at any rate, nonconsequentialist lines, must be independent of future benefits; and it

rejects injustice to individuals, regardless of any benefits to others. Defiance as a moral act defies unjust demands for the sake of justice, regardless of other benefits.

I have given no voice to those who would be sacrificed or saved. Given a voice, those to be saved at the expense of others might prefer to perish with them, or those to be sacrificed might volunteer to save the others. The problem of social ethics would dissolve into a series of moral problems for individuals. These problems are not quite analogous, since social morality includes the order of fiduciary obligations to third persons, and the right of the law to compel individuals, as well as the morality of government policies and rules.

It also makes a world of difference whether the persons the bystander is asked to shoot are among the one hundred the tyrant is about to kill—in which case the bystander kills ten doomed persons to save the remaining ninety; or whether he is asked to kill ten previously not doomed persons to save the one hundred prisoners—in which case he must kill ten persons who would have survived were it not for his killing them to save the one hundred who would have been doomed.

Finally, distress is greater if one fails to save, or is asked to kill, persons one knows and cares for, than if one is merely aware that anonymous prisoners are going to be executed because of one's refusal to kill others. Should people one knows count more than people one does not know? To demand that all personal bonds be ignored may be pushing egalitarianism too far. Yet the life of a person does not become more valuable in itself if I know that person, although his life is more valuable to me.

The Consequentialist View Accepted

Historically, the medieval legend of a dragon who requires the annual sacrifice of a virgin to spare the town from destruction appears to indicate the general acceptance of a consequentialist view. The population customarily complied with the dragon's demand. The problem is never reported to have been met by a refusal to offer the virgin as a matter of deontological principle. Her interest in her innocent life simply was valued less than the interest of the community in its survival. Her rights, if any, were ignored. The legendary hero's heroism consisted of killing the dragon, i.e., eliminating the problem. He never met the problem by protecting the virgin from her fellow citizens. The slaying of the dragon certainly was a better solution—but one without philosophical relevance.

Is defiance of a demand for innocent lives justified if the defiance leads to the loss of more innocent lives than compliance would? Or is it better to comply, to permit, or even to commit injustice to some, in order to prevent injustice and harm to more persons? Is the consequentialist rule: 'justice to individuals must sometimes yield to social welfare' correct?[54] Or must we insist on a Kantian rule: 'justice to individuals can never be sacrificed for any social end, including saving the lives of other individuals'? Surely in this form even Dworkin admits the rule won't do.[55] Indeed, the notion of an indefeasible right to innocent life becomes useless in any situation in which the indefeasible right of one — e.g., his right to innocent life — requires the defeat of the indefeasible right of another — his right to his innocent life.

If the bystander confronted by the tyrant refuses to shoot ten innocents, he allows to be condemned to death ninety who would otherwise survive. Similarly the judge who refuses to find ten innocents guilty implicitly allows ninety or a hundred innocents to be executed. Shooting ten innocent people is hard. So is finding them guilty, contrary to one's judicial duty. The judge has no legal grounds to find the innocents guilty, and he violates his judicial duty by yielding to extra-legal pressures to find them guilty. But he is acting under duress, even if the lives at issue do not include his own. The tyrant, not he, is morally responsible for the loss of life. The judge is responsible for saving innocent lives by failing to do his judicial duty, although he also is responsible for dooming some innocents — fewer than he saves.

Prudential objections to compliance are often disguised as moral ones. But if one abstracts from prudential objections, however disguised, and considers only the purely moral question, objections are reduced either to Kantian categorical reasoning,[56] or to an attempt to save one's own soul, regardless of the consequences to others. Yet, if life is valuable, how can it be right to let ninety or one hundred innocents die to save ten?[57] Does a wish to avoid guilt by avoiding participation in wrongdoing justify letting ninety or one hundred innocents die whom one could have saved? Certainly not if the ten are among those who would be killed anyway. And not even if the ten are not.

To Govern Is to Presume Fungibility

The innocent person, killed to save others, is not helped — perhaps not even comforted — by knowing that his death saves others. He has only one life, his, and he is losing it. His death is involuntary: he is innocent, yet used as a means to save others. To kill him is to commit a wrong. But if killing one innocent person by commission is wrong, is letting more than one die by ommission not more wrong?[58] It must be, unless, somehow, a quantity discount is presumed.[59]

As far as their possessors are concerned, human lives are never fungible. Not even appetites are. Still, both must be treated as fungible by governments. My thirst is not quenched when you drink, nor my life lived when you live. To the government, however, thirsts and lives must be fungible: if it has to choose, it will find it more equitable to slake the thirst of several at the expense of one person. *Social, as distinguished from individual, life, in war and in peace, is not possible unless human lives are implicitly treated as though fungible, at least in some circumstances.* Fungibility is both a matter of prudential reasoning and of power. The deontological view quoted above holds that an individual never can be denied his "rights" or entitlements in favor of a social interest. This view cannot be defended without resorting to natural rights, or to reason as a lawgiver, and these notions have already been rejected.

It is necessary to make some distinctions here. One's interest in one's innocent life cannot be overridden by anything but possibly the interest of others in theirs. But what about heterogeneous interests? It is here that the fear of those who cling to deontological rights has its legitimate source. In crude utilitarian terms, they fear that, if the happiness of ten thousand persons is increased by one point for each person, through eating ice cream, and if that becomes possible only by imposing life imprisonment on one person, whose happiness is decreased by nine hundred points, he might be imprisoned, because total happiness is increased thereby. This imprisonment would be unjust and contrary to our moral intuition. Hence, deontologists want to protect the individual with indefeasible rights. However, the objectionable decision is linked to a crude form of utilitarianism to which consequentialists need not be committed. They may well weigh interests in terms other than of happiness. Surely the individual's interest in his life should prevail over less fundamental interests of others, even if many.[60] I'm not sure how interests should be weighed. But I'm sure that they need not be weighed along utilitarian lines.

Arcana

While justice to some individuals must at times yield to justice to more individuals, the public acceptance of this rule may have a demoralizing and corrupting influence. It may encourage mobs and tyrants to make unjust threats, and authorities to yield to them more readily than they should. The rule also may inspire fear in everyone: his welfare, even his life, and any of his interests may be sacrificed to the welfare or life of a greater number. Thus, if the rule is beneficial, its public proclamation is not. This leads to an unpleasant yet inescapable conclusion. The consequentialist rule should be followed, but it should not be proclaimed. The rule should be treated as one of the *arcana imperii*; officially, the indefeasibility of legal individual rights must continue to be proclaimed for prudential reasons then. This is, like it or not, a description as much as a prescription—i.e., it is what has happened historically.

Salus Publica vs. *Justitia*

Sacrificing individual justice to social interests (including justice to other individuals) implies that individuals are fungible. This is repugnant to us. We do not feel that we are fungible. Fortunately, the extreme situations in which the sacrifice of individuals and of their interests or rights to others can be justified are rare. Even in reconsidering the mob or tyrant illustrations, I find it hard to free myself of the lingering suspicion that the defiant stand is attractive (apart from the psychological factors mentioned) because of the implied prudential idea of a duty to avoid setting a demoralizing precedent, which, ultimately, would cause a net loss. However, were we rigorously to abstract from this prudential matter, consequentialist moral reasoning would lead us to compliance rather than defiance.

Fortunately, few situations call for a moral choice uncontaminated by prudential considerations. Nevertheless, when such situations occur, there is an antinomy between consequentialist theory, which gives priority to social survival[61] and, for its sake, treats individuals as fungible, and a theory that gives priority to justice to individuals. Heedless of consequences, deontologists would defy the tyrant's or the mob's demand and refuse to commit the unjust act necessary to prevent injustice to more numerous innocent victims. There would be an irresolvable conflict between doing what is just to individuals — *fiat justitia pereat mundus* and doing, at their expense, what is helpful to society (to a greater number of other individuals) — *salus populi suprema lex.*[62]

If it is a choice between actively doing an injustice to some persons and letting the same injustice happen — by passivity — to more persons, I think one should choose to do the first even though it is more difficult. In this respect we should act as though people are fungible. If killing of one person is wrong, killing of two persons must be more wrong. So with injustice or suffering. Although one's degree of participation must make a legal and also a moral difference, that difference cannot be decisive when the choice is clear-cut.

If we accept Ulpian's principle *neminem laede* — do not harm innocent persons — we should add, 'unless it be to avoid harm to a greater number of innocents.' The airplane pilot who crashes his plane in the least populated area follows this principle. In some situations we should not do otherwise, if we believe, as I do, that life is valuable and that the lives of unknowns must all be deemed to be equally valuable.

VI   Fungibility and Narcissism

Confiscating Parts of the Body?

Let me now turn to some less exceptional, indeed potentially common situations, in which natural law and rights prescriptions as well as Kantian ones clash with consequentialist prescriptions that prescribe actions contrary to our moral intuition if, as stipulated, consequentialists assume that the life of each person has an equally high value, as far as society is concerned.

1. A healthy and happy twenty-five-year-old man comes to a hospital for a visit with a patient. There are in that hospital ten healthy and happy twenty-five-year-old men who cannot survive unless a diseased organ is replaced but will if it is. That organ can be taken from the visitor and shared among them. The visitor is unwilling to have it removed because of one of the following reasons: (*a*) some inconvenience is involved, (*b*) some risk to his health is involved, (*c*) his certain and almost immediate death will be caused by the removal.

Current law leaves the decision entirely to him and imposes no obligation whatsoever on him. Current moral views probably would suggest that he volunteer if (*a*) only inconvenience is involved; perhaps also if (*b*) some risk is involved; but only some religious moralities might encourage volunteering if (*c*) his certain death is involved.[63] No moral view known to me would suggest compelling the visitor to have his organ removed, regardless of whether (*a*), (*b*), or (*c*) is involved.

2. There may be variations on this situation. For instance, medicine that Jones owns can be used to cure him alone, or to cure ten other people doomed to die without it. It can also be used to cure him and five others, perhaps at some risk to him. Is Jones morally entitled (as he is by current law) to use the medicine only for himself?[64]

Is present positive law justified, as deontologists and believers in natural rights might claim, in declining on principle to compel the sacrifice of one person, or of his convenience, or of his property, to ensure the survival of many others? Or is the refusal of the law justified on purely prudential grounds? Or is it not justified at all?

There is a second set of questions. Why is a legal compulsion to give parts of our bodies to others so contrary to our moral intuition? There are but a few reluctant exceptions, such as involuntary military service, taxation, and eminent domain, and perhaps also some cases involving property, though certainly no cases involving one's ownership of oneself, one's bodily integrity.

The argument for compulsory confiscation of body parts must be basically utilitarian: the sacrifice of an individual, of his convenience, his property, his organs, or his life is demanded because it would increase aggregate happiness. Before scrutinizing that argument per se, let me draw attention to some prudential matters, which, I think, may motivate intuitive opposition, and perhaps even deontological arguments, against the compulsory sacrifice of the individual.

Prudential Considerations Once More

1. Although the illustration stipulates that the sacrifice would lead to the desired result, this is less than certain in the reality known by experience. Hence people feel, at least subconsciously, that actual welfare, or even life, may be sacrificed to potential life or doubtful improvements.

2. Compulsion would require immense "transaction costs," as economists call them. Some kind of judicial agency would have to determine who has to give what to whom. It is unlikely that, even at great cost, anything like an equitable system (granted the premise) could be enforced. A bureaucratic nightmare is more likely. The attempt may result in more injustice, or unhappiness, than it prevents, even if the compulsory redistribution, could it be carried out frictionlessly, without transaction costs, would actually maximize happiness.

The limited redistributive efforts now made by governments, efforts that exempt one's property and oneself (military service excepted), and, indeed, nearly anything other than income, demonstrably are of doubtful effectiveness. The undesired effects are costly and horrendous. The prudential case for reducing redistributive efforts is better than the case for expanding them.

3. The effect on incentive will be depressive. Why care for one's health if it will be redistributed? Why avoid cirrhosis of the liver if it entitles one to a new liver? Why work to buy medicine (or, ultimately, anything) if one can get it at the expense of others?

4. If we were to be in constant peril of having our organs confiscated by, or for, others who are in need of them and to whose happiness they would contribute more than to ours, whether because there are more of them, or because they have greater hedonic capacity, we would all lead a very insecure life. Aggregate happiness may be decreased by more than it is increased by the threat of redistribution, whether or not the latter is as predictable as taxation is, or, more likely, even less so. The peril would distort our actions and relationships, for we would all try to escape confiscation. Indeed this might become our major endeavor in life, to the detriment of all other activities.

These prudential reasons seem quite sufficient to justify the general rules of current positive law that protect our bodies from being appropriated by others. There is no need to resort to any deontological norms, or natural rights. Which is fortunate. For neither natural law nor natural rights, and, therefore, moral rights, in the deontological sense, have been justified.

Fungibility and Uniqueness

Let us now inquire into what outrages us so much about the utilitarian principle when it is driven as far as it has been driven above. Apart from prudential considerations, masquerading as objections to the principle, there is one important feeling, rationalized as a moral right. The utilitarian principle pushed as far as we have pushed it implies an unlimited fungibility of individuals. This is altogether contrary to the feeling each person has about himself. Our proprioceptive feeling is propriocentric. We are all unique to ourselves, and none feels he is exchangeable for others. Wherefore, in Kantian terms, we feel exclusively as ends in ourselves, and resent ever being treated as mere (involuntary) means. We want rights to protect us from the threat of being used for the benefit of others.

Our feelings about ourselves, being a feeling, is neither right nor wrong. Viewed from the outside, it can be shown that each of us is unique, yet fungible too. But we are fungible only to others, never to ourselves. We are fungible as taxpayers, soldiers, voters, and objects of scientific taxonomy. Indeed we are fungible as objects; but not as subjects. No two individuals are identical physically or psychologically,[65] and no individual feels himself to be identical to any other, or exchangeable. It is this feeling of uniqueness, of nonfungibility, that is outraged by utilitarianism, if driven far enough. Yet governments treat people as potentially fungible, and they will stop only where transaction costs nullify the benefits to society, which is likely on the whole to be the point at which—could it be an accident?—deontological reasoning also tells governments to stop.

Can We Have "Aggregate Happiness"?

So far I have implied that we know what it means to maximize "aggregate happiness." We don't. The objections to the concept, to its quantification, and to attempted measurements and distributions are too well known to need rehearsing. These objections cast all redistributive schemes into dubious light, the more so the more important what is to be redistributed is to us.[66]

Why bother then? I did make a case for fungibility, and for what I called injustice to individuals in favor of others in certain situations. I felt, therefore, that I should explore the limits of the case, and have tried to do so.

NOTES

1. Sophocles' tragedy *Antigone* clearly illustrates this point.

2. Sophocles' Theban Tragedies are among many illustrations of this belief.

3. In early times, liability for offending nature did not necessarily imply personal guilt as it might now. Even *scienter* was not required for guilt. The legal concept of "strict liability" thus actually was invented before personal guilt was required for liability.

4. From the observable purposefulness of our actions Alan Gewirth, by an odd though intriguing piece of reasoning, infers human rights: since we all may act purposefully we all have the right to the freedom and other necessary conditions required to achieve our purposes. Since our purpose, by definition, is our welfare, everybody has a right to it; for we can claim rights by our action for ourselves only if we grant them to others. Thus, if we do or logically must claim rights, we *eo ipso* get them and must grant that others have the same rights. (See Alan Gewirth, *Reason and Morality* [Chicago: University of Chicago Press, 1978].)

5. Where moral rules are not conceived as invariable and universal, one wonders to what extent they should be defined as "rules." Where they are thought to be dictated by reason it is usually argued that not to justify them is inconsistent, and not to follow them is to behave incoherently.

6. My interpretation is deliberately free, but, I think, justifiable.

7. Contrary to what Bruce Aune writes (*Kant's Theory of Morals* [Princeton, N.J.: Princeton University Press, 1979], p. 120): "The fundamental weakness of Kant's moral theory lies in its appeal to a teleological system of nature," Kant makes no such appeal. His work was to supersede natural law by a priori reason. The "fundamental weakness" is in Professor Aune's understanding of Kant.

8. *The Concept of Law* (Oxford University Press, 1961), pp. 181-207.

9. Cambridge, Mass.: Harvard University Press, 1977, pp. 151-81 *passim* and specifically pp. 177-78.

10. People are expected to choose their own interests, to be maximized in a utilitarian manner, but protected against some kinds of aggregation by becoming rights. The result is more interesting than convincing. (See John Rawls, *A Theory of Justice*, 1971.)

11. See his *Anarchy, State and Utopia*, New York, 1974. Nozick proceeds brilliantly once his natural rights premise is granted. His articulation and his illustrations of justice as noninterference with natural rights are illuminating and his incidental points are often original and striking.

Interestingly, Nozick's natural rights are quite different from Dworkin's. At least the conclusions drawn are. They must have different natures.

12. Ockham was perhaps the first to define "natural right" explicitly as independent of "agreement" (positive law), whereas only "natural law" had been so defined before.

13. *De Jure Belli et Pacis* (1625).

14. *De re publica.*

15. However, modern proponents, such as Rudolph Stammler, feel that natural law may develop or become known, i.e., that, in practice, it changes. This view minimizes the difference between natural and positive law and indeed makes the former no less arbitrary than the latter.

16. See Appendix B (pp. 35–47) of my *Political Violence and Civil Disobedience* (New York: Harper Torchbooks, 1972). "Passing a law" Dworkin writes (op. cit. p. 192) "cannot affect such rights as men do have." "Law" here includes legally valid court decisions.

17. Cruelty is "gratuitous" when it serves an end not thought to justify it, such as pleasure directly derived from the cruelty. When this pleasure is not the end, cruelty is often thought not to be gratuitous. When incidental to commercial ends, or when, generally, a means to something less frivolous than pleasure, such as food, cruelty is thought less immoral, even when the food itself is eaten mainly for pleasure (e.g., *foie gras*). There seems to be an aversion not so much to cruelty but rather to pleasure directly derived from it. There is much less aversion to pleasure derived from the products of cruelty.

18. The incurably insane have rights only in as much as they belong to a class, "humans," that does. Else we only would have duties toward them.

19. For a brief and incomplete analysis of the right to escape, see Dworkin, op. cit., p. 189. Had Dworkin completed his analysis by deriving the apparent inconsistency between the rights and duties of guards and prisoners from their allegiance to different sovereigns, he might have reconsidered his claim that rights are independent of the commands of sovereigns, and supersede them.

20. *Taking Rights Seriously,* p. 184. Dworkin gives no source but must have referred to the passage I quote in the text, which is found in *Works of Jeremy Bentham,* ed. J. Bowring (New York, 1972), vol. 2, p. 105.

21. The meaning of the phrase becomes most dubious if one tries to apply it to a concrete situation. If I have a right to innocent life, or to spaghetti, or to welfare in some sense, is it "wrong for the government to deny it" to me, even if that is the only way to protect the innocent lives, the spaghetti, or the welfare of ten other persons who have the same rights as I do?

22. I am cautious here. What two hundred years ago would have been held to be inherent, e.g., inability to see or hear at great distances, or to fly, is not necessarily so. And cogent alternatives to Euclid's geometry have been found applicable to unforeseen conditions.

23. Matters are not helped by insisting that our need for something—be it liberty, food, or air—leads us to demand it and thereupon to grant it to ourselves and to others similarly in need, as a right. An interest cannot be transformed into a moral or natural right either because satisfaction is indispensable or because it is universal, unless we have shown that the morality of conditions can be inferred from their indispensability or universality. But my natural wish to have my interest protected does not transform it into a right, nor does it morally obligate me to protect your interest.

24. I assume that by reason more is meant than consistency—something like an inherent prescription.

25. The broken but genuine promise is not important here, because the intention was to keep it.

26. We also can define promises as morally binding. But in doing so we bind ourselves to our definition, i.e., we, not nature, made a moral rule.

27. The parental voice is introjected ultimately to become an autonomous conscience; and projected to become the transcendent moral law that inspires conscience. But this psychological genesis is philosophically irrelevant. Nonetheless, it may be noted that Freud's notion of superego command (issued because morally required) as distinguished from an id demand (issued for the sake of pleasure) or an ego demand (issued for the sake of realistic self-preservation) coincides with Kant's notion that the "moral" is that which is done for moral reasons alone. We certainly do

feel and act at times as Freud described and Kant prescribed. It does not follow that the moral can be shown to be objectively so nor that we are bound to its imperatives. (In Kantian terms Freud's superego is more heteronomous than Kant would like morality to be.)

28. Things were different when philosophical proofs for the existence of God were respectable. Today religion must rely on faith, buttressed, but not produced by reason.

29. *Reason and Morality,* Chicago, 1978.

30. Here Gewirth seems to stand Kant on his head. Kant argued that universalizability is the condition of morality. Gewirth seems to say that morality (or right) follows from the universality of claims.

31. Because of my own interest I want positive law to grant a right to freedom. But it comes into being only when granted by positive law—even though nature may have created my interest. How it can create rights eludes me altogether.

32. See Note 7.

33. Note that the contents of natural law are similarly indeterminate.

34. I owe most of the foregoing argument to my friend Michael Levin. See his "Kant's Derivation of the Formula of Universal Law as an Ontological Argument" (1947). He is not to be held responsible for what I learned from him.

35. Oddly enough, those who argue that there must be natural law, because its absence would have terrible consequences, rest their argument on a consequentialism quite alien to natural law tradition and principle. It is, moreover, a perverted consequentialism. Consequentialists do not believe that, if the consequences of something being untrue, unwarranted, or incorrect, were bad, it would become, or have to be, true. They believe that actions should be evaluated in the light of their consequences, not that ideas are true or untrue depending on the desirability of their social effects. (I cannot vouch for some pragmatists. But consequentialists need not be pragmatists.)

36. On the notion of "essentialism," see Karl Popper, *The Open Society and Its Enemies,* and also Friedrich von Hayek, *Law, Legislation and Liberty.* I have some reservations on Popper's version of history and on Hayek's utilitarianism but they do not weaken the general point made above.

37. I have not changed my position on this matter since my "Open Letter to Sidney Hook," published in *Partisan Review* (1950) and republished with his rejoinder in Hook's *The Quest for Being* (New York, 1961).

38. I have not met anyone who calls himself a relativist, although I have met people who accuse others of being relativists.

39. Science, of course, is concerned with the demonstrable, often only with the demonstrated. What is demonstrable must be true. But what is true may not be demonstrable, at least not by scientific methods. Hence, philosophers should not pretend to be scientists. Note that my argument heretofore tried to show that natural rights and natural law had not been demonstrated to exist or to be meaningful, and that alternative explanations for what they are meant to accomplish or explain are better. I have not tried to show nonexistence.

40. What is here said about moral values seems as true about aesthetic values.

41. See my "Liberty: Negative or Positive," *Harvard Journal of Law and Public Policy* 1 (1978).

42. Provided that happiness itself does not become an end, but is recognized as a by-product of achievement.

43. Everything said about the insufficiency of consequentialism applies to "naturalism" and "pragmatism" as well. My objection to these theories is that they attempt, albeit unsuccessfully, to supply moral norms from nowhere. (It should be noted that all these philosophies can be used to defend or to suppress freedom.)

44. There is nothing in consequentialism to prevent such sentiments as *"dulce et decorum est pro patria mori,"* or any transcendent duty, from being accepted or demanded. But duties, norms, or rights must be evaluated in terms of consequences, and are imposed by human decision, not prescribed by nature.

45. *Right and Wrong* (1979). It does not matter here what "unjust" means. Fried might have written, "We must never violate principle X" to be as unreasonable as I believe he is.

46. Op. cit.

47. "Right," "just," or "justice to individuals" are here stipulated along the lines of Ulpian's maxims, or along Roman and Common law lines. I argue from these stipulative definitions without attempting to demonstrate what I think is not demonstrable.

48. Such a recognition need not be dictated by nature, but by one's own will. And the axioms may be derived from shared interests. Hereafter I simply stipulate them as recognized principles of moral and legal reasoning, disregarding questions about their foundations.

49. Injustice to individuals here consists in deliberate violation of the rights (recognized interests) they are conceded to have, including the right to innocent life.

50. I have not fully separated here evil caused, from evil not prevented, and various degrees of active and passive participation. Although of some moral importance, and of great legal importance, these distinctions need not be made at this point.

51. Much depends on the degree of responsibility felt for the beneficiaries of charity. *Volente nolente* we must admit to a greater responsibility to those near to us—with whom we can, and do, identify—than for those far away, or culturally distant. (Here, incidentally, lies the answer to the abortion problem: it is the degree of identification with fetuses at various stages of development that determines the protection they will and, perhaps, should be accorded.)

52. I include here under "moral reasoning," for the sake of convenience, what may as well be called an analysis of the appropriate relationship of individual to social interests, as well as deontological reasoning. A "prudential" justification in this terminology is one that meets the problem in terms of contingencies without addressing that which must be addressed in either deontological or consequentialist terms.

53. There is an empirical problem: what will the effects be? and a partly moral problem, about the weight to be given to these effects. However, these matters must not be conflated with the purely "moral" problem: would compliance with the wrongful demand be justified if it had no effects other than the avoidance of the threatened wrongful action?

54. Adam Smith had no doubt: "When the preservation of an individual is inconsistent with the safety of the multitude, nothing can be more just than that the many should be preferred to the one." See *The Theory of Moral Sentiments* (*Adam Smith's Moral and Political Philosophy*), H. W Schneider, ed. New York, 1970, pp. 129–30.

55. Op. cit.

56. Natural law reasoning probably would have favored compliance, natural rights reasoning probably not.

57. The valuableness of life is here stipulated, neither demonstrated, nor derived from any theory.

58. The omission here is not one that would lead to legal liability: no negligence is involved. But one is morally liable for not doing what one could have done to save others when one could have done it without risk to oneself and without any but moral discomfort. I don't believe that moral discomfort should be a moral excuse.

59. If the bystander has a special relationship to any of the persons to be killed, or spared, the quantitative considerations have to be modified by giving different weights to different persons. Discussion of these modifications is beyond my present scope.

60. Social policy follows this prescription only fitfully. People rarely are compelled to lose their lives to make ice cream available to others. But they often are induced to take risks by rewards held out to them for the sake of trivial amusement of others. This risk-taking cannot be objected to if voluntary: it is part of liberty. But risk-taking is not always all that voluntary.

61. By stipulation. Even if not defined as happiness, social welfare will include the survival of the greater number of innocents.

62. Usually the task of doing justice to individuals is left to the courts while governments—by exercising emergency powers or pardon powers—implicitly reserve the right to overrule courts in special and extreme situations. But in some cases the courts too have to overrule justice to individuals.

63. The religious reason for the sacrifice often lies in the merit found in sacrificing, not in the consequences for the beneficiaries. This matter goes beyond my present scope.

64. One can vary degrees of risk and of benefits available to various recipients *ad infinitum*.

65. Monozygotic twins are more identical than others—but not identical either.

66. However, in my opinion, these objections do not suffice to overwhelm the case for the injustices to individuals discussed in Section V above.

LEWIS S. FEUER

The Genetic Fallacy Re-examined

I The Divergence Among Empiricists Concerning Psychoanalysis

Genetic considerations are those bearing on the circumstances under which belief in a given proposition arises. In the view of many philosophers, such considerations are irrelevant in determining the truth or falsehood of any philosophical or scientific proposition. The "genetic fallacy" is taken to be a class name for all arguments that assume that the extralogical circumstances—social, historical, psychological—under which belief in a given proposition originated are relevant to deciding its truth or falsehood.

In this essay, I shall inquire as to whether indeed there is such a fallacy as a "genetic fallacy" and whether its invention was indeed meant to obstruct philosophical inquiry. Ever since Henry Sidgwick asserted that to trace "the Origin of the psychical facts which we call Intuitions" has no bearing "on what I have called their Validity,"[1] the "genetic fallacy" has acquired the status of a philosophical axiom.

Genetic considerations, however, thrust themselves upon every student of contemporary philosophical ideas. Take, for instance, the divided opinion among contemporary positivists and scientific philosophers concerning the scientific validity of Freud's psychoanalytical theories. Virtually all the Austrian and German logical positivists and scientific philosophers have been sympathetic to psychoanalytical work. Hans Reichenbach, for instance, "had a serious interest in psychoanalytic theory" and became an honorary member of a psychoanalytic institute;[2] Richard von Mises, the distinguished theorist of the foundations of probability, declared: "The extremely vigorous objections raised in many circles to the acceptance of the psychoanalytic theory are in large part of a nonlogical nature . . . There can be no doubt, however, about factual agreement with many observations, and hence about a certain practical usefulness of the theory.''[3]

American empiricist philosophers, on the other hand, especially those in New York City, though sharing some of the cultural background of their European colleagues, were hostile toward psychoanalytical ideas. How did it happen then that philosophers adhering to a common standpoint differed so sharply when it came to questions of mental phenomena, conscious and un-conscious? Had the Europeans been affected by a literary-cultural milieu of sexual emancipation that deflected their scientific reasoning? Or had the New York students been determined in their late adolescence by their teacher, Morris R. Cohen, who all his life disliked vehemently any intrusion of psychological considerations, above all, psychoanalytical ones? I addressed these queries to Sidney Hook after reading how surprised he had been in 1928-1929 upon first discovering Reichenbach's psychoanalytical interests. Professor Hook had narrated:

> I recall also a matter of mutual shock at the time. He [Reichenbach] was startled when I asserted that the theory of psychoanalysis, especially in its Freudian for-mulation, was unscientific, and I was startled when he insisted that it was. It seemed clear to me that on his own criteria of scientific verification that psychoanalysis was no more scientific than Christian science. In passing, I should note the curious fact that all the logical empiricists or positivists I have known were quite vehement in defending the scientific validity of Freud's basic views—something which in my obtuseness I could never square with their professed philosophy of science.[4]

Doubtless, if both groups of logical empiricists, the Central European and the New York, were aiming to apply the same principles of scientific logic to their evaluation of psychoanalysis, then genetic considerations would have to be invoked to explain how at least one of them was constrained by emotional, perhaps unconscious, factors from adhering rigorously to those scientific prin-ciples. If so, which one?

To my question as to how this divergence in philosophy could be explained, Professor Hook kindly responded:

> I do not know how to explain the partiality of the logical positivists toward psychoanalysts—and, as I wrote you, not only of them but of people like Kurt Lewin and Lazarsfeld who agreed with all of Ernest Nagel's methodological stric-tures but nonetheless said "but it's true."
>
> I don't recall whether it was you or Meyer Schapiro who explained my posi-tion and Ernest's as due to the influences of Morris Cohen, but we broke away from Cohen on so many points it is hard to explain why we remained critical. Perhaps it was the presence of too much shoddy in the popularizers. I really read and *enjoyed* Freud but couldn't take *Civilization and Its Discontents* seriously or accept *Moses and Monotheism* . . . I greatly admired A. A. Goldenweiser, whose criticisms of Freud's excursions in anthropology were more persuasive to me

than his defence of his concepts in personal psychology . . .[5]

Now it is noteworthy that, quite apart from its theoretical explanation, there does then exist a verified empirical correlation, or empirical law, that the Viennese and Berlin empiricists were philo-psychoanalytical while the New York circle was anti-psychoanalytical. Genetic correlations of this kind stand quite apart from their theoretical explanation, but only the latter will help enlighten us as to at least which of the two (or possibly both, or neither) is irrationally motivated. If, however, on presumably independent grounds, we already knew the truth of psychoanalytic hypotheses and were then to explain the irrational opposition of the anti-psychoanalysts, "genetic considerations" might reinforce the validity of the psychoanalytic hypotheses. On the other hand, if such independent evidence for the validity of psychoanalytical ideas is regarded as unconvincing, we would appear to be begging the question in assuming their validity in determining which cultural circle of philosophers was contra-rational.

Actually, however, it is precisely through genetic investigations of this kind that the truth or falsity of psychoanalytical theories is established. We undertake to explain the divergence between the two rival schools of thought concerning the truth or falsehood of basic psychoanalytic hypotheses. If we assume the latter's truth, we shall then have to advance subsidiary hypotheses as to what elements in their social environment exerted an emotionalizing impact on the New York school. Were they shaped by the transmitted American Puritan culture, or the New York lower-class, Jewish, anti-sexual immigrant culture, or a City College philosophical milieu dominated by a would-be father figure who was himself tormented by emotional resistances,[6] or the influence of their next father figure, John Dewey, who retained a Vermonter's distaste for sexual motives, or by the impact of Marxism after the First World War that placed economic motivations higher in the historical hierarchy than the more bourgeois sexual ones.

We may, on the contrary, begin by assuming that the basic psychoanalytic theories are false. In that case, we shall invent all sorts of subsidiary hypotheses to try to explain why the Central European empiricists were misled into accepting them. Experiencing the full impact of defeat and disillusionment after the First World War, they were attracted perhaps toward a psychological theory that might unmask the bogus ideas of militaristic tradition, dedication to the emperor, and battlefield romanticism, as stemming not from some higher metaphysical source but from phenomena as lowly as toilet-training or a domineering father. Perhaps, moreover, as children of the Viennese middle and upper classes, especially its Jewish sector, growing up in an unwonted economic security but with their marriages delayed because of professional exigencies, and their traditional religious restraints obsolete, they gave themselves to uninhibited sexual activities; their sexual overemphasis, in theory as well as practice, was then class-biased and historically strained.

Such genetic considerations would themselves help decide which rival alternative concerning the Central European and New York empiricists was true. If the subsidiary hypotheses concerning the New York school were validated, then weight would be lent to the notion that their scientific judgment had been perturbed or warped by psychoanalytical fixations. Or, if the subsidiary hypotheses concerning the Central European school were confirmed, then we would accept the proposition that class-originated aberrations rendered them susceptible to an acceptance of psychoanalytical ideas contravening their own scientific criteria.

From this standpoint, genetic analysis is comparable to the astronomer's concern with the purity and resolving power of his telescopic lenses. An unusual photographic image may trouble him: Is it the image of a distant star or the consequence of a speck of dust on the great lens or mirror? Is the bit of color on the photograph a record of a "red-shift" in the light from a distant star or possibly a chromatic aberration grounded in the physical structure of the telescopic lens itself? No astronomer would reject such considerations as examples of an "optical fallacy"; why then should a philosopher invoke a "genetic fallacy" to exclude analogous considerations concerning philosophical theses? There is then no "genetic fallacy" as a class of fallacies; rather there are genetic considerations that are well-founded, strong genetic evidence, just as there are cases of purported genetic considerations that are weak, insubstantial.

Leibniz, in his philosophic debate with John Locke over the existence of "innate ideas," thus refused to invoke a "genetic fallacy." Locke had argued that the purported innate ideas were rather the effects of a parent's or nursemaid's admonitions in our early childhood.[7] Leibniz rebutted Locke by saying that the latter hadn't carried his genetic analysis far enough. He agreed that Locke had done well in showing how "under the name of innate principles one often maintains his prejudices," that "under the specious pretext of innate ideas" people avoid "investigating . . . the sources . . . and the certainty of this knowledge. In that I am entirely agreed with him," wrote Leibniz, but he added, "I go even farther." He argued that the human mind is not a blank tablet, that if one probes more deeply one finds ideas that are, as it were, "engraved" in us "by a species of instinct," ideas indeed "of which we are not always actually conscious," truths that "are for us as innate as inclinations, dispositions . . ."[8] Of course, from this Leibnizian standpoint, much further investigation was needed to establish what unconscious ideas were actually "engraved" in the human mind. Leibniz nonetheless calls for a genetic analysis that reaches indeed to origins in a way that Locke's reportage does not. For the rationalist Leibniz, there is thus no "genetic fallacy," only genetic considerations that are relevant, and those that might be irrelevant, that is, perhaps not truly genetic.

II Genetic Privilege and Genetic Handicap

An "antinomy of genetic method" (as I might call it) arises, however, in practice to haunt both Leibnizian intuitionist and Lockean empiricist, both Marxist historical materialist and "bourgeois" idealist, indeed all genetic analysts. In actual use, the genetic facts often seem insufficient to determine whether the given thinker or school of thinkers was "genetically handicapped," or, on the contrary, "genetically privileged." A genetic privilege exists for a person, with respect to some domain of truths, when his character, configuration of emotions, social circumstances, and historic experiences are such as to place him in a favorable situation for perceiving, receiving, or imagining those truths that will not be thus experienced by people not so constituted. A genetic handicap, on the contrary, exists when a person's character, emotions, and social and historic background are such as to render him impervious to, or desirous of repressing, the existence of certain phenomena that he otherwise might have perceived, received, or imagined.

Genetic analysts, from Marxist to Bloomsburyan, tend arbitrarily to regard their favored class or circle as privileged for access to knowledge, as not being handicapped. The homosexual circle, for instance, that constituted the Cambridge Apostles gave great support to the formation of the intuitionist doctrine of G. E. Moore, to his notion that all utilitarian or scientific definitions of "good" were examples of a "naturalistic fallacy." Lytton Strachey "saw in *Principia Ethica* a justification for homosexuality," and Moore "was not inclined to correct Strachey."[9] G. Lowes Dickinson, a sensitive Platonist and an idealistic advocate for the League of Nations, had together with John McTaggart transmitted to Moore "the romantic idea of Apostolic homosexuality";[10] McTaggart, a sharer of homosexual and philosophical interests with Dickinson, contributed as many as eighteen papers to the Society, one of which, "Violets or Orange Blossoms?" was an explicit "defence of homosexual love."[11] Not only did sexuality by 1894 become "the Apostles' chief interest," but Moore's paper "Achilles or Patroclus?" suggested the underlying homosexual tone: "It was obligatory to make the humorous assumption that all sexual relations were homosexual ones, so that even heterosexual love had to be treated as only a special case of the Higher Sodomy."[12] Moore even ventured the cosmological speculation that the active-passive structure of homosexual relations was connected with the structure of the universe. In a more terrestrial vein, he asserted that copulation was a disagreeable activity, a trial and a trouble, so that a man and a woman who loved one another engaged in sexual relations only because it was necessary for the begetting of children.[13] Moore's candor in talking about his own sexual shame and pruriency evidently had a profound effect on his fellow Apostles.[14] Ethical intuitionism, ethical anti-naturalism, became the ideology of this homosexual circle.

Does its homosexual origin, however, discredit the philosophy of *Principia Ethica?* Does its origin bear upon its validity? Moreover, might one indeed affirm that, far from having handicapped their philosophical vision, the homosexuality of the Apostles made them more perceptive of underlying realities? The homosexual experience, according to this argument, makes its practitioners more spiritual, liberated from materialistic constraints in much the same way that the mathematical imagination liberates one to conceive pure possibilities. The homosexual thinker, from Plato and Socrates on, it is argued, has been genetically privileged, a metaphysical aristocrat, with an access to a pure idea that is not vouchsafed to the vulgarian, the unspiritual heterosexual. By contrast, however, to the claim for homosexual "epistemological privilege," the famed English geneticist and then Marxist J. B. S. Haldane argued that, apart from slavery, it was sodomy that killed Greek science: "Plato and other idealists were extremely tolerant of this latter aberration . . . Today it is common in literary circles, and rare among scientists. For it is a second-rate imitation, like the substitution of words for things, with which it is associated today as it was in Athens."[15] Scientific biologists who have written on questions of ethics have evidently found G. E. Moore's argument on the "naturalistic fallacy" a feeble one. Such scientists as C. H. Waddington, Haldane, and Julian Huxley, who continued to probe the evolutionary and psychological origins of "good," have regarded their work as contributing to a scientific analysis of "good."[16]

Some philosophers likewise have found insubstantial Moore's argument that "good" is unanalyzable;[17] to psychological naturalists, indeed, the doctrine of the "naturalistic fallacy" seems rather to be the functional formula of a resistance mechanism to scientific, reductive analysis. From the psychoanalytical standpoint, the word "good" carries all the overtones of our early conditioning by our parents; to do what is "good" is to enjoy the unconscious reassurance of parental love; to do contrary to "good" ignites feelings of guilt, the threat of withdrawn parental affection and its introjected consequence, self-hatred.[18] From the genetic standpoint, it was bound to seem clear to Moore that "pleasure is good" is not at all equivalent to "pleasure is pleasure," because the word "good" signalizes as well the associations superadded by our moral education that endure recessively in our unconscious. Presumably, these unconscious meanings can be brought to consciousness by psychogenetic analysis. What then remains of the "naturalistic fallacy"? Evidently it expressed Moore's lifelong repugnance toward genetic analysis. He had objected very early to Santayana's ethical naturalism, because Santayana's arguments were so largely founded on psychological and biological facts. "The primitive origins of the various human activities," wrote Moore, have no "direct bearing on . . . the enumeration of goods."[19] Then, many years later, Moore told the eminent genetic psychologist Jean Piaget that the latter's studies were "of no interest at all, in substance, because the philosopher is concerned with true ideas, while the psychologist feels a sort of vicious and incomprehensible attraction for the study of false ideas."[20] This is like saying that the laws of optics are of interest to an astronomer only to inquire into the aberrations of his telescope, but not to explain its effective range and resolving power. Obviously, genetic considerations explain the possibility of knowledge, as Bacon saw, even as they do that of ignorance. The discoveries of great scientific truths—Darwin's theory of natural selection, Einstein's theory of relativity—were also based on genetic vectors, psychological and social, which provided their perhaps indispensable matrix. Truth has no immaculate conception, as most every historian of science knows.

Generally speaking, when a philosopher makes a basic change in stand point, it is highly likely that that change is grounded in some basic emotional alteration. Bertrand Russell, for instance, after having been an intense intuitionist of objective ethical absolutes, found himself persuaded, he writes, to relinquish such absolutes in part by Santayana's arguments on behalf of ethical relativism.[21] Now Santayana's arguments were the ones well known since Locke's time to the English-speaking world. Why did these arguments have a valence for Russell at one time and not earlier? The genetic analyst cannot but observe that Russell's years of intuitionism coincided approximately with his "years of tense self-denial," of sexual abstinence. Santayana's criticisms of Russell's "hypostatic ethics" were published in August 1911.[22] Russell's persuasion to ethical relativism was evidently prepared when, in March 1911, his years of sexual repression ended. To which one still queries: Was sexual abstinence perhaps a genetic privilege that enabled its possessor to intuit higher, spiritual truths?

When philosophies are discarded as obsolete, a kind of unwritten psychogenetic and sociogenetic analysis has usually shown the attraction of those philosophies to have been based on emotions that have in the meanwhile dissolved. John Dewey once observed: "We do not solve them [philosophic questions]; we get over them. Old questions are solved by disappearing . . ."[23] Genetic analysis is precisely the intellectual articulation of this process of "getting over" a question. Many American intellectuals, for example, after the Second World War, abandoned historical materialism for existentialism; with the destruction of the Nazi incubus and the resurgence of the American democracy, they were disenthralled from anxieties that had sombered their thought. Otherwise, virtually no novel argument or evidence had been presented.

Does genetic analysis then terminate in a genetic indeterminacy, that is, an inability to infer from any genetic analysis whether the conditions it analyzes constitute a genetic privilege or a genetic handicap? In that case, a form of the "genetic fallacy" could be affirmed, namely, that we can infer nothing concerning the validity of a proposition by knowing its origins so long as we have no way of knowing independently whether the latter brought privilege or handicap. In which case, the truth or falsehood of any given proposition would have been decided antecedently quite apart from any genetic analysis.

This negative inference concerning genetic analysis, however, is unwarranted.

What it overlooks is that genetic analysis is the most searching instrument for studying the epistemic bases for the truth claims of basic philosophical propositions. Descartes's philosophy, for instance, rested on a claim that certain innate ideas existed: the truth of this claim could be validated only by its being able to withstand the kinds of genetic criticisms that Locke made. The epistemic claim of Sidgwick and Moore that an ethical intuition is part of our mental equipment would similarly have to withstand the genetic analysis that aimed to dissolve that "intuition," by making the intuitionist aware that it blended unconscious residues with a resistance-formation. Kant's claim that the Euclidean space and time were a priori forms of intuition was thus shaken by Ernst Mach's inquiry into the origins of the ideas of absolute space and time. The notion that the idea of God is inherent in our consciousness would have to stand unfalsified by Freud's genetic evidence that the idea of God is a projection of the child's fear of its father. The notion of a "genetic fallacy" would simply exclude arbitrarily any empirical testing of the sources of knowledge claims.

Whether a given social or psychological base provides a genetic privilege or a genetic handicap is determined in accordance with the customary scientific criteria. The claim that homosexuality confers an epistemic privilege is sorely contravened by the evidence that homosexuality is virtually unknown among the outstanding contemporary physicists.[24] The ideas of an intuited absolute space and time which were dominant in the homosexual culture-circle of the Cambridge Apostles, and the verbal arguments with which they were demonstrated, scarcely proved as heuristic as those of Einstein and his comrades in the genetically minded, Machian circle of Zurich-Berne students.

Auxiliary hypotheses can, however, be invoked in such disputes. The homosexualists might claim that in the spiritual sciences, involving ethical and aesthetic insight, their genetic status conferred an epistemic privilege.[25] They might claim that sexual energies diverted from female objects rendered one more sensitive to spiritual entities, which coarsened, vulgarized personalities could never apprehend. The discussion and weighing of epistemic claims would thus continue. However, a claim that can be sustained only by multiplying auxiliary hypotheses would run dead against the principle of parsimony, Occam's Law.[26]

Under what logical conditions, then, would genetic analysis invalidate a claim to a metaphysical intuition, that is, a direct, immediate experience of a transempirical reality? The controlling principle is indeed that of Occam's Law: thus, if the genetic analysis establishes a causal chain all members of which are natural occurrences and that terminates, in accordance with causal laws, in an event characterized by all the introspective traits of the purported intuition, then the claim of that intuition to have been generated by some transempirical interrelation, as by some influx of divine energy, or some spiritual interaction, would have to be judged as otiose, as a superfluous, unnecessary hypothesis, to be ruled as contravening Occam's Law.[27] Genetic analysis, for instance, as John Stuart Mill practiced it, thus tried to undermine the intuitionist epistemic claim by using what he called "Psychological Theory." Mill, in effect, defined the role of genetic analysis as showing that such concepts as "intuition" were unnecessary because a reductive psychogenetic explanation could be given of every trait of the alleged intuition;[28] to assume that such a faculty of intuition existed was as scientifically redundant as to hold today to the hypothesis of the physical ether.

III The Incompleteness of Genetic Analyses

The aim of genetic analysis in the history of empiricism has thus been founded on a valid principle of scientific logic if one can take the propositions concerning such metaphysical ideas as God, intuition, freedom, natural right, and show how their origins, their formulation, and the belief in their existence are explicable on the basis of observable psychological facts; if, in other words, a causal line can be established in which all that is asserted concerning these metaphysical entities can be shown to be the consequence of psychological data and laws, with no supervenient fact concerning the character and existence of these metaphysical entities remaining that cannot be explained through such causal lines, then that entity or belief is logically unnecessary. Thus, Arthur O. Lovejoy, America's foremost historian of ideas, though himself devoted to a purely formal account of the filiation of ideas, declared that the genetic analysis of the "immediate certitude of religious experience" had undermined its claims: "The destructive effect of this criticism of the ordinary argument from subjective religious experience to objective theological entities cannot, it seems to me, be denied by a serious and honest reasoner. . . ." How many persons who have believed themselves to possess religious "instructions, even visions" have subsequently come to doubt, noted Hastings Rashdall, whether they were "anything but the outcome of subjective wishes or a disordered brain."[29]

The fact of the matter, however, is that no genetic analysis has really fulfilled the strict scientific canons to an extent that would justify affirming that "God" and "intuition," for instance, can be eliminated on Occamite grounds. In other words, empiricists have never met Leibniz's challenge to Locke. Freud never actually showed that the predisposition to believe in God was simply the outcome of parental scares and fears; the recrudescence of belief in God among Soviet intellectuals, despite all the contrary forces of societal and parental conditioning, might even suggest the existence of an underlying intuition.

Genetic analysis, at the hands of even the most remarkable of its practitioners, tends to claim a completeness that the actual observational facts are too meager to support. Jean Piaget, for instance, declared that "the theory of the filial origin of the religious sense seems to us singularly convincing . . .";[30] according to his account, moral commands seem to a child to be endowed with a transcendental origin only because very young children have difficulty in distinguishing between what they have invented and what is imposed upon them from without by adults; a superpersonal transcendence thus apparently absorbs what were originally adult-ordained mandates. How then, one asks, do children advance upon the moralities inculcated in them by their parents and their societies? By what criterion does criticism of the received parental morality become possible? The geneticist responds: The very conflict among rival adult moralities helps to develop the young person's autonomous moral conscience. But we ask further: Has such a causally determinist explanation of the genesis of the moral conscience ever been verified? Has it been shown that its developing autonomy is not guided by an implanted intuition, possibly linked to a biogenetic base? Has the psychogenetic causal line been traced in its sequential members so as to enable us to exclude altogether any suggestion that a transcendental component has been operative in the human ethical evolution? Piaget has given a fascinating account of his own "philosophical crises of adolescence"—his devout Protestant mother; their minister, with his weak proofs for God's existence; his father, a scholarly, unchurched historian; his godfather, an enthusiast for Bergsonian creative evolution; and himself, devoted to collecting mollusks.[31] Was Piaget's own intellectual route to his positivist inference the outcome of an overdetermination in emotional rebellion that led him to conclusions that far exceeded the bounds of his observational support?

The notion that, independently of sociogenetic circumstances, a marked propensity to believe in the existence of a divine being is implanted in men still remains consistent with the evidence. Perhaps such a theistic propensity has a biogenetic basis; possibly an intuitive ingredient has acted autonomously.

Genetic analysis, as pursued by its proponents, even Mill and Marx, has indeed been woefully lacking in rigor. Mill, for instance, in justifying his concern with inductive logic, said that he wanted to undermine the belief in intuited political principles, because the latter served the purposes of the conservative party. Whether Mill's *Logic* showed that such principles can altogether be dropped as unnecessary is a question beyond our purview.[32] What is clear, however, is that intuitionism has probably animated liberal political creeds as frequently as it has conservative ones. Jefferson, writing in the Declaration of Independence of truths held to be "self-evident," was appealing to the laws of reason, instilled by God and confirmed in the "common sense" of mankind.[33] Socialists, such as R. H. Tawney, assailing the "acquisitive society," grounded themselves on purported ultimate religious intuitions of human equality and fellowship; and more among the founders of the British Labor Party were intuitionists than were reductive, genetic utilitarians.[34]

Stratogenetic analysis, indeed—that is, one founded on the assumption that the class, social origins, or affiliations of thinkers are the primary extralogical factor in determining their philosophic beliefs—is apt to eventuate in far-fetched, caricatural genetic accounts. Thorstein Veblen, for instance, argued that the positivist philosophy was especially congenial to members of the French commercial middle-class who were divorced from physical contact with mechanical productive processes.[35] All of which sounds bizarre when we recall that the greatest proponent of positivism at the end of the nineteenth century, Ernst Mach, was an experimentalist of a high order, who helped inspire the formation in Einstein's mind of the theory of relativity. John Dewey argued that the Greeks' theory of knowledge reflected the separation of social classes; according to Dewey, the "disesteem entertained for the manual worker" expressed itself in a corresponding low esteem for the "prosaic matter of fact knowledge" and the corollary that Pure Ideas, unsullied by empirical impurities, and given only to the aristocratic nonworker, constituted Truth. It followed, from Dewey's point of view, that the genesis of modern science was founded on the growth of a democratic polity that brought "the substitution of a democracy of individual facts equal in rank for the feudal system of an ordered gradation of general classes of unequal rank."[36] The historical facts, however, contravene Dewey's stratogenetic account; actually, British aristocrats, together with King Charles II, were the social mainstay in founding the Royal Society in the seventeenth century; furthermore, the chief centers for scientific research in the first part of the twentieth century were part of the absolutist, undemocratic German Empire, whereas the American democratic states were for a long time quite averse to helping encourage projects of scientific research. Perhaps a genetic analysis of Dewey's rendition of intellectual history would indicate that his own democratic, emotive a priori imposed a pattern that did violence to the historic facts;[37] the democratic outlook might constitute with respect to some questions a genetic handicap rather than the privilege that Dewey took it to be.

Of all the philosophers in the modern era, Leibniz, curiously, was the one most concerned with industrial processes; nevertheless, he, like Spinoza the lens grinder, also believed in pure ideas and the givenness to rational intuition. We might note parenthetically, however, that Leibniz was brought to grief by his industrial interests. Wishing to bring the labor of workingmen under the rational direction of philosophers, he contrived a scheme in 1679 that aimed to enable the Harz state silver-mines to use wind as well as water for keeping the pumps operating continuously. The windmill, however, failed; much worse, the miners threatened to strike unless Leibniz was removed from the premises; he was, they said, "a dangerous man with whom it bodes ill to have any dealings." This was the first recorded rift in history between philosophy and the proletariat, between the intellectual and the working classes. For several years, Leibniz persisted in his project, though his "cost overrun" by 1683 came to more than sevenfold. Finally, the Duke of Hanover, troubled by the miners' unrest, terminated the experiment; Leibniz was deeply disheartened.[38] But his philosophical idealism and intuitionism was thoroughly consonant with his desire to bring science to bear on industrial life.

IV   The Modes of Genetic Analysis

Psychogenetic analysis has been important in the history of philosophic thought; stratogenetic analysis, on the other hand, has had little significance. As far as political ideologies are concerned, however, the stratogenetic determination has been the more primary variable. The various modes of genetic analysis that have been used, and not infrequently confused, need be distinguished; for the "genetic fallacy" is often directed against some irrelevant mode of genetic analysis. The psychogenetic approach itself consists of several varieties. First, there is what we might call the "protogenetic" kind that is concerned with the influence of family and upbringing in one's early years, of the sort that John Locke emphasized. Underlying that level, there is the biogenetic substructure; if diversities in temperament do have a basis in the variant structures of genes, then the character-types underlying the rival philosophies would be denominated as "biogenetically founded." When William James classified philosophies as "tender-minded" and "tough-minded," he was delineating a spectrum of philosophies that might well have its source in biogenetic variations. Such a spectrum would repeat itself throughout the range of different social structures. Under different social systems—capitalist, communist, feudal, primitive—the spectrum of biogenetic characters and their corresponding philosophic propensities would tend to reappear.

Superimposed are the impacts on both personal character and the social climate that are exerted by the events in one's historical place-time. The steady progress of Britain during the nineteenth century, for instance, evidently imparted to Herbert Spencer's thought an optimistic overtone that was not altogether in keeping with his nervous propensity to depression.[39] The events of the First World War and the recurrence of pogroms, by contrast, may have elicited in Sigmund Freud his theory of the death wish, projecting itself far beyond what either the evidence or his own cultural background of Jewish optimism would have endorsed. We might call this mode of genetic analysis "historico-genetic."

Successive generations moreover tend to revolt against the dominant philosophies of their predecessors. Rough cyclical rhythms are defined in which materalists rebel against idealistic forebears, and vice versa, in which disbelievers rebel against theists, and vice versa. James conjectured that each philosophy expressed some ingredients in our underlying emotional character, and repressed others. The waves in philosophic ideas, their alternation, might then be due to the returns of the successively repressed and incompatible elements of longing.[40] I would call this mode of genetic analysis "generational-genetic."

If there are generational waves underlying the cyclical patterns of philosophic ideas, it is also true that the progressive evolution of technology has given new analogies, fresh models, to those successive generations. Veblen especially was a practitioner of what we might call "technogenetic analysis."[41] Such inventions as the bow and arrow, the weighing scale, the lyre, the wheel, the mirror, the clock have each provided a new fulcrum around which philosophic alternatives could pose themselves; cosmologists could ponder whether the world with its recurrent movements was propelled by a wheel of fate, even as they later argued whether the universal clock presupposed a clock-maker, or even a deity who synchronized the mental and physical chronometers. Leibniz and Robert Boyle both responded to the technological inspiration of the clock. Veblen carried technogenetic analysis to the point of unlikelihood; he argued, for instance, that the workingmen in machine factories were shaped in their thinking to an impersonal, causal standpoint, and consequently led to revolt against a system of business enterprise that they regarded as committed to personal, teleological categories. The ideologies of, on the one hand, trade unionists seeking higher wages, security, and better conditions on the job, and, on the other, of the revolutionary unionists, articulating the feelings of the footloose, restless, usually unattached single men, wandering through mines, prairies, fields, and grouping themselves loosely in the Industrial Workers of the World, had nothing to do with Veblen's presumed causal psychology of the machine worker.[42] Veblen's chief disciple, Robert Hoxie, struggled to fit the facts to Veblen's technogenetic analysis; deciding finally that it had all been "bunk," and depressed with his "deconversion from Veblen," he committed suicide.[43]

One could multiply the varieties of genetic analysis, some altogether spurious, that have multiplied.[44] The Nazi claims for a acial-genetic repudiation of the theory of relativity as "Jewish physics" provide the ugliest chapter in the degradation of scientific categories; their counterparts have been the Soviet theses that held the theory of relativity was genetically handicapped by Einstein's bourgeois origin (today it might be "Zionist") and that Mendel's genetics was the distorted intellectual emanation of a Catholic monk.

Every school of philosophy, indeed, tends to be friendly to that mode of genetic analysis which reinforces what it regards to be the proper method of philosophy. Thus, the vogue of linguistic philosophers has been associated with a linguo-genetic thesis, namely, that the structure of a given language tends to determine the basic character of its users' philosophy. The linguo-genetic approach merges partially with the psychogenetic; for, as Franz Boas long ago noted, "linguistic notions never rise into the consciousness of primitive man, and the basic categories are unconsciously formed."[45] The logical-positivist school, however, holding that the proper office of philosophy was the explication of the methods of science, inclined toward a scientogenetic account of philosophic ideas; thus, the dominant scientific advance of a given era, whether Newton's physics or Darwin's theory of natural selection, or Einstein's theory of relativity, or Heisenberg's principle of indeterminacy, was held to have originated a corresponding set of novel philosophies. Religious myths of creation were, from their standpoint, the proto-scientific theories of primitive man which, for reasons of cultural lag, still survive among the backward or unintelligent parts of the population.

The linguo-genetic theory, however, has little evidence in its support. Bertrand Russell used to argue that the problems of being arose because Latin (or Greek) had the verb "to be";[46] yet the same problems preoccupied the medieval Jewish philosophers, though the Hebrew language in its classic form lacked the verb "to be." And the spectrum of diverse philosophical standpoints seems a near-invariant; how much would the distribution among British philosophers of empiricists, idealists, realists, materialists, and commonsensists in 1910 have differed from what it was two hundred years previously, in 1710? Moreover, every scientific advance is shortly accommodated to the diverse philosophical standpoints. William James, Henri Bergson, and C. Lloyd Morgan assimilated the discoveries concerning biological evolution to their respective theistic standpoints; absolute idealists recognized a corresponding insight of their own eternalistic nontemporalism in Einstein's view that the distinction between past and future grows unreal with the advance of physical theory.

Of all the modes of genetic analysis, the psychogenetic, beginning with Locke, has been the most effective critical instrument in the history of empiricism. And the history of the idea of a "genetic fallacy" itself deserves to be studied psychogenetically. The "genetic fallacy" seems to have been invented as a notion for repressing all one's own inner doubts concerning the origins of one's intuitions or one's a priori affirmations concerning ethical, metaphysical, and religious notions; the notion of a "genetic fallacy" serves as a device for maintaining intact the repression of genetic facts in one's unconscious; lastly, it authorizes excluding from the philosophic community whosoever would import genetic considerations into philosophic discussion.[47]

Within the social sciences, sociogenetic and psychogenetic considerations have contributed in recent years to the most basic critique of the Marxist social doctrines. The genetic analysis of the aims of intellectuals was first opened by such writers as Waclaw Machajski and Robert Michels, who noted that the latent motive of the Marxist critique was the desire of the intellectuals to emerge as the ruling class or elite of society. John Stuart Mill had once observed that when he analyzed the social motives underlying the schemes of revolutionists, he invariably found that they housed a project of "liberticide."[48] Schumpeter's writings on the anti-capitalist mentality of the intellectual class further illumined their unconscious aims, helping explain the appeal to intellectuals of Lenin's call in *What Is to Be Done?* in disregard of its possible regressive social consequences. Marxist ideologists have shown the same hostility to genetic analysis when it is applied to themselves as the intuitionists have shown in philosophy; Marxists themselves do not hesitate to use a crude stratogenetic analysis against "bourgeois" thinkers; they experience an anxiety, however, when such considerations are directed against themselves, because they wish to preserve the Marxist unconscious intact, to maintain the "facade" that they speak with the genetic privilege of the proletariat when theirs perhaps frequently is the genetic handicap of the semi-intellectuals, afflicted by jealousy and a compensatory drive for power, or of "high intellectuals," yearning to be philosopher-kings.

. Nonetheless, even the most elevated intuitionists have similarly not been unready to avail themselves of genetic considerations to discredit, or ridicule, theories they disliked. John Maynard Keynes, for instance, derided what we might call the "Jevonian anxiety";[49] its exemplar, the economist William Stanley Jevons, feared (as Keynes narrated) that Britain's coal reserves might within a few generations be depleted. Jevons's melancholy conclusions were influenced, Keynes wrote, "by a psychological trait, unusually strong in him, which many people share, a certain hoarding instinct, a readiness to be alarmed and excited by the idea of the exhaustion of the resources." Jevons indeed did so much apprehend an approaching scarcity of paper that he accumulated large reserves of writing paper; a half-century later his children were still using them.

The "Jevonian anxiety," however, it transpires, conferred a genetic privilege on its bearer, not a genetic handicap. Jevons, struggling with poverty, and observing at first hand the brutalities of the gold mining rush in Australia, had grasped the tenuousness of the equilibrium between the human species and its available natural resources.[50] Perhaps the homosexual outlook of the Cambridge Apostles tended in their economic thinking to repress the crude reality of material resources even as in their metaphysical thinking they deprecated naturalistic realities.

In short, genetic analysis opens a path of all sorts of hypotheses for investigation, vertification, contravention. It becomes a matter for empirical investigation to determine whether a particular standpoint constitutes a genetic handicap or a genetic privilege. As applied in philosophical arguments, however, genetic analysis is more likely to terminate in decisions "genetically indeterminate" than is the case with regard to economic or physical problems. Quite apart from their diversities in psychological traits, Jevons and Keynes would have tested their rival hypotheses in terms of their contrary, approximate predictions concerning the depletion of Britain's coal reserves. Even such approximate predictions are not available to philosophers, who may dispute, for instance, with no available crucial test, whether a set of causal laws and conditions are indeed sufficient for explaining the advent of an intuition. In the social sciences, however, the genetic analyses of Marxist ideologies have made a significant contribution; by showing how intellectuals project their own ambitions, language, and even neuroses upon their theories of "historical mission" and "the proletariat," they have tended indeed to undermine the claims to "ideological truth." The intrinsically indeterminate character of philosophical questions, on the other hand, reflects itself in a corresponding indeterminacy with respect to determinations of genetic privilege or handicap.

Curiously, moreover, genetic analysts themselves seem to recognize exceptional processes in which the person "transcends" his social origins and influences. Are there such epigenetic intellectual events that would indeed elude all genetic explanation?[51] Karl Marx wrote of intellectuals ("ideologists"), who, having grasped the direction of history, thereupon decided to renounce their bourgeois background and to commit themselves to the proletarian cause. If this account, presumably a projection of Marx's own personal history, were accurate, then social acts have occurred that "transcended" the laws of historical materialism. Likewise, the English factory inspectors, though presumably agents of the British capitalist system, had, according to Marx, a vocation for truth that was higher than their economic interest. Their Blue Books were a mine of facts for Marx's *Capital.* And Freud too named Popper-Lynkeus as one whose pure character transcended the trammels of neurosis. Genetic analysts themselves thus seem to wish for exceptions to their deterministic genetic causal lines.

Lastly, genetic analysis has sometimes been likened to the cross-examining of a witness in court, where the aim, for instance, is to discredit that witness as a habitual liar, or as a previously convicted perjurer. The genetic analyst is only superficially like the cross-examing lawyer. For the genetic methods are, above all, concerned with establishing *unconscious* influences and *unconscious* determinants of ideas; the suborned witness, on the contrary, is usually a conscious liar. Nor is the genetic analyst, if scientific in his calling, a polysyllabic enlarger of ad hominem argument. The user of an ad hominem argument appeals to a popular prejudice; he does not investigate whether the given genetic conditions constitute a privilege or a handicap; he is not concerned with tracing genetic causal lines. Hitler hated the theory of relativity as begotten by a Jew; Einstein, by contrast, was prepared humorously to accept his theory as "Jewish physics" but would then have inquired as to what elements in the Jewish character or its circumstances had made it sympathetic to the notion of rational, invariant principles.[52]

The probative significance of genetic analysis thus varies greatly as one moves from philosophy to the social sciences and, lastly, to the natural and physical ones. In the social sciences, the genetic hypotheses concerning the rival schools are tested by independent evidence and become part of the observational consequences relevant to the accepting or rejecting of, for example, psychoanalytical ideas. In such cases, the origin of the ideas is relevant to the judgment of their validity, and the "genetic fallacy" is little more than an inflated resistance mechanism. When it comes to metaphysical questions, however, such as that concerning a Jamesian divine inspiration, or determinism and free will, genetic analysis, to be decisive, would have to approximate to the limit of possible explanation; then it might judge whether any lacunae in the causal lines still remained through which a divine ingredient, for instance, or a free decision might operate. Genetic analysis of metaphysical ideas therefore tends to culminate in a domain of indeterminacy, for it cannot claim such explanatory completeness. The physical sciences, happily, work with hypotheses which, through their predictive consequences, are usually contravened or verified; herein, the role of genetic considerations approaches a minimum. The sociology of scientific ideas, however, has meanwhile emerged as a science concerned with the extralogical and, indeed, nonlogical genetic factors in their discovery. Einstein's emotional adherence to determinism, in a Spinozist form, had much to do with his reaction to German anti-Semitism, but his scientific efforts at a field theory would usually not be evaluated with reference to that premise. If he had evidently been resolved to adhere to that standpoint, despite an accumulation of contrary evidence, his fellow physicists might well have deemed it relevant to note the psychogenetic and sociogenetic grounds from which his determinist postulate derived.

NOTES

1. Henry Sidgwick, *The Methods of Ethics,* 4th ed. (London: 1890), p. 212; J. B. Schneewind, *Sidgwick's Ethics and Victorian Moral Philosophy* (Oxford: 1977), p. 206; cf. William F. Quillian, Jr., *The Moral Theory of Evolutionary Naturalism* (New Haven, 1945), p. 85 ff.

2. Wesley C. Salmon and Maria Reichenbach, in *Hans Reichenbach: Selected Writings, 1904-1953,* vol. 1, ed. Maria Reichenbach and Robert Cohen (Dordrecht: 1978), pp. 76-77, 80.

3. Richard von Mises, *Positivism: A Study in Human Understanding* (New York: 1956), p. 327; Philipp Frank, "Psychoanalysis and Logical Positivism," in *Psychoanalysis, Scientific Method and Philosophy* (New York: 1959), pp. 308-09: "It is a matter of fact that among the founders of Logical Positivism, the members of the Vienna Circle, there have been quite a few scientists who exhibited a certain sympathy with the teachings of psychoanalysis . . . This has been the opinion of Rudolf Carnap and other positivists."

4. Sidney Hook, in *Hans Reichenbach: Selected Writings, 1904-1953,* vol. 1, ed. Reichenbach and Cohen, pp. 33-34.

5. Letter of Sidney Hook to the writer, February 6, 1981; cf. Lewis S. Feuer, rev. of *Psychoanalysis, Scientific Method and Philosophy,* ed. Sidney Hook, *Philosophy and Phenomenological Research,* 20 (1960), 550-52.

6. Heinz Eulau, "Cohen and Freud," *Antioch Review,* 9 (1949), 414-19.

7. John Locke, *An Essay Concerning Human Understanding,* Book I (London: George Routledge and Sons), p. 39.

8. Gottfried Wilhelm Leibnitz, *New Essays Concerning Human Understanding,* trans. Alfred Gideon Langley (Chicago, 1916), pp. 71, 72, 46.

9. Paul Levy, *Moore: G. E. Moore and the Cambridge Apostles* (London: Oxford University Press, 1979), p. 238.

10. Ibid., p. 98.

11. Ibid., p. 103.

12. Ibid., pp. 139, 140.

13. Ibid., p. 142.

14. Ibid., pp. 144-45.

15. J. B. S. Haldane, "How Slavery Killed Greek Science," *Labour Monthly,* 27 (June 1945), 190. Haldane maintained that sodomy (like celibacy and prostitution) was "undesirable and that propaganda in favor of all of them should be discouraged." See also J. B. S. Haldane, *Science and Life: Essays of a Rationalist* (London, 1968), p. 68.

16. C. H. Waddington, *The Ethical Animal* (Chicago: University of Chicago Press, 1967),

pp. 6, 54; T. H. Huxley and Julian Huxley, *Touchstone for Ethics, 1893-1943* (New York: Arno, 1947), pp. 157-63.

17. Anthony Quinton writes, "Moore's technique for proving the anti-naturalist principle was crude and unsatisfactory. His successors have discreetly drawn a veil over it . . ." in *Biology and Personality*, ed. I. T. Ramsey (Oxford: 1965), p. 108.

18. "The molding of the newborn infant . . . involves a most surprising process of projection and re-introjection of certain of his own impulses . . . and a whole peculiar mechanism which is described in terms of such concepts as the super-ego . . . At first sight, the story of the psychoanalysts may seem unlikely, but it seems to me they have now produced enough evidence to make it rather plausible . . .": C. H. Waddington, *The Evolution of an Evolutionist* (Ithaca: 1975), p. 227. Through "socio-genetic transmission," ethical beliefs emerge as part of a new evolutionary mechanism: ibid., p. 278. C. H. Waddington, *Science and Ethics*, London, 1942, p. 137. Such grouplets as the Bloomsbury Circle are useful to mankind in general. By confining their homosexual advocacy and practices to small "endogamous" circles, who then eliminate themselves through a low number of descendants, they are advantageous to society as a whole. Cf. J. B. S. Haldane, "Science and Ethics," in *Science and Human Life* (New York: Arnot, 1933), pp. 98 ff.

19. G. E. Moore, "George Santayana: The Life of Reason," *International Journal of Ethics*, 17 (1907), 253.

20. Jean Piaget, *Insights and Illusions of Philosophy*, trans. Wolfe Mays (New York: 1971), p. 25; Margaret A. Boden, *Jean Piaget* (New York: 1979), p. 97: "Anglo-Americans likewise regard psychological facts about the history of a concept or belief as in principle irrelevant to its philosophical justification or epistemological worth. As a result, such philosophers feel that there is no need for them to read Piaget—and if they do, they accuse him of systematically committing the genetic fallacy."

21. George Santayana, "Russell's Philosophical Essays: III. Hypostatic Ethics," *Journal of Philosophy, Psychology and Scientific Methods*, 8 (1911), 421-32; Russell wrote: "It was Santayana who first led me to disbelieve in the objectivity of good and evil . . ." (Bertrand Russell, *Mysticism and Logic* [New York: 1929], p. v).

22. *The Autobiography of Bertrand Russell*, vol. 1, pp. 200, 274.

23. John Dewey, *The Influence of Darwin on Philosophy, and Other Essays in Contemporary Thought* (New York: 1910), p. 19.

24. A study of "life-styles" of forty research scientists at a West Coast university was done by a clinical psychologist, Bernice T. Eiduson. Although, as she acknowledges, her interviews "were not so sustained or so intensive that extremely intimate material was proffered," none of the scientists indicated any homosexual propensity. Their sexual behavior was generally conventional, and she noted: "The scientific community as a group, however, seems to uphold these conventions." Cf. Bernice T. Eiduson, *Scientists: Their Psychological World* (New York: 1962), pp. 204-26.

25. Benjamin De Mott, *Supergrow: Essays and Reports on Imagination in America* (New York, 1969), pp. 24-25.

26. Lewis S. Feuer, "The Principle of Simplicity," *Philosophy of Science*, 24 (1957), 113-14.

27. Lewis S. Feuer, "The Bearing of Psychoanalysis Upon Philosophy," *Philosophy and Phenomenological Research*, 19 (1959), 333-34; Lewis S. Feuer, *Psychoanalysis and Ethics* (Springfield: 1955), p. 7. Many years ago the writer presented this standpoint to the last Unity of Science Congress at the University of Chicago, in 1941. The paper was absorbed into one published as "Ethical Theories and Historical Materialism," in *Science and Society*, 6 (1942), 242-72. Its use of psychoanalytical ideas elicited a collective rejection by several Marxist writers. Evidently the application of the genetic method to the Marxist ideology itself aroused anxieties in Marxists' unconscious.

28. Thus Mill tried to refute Hamilton's view that we have an "intuitive knowledge" of an external world by showing that "the Psychological Theory" could explain all the traits of the alleged intuition without going beyond "the order of our sensations coupled with memories"; one could further explain how the belief itself in an intuition of the external world arose from these verifiable

psychological facts. See John Stuart Mill, *An Examination of Sir William Hamilton's Philosophy* (New York: 1873), vol. 1, pp. 203, 236, 243.

29. Arthur O. Lovejoy, "James H. Leuba, A Psychological Study of Religion: Its Origins, Functions and Future," *International Journal of Ethics,* 24 (1914), 218; H. Rashdall, rev. of *Varieties of Religious Experience,* by William James, *Mind,* 12 (1903), 250; Herbert Feigl, "Critique of Intuition According to Scientific Empiricism," *Philosophy East and West,* 8 (1958) 14-15.

30. Jean Piaget, *The Moral Judgment of the Child,* trans. Marjorie Gabain (New York: 1932), pp. 88, 385-86.

31. Edwin G. Boring, et al., *A History of Psychology in Autobiography,* vol. 4 (Worcester: 1952), pp. 239-40.

32. *Autobiography of John Stuart Mill* (New York: 1924), pp. 192-93.

33. Carl Becker, *The Declaration of Independence: A Study in the History of Political Ideas,* 2nd ed. (New York: 1942), rpt., n.d., p. 26.

34. Cf. my *Ideology and the Ideologists* (New York: 1975), pp. 64, 118.

35. Thorstein Veblen, *Theory of Business Enterprise* (New York: 1904), p. 367.

36. John Dewey, *Reconstruction in Philosophy,* pp. 12, 13, 65, 66. Similarly, according to the Bolshevik sociologist Nikolai Bukharin, the *Summa Theologica* of Thomas Aquinas "clearly reflects the feudal conditions of his philosophy." *Historical Materialism: A System of Sociology,* tr. (New York: 1924), p. 186. N.I. Bukharin, "Theory and Practice from the Standpoint of Dialectical Materialism," in *Science at the Crossroads* (London: 1931), pp. 14-18.

37. A. Hunter Dupree, *Science in the Federal Government: A History of Policies and Activities to 1940,* (1957; rpt. New York: 1964), pp. 19, 21, 24, 40.

38. Cf. R. W. Meyer, *Leibnitz and the Seventeenth-Century Revolution,* trans. J. P. Stern (Chicago: 1952), pp. 108-09; Ronald Calinger, *Gottfried Wilhelm Leibniz* (Troy: 1976), p. 18.

39. Cf. Richard L. Schoenwald's psychogenetic study of Spencer, "Town Guano and 'Social Statics,' " *Victorian Studies,* 11 (1968), 699 ff.; Herbert Spencer, *An Autobiography* (New York: 1904), vol. 1, pp. 553-55, 579-80.

40. See my *Ideology and the Ideologists,* p. 59. The phenomenon of fashions in ideas is related to the generational wave. The philosopher-sociologist L. T. Hobhouse observed of his students at the London School of Economics: "These generations are extraordinarily short-lived. I can count up the intellectual fashions that have taken and held my students for a brief space. When I began in 1907 there was a wave of social idealism. Then very soon came suffrage, then syndicalism, then the war, then guild socialism, then Freud. Freud, nothing but Freud, for three or four years; now, thank goodness, that is going out, and we have mostly Elliot Smith and the Diffusion Theory . . . Each of these waves absolutely submerges everything for the time being . . . It's lost labour to refute these things. They just die out in time." See J. A. Hobson and Morris Ginsberg, *L. T. Hobhouse* (London: 1931), p. 68.

41. Thorstein Veblen, *The Theory of Business Enterprise,* p. 367.

42. Cf. Cornelia Stratton Parker, *An American Idyll: The Life of Carleton H. Parker* (Boston: 1919), pp. 144-48; cf. Selig Perlman's notion of "job consciousness," in *A Theory of the Labor Movement* (New York: 1928), p. 169.

43. Alvin Johnson, *Pioneer's Progress: An Autobiography* (New York: 1952), pp. 206-07; Robert Franklin Hoxie, *Trade Unionism in the United States,* 2nd ed. (New York: 1926), pp. 365-67; Joseph Dorfman, *Thorstein Veblen and His America* (New York: 1937), p. 311.

44. Thelma Lavine, in a keen essay, applied what she called the "four basic laws of situational logic" to give a rationale for genetic analysis. Basically, she founds it on the notion that beliefs that were designed to solve the problems of one period may be presumed inadequate for those of a later one. Is this "law" helpful? The Protestant virtues, thrift, frugality, industry, may have had in mind the problems of early capitalist accumulation, but all societies have found them valuable. Genetic analysis is at its best in confuting solipsism, though the recurring doctrine hardly provides an answer to some previous "problematic situation" (T. Z. Lavine, "Reflections of the Genetic Fallacy," *Social Research,* 29 [1962], p. 333).

45. Franz Boas, Introduction to *Handbook of American Indian Language* (Lincoln, Nebr.: 1966), pp. 63-64, 66.

46. Lewis S. Feuer, "Sociological Aspects of the Relation Between Language and Philosophy," *Philosophy of Science,* 20 (1953), pp. 85-100; rpt. Robert A. Manners and David Kaplan, eds., *Theory in Anthropology* (Chicago: 1968), pp. 411-421.

47. Cf. J. B. Schneewind, *Sidgwick's Ethics and Victorian Moral Philosophy* (Oxford: 1977), pp. 205-206.

48. Lewis S. Feuer, "John Stuart Mill as a Sociologist," in *James and John Stuart Mill: Papers of the Centenary Conference,* ed. John M. Robson and Michael Laine (Toronto: 1976), pp. 89, 104-05; F.A. Hayek, ed., *John Stuart Mill and Harriet Taylor: Their Correspondence and Subsequent Marriage* (Chicago: 1951), p. 216.

49. John Maynard Keynes, *Essays in Biography,* new ed. (London: 1951), p. 266. Bertrand Russell much annoyed John Dewey by characterizing the pragmatic theory of knowledge as an expression not of the scientific mentality but of American industrial motives; cf. P. A. Schilpp, ed. *The Philosophy of John Dewey* (Chicago: 1939), pp. 156.

50. *Letters and Journal of W. Stanley Jevons,* ed. H. A. Jevons (London: 1886), pp. 66, 101, 123, 127, 129; R. D. Collison and Rosamond Konskamp, *Papers and Correspondence of William Stanley Jevons* (London: 1972), vol. 1, p. 38.

51. Lovejoy once noted: "If the thing to be accounted for is truly something new, an 'emergent' or pure 'mutation,' then, though the theory may correctly describe the circumstances preceding, or attending its emergence, it cannot deduce the necessity of its emerging . . ." In this sense, "it is of the nature of really genetic theories *not* to explain" (Arthur O. Lovejoy, *Reflections on Human Nature* [Baltimore: 1961], pp. 85-86).

52. Cf. Raphael Patai, *The Jewish Mind* (New York: 1977), pp. 352-53.

PART V

Pragmatism

DANIEL BELL

The Pragmatism of Metaphysics

In 1927, Sidney Hook published his first book, *The Metaphysics of Pragmatism,* his doctoral dissertation at Columbia University.[1] No matter in what ways Hook's political views have changed, his philosophical views, as a pragmatist and as an exponent of John Dewey, have been consistent. He believed then, as I think he believes now, that mind is an instrument and that thinking is instrumental, a tool to explore the world rather than as a reflection or a picture of the world.

What is curious is that the target of Hook's attack was Kant. Now Kant did not believe that mind reflected the world or built up a picture of the world from perceptions, sensations, or images. In a famous passage in the *Prolegomena,* Kant remarked in an italicized sentence: *"The understanding does not derive its laws from, but prescribes them to, nature."* In fact, it is clear that Kant had an "activity theory" of knowledge, albeit that activity was a property of mind.[2]

Hook never took up that aspect of Kant's thought, but levied his charges on two other aspects. One was the use of a priori categories. In that first book, Hook wrote:

Categories are bound up with distinctions we make in analysis. Analysis starts *from* something given and with something *taken.* . . . It follows, therefore, that Being is not a category and Experience is not a category. Neither is Space-Time nor subsistence nor any other denotative indication of the sum total of actual and possible existents. A fundamental term which has no intelligible opposite describes nothing because its apparent import is to describe everything. [p. 116]

The second was the alleged psychologism that underlay Kant's and the neo-Kantian view of experience. Again:

. . . the various forms of the Kantian tradition must be rejected because of the mistaken and gratuitous psychological views. . . . The neo-Kantian deduction of the categories is generally effected by the rattling of a psychological colander of remarkable complexity through which somehow or other the world is precipitated. If the psychology were empirical, the analysis would be significant although inadequate as far as determining answers to questions concerning the extent and limits of the validity of categorical laws. However the Mind (or Self or Subject) of Neo-Kantianism is transcendental; not a function of temporal analysis. [pp. 114–15]

Against these views, Hook emphasizes time and again throughout the book (and through all of his other philosophical works) that pragmatism (though coming "of age in a complex industrial era . . . may be regarded as the culminating expression of one of the great philosophical motifs in the history of thought") revolves around a conception of man as "homo faber," and that "the clear indication of the primacy of the practical may be accepted as the defining emphasis of the pragmatic point of departure."[3] And the emphasis on the practical, or the problematic, leads to the view of thinking as instrumental, as the means to deal with the difficulties, as the effort to overcome the puzzles and dilemmas that have given rise to our concerns and to thought and action.

Now if instrumentalism was meant as a psychological theory, as how thought is prompted, it surely could be accepted more readily than a mimetic or reflective or contemplative theory of thought. But it is the claim, expressed by Hook, that the view extends beyond psychological notions into "the root problems of metaphysics" that provides the difficulties.

In the more than fifty years since the publication of Hook's first book a large number of difficulties with this claim have become apparent. In one sense, instrumentalism merges with an inductivist view of generalization. If the consequential conditions are the test of a proposition, how can we generalize from what will, necessarily, be a limited number of experiments? One can go, then, either to a complete hypothetical-deductivist view, with the notion of a "covering law" as the basis of adequate ground of judgment, or some notion of conjecture and refutation (with which Dewey's pragmatism would be compatible), although propositions could never be wholly established, only falsified.

But, out of these debates, we seem to return to one anchorage of Kant, that knowledge is theory-laden and mind-dependent. As Hilary Putnam puts it: "It is not that the thinking mind *makes up* the world on Kant's view; but it doesn't just mirror it either."[4] To formulate it somewhat differently: for experience, the factual order is primary; for meaning, the logical order. We are back to the old thought of Henry James: "The intellectual life of man consists almost wholly in his substitution of a conceptual order for the perceptual order in which his experiences originally comes."[5] The crucial qualification is the phrase "originally comes." While, in any unthinking sense, the world is a blooming, buzzing confusion, the meanings we *impose* on that perceptual flux derive from the categories we use and the theories in which they are embedded.

The starting point, necessarily, is the categories; that is inescapable from the proposition of reality being, crucially, mind-dependent.

Hook's argument, given his instrumentalism and emphasis on process, was entirely against the idea of a priori categories. Kant's insistence on the fixity of these categories (or at least the fundamental organizing frame of space and time) made it easy to object to their character. Nor did it help for Paul Natorp and Hermann Cohen to assert that the a priori categories are basically logical or mathematical, since these only emphasize the formal nature of these categories. Yet, if we return, as I think we have, to the primacy of theory (or mind) the real difficulties are not those with which Hook attempted to deal but with the exact opposite: the historicism and relativism that is implicit in the nature of such theorizing.

The root of the problem is already there in the original formulation of Kant that we do not derive our ideas (images, sensations, perceptions) *from* nature, but prescribe them *to* nature. For what if these categories are prior, but not fixed? What if these "organizing frames of reference" shift over time, or change with the perspectives of different cultures? As Dilthey, Durkheim, and the later Wittgenstein have argued in different ways, categories, meanings, and rules are socially shared and become meaningful only through an implicit consensus. How, then, do we transcend time and place and make such understandings a common property beyond the particularities that social usages define? This is the problem Hook once formulated brilliantly. In his essay on "Materialism" in the *Encyclopedia of the Social Sciences,*[6] Hook wrote:

> If it is true as Marx states in *Das Kapital* that in changing his external environment man changes his own nature, then human nature under ancient slavery must have been different in some respects from human nature under modern capitalism. But if this is so, how is it possible to understand present experience, since understanding presupposes an invariant explanatory pattern? That is a problem which confronts not only historical materialism but all philosophies of history. . . . [p. 219]

The crux of the matter, and it is a metaphysical question, is the nature of invariance. Theories about phenomena are either constitutive of nature or history, or they are primarily conceptual prisms. If they are the former, then there have to be specific rules for their correspondence to truth. If they are primarily conceptual prisms, then one has to specify their utility in relation to the questions one seeks to answer. Phenomena, I would say, are either "constitutive" or "constructed." The modes of inquiry are a search for invariance (either intrinsic to the phenomena or imposed by the observer) and then causal and functional relations can be established, or the inquiry is largely interpretative, in which multiple meanings and changing perspectives are possible.[7] In the one frame, to follow Collingwood,[8] one can establish a logic of propositions; in the other, we know through the logic of question and answer. These are gnomic statements. In the few pages that follow, I can only sketch an outline of this dualistic, largely neo-Kantian, framework.

A number of years ago, the Rand Corporation published a book entitled *A Million Random Numbers and a Hundred Thousand Digits*. It did so because statisticians need true random numbers for certain experiments; but the human mind, asked to generate numbers "at random," will fall into repetitive chains and a weird order will have been produced.

We cannot escape this search for order, which underlies all the things we do. There is a thema, the one and the many, that circumscribes this quest. There are the many: the division of mind and body, the dualism of observable phenomena and unknowable noumena, the distinction between nature and culture, all within a pluralistic universe. And there is the one: the quest for a single all-embracing scheme, a single prime mover, a single noetic mode; and this effort twists the diverse threads of myth, religion, science, and philosophy into the search for the unity of knowledge, a unity within the great chain of being, or a single explanatory pattern.

In the *Theatetus*,[9] we find Socrates sending this hare down the tricky course of the dialectic. Theatetus, the red-cheeked young innocent, in seeking to define knowledge, points to the different kinds he has learned: about the relation of geometry to the sciences, or the craft of the potter and the different uses of clay. To which Socrates replies:

> But the question you were asked, Theatetus, was not about what are the objects of knowledge, nor yet how many sorts of knowledge there are. We did not want to count them, but to find out what the thing itself — knowledge — is. [146 E]

Socrates then leads the young man on to show him the commonality between the different kinds of clay, and to demonstrate the single term that solves the difference between like and unlike numbers; and he concludes:

> Forward then. . . . Just as you found a single character to embrace all the multitude, so now try to find a single formula that applies to many kinds of knowledge.

Here is the grail: unity behind multiplicity, structure beneath flux, reality underneath appearance, all moving through the dialectic ascent to the noetic unity that is the knowledge of the eternal oneness of it all.

What Plato sought to establish by dialectic, Aristotle did by logic: through observation, classification, deduction, to find the *prote aitia*, the first cause. When Aristotle reduced all the changes that come under our observation to four kinds of motion, and further reduced these four kinds to locomotion, positing then a prime mover, which or who was itself immovable, he thought he had established the principle of the uniformity of the laws of nature.

Classical thought never doubted the unity of nature and the unity of culture, and the fusion of the two into the unity of knowledge. But there was one essential element to that understanding, the belief that knowledge was inherently normative: that it embodied purposes, natural and human, and that understanding, in crossing that dividing line from the visible to the intelligible, from the existent to the ideal, would allow us to achieve the inherent design of the true, the good, and the beautiful, the realization of matter (and of art and of human nature) in its perfected form.

None of this, of course, was automatic. If there was *physis,* the structure of matter, there was also *nomos,* the laws of justice. If there is *techne,* the instrumental arts, there is also *themis,* the union of conscience and honorable conduct, which is the principle of civilized life. The purpose of knowledge (the move from *doxa* to *epistme*) was to understand the entelechy of things, their intrinsic design, so that we could conform to their principles, or eliminate any hindrances, in order to be able to realize the potential of form, the potential of nature.

The unity of knowledge—which was therefore the unity of philosophy—was not just the delimitation of the "order of things," but the knowledge of *telos,* the normative ascent, not semantic but substantive, to the highest, the true ends.

Central to all this is the distinction, as in Aristotle, between the natural and the unnatural. The natural is that with its immanent telos, the course inherent in its design and ascent. The unnatural is that from without, accidental or contingent, or distorted by excesses or fevers in which one dimension alone predominates and interferes with the unfolding of a *telos.* Motions are natural: smoke, being of the air, rises; clay, being of the earth, falls. Violent motions are those from without, disturbing the order of things. Similarly in the polity: the *oikos* is the prudent management of the household in accordance with natural needs; *chrematique* is the unnatural, avaricious desire for riches, or, as in *The Republic* when unrestrained appetite created the fevered city.

Modern science, of course, sunders and dissolves these distinctions between the natural and the unnatural. In physics, there are only motions, unified by sets of equations and laws. In psychology, behavior is distributed along a curve, and the pathological is less a difference in kind than a skewed tail of a continuum of traits. Similarly, science rejects the idea of *telos.* Nature has no purposes. There are no higher or lower motions, and natural philosophy becomes natural science—though we may wonder why it still retains the word "natural."

We come, then, to the first divide: if man is wholly, or largely, a part of nature, are his actions "reducible" to the facts of nature? What do we say of purpose and design? If these are not intrinsic to nature, in what ways are they emergent or transcendent; or are these only blind illusions in a mechanistic world, as even some of the Enlightenment followers of Newton, such as de la Mettrie, thought: that man is a machine. (De la Mettrie, as has been pointed out, was a gourmand who died of the gout; probably from stoking the machine too much.)

If Galileo did the first act of sundering, that of eliminating *telos* from nature, Kant completed the building of the divide. For Kant there can be no totality; all is duality. Mind only knows through categories: we can never know the *Dinge an sich,* the world itself. There is a physical order, sensory and perceptual; and a conceptual order, the world of fact and flux, ordered through logical categories. What we know is ineradicably mind-dependent. There is a world of objects and a world of subjects; a world of nature that is determinate and bound by causality, and a moral realm that is open to desire and design and, as Dewey argued in *Art as Experience,*[10] to re-design, re-ordering and re-shaping in accordance with human purpose.

Since Kant, there have been two broad currents that have, in effect, tried to bridge that divide. One is the Hegelian tradition (including Marxism), which has sought to re-assert the possibility of totality, of overcoming the separation of man from nature, of subject from object, but places that project at the end of history. The Aristotelian frame is thus re-drawn: realization of form (with its languages of biological unfolding, even in art) is replaced by the realization of history (through the cunning of reason or the unfolding of self-consciousness). Thus we have the restoration of a *telos,* and of a normative order that judges the existent from a specific ideal standpoint, that of the "end of history." (But what if history is not obedient to the bugle of that *marche generale,* and from what moral standpoint is man to judge the present if transcendence is denied?)

The other current has been scientific positivism in various guises: from a radical behaviorism to a logical empiricism. As such, the unity of philosophy is replaced by the unity of science. But in so doing, a different kind of divide is introduced. In one version, the unity of science is a substantive skein, a great chain of being in which, from molecule to man, there is a single ladder of nature. And the expansionism of modern biology provides a double set of rungs: physiology, which links molecular biology to chemical and physical processes at one end, and evolutionary biology, linking behavior and culture to the genetic leashes on human purposes.

In the different version, the unity of science is not sought through a common structure within the factual order of things, but through a common logic of application applicable to all diverse realms, from history to physics. Thus, if statements about phenomena are to be accepted, *as science,* they must follow certain common canons about the nature of explanation, generalization, verification, falsification, a covering law, or some such similar stipulations.

I leave aside the historicist arguments (e.g., those of Stephen Toulmin) that even these stipulations of explanation are not simply logical but themselves are contextually and historically derived. What concerns me is that the overall project itself, though dealing (in some versions) with the evaluative, excludes the normative. Questions of ends and values and purposes are seen, in one extreme version (now largely discarded), as preferences or as emotive or nonrational and therefore unprovable. Or, even in the more "humane" pragmatic versions, values are seen as statements of consequence, to be tested like descriptive statements, but not to be judged as ends in themselves.

I believe that both streams, Hegelianism (including its contemporary expressions, such as those of Lukacs) and positivism (in psychology and economics), are drying up; and we do not have to step in that same stream twice. What is striking is that in so much of philosophy the theme today is "back to Kant." But if so, how to go forward?

The Kantian starting point is the acceptance of two realms: the world of nature, wherein one seeks causal laws, and the world of culture, in which the quest is for meanings. Put in my own terms, these are the worlds of invariance and of interpretation, and each is obedient to a different axial principle. The acceptance of this division is the necessary ground for the reconstruction of philosophy.

To restate this division in a modified Kantian language: there are constitutive worlds and constructed orders, the one whose structure is intrinsic, often masked and obscure, and which has to be inferred and discerned; the other is an order shaped by design and purpose, question and answer.

A constitutive structure is one of invariance where there are stable relations, repeatable sequences, or a given order of procession, or where "transformation rules" can take relations that are co-variant in one frame of reference and make them invariant in all frames of reference. Thus, the laws of physics hold through the entire structure of the universe, from microcosm to macrocosm. Even when the angles of vision are complementary, and the observer, being himself within the field, makes the measurement of the phenomenon difficult, or if the determinate relations be stochastic and probabilistic rather than mechanistic, the phenomena has an intrinsic order of its own. That order is not constructed by mind, though our knowledge of it, and the way we conceive of it, is sometimes mind-dependent. But truth is necessarily a correspondence between the logical frame (or the mathematical formulation) and the outside structure of reality — even when mathematicians and physicists marvel at the fact that the mathematical constructions by mind seem to be so congruent with the reality.

The cultural world is a constructed order (subject to constraints, for it cannot be completely fanciful or utopian), in which the relations we single out as significant derive from our need to interpret these actions and symbols in accordance with diverse perspectives and values and the different histories of human groups.

Within this frame, I reject the biological reductionism that places culture at the end of a genetic tether. I reject the psychological reductionism of the behaviorism that sees all actions as responses to the environment and to others (for if we are others to one another, is there not a question of intersubjectivity as well?). And I reject, too, the social Darwinism of a Menger or a Hayek, who see society as the spontaneous adjustment of human beings to one another, through the market or assortative mating, and where common purposes, for them, are impossible or defeat the "natural" processes of adjustment.

Nor does this distinction repeat the division suggested by Dilthey between the natural and the cultural sciences, or by Rickert between the nomothetic and ideographic disciplines. Invariance, as a mode, may be common to all fields. One sees the search for invariance in economics (in the effort to identify stable relationships, or the assumptions of the movements of markets to equilibria), for how else could one "model" the real world? And one sees the search for invariance in structuralism, where Levi-Strauss, for example, has sought to apply "transformation rules" derived from linguistics to stipulate invariant (through formal) homologies in diverse cultural myths. And, conversely, one finds in the natural sciences (as Gerald Holton has shown) how commitments to philosophically grounded interpretative thema (such as seeing the world as continuous or discontinuous, as deterministic or probabilistic) shape the inquiries and research experiments in science.

The distinction between invariance and interpretation cuts across the traditional division of the disciplines, yet remains necessary in identifying two radically different consequences from these modes of inquiry. Invariance tells us the constitutive, intrinsic structures and rules of order, rules that, once, known, may become instrumental for human purposes to be re-ordered and re-designed. The realm of social constructions is the realm of meanings; but meanings not just in the technical, epistemological sense of the relation of words to objects, or of *sinn* to *bedeutung,* for these are the *semantics* of science. The study of socially meaningful behavior raises questions of sense to reference in a way that the study of nature does not, for these are meanings that prompt *reciprocal* conduct, or conflicts of purposes, or norms of behavior that arise when the construction of recognitions is also the work of *re*-cognitions.

That there is a unity of nature (as C. F. von Weizsacker, for example, proposes) I would accept as a constitutive fact. And it is the task of science to discern that order. That there is a unity of nature and culture, I am prepared to deny, and I have only given the outline of my reasons here.[11]

I close, however, on a simpler problem and a more difficult solution. Science has defined its role — the study of nature — though there is the question, as I have indicated — of the reach of that inquiry. But where is philosophy? Pushed out of the "natural" world by science, eschewing the domains of metaphysics, it has been, in the old phrase of Locke, the "under-laborer," the street-cleaner of the mind, clarifying sentences, multiplying distinctions, establishing rules of reference, polishing the bite of language. Yet, if we go back to the classical heritage, one large task has been largely ignored: to re-establish the normative as a legitimate field for philosophy. Purposes, values, and meanings are also kinds of knowledge, since they are judgments of alternative realities. Justifications and moral evaluations are not just assertions or preferences, but claims that can be judged adequate or inadequate, as morally enhancing or morally diminishing, within the field of rational discourse, which is, I would hold, congruent with the definition of philosophy.

It has been the glory of Sidney Hook, as philosopher and humanist, that the question of values has played a central role in his thinking and actions.

And that concern has led him to his conception of the tragic sense of life: the inescapable fact that often values are incompatible and "every genuine experience of moral doubt and perplexity in which we ask, 'What should I do?' takes place in a situation where good conflicts with good." As Hook concludes:

> No matter how we choose, we must either betray the ideal of the greater good or the ideal of right or justice. In this lies the agony of choice. . . . The pragmatic perspective on life . . . is an attempt to make it possible for men to live in a world of inescapable tragedy — a tragedy that flows from the conflict of moral ideals — without lamentation, defiance or make-believe.[12]

That, in a way that perhaps Hook had not completely intended, is also a metaphysics of pragmatism.

NOTES

1. Open Court, Chicago, Ill., 1927.

2. In fact, that very activity theory posed a problem for Marx and the first generations of Marxists. As Hook was one of the very first to point out (in *Towards the Understanding of Karl Marx* [1933]), the "young Marx" did have an activity theory of knowledge, but the difficulty was to reconcile this with the simple-minded materialism of matter that Engels held to be the hallmark of science. Thus, in *Anti-Duhring* and in the *Dialectics of Nature,* Engels put forward the absurd position that matter moves dialectically and that through *ein spiegelbild* or copy image we catch the reflections of change. What is difficult to understand, of course, is why Marx did not object to these vulgar formulations in *Anti-Duhring,* which he read, and to which he contributed a section.

3. In attacking Kant's idealism, Hook also wrote: "Practical reason meant the demands of the ethical consciousness rather than the primacy of biological adaptation." I wonder whether Hook would still hold to the view of the primacy of biological adaptation? The implicit "reductionism" has always been one of the more troublesome aspects of a "naturalistic" view of man.

4. Hilary Putnam, *Meaning and the Moral Sciences* (London: Routledge & Kegan Paul, 1978), p. 1.

5. William James, *Some Problems of Philosophy* (New York: Longmans, Green, 1916, p. 51).

6. Vol. 10, Macmillan, New York, 1933.

7. To return, as with Hook, to Marx's thought and the character of historical materialism: Fundamental to Marx is the emphasis on the mode of production as determining (in the first instance or the last) all other dimensions of society. Yet is the "mode of production" *constitutive* of all society and of history? Is it, so to speak, an intrinsic structural feature of all societies as a determining force? Or is it, largely, a "conceptual prism" that has greater or lesser focusing power, depending upon the historical question one is asking? If one argues that it is "constitutive" of society, as the "vulgar Marx" and the "vulgar Engels" seemed to imply, how does one "falsify" the proposition? If it is a "conceptual prism," then its theoretical status is like that of Max Weber's "modes of domination," a scheme that one can apply with great results to our understanding of society. Yet it is important to note that Marx's "modes of production" and Weber's "modes of domination," even though they are each given time-frames, are not at all historically congruent. One cannot be an overlay on the other. One uses each for different questions. This is, I think, a testament to the power of Collingwood's formulation.

8. R. G. Collingwood, *An Autobiography* (Oxford: Clarendon Press, 1939).

9. In Plato, *The Collected Dialogues,* ed. by Edith Hamilton and Huntington Cairns, Bollingen Series, no. 71 (New York: Pantheon Books, 1966).

10. Capricorn Books, New York, 1958 (original publication, 1934).

11. That there is a "unity of culture" I would be prepared to affirm, though this cannot be the place to do so. I believe that there are cultural universals, but not in the narrow anthropological sense of language of language structures or taboos, though these may be true. I believe that the cultural universals arise out of the common existential predicaments and situations that each human group faces and which call for some coherent answer to a set of symbolic meanings. These are the existential situations of death, obligation, tragedy, love, courage, and the like. The answers vary, but that is the *history* of human culture; but the questions are the same. I have elaborated this argument in my essay, "The Return of the Sacred," in my book, *The Winding Passage: Essays and Sociological Journeys, 1960–1980,* especially pp. 335–45.

12. Sidney Hook, *Pragmatism and the Tragic Sense of Life,* Basic Books, New York, 1974, pp. 15, 22.

RICHARD RORTY

Pragmatism Without Method

American pragmatism has, in the course of a hundred years, swung back and forth between an attempt to raise the rest of culture to the epistemological level of the natural sciences and an attempt to level down the natural sciences to an epistemological par with art, religion, and politics.

C. S. Peirce sometimes thought of himself as carrying the methods of laboratory science into philosophy and sometimes (in the manner later made fashionable by Russell) claimed to deduce all his philosophical views from the results of mathematical logic. But at other times he subordinated logic to ethics (and ultimately to aesthetics) and raged against the positivism of his "nominalist" opponents.

William James sometimes comes on as tough-minded, empirical, in love with hard facts and concrete details. But at other times, notably in "The Will to Believe," it becomes clear that his principal motive is to place his father's belief in Society as the Redeemed Form of Man on a par with the theories of the "hard" sciences. By taking a true belief as a successful rule for action, he hoped to rub out the purported difference between scientific beliefs as "evidenced" and religious beliefs as adopted without evidence.

Dewey, in turn, was grateful to natural science, especially as represented by Darwin, for rescuing him from his early Hegelianism. But Hegel had taught him to (in a phrase I borrow from Marjorie Grene) "treat history as our basic phenomenon and draw the world of science, as a limiting case, out of historical reality." Dewey's insistence that *everything* could be made "scientific" often seemed to his positivist critics merely to make science itself look unscientific by softening the contrast between it and the rest of culture.

One can describe these two sides of pragmatism in another way: as the side turned toward the general public and the side turned toward competitors within the philosophical profession. On the public scene, the principal social and cultural function of this movement has been to break through the crust of convention, to favor receptivity to the new rather than attachment to the old, and in particular to shake a nation free from the religious culture in which it began and which still permeates its public life. On this side, it has tried to break down the influence of old moral codes and replace them with an "experimental" attitude, not afraid of seemingly revolutionary social legislation, nor of new forms of artistic and personal freedom. So this side of pragmatism has been scientific. It has spent its time holding up the experimental scientist as a model to the rest of culture. Among their fellow philosophy professors, however, the pragmatists have differentiated themselves from other brands of scientism — utilitarianism, sense-data empiricism, and logical positivism. Within the philosophical community, they are best known as holists. Like the idealists, they are dubious about the suggestion that we can isolate little building-blocks called "meanings" or "sensations" or "pleasures and pains" and construct something interesting out of them. Notoriously, they share the idealists' doubts about the idea that "truth is correspondence to reality" (although they hasten to distinguish themselves from the idealists by making "the ideally coherent set of representations" a future human product rather than a pre-existent reality).

These various ambiguities have sometimes made pragmatism seem a very muddled movement indeed — neither hard enough for the positivists nor soft enough for the aesthetes, neither atheistical enough for descendants of Tom Paine nor transcendental enough for descendants of Emerson, a philosophy for trimmers. As David Hollinger has remarked, the cliché that pragmatism was *the* philosophy of American culture suddenly ceased to be heard around 1950, just before Dewey's death. It was as if pragmatism had been crushed between Tillich and Carnap, the upper and the nether millstones. Carnap, with his return to hard-edged empiricism, became the hero of the philosophy professors, but most American intellectuals turned their back on pragmatism and on analytic philosophy simultaneously. They began to look to Tillich, or Sartre, or Marcuse, or some other philosopher who sounded deeper and more intellectually ambitious than the Deweyan anti-ideological liberalism on which they had been reared. Liberalism had come to strike them as, at best, boringly platitudinous, or, at worst, a defensive apologia for the status quo.

This anti-ideological liberalism is, in my view, the most valuable tradition of American intellectual life. We owe a great debt to Sidney Hook for his sustained and courageous efforts to keep it alive, in a period in which it has become fashionable to despise it. In what follows, however, I shall be arguing against some of the tactics Hook has employed in doing so. In particular, I think he was wrong to opt for the "let's bring the scientific method to bear throughout culture" side of pragmatism, as opposed to the "let's recognize a pre-existent continuity between science, art, politics, and religion" side. Hook's adoption of this tactic — his identification of liberalism with "being scientific" or "the use of intelligence" — has led him into two positions that, I think, pragmatists ought to avoid. First, it has made him more positivistic than

than he needs to be. Post-positivistic philosophy of science (what Clark Glymour has called "the new fuzziness" — the common denominator of, say, Kuhn, Hesse and Harré) has left his account of "scientific method" in the lurch. Second, it has led him to be more antagonistic to "Continental" (and, specifically, Heideggerian) philosophy than he needs to be. I think that by developing the other side of pragmatism — the holistic and syncretic side — one can make a better case for liberalism (a better "Defense of the Enlightenment," to use the title of Hook's essay on Polanyi) than by attempting to isolate the essence of "science."

Consider the following passage from Hook's 1955 essay "Naturalism and First Principles":

> My contention is that what makes any reason in science a valid reason for believing an hypothesis is not historical, but invariant for all historical periods in the growth of science. But whether a reason is a strong reason for believing an hypothesis varies with the presence or absence of other leads and evidence for them.[1]

Hook is here making a distinction between "the logic of the scientific method" (which pronounces on "validity") and the various historical factors that influence theory-choice at a given stage of inquiry (and make for "strength"). This is just the distinction that, in the decades since Hook wrote, has come to seem more and more dubious thanks to (ironically enough) the "pragmatist" holism of Quine and Kuhn. These writers made clear the difficulties involved in holding language and world, theory and evidence, apart, as the positivists wanted to do. Whereas Hook attempted to enlist positivistic philosophy of science as an ally, and to interpret Dewey's talk about "scientific method" in those terms, most philosophers of science have been moving in the direction of Dewey's suspicion of attempts to contrast an objective "given" (e.g., "the evidence," "the facts") with human "takings."

Hook continues, shortly after the passage I just cited, by saying:

> If the foregoing is sound then I think it constitutes some reason for believing that there is only one reliable method of reaching the truth about the nature of things anywhere and at any time, that this reliable method comes to full fruition in the methods of science, and that a man's normal behavior in adapting means to ends belies his words whenever he denies it. Naturalism as a philosophy not only accepts this method but also the broad generalizations which are established by the use of it; viz., that the occurrence of all qualities or events depends upon the organization of a material system in space-time, and that their emergence, development and disappearance are determined by changes in such organization.

Let me call the claim that there is such a "reliable method" "scientism" and the the "broad generalizations" Hook offers "naturalism." By redefining "naturalism" in this way I can say that the other — holistic — side of pragmatism would like to be naturalistic without being scientistic. It wants to hold on to the materialistic world-view that typically forms the background of contemporary liberal self-consciousness, while refraining from the claim that this view has been "established" by a *method,* much less the "one reliable method for reaching the truth about the nature of things." If one takes the core of pragmatism to be its attempt to replace the notion of true beliefs as representations of "the nature of things" and instead to think of them as successful rules for action, then it becomes easy to recommend an experimental, fallibilist attitude, but hard to isolate a "method" that will embody this attitude.

Hard though it may be, there is an obvious temptation to do so. For pragmatists would like some stick with which to beat the people who refuse to share their naturalism, once they have deprived themselves of the ability to say that their antagonists are not "corresponding to the nature of things." The claim that anti-naturalists are being irrational, or not using "intelligence," seems the obvious alternative. For this suggests that there is some neutral ground upon which naturalists and anti-naturalists can meet, and naturalists conquer. Unless there is some such ground, the specter of "relativism" looms. So ever since "correspondence to reality" began to look dubious, "rationality" has been used as a substitute. Dewey's way of doing this was to emphasize the difference between the priests and the artisans, the contemplators and the doers. Hook reiterates this contrast when he says, for example,

> Science and technology represent two different attitudes toward the mysterious: one tries to solve mysteries, the other worships them. The first believes that mysteries may be made less mysterious even though they are not cleared up, and admits that there will always be mysteries. The second believes that some specific mysteries are final.[2]

This distinction hooks up with that between the cognitive and the noncognitive, as when Hook says that "all knowledge that men have is scientific knowledge"[3] and quotes with approval the remark, "If scientific statements are to be called truth, then religious statements should be called something else — comforts, perhaps."[4] When "truth" is used in this contrastive way, we are clearly a long way from "The Will to Believe" and from the laissez-faire attitude that sees religion and science as alternative ways of solving life's problems, to be distinguished by success or failure, rather than rationality or irrationality.

The anti-scientific, holistic pragmatist who adopts the latter attitude wants us to adopt naturalism without thinking of ourselves as more rational than our theistic friends. He begins by granting the Quinean point that anything can, by suitably reweaving the web of belief, be fitted either into an anti-naturalistic world-view in which Divine Providence is a central element *or* into a naturalistic world-view in which men are on their own. This is to admit that James was right against Clifford: "evidence" is not a very useful notion when trying to decide what one thinks of the world as a whole. Such an admission only looks relativistic if one thinks that the lack of general, neutral, antecedently formulable criteria for choosing between alternative, equally coherent, webs of belief means that there can be no "rational" decision. Relativism seems a threat only to those who insist on quick fixes and knock-down arguments. To the holist, it is enough to debate naturalism and anti-naturalism in the old familiar, inconclusive ways. If one drops the idea that there is a common ground called "the evidence," one is still far from saying that one person's web is as good as another. One can still debate the issue on all the old familiar grounds, bringing up once again all the hackneyed details, all the varied advantages and disadvantages of the two views. One will talk about the problem of evil, the stultifying effect of a religious culture upon intellectual life, the dangers of theocracy, the potentiality for anarchy in a secularist culture, the *Brave New World* consequences of a utilitarian, secular morality. One will contrast the lives of one's secularist and of one's religious friends and acquaintances. One will do, in short, just what the "new fuzzies" in philosophy of science say scientists do when some relatively large-scale proposal to change the way nature (or part of nature) is pictured is up for discussion. One will muddle through, hoping that some reweaving will happen on both sides, and that some consensus may thus emerge.

There is, in our culture, a sociological difference between the naturalists and the anti-naturalists. The former, on the average, have been in school longer and been exposed to more books. They are faster on their feet in developing the implications of views they like and in finding objections to views they don't. So it is tempting to think of the latter as having been insufficiently rational in adopting their views. The atypical anti-naturalists—those who fit nicely (e.g., as professors of physics or philosophy) into the modern *entzauberte* world of means-end rationality but for whose lives religious belief is still central—are accused by scientific naturalists like Hook of intellectual schizophrenia, or applying one method on weekdays and another on Sundays. But this accusation presupposes that one ought to formulate general methodological principles, that one has a duty to have a general view about the nature of rational inquiry and a universal method for fixing belief. It is not clear that we have any such duty. We do have a duty to talk to each other, to converse about our views of the world, to use persuasion rather than force, to be tolerant of diversity, to be contritely fallibilist. But this is not the same thing as a duty to have methodological principles.

It may be helpful—it sometimes has been helpful—to formulate such principles. It is often, however—as in the cases of Descartes' *Discourse* and Mill's "inductive methods"—a waste of time. The result is often just a string of platitudes, hoked up to look like an algorithm. The advice to profit by the example of some notably successful piece of inquiry makes sense if it means: look at the rest of your beliefs and see if the new beliefs you have acquired as a result of that success don't suggest some useful readjustments. This was one of the things that was said by admirers of the New Science to the orthodox of the seventeenth and eighteenth centuries. But unfortunately these admirers also thought that one could isolate the *method* used by the New Science. They made some good tries at describing such a method, but I take the history of epistemology to show that none of their attempts panned out (and the triumph of the new fuzziness to show that philosophy of science did not succeed where epistemology failed). The advice to see if it might not pay to reweave your web of belief in the interests of a better ability to solve your problems is not the advice to formulate epistemic principles. The one piece of advice would only entail the other if experience had shown that having a conscious epistemological view were always an efficient instrument for readjusting old beliefs to new.

But experience does not show this, any more than it shows the opposite. Having general epistemic principles is no more intrinsically good or bad than having moral principles—the larger genus of which epistemic ones are a species. The whole point of Dewey's experimentalism in moral theory is that you need to keep running back and forth between principles and the results of applying principles. You need to reformulate the principles to fit the cases, and to develop a sense for when to forget about principles and just rely on know-how. The new fuzzies in philosophy of science tell us that the apparatus of "the logic of confirmation" got in the way of understanding how science had been operating. This is a plausible, though not a self-evident, claim. As such, it resembles the claim Dewey made in *Human Nature and Conduct* (a book that has been ably defended by Hook against those who found *it* fuzzy). Dewey there urged that the traditional attempt to describe moral problems in terms of clashes between Kantian and utilitarian principles was getting in the way of an understanding of moral deliberation. His central argument was that the use of new means changes ends, that you only know what you want after you've seen the results of your attempts to get what you once thought you wanted. Analogously, post-positivistic philosophy of science has been saying that we only know what counts as being "scientific" in a given area, what counts as a good reason for theory-change, by immersing ourselves in the details of the problematic situation. On this view, the wielder of an ahistorical scientific method— a method for judging "validity" rather than mere "strength"—is on a par with the ideal wielder of practical syllogisms, the person who knows in advance what results he or she desires and has no need to adjust his or her ends. Such idealizations may sometimes be heuristically useful, but we have no special duty to construct them.

This comparison of Dewey on morals with the new fuzzies on science brings me to a final formulation of my doubts about Hook's use of the notion of "scientific method." Hook wants this notion to stretch as far as morals and politics, but he does not want it to stretch as far as, e.g., Tillichian theology. I doubt that this can be done. If we stretch it as far as morals and politics, then we shall have to cover cases in which we are not choosing between alternative hypotheses about what will get us what we want, but between redescriptions of what we want, of what the problem is, of what the materials to hand are. We shall have to cover just the sorts of cases that Kuhnians emphasize in the history of science: cases in which the description of the problem to be solved changes, thus changing the "observation language" used to describe the "evidence." This is not to say that we cannot, retrospectively, describe the problems and the data of all earlier epochs in a single, up-to-date, commensurating vocabulary. But the ability to commensurate by hindsight—the ability to say that what Aristotle was looking for was what Newton found, or that what the Roman plebians were trying for was what the United Automobile Workers later got—should not mislead us into trying to describe our favorite ancestors as using "the hypothetico-deductive observational method" (as Hook sometimes characterizes "scientific inquiry."[5] Dewey's description of moral and scientific progress is much more like somebody's description of how he or she managed to get from the age of twelve to the age of thirty (that paradigm case of muddling through) than like a series of choices between alternative theories on the basis of observational results.

Let me turn now to what I have described as a second disadvantage of Hook's scientistic strategy. This is his treatment of the various figures currently lumped under the heading of "Continental philosophy." Tillich is a convenient example with which to begin, since he is the one whom Hook has discussed in most detail. But I have another, autobiographical reason for discussing Tillich in this connection, I was assigned years ago to teach a course in the philosophy of religion. Looking around for some interesting books on which to lecture, I picked, among others, Dewey's *A Common Faith* and Tillich's *Dynamics of Faith*. After making up a syllabus with neat little divisions ("analytic philosophy of religion," "pragmatist philosophy of religion," "existentialist philosophy of religion," "fideist philosophy of religion," etc.), I encountered a problem. When I actually got down to writing the lectures I couldn't see any difference between the pragmatist and the existentialist, between Dewey and Tillich. My syllabus suddenly appeared repetitive, for my lectures were making Tillich sound just like Dewey, and conversely. I could not seem to differentiate between Tillich's "ultimate concern" and Dewey's "moral faith," nor between Dewey's attempt to distinguish the religious from the supernatural and Tillich's to distinguish genuine from idolatrous faith. Tillich's "God beyond the God of theism" looked just like the God Dewey defined as "the active relation between ideal and actual."[6] Eventually I gave up and told my students that they should treat Dewey and Tillich as saying the same things to different audiences. When they asked why they should call this funny thing that both men were talking about "God," I could do no better than cite Dewey:

> One reason why personally I think it fitting to use the word "God" to denote that uniting of the ideal and actual which has been spoken of, lies in the fact that aggressive atheism seems to me to have something in common with traditional

supernaturalism. . . . What I have in mind especially is the exclusive preoccupation of both militant atheism and supernaturalism with man in isolation. . . . A religious attitude, however, needs the sense of a connection of man, in the way of both dependence and support, with the enveloping world that the imagination feels is a universe. Use of the words "God" or "divine" to convey the union of actual with ideal may protect man from a sense of isolation and from consequent despair or defiance.[7]

Dewey's seemed, and still seems, a good way to keep the term "God" in one's vocabulary, thus enabling one to keep some of the strands in one's web of belief which, at the time one became a naturalist, one had feared one might have to tease out. Hook disagrees. He tells us that the only thing he protested in the manuscript of *A Common Faith* was Dewey's "use of the term 'God' for faith in the validity of moral ideals." Part of Dewey's response, he says, was

. . . there are so many people who would feel bewildered if not hurt were they denied the intellectual right to use the term "God." They are not in the churches, they believe what I believe, they would feel a loss if they could not speak of God. Why then shouldn't I use the term?[8]

This parallels the response that Tillich used to make when people asked why he didn't stop pretending to be a Christian theologian and instead bill himself as a Heideggerian philosopher. He would say, in effect, that it was precisely the job of a Christian theologian these days to find a way of making it possible for Christians to continue using the term "Christ" even after they had given up supernaturalism (as he hoped they eventually would).

Some beliefs best expressed by using the word "God" were part of both Dewey's and Tillich's web at the points in their lives when they were converted to naturalism. They both asked themselves whether they could hang on to some of these and experimented with various reweavings of the web that might enable them to do so. Tillich also thought that he could hang onto some beliefs best expressed using the word "Christ," though Dewey did not. Both were, as far as I can see, doing the same thing—keeping as much of the old as they could in the face of the new. Their various reweavings do not seem different in "method" or "logic" from the tinkering that scientists engage in when trying to keep anomalous occurrences within the framework of old ways of picturing things or, conversely, to make a new way compatible with old observations. Dewey was, in writing *A Common Faith,* doing just the sort of creative problem-solving that he thought was illustrated in both scientific and moral progress. So, to repeat my previous point, I do not think that one can stretch "scientific method" as far as Dewey and Hook want to stretch it and still accuse Tillich of not using it.

This may, however, seem to be letting Tillich off the hook too easily. For what about his weird use of the term "Being-itself"—a habit for which he was frequently castigated by Hook? And, in any case, what about Heidegger's use of it? Heidegger is harder to make resemble Dewey than is Tillich. He would have been much less inclined, as Hook tells us Tillich was in debate, to "reply with manifest sincerity 'I agree with everything you have said'" and to embrace Hook "as a fellow religionist crusading for the Holy Grail of Being."[9] Even if Tillich, the conversable social democrat, can be excused for finding naturalism inadequate to express his ultimate concern, can Heidegger, the hermetic quasi-Nazi, also be seen as just another pragmatic reweaver?

To begin with what Hook calls "the quest for Being," I agree with Hook and Carnap that we are not going to find a property that distinguishes the existent from the nonexistent, that we should not treat the existential quantifier as referring to an activity (what Austin called "quietly ticking over, in a metaphysical sort of way"), and, more generally, that the word "Being" is just more trouble than it is worth. I would be happy if Heidegger had never employed it and if Tillich had never picked it up from Heidegger. But Heidegger and Tillich would have agreed with Carnap and Hook too. I do not think that the word "Being" was essential to the thought of either. My attitude toward its use in their work is the same as Hook's toward Dewey's use of "God" in *A Common Faith*—it is a rhetorical blemish, a misleading way of getting one's point across. At best, its use is a technique for relating to an audience. The reason Heidegger used it, I think, was to tie himself into a tradition he admired, a tradition that he thought ran through Aristotle's *Metaphysics* and Hegel's *Logic*. He thought both philosophers had shared his goal of getting beyond the "ontic" to the "ontological," and that the distinction between Being and beings was a good starting point for telling the sort of story about man and his situation he wanted to tell. As Hook wrote in 1930 about his student year in Germany, German philosophers of that period took German idealism "not as one of a number of possible logical alternatives but rather as a national possession, the blazing jewel in Germany's cultural crown."[10] Heidegger—nothing if not a "national" philosopher—was using "Being" to place himself in the context of this national tradition, thus differentiating himself from three movements he despised—the neo-Thomism of his youth, *Lebensphilosophie,* and the Haeckel-like naturalism that had been part of the nineteenth century's reaction to Hegelianism.

A few years after *Being and Time,* however, Heidegger dropped the notion of "ontology" altogether—though not, alas, before his admiring professional rival Tillich had become thoroughly imprinted with the earlier jargon. Ontological talk about "the Nothing" makes a brief appearance in the early thirties, just long enough to be satirized by Carnap, and then it too disappears. From then on Heidegger gradually got down to what, as it turned out, he was really good at—telling stories about the history of Western philosophy designed to show how a decisive turn of thought, already taken by Plato, had created the Western philosophical tradition. Instead of doing "phenomenological ontology," Heidegger now tries to "overcome" the "onto-theological tradition," precisely the tradition that linked Aristotle to Hegel. As I have argued elsewhere, in this later period Heidegger's account of what is wrong with the presuppositions of the great European philosophers is not clearly distinguishable from Dewey's.

But still, why does Heidegger call what is wrong with the tradition "forgetfulness of Being"? Maybe ontology goes in the later Heidegger, but Being is still around—or rather, not around, but absent, concealing itself, *absconditus.* One can sympathize with Hook's 1930 remarks, referring to *Being and Time* and "On the Essence of Reasons," that "there is a mystical doctrine of creative emanation at the bottom of Heidegger's thought," and that "Heidegger is really asking theological questions."[11] These remarks are still in point for Heidegger's later work. But I would want to modify what Hook says by urging that, in his later work, it becomes clear that what Heidegger really wanted to do was to find a way of getting himself out from under theology while still keeping in touch with what theology (and the central books of the *Metaphysics* and the *System of Logic*) had been about. Like Plato and Plotinus before him, he wanted to get away from the gods and the religion of the times to something "behind" them. So, although in one sense he is indeed still asking theological questions, in another sense he is trying to find some better questions that will replace theological (or, as he was later to say, "metaphysical") questions.

This is not a perverse or self-deceptive thing to do. I have suggested that it was just what Dewey was doing in *A Common Faith* (and elsewhere, as in parts of *Art as Experience*). Dewey was right, in responding to Hook's report of *Being and Time,* when he said, "It sounds like a description of 'the situation' in transcendental German."[12] That book's discussion of the priority of the "ready to hand" over the "present at hand" covers a lot of the same ground as Dewey's insistence on the "interactional" relationships between experience and nature. But, more important, this ground was covered in aid of a project Heidegger shared with Dewey—getting us out from under the metaphysical urge to find some ultimate, total, final context within which all our activities could be placed. Whatever motivated Heidegger's short-lived flirtation with the idea of "phenomenological ontology," it seems clear in retrospect that this discipline was intended as an anti-metaphysical enterprise. It was not just a joke when he later borrowed Carnap's title for his essay "Ueberwindung der Metaphysik." As it also did to Carnap, "metaphysics" means to Heidegger the objectionable idea of a superscience—something that would establish that what Dewey called "moral ideals" were pre-existent realities. If he can be imagined agreeing with anybody, Heidegger would agree with Dewey that

> men have gone on to build up vast intellectual schemes, philosophies and theologies, to prove that ideas are real not as ideals but as antecedently existing actualities. They have failed to see that in converting moral realities into matters of intellectual assent they have evinced lack of moral faith.[13]

What Heidegger gives us that Dewey doesn't is a detailed treatment of the history of European philosophy showing how such "inauthentic" conversion of moral faith into superscience expressed itself at various periods. The role of the term "Being" in this treatment comes to be that of a name for what moved people to be metaphysical, but could not itself be an object of quasi-scientific inquiry. This is just the role of Dewey's "moral ideals," or, more exactly, the role of what Dewey calls "the sense of a connection of man, in the way of both dependence and support, with the enveloping world that the imagination feels is a universe."[14]

Heidegger would, of course, object to every word in this quotation from Dewey. For he thinks that just about *all* the words in currency nowadays are useless for what he calls "Thought"—the activity that replaces "phenomenological ontology" in his later work. He thinks that notions like "moral ideals," "imagination," "man," "support," and the like have been so cheapened by their use in ordinary *Gerede* that they are useless to the Thinker. That is why a lot of late Heidegger is in Greek, Greek which we are supposed to translate to Heidegger's own idiosyncratic specifications. Heidegger ended up not (alas!) as a reweaver of a web of beliefs, but as a thinker who tried to get away from beliefs, rules for action, altogether. He wanted a language that was not hammered out as an instrument for communicating, for helping us get what we want, but one that "is what it says" (a compliment he once paid to Greek). He wanted to discover a language that was as close to silence as possible, rather than to reweave the connections between the various things we want to say. *Being and Time* was (like *A Common Faith* and the first volume of *Systematic Theology*) a proposal to teach us a new way of talking—one that would let us ask about God or Being without thinking of ourselves as superscientists. The later work only hopes to show us how to be suitably still.

So, to answer the question I posed earlier, I do *not* think one can view Heidegger—the later, more important, Heidegger—as one more pragmatic reweaver. Here, if anywhere, one finds a figure who *cannot* be said to have used "the scientific method" (in the broad, fuzzy, un-Hookian sense of "muddling through"). He leans over so far backward to avoid being one more superscientist, one more metaphysician, one more theologian, that he ceases to reweave. He merely points and hints. But that means that we cannot criticize him for employing an alternative method to the method of science. He doesn't employ *any* method. He is not, in *any* sense, competing with science. He would not dream of offering "knowledge that is not scientific knowledge." He has nothing whatever to say against naturalism, for example, since he thinks that Thinking has nothing to say about the way things work, or about their causes, or even their "grounds" (if "ground" means what emanationists like Plotinus meant). Just as, in his early days, he redefined every important word he used so that it had an "ontological" rather than an "ontic" sense (thus making it impossible to converse with him about whether it was the right word for his purpose), so in his later work he takes care to assert only sentences that cannot be construed as "rules for action," as beliefs (thus making it impossible to converse with him at all).

The thing to criticize in Heidegger is not an attempt at a superscience that would use a different method (e.g., a "phenomenological" method) from that of the natural scientists. That attempt was, at most, an aberration of his early middle age. Rather, what needs criticism is his inhumanism—his attempt to find Dewey's "connection of man, in the way of both dependence and support, with the enveloping world that the imagination feels is a universe" by cutting himself off from connection with other men. Whereas Dewey saw European culture as moving in the direction of what he called "the aesthetic" by virtue of the leisure and freedom that technology had made possible, Heidegger saw nothing in technology save the punishment for our original Platonic sin. Dewey optimistically thought of Plato not as a disaster but as one of the important early steps in getting ourselves out from under religion, even though one of the prices paid was the invention of metaphysics. Pragmatically, he thought that you had to weigh the bad against the good consequences, and that on balance Plato came out ahead. To Heidegger, technological civilization was something so un-Thoughtful, so un-Greek, that only refusal to speak any of the words associated with it could help. But this could help only a very few. For Heidegger there is no community that plays the role that the Christians played for Tillich or the Americans for Dewey. So there is no attempt to help such a community find its way by helping it to reweave its beliefs, and thus its language.

To sum up what I have been saying: I take "Being" to be, in Heidegger and again, derivatively, in Tillich, merely "transcendental German" for a "connection of man with the enveloping world," which naturalism, construed as the generalization that "the occurrence of all qualities or events depends upon the organization of a material system in space-time," does *not* help us envisage. This is what certain forms of art (when not construed romantically and transcendentally as a peep into another world) and certain forms of religion (when not construed as an encounter with a pre-existent power that will rescue us) *do* help us envisage. But vision is not knowledge. If "knowledge" is to mean (as it is, on the whole, convenient that it should) the sort of proposition that can be tested against explicitly formulated public criteria, then Hook is quite right in saying that "all knowledge which men have is scientific knowledge." But this use of "knowledge" merely forces us to find some new terminology for forms of discourse that are not subject to such criteria but which are nevertheless necessary for our lives. In *A Common Faith,* in some of his more Hegelian remarks about the social functions of philosophy, and in some of his equally Hegelian remarks about the function of art, Dewey tried to work out such a terminology. On my interpretation, this is also what Tillich and (sometimes) Heidegger were also doing.

Let me now try to bring together my doubts about scientific method with my attempt to make "the quest for Being" look respectable. As I see the matter, both pragmatism and "Continental" philosophy have a common interest in debunking a certain traditional conception of philosophy. This is the conception of a discipline that unites the argumentative rigor made possible by an appeal to commonly shared criteria with the ability to decide issues of ultimate significance for our lives. The traditional image of philosophy is of a discipline that will (any day now) produce noncontroversial results concerning matters of ultimate concern. The scientistic side of pragmatism—best represented by Hook—debunks this image in the form of philosophy as a superscience, employing a privileged method of attaining a kind of knowledge not available to the mere natural scientist. The holistic side of pragmatism—best represented by James—debunks it in the form of the suggestion that the results of the natural sciences suffice to give meaning to our lives (and the corollary that the unscientific attempt to do the latter is somehow a second-rate kind of intellectual activity, one which should be satisfied with painting pictures or writing lyrics, rather than attempting discursive prose). It wants to avoid having the natural scientist step into the cultural role which the philosopher-as-superscientist vacated, as if the naturalistic world-picture were somehow enough to serve the purposes for which the gods, the Platonic Ideas, and the Hegelian Spirit were invented. It wants that cultural role to *remain* unfilled.

Heidegger's protest against the "metaphysics of presence" and Tillich's against "idolatry" share this aim of debunking the idea that either a superscience, or just plain science, are going to give us what we need. Both men see positivism and Hegelianism as two sides of the same coin—the attempt to be methodical about what will not allow of method, to transport techniques of relating various bits of the world to one another into the attempt to "imagine the enveloping world as a universe." The main theme of "Continental" philosophy in our century has been criticism of the presupposition common to Hegel and Carnap—that what matters is being "scientific" in the sense of rigorously carrying through some procedure (dialectical, inductive, hypothetico-deductive, analytical, or whatever). Just as Hook has debunked "Being" in the name of "method," Heidegger has debunked "method" in the name of "Being." I am suggesting that both Hook and Heidegger were right in debunking what they debunked, but that both sometimes found themselves using weapons that belonged to the tradition they were attacking. These weapons should now be thrown away.

If we do throw them away—if we try to have pragmatism without method and Heideggerian philosophy without ontology—then I think that Tillich, James, and the more holistic and syncretic side of Dewey suggest how intellectual life might be led. It would be pursued without much reference to the traditional distinctions between the cognitive and the noncognitive, between "truth" and "comfort," or between the propositional and the nonpropositional. In particular, it would not make much of the line between "philosophy" and something else, nor try to allot distinctive cultural roles to art, religion, science, and philosophy. It would get rid of the idea that there was a special sort of expert—the philosopher—who dealt with a certain range of topics (e.g., Being, reasoning, language, knowledge, mind). It would no longer think that "philosophy" was the name of a sacred precinct that must be kept out of the hands of the enemy. People in other disciplines would no longer come around to philosophy professors to get their concepts properly "clarified" (like the student of Mary McCarthy, who, after finishing her short story, needed help in putting in the symbols).

If we could get rid of the notion that there was a special *wissenschaftlich* way of dealing with general "philosophical" ideas (a notion Dewey did his best to discountenance), then we would have much less trouble thinking of the entire culture, from physics to poetry, as a single, continuous, seamless activity in which the divisions were merely institutional and pedagogical. This would prevent us from making a moral issue of where to draw the line between "truth" and "comfort." We would thus fulfill the mission of the syncretic and holistic side of pragmatism — the side that tries to see human beings doing much the same sort of problem-solving across the whole spectrum of their activities (*already* doing it — not needing to be urged to start doing it).

I shall conclude, in suitably pragmatic style, by remarking on the relevance of what I have just been saying to a particular problem in contemporary American culture — the disdain for traditional American anti-ideological liberalism that I mentioned at the outset. Dewey and Hook fought, jointly and with great success, against the temptations that Marxism held out to American intellectuals in the thirties. Specifically, they battled the temptation to think, as we Americans so easily do, that our naive domestic forms of cultural life had been superseded by a more sophisticated import. The Stalinists and the Niebuhrians were at one in telling us American liberals that we were indeed naive. Dewey and Hook had a good time debunking both at once. Thanks to them most American intellectuals in the pre-war period were not buffaloed by German depth or French subtlety. But things are different nowadays. Some of our best students take Althusser seriously. The idea of "philosophical depth" is in the air once again, and this means, inevitably, a trip back to the Continent. This trip is by no means a bad thing in itself, but it has become associated with the idea that liberalism is both intellectually lightweight and in need of being "diagnosed." So we now have the dismal spectacle of what Hook used to call "knee-jerk liberalism" (i.e., trying to figure out how to blame anything bad that happens on American ruling circles) combining with specifically philosophical *Tiefsinnigkeit* in the claim that we need "new philosophical foundations" for criticism of "contemporary bourgeois society" (i.e., the surviving parliamentary democracies).

It would be absurd to blame the post-war failure of American nerve on the presence or absence of various views about philosophy. It is a much more massive phenomenon — the loss of America's hope to lead the nations. The frustrations and dilemmas of the last four decades may have made this loss inevitable. But it does not seem inevitable that it should have been accompanied by the sense that we have been found *morally* unworthy of the role we once thought we might play. Such self-indulgent *Schadenfreude* is, I think, the origin of the idea that Deweyan experimentalism, the dominant intellectual movement of a more hopeful time, was not "real" philosophy, but merely a rationalizing apology for certain institutions.

This latter suggestion has, of course, its grain of truth. Dewey and his followers were, to be sure, betting that reformist politics (internally and internationally) could do what Marxists think only revolution can do. More generally, pragmatism is the sort of movement that is only conceivable within a certain kind of polity with a certain kind of history. But, having admitted all that, one should continue to resist the individious distinction between expressing the spirit of a time and place (and thus of various institutions) in philosophical terms and "real philosophy." The latter notion means, if it means anything, a discipline that would produce *more* than such an expression—that would detach itself from a time and place and see reality plain.

Such notions embody the hope that some new jargon is about to do (any day now) what no old jargon has done—take us right down to the things themselves, stripping away opinion and convention and the contingencies of history. They represent the old Platonic dream. Dewey and Hook helped several generations of American intellectuals to avoid falling back into this dream, to avoid "philosophical depth" and thus to turn to the detailed, particular dangers of their times. My criticism of some of Hook's tactics—those he adopted when dealing with some of his fellow philosophy professors, as opposed to those he adopted on the wider, public scene—has been intended as an assist to his over all debunking strategy. If pragmatism (stripped of "method") and "Continental" philosophy (stripped of "depth") could come together, we might be in a better position to defend the liberalism that is exemplified by Hook's contributions to American political life.

NOTES

1. Sidney Hook, *The Quest for Being* (New York: Greenwood, 1963), p. 185.
2. Ibid., p. 181.
3. Ibid., p. 214.
4. Ibid., p. 181.
5. Sidney Hook, *Pragmatism and the Tragic Sense of Life* (New York: Basic Books, 1974), p. xi.
6. John Dewey, *A Common Faith* (New Haven: Yale University Press, 1934), p. 51.
7. Ibid., pp. 52–53.
8. *Pragmatism and the Tragic Sense of Life,* p. 114.
9. Ibid., p. 193.
10. Sidney Hook, "A Personal Impression of Contemporary German Philosophy," *The Journal of Philosophy,* 27 (1930), 145.
11. Ibid., p. 156.
12. *Pragmatism and the Tragic Sense of Life,* p. 103.
13. *A Common Faith,* p. 21.
14. Ibid., p. 53 (quoted above).

JACK KAMINSKY

Ontology, Formalism, and Pragmatism

One important way of defining ontology, in contemporary philosophy, is in terms of Quine's criterion.[1] What has being, what exists, is determined by: (1) the translation of statements about being and existence into a formal language and (2) the kind of variables that are required to be quantified in that language. What is presumably real, what entities can be said to have being, is discoverable by noting the entities that are taken to be values of the quantifiable variable. Thus the meaning of such expressions as "being," "exists," and "nothingness" is found in the way such expressions are incorporated into a formal language. "Nothingness," for example, is usually regarded as a synonym for "nothing." But the expression "nothing" does not satisfy the identity criterion for names, e.g., "Nothing is identical to everything" cannot, without a change in truth value, be converted into "Everything is identical to nothing." The expression, therefore, loses its traditional status as a noun to which predicates can be attached and becomes a simple negative existential quantifier. Similarly, as is well known, "exists" has lost its predicate status, and hence its crucial position in the ontological proof for the existence of God, and has become the ordinary positive existential quantifier. "Nothing" is not a name and "exists" is not a predicate. Only by aggrandizing natural language do we come to believe that whatever acts as a name or a predicate must, in the logical sense, also be retained as a name or a predicate.

On the basis of his criterion Quine leans, for the most part, toward a traditional nominalistic position even though, in a famous footnote in *Word and Object* and in his *Set Theory and Its Logic*,[2] he begrudgingly calls himself a Platonist. In his view most natural-language sentences are translatable into a formal language consisting of general terms (predicates that are "true of" individuals but do not denote any properties), logical connectors, quantifiers, and individual variables and constants. Since quantification occurs only over the individual variable, nominalism, the view that only individuals exist—rather than classes or properties or universals—seems to be Quine's primary ontological preference.[3] But he is forced to resort to a Platonistic position because (1) the ancestor relation can still not be defined without a reference to classes, (2) not all classes in set theory can be reduced to "virtual" classes, i.e., those that simulate but are not really classes, and (3) sentences whose prenex quantifiers are mixedly universal and existential force a commitment to classes. Thus whereas the following statement, which contains class quantifiers:[4]

$$(\exists \alpha)\,((\beta)\,(x)\,(x\epsilon\beta\cdot\supset\cdot x\epsilon\alpha) \supset (\exists \gamma)\,(\exists x)\,(x\epsilon\gamma\cdot x\epsilon\alpha))$$

can be transformed through stages to:

$$(x)\,(Gx \supset Fx) \supset (\exists x)\,(Hx\cdot Fx)$$

in which class quantification disappears, class quantification cannot be eliminated in the following:

$$(\alpha)\,(\exists \beta)\,(x)\,(x\epsilon\alpha\cdot\equiv\cdot x\epsilon\beta)$$

$$(x)\,(y)\,(y)\,(\exists \alpha)\,(x\epsilon\alpha\cdot\equiv\cdot y\epsilon\alpha)$$

in which the prenex quantifiers are mixedly universal and existential.

In any event, even if the class statements above could eventually be shown to be free of class quantifiers, the criterion for ontology would remain intact. An ontological commitment depends upon the kinds of quantifiers needed in a formal language. If all the sentences of the social and natural sciences can be stated in a formal linguistic structure that utilizes only individual variables, then science can be regarded as nominalistic, which obviates the need to introduce abstract entities or universal properties that quickly become transformed into essences. It should be noted, in this connection, that all the fuss about subjunctive conditionals, theoretical terms, dispositional predicates, and oblique contexts becomes quite understandable. They are the crucial issues for determining whether the population of the universe is to be taken as consisting solely of individuals or of both individuals and abstract entities. Carnap's bilateral reduction sentences, had they been adequate for explicating sentences with dispositional predicates or subjunctive tenses, would have given a great victory to the nominalist position.[5] Similarly, if Davidson had succeeded in showing that oblique sentences could really be stated extensionally, the nominalist position would have been reinforced.[6] Unfortunately—for the nominalist—both subjunctive and oblique sentences have eluded translation into a formal system.

However, no matter what the ontological commitments in a formal language turn out to be—regardless of whether quantification occurs only over the individual variable or over property and perhaps even propositional variables—Quine's formal criterion for ontology is damaging to traditional views of ontology and its handmaiden, metaphysics. Not only does Quine's analysis eliminate from serious consideration several important metaphysical issues, such as those concerning "exists" and "nothing"; it also makes certain statements unallowable. Wittgenstein's distinction, in the *Tractatus,* between saying and showing and Carnap's differentiation of the formal from the material mode of language are all incorporated in this new view of ontology. Such statements as "There are things" and "There are universals" and "There are propositions"—the very basic sentences of probably all metaphysical systems—become unsayable in any formal construction. The very avenues into traditional metaphysical speculation become blocked because these basic statements that lead to such speculation cannot be stated without paradox or contradiction. Thus if "There are things" is stated as $(\exists x)Tx$, a contingent statement, then its negation is also a contingent statement. But $(x)\text{-}Tx$ yields the paradoxical statement "Nothing is a thing." Similar problems arise with "There are universals" and "There are propositions." They are not formally statable.

But the most damaging consequence of Quine's restatement of ontology is that it brings a built-in relativism to all ontological speculation. Ontology becomes redefined from the investigation of what entities exist essentially into an investigation of what entities are essential for the adequate formulation of a rigorous scientific language. If the construction of mathematical systems requires the inclusion of class variables, then there are classes. Otherwise not. If a definition of identity requires a commitment to Leibniz's identity of indiscernibles and, therefore, a quantification over predicate variables, then there are universals. Otherwise not. If it turns out that the only way to account for vacuous names is by means of Meinong's subsistent entities, then there will be subsistent entities. Ontology is never absolute. The commitment to what exists is always made in terms of the formal languages available at a given time and also in terms of the language that can most successfully handle the verbalized data pouring into it from the various sciences. Traditionally, ontology was the study of what exists essentially. But now we must ask what exists essentially for some formal system. Carnap argued that there are two kinds of questions: What exists? What really exists? We can always answer the first question. There are chairs, tables, houses, lions, tigers, men, women, etc. But the second question is not a question at all since its answer would be outside the structure of any linguistic system, either formal or informal. It would bring us back to Kant all over again. Yes, we recognize that we perceive what we perceive, but what is the world like aside from the many modifications made on all sense-perception by our particular biological and mental characteristics? The answer to the question is not forthcoming since, to use an expression of Wittgenstein's, our form of life is what it is. We are stuck with seeing the world through our kind of linguistic spectacles. Show me, if you can even by gesture, where the noumena are!

Pragmatism, at least as it is defined in the works of John Dewey and Sidney Hook, is in agreement with many of the basic tenets of contemporary formalism. At one time pragmatists and formalists disagreed about the nature of logic. Wittgenstein had apparently proved once and for all the incorrigible character of logical truths by showing them to be tautologies and therefore true in all possible worlds. On the other hand, John Dewey, in his classic work *Logic: The Theory of Inquiry,* had argued that logic is a "progressive discipline" whose subject matter is always tied to scientific inquiry. "As the methods of the sciences improve, corresponding changes take place in logic."[7] The differences between Deweyan pragmatism and Wittgensteinian formalism seemed to be basic. But in his famous paper on the dogmatisms of empiricism, Quine drew the startling conclusion that there are no sharp distinctions between the analytic and the synthetic and, therefore, it is clearly possible that a future logic might be quite different from the present one.[8]

In fact, Putnam took the much stronger position that change might be required immediately.[9] If quantum mechanics is to be stated in a formal language, then some of the most fundamental theorems of classical logic must be revised or rejected outright. His argument is not very complicated. Consider a one-particle physical system. In such a system I can construct a statement recording the position, *p,* of that particle at a given time. I can then also construct a series of statements, *q, r, s,* etc., which represent all possible momenta the particle can have. But, since in quantum mechanics the position of the particle cannot be simultaneously conjoined with its momenta, *pq* and *pr* and *ps,* etc., are all false. Given then *-(pq)* and *p* we can infer, by classical logic, that *q* is false. By similar reasoning we can infer from *-(pr)* and *p* and from *-(ps)* and *p* that *r* and *s,* respectively, are false. We would have inferred that the particle has no momenta. But, of course, *q, r,* and *s* are all true. So here the laws of classical logic conflict with the needs of quantum mechanics. In a similar way, *p (qvrvs)* is true for quantum mechanics. The position of the particle does have one of the momenta *q* or *r* or *s.* But if we employ classical logic we obtain, by the rule of distribution, *pqvprvps,* a statement that is in fact false, since in quantum mechanics each disjunct is false. So Putnam's conclusion is that logic must be revised when scientific inquiry requires it. This is not very different from the pragmatist position of Dewey and Hook.

The pragmatist not only denies the absolute nature of logical systems, but he also favors the formalist rejection of essences, a metaphysical concept that is suddenly threatening to become philosophically respectable now that Kripke has made his damaging criticisms against Russell's theory of descriptions. According to Kripke, names and common nouns, unlike definite descriptions, are rigid designators.[10] Water is necessarily H_2O. But this means that in all possible worlds whatever is called "water" is H_2O. Water, then, is characterized by an essential property, i.e., it has an essence.

Formalists have, like pragmatists, reacted to the new appearance of essentialism. Quine has made some of the major criticisms. (1) Modal statements—those that make claims about what is possible or what is necessary—are opaque. The rule of substitution—a crucial rule in any formal system and, perhaps, even in any linguistic system—is not applicable to the terms of a modal sentence. If $a = b$ is a true identity, it does not follow that their mutual substitution will preserve truth value. Modal sentences behave like oblique sentences and have similar problems. (2) The rules of quantification do not function in modal contexts. From "Necessarily 9 is greater than 7" we cannot infer "$(3x)$ (necessarily x is greater than 7)" since replacement of "x" by an expression equivalent to "9," namely, "the number of planets," produces a false substitution instance. (3) The designata of names in a modal context, if there can be such designata, turn out to be intensions—"creatures of darkness" as Quine calls them. All of these arguments would be regarded sympathetically by the pragmatist. The objection to essences—to the existence of certain generic traits of being—is fundamental to the pragmatist position, and we shall shortly see why. The objection permeates Dewey's *Experience and Nature* and *The Quest for Certainty;* it is a basic claim in Hook's *The Quest for Being.* Hook especially regards the notion of essence as not merely false but detrimental to what Hook regards as the creative view of reality in which human beings have "the power to make themselves and the world around them better or worse."[11]

The pragmatist would also not quarrel with the formalist contention that what is taken to exist is determined by means of the language of science and not by natural language. For this reason neither the pragmatist nor the formalist is attracted to Chomsky's attempt to invest natural language with certain inherent and inalienable properties evidenced by means of transformational grammar. But, even if Chomsky is right and natural language reflects a set of innate biological categories, this does not mean that we are necessarily committed to a given deep structure syntax. We are biological animals born with a certain kind of biological structure; but someday hearts may be constructed and placed into the human body, and they will be better than the biological ones. They will hold up better and be averse to the build up of cholesterol. The bionic man and woman are television fantasies, but they are both logical and technological possibilities. Similarly, a biological commitment to a given transformational deep structure syntax does not entail its necessity. As Russell once pointed out,[12] it may seem "natural" and intuitively correct to say, "This is red." But it may be better, for certain logical purposes, to change this sentence to "Redness is compresent with centrality." "This house is white and that ball is white" might be converted, if we believed that a phenomenalistic language best expressed scientific data, into "The same phenomenal *quale* white is a member of two different classes, the house class and the ball class." Nothing we are born with—linguistic or otherwise—is sacrosanct. Chomsky seems to be saying that deep structure sentences are fundamental to any and all languages. But of any linguistic component, deep or surface, it is always legitimate to ask: ought we to transform it into this or the other form that will fit some logical or scientific need? "The present king of France is bald," prior to Russell's analysis, may have turned out to be a legitimate deep structure terminal string containing the appropriate lexemes and auxiliaries. But no one denies that the conversion it undergoes in Russell and Whitehead's *Principia Mathematica* system is an improvement if we regard logical inference as an important human value. This does not mean that Russell's analysis is the final answer to the problem of dealing with definite descriptions. Kripke has surely raised serious questions. But this does not alter the fact that linguistic structures are not *inherently* and absolutely unalterable. (It should be noted that Chomsky's view of the innateness of certain transformational structures is not accepted by many linguists.) Human bodies and whatever is innate in them can and do change, sometimes by evolution and other times by human intervention.

The pragmatist and the formalist, therefore, agree about many important philosophical points, e.g., the repudiation of essences and the reliance on scientific knowledge. We should remember that for both Dewey and Hook scientific inquiry and its methodology have been a major emphasis. Hook's position on social, political, economic, and educational problems has always been very clear. Approach these problems with the same notions of verification, reliance on empirical data, confirmation of hypotheses, and criteria for rejectibility as the physicist employs in dealing with difficulties in physical theory. Scientific methodology ought to characterize both the natural and the social areas of inquiry. Few philosophers have argued this position with Hook's effectiveness and cogency.

The pragmatist, then, is allied with the formalist on certain major issues. But in spite of this alliance the pragmatist still has an important axe to grind with the formalist. With all his enthusiasm about science and scientific language the formalist, according to the pragmatist, gives us a static view of the universe. Quine may adore desert landscapes and indeed these are to be preferred to the bloated universes posited by many metaphysicians. But the universe—especially the way human beings picture it—is not a desert landscape. Quine's universe is a cold, bare place in which individuals—sometimes called "posits" by Quine[13]—move in and out of class relationships. (And since for Quine individuals are often no more than unit classes there is sometimes a question as to whether Quine's universe contains anything except classes![14]) This may be a remarkably precise and well-organized universe to which set theory and extensional logics are admirably adapted. But it is more like a sketch, a diagram, and not the full-color production that human beings constantly encounter. There are neither processes nor properties—monadic or polyadic. The values of the variable can be objects that are chairs, or human beings, or buildings, etc. But there is no place for objects that are in the process of being made or which one is planning to make or which it is possible to make. "There are chairs" can easily be stated in a formal language, but there are no formal tools for incorporating "There is a chair being made for John" or "John is making a chair"—and this for the simple reason that such verbs as "making," "constructing" and "planning" are polyadic predicates in which at least one term is not open to quantification. In "John is making a table" quantification is applicable to "John" but not to "a table" because the table has not yet been constructed and perhaps never will be constructed. It might be argued that "is constructing a table" could be treated as a one-place predicate, and that this would eliminate the quantification problem. But under such circumstances there could be no backward reference to a table. That is, we could not say "John is making a table and it will be used for the party" since there would be no reference for "it." Once we incorporate the object of a construction verb into the predicate there is no breaking into it with an outside pronoun. It is in order to permit such breaking and entering that we unpack complex expressions into more basic conjuncts and disjuncts. Furthermore, the avoidance of the quantification problem would lead to a loss of important inference power. It is difficult to see how we would deal with "John is making all the tables" and "John is making some of the tables." If what we have here are simple monadic predicates, the obvious logical derivation of "some" from "all" by universal instantiation and existential generalization would fail. Thus to make sense of what I have called "construction" verbs and other such expressions, we must be able to account for terms that do not have denotations. But in the usual extensional formalist systems, terms that do not have denotations either are not permitted in the system or—when they are definite descriptions or translatable into definite descriptions—produce false sentences. But "John is making a table," unlike those problematic sentences with psychological or subjunctive verbs, is as respectable a sentence as one could find. We do not only observe objects and groups of objects, but we are also constantly watching objects beings made. Things are being constructed even though such attempts often fail. Thus the charge of the pragmatist is that the formalist has not dealt with some of the most important sentences—more important perhaps than even subjunctive conditionals and indirect discourse. If we can be sure of anything it is that we have science and also technology. The making of objects is as important as their discovery, and no formal system will be adequate until the pragmatic and technological demand is satisfied.

Russell may indeed have shown us a way of dealing with subsistent and other worldly entities. But the price paid for accepting Russell's theory has not been cheap. Philosophers have become extremely suspicious of dealing with expressions that *may* but do not yet and perhaps never will denote. "The ideal automobile will have a nonrusting body" turns out to be a false sentence because the description is not satisfiable. But no engineer would call it false. "The complete control of the weather may be realized someday" is true to the meteorologist but false on Russell's analysis. Nor would it help to extract by transformation rule a deep structure sentence such as "Someday the weather will be controlled," since there is no such day and perhaps never will be. So the pragmatist's criticism of the formalist is that the ontology he presents us with, the universe he pictures, leaves out one important characteristic—the existence of man-made objects. A statement about a human world is simply false on the face of it if it does not include reference to the fact that things are being made or being changed or being planned. Both Dewey and Hook have made the point well: what is needed is a view of reality that will present itself to human beings as marble presents itself to the sculptor. William James has given us the most incisive statement: "On the pragmatist side we have only one edition of the universe, unfinished, growing in all sorts of places, especially in the places where thinking beings are at work."[15]

What then are the demands a pragmatist might present to the formalist? The first demand might be to reappraise the formalist's domain of entities, a domain which, emptied of everything except objects, would seem to consist only of bare particulars. Predicates, we should remember, do not denote. But, aside from names, constants, and variables, predicates are the only nonlogical expressions remaining in the formal system. So if we are to begin improving Quine's desert landscape we should inquire into the role of predicate terms. Quine insists that our ontological commitment rests solely with the quantifiable variable; there is no such commitment when terms are not quantified. Thus we can say there are individuals, but since predicates function as general terms and do not undergo quantification we cannot speak of properties. But then exactly what is the role of these predicates? When they are changed into predicate variables and then used with a predicate quantifier, there is no ambiguity. The elements of the domain become populated not only with individual objects but with universals as well. We are making the Platonistic claim that something exists that two individuals can share. (We might note that the notion of quantification over variables makes precise the distinction between Platonism and Aristotelianism. For the Platonist $(\exists F) - (\exists x)Fx$ is true; for the Aristotelian, for whom universals are always *in re,* the statement is false.) We are stating that *both* individuals and universals are elements of the domain. But the question still remains: When predicates are not involved with quantification, what is their function? Quine says that predicates are true of objects, but they do not denote properties. Yet we usually say that a term is true of an object not in any arbitrary manner but because there is something about the object that permits the application of the term. Permission is usually granted when a characteristic of the object is noted. So that we are in the curious quandary of saying that, if there exists an x that is red, then there must be a characteristic—I think we can safely call it a property—that x has. How could it be otherwise? We could resort to classes so that predicates have classes as their designata. But this would be to permit general terms to become class terms, a change, as we have seen, Quine permits only under very special circumstances. So if we cannot have properties and we cannot have classes, how are we to deal with general terms? In order to answer this question adequately we ought to ask again why there is strong objection to predicate quantification. Such quantification commits us to universals, and this kind of blatant metaphysics is anathema to both Quine and pragmatists in general.

Is there, then, some way of having our cake and eating it too? Can we permit predicate terms to have their, apparently, normal function of designating properties and yet deny them the status of universals? I think the answer begins to appear if we mix a bit of Carnap with a bit of Wittgenstein. Carnap did not approve of Quine's reduction of properties to classes for the simple reason that equivalence of classes did not entail identity of properties. If the class of round objects is logically equivalent to the class of red objects it does not follow that being red is identical to being round. So for Carnap predicates designate two elements—classes and properties. But he insists that this does not automatically commit him to the existence of universals. The use of such terms as "property"—or intensional terms in general—he warns, "does not involve hypostatization."[16] The use of "red" with a small *r* does not commit us to the use of "Red" with a large *R*. Predicates do designate properties, but the fact that we often want the same predicate to apply to different objects, i.e., that we want to admit predicate quantification, does not imply that there is one property that is shared by many objects. Carnap refuses to be accused of introducing an "absolutist metaphysics" merely because he uses propositional and predicate variables. "Such an accusation," he argues, "must be based on an analysis of the statements or pseudo-statements which (one) makes with the help of those signs."[17] Unfortunately Carnap does not elaborate. We are not told what uses are legitimate and what are not. But by introducing Wittgenstein's notions of language games and family resemblances we may be able to overcome Carnap's deficiency.

For Wittgenstein there are no common properties—no essences—even though there are common nouns. To use Wittgenstein's famous example "game" may be applicable to many activities, but it does not at all follow that there is some characteristic that all games have in common. One game may be characterized by F, G, and H, another by H, I, and J, and still another by J, K, and L. Like the strands of a heavy rope no one strand is required to run through the entire length. So that when we say that F is applicable to two or more objects no common property, Fness, is implied. We are merely indicating a family resemblance that the objects involved reflect in various degrees. But no one degree is ever necessary. As in every family not everyone is an uncle. Even with such a basic predicate as "red," which is used with an indefinite variety of overlapping shades, no one would maintain that any one shade must always prevail. Shades, like uncles, will continue to come and go; but colors and families will probably remain. Properties, then, both monadic and polyadic, ought to be part of the domain of a formal language. At least this gives us a picture of what exists that is more closely allied to what most human beings believe exists. Formalists need no longer be closet nominalists—those who are committed to individuals but keep constantly surreptitiously introducing properties. There are properties, but no common ones.

A second demand that the pragmatist can make of the formalist is that he —the formalist—reconsider his analysis of vacuous terms. If construction sentences are ever to be fully explicated, we must be able to speak of objects that do not exist and cannot exist in a system that incorporates Russell's theory of descriptions. "The ideal automobile" as well as "Hamlet" are used in sentences that are very often taken to be true by engineers and scholars, respectively, but false on Russell's analysis. ("Hamlet" becomes "the moody Dane," a description that is never satisfiable.) In the remainder of this paper I should like to recommend a small change—or what I consider to be a small change—in Russell's theory that I believe will permit the use of vacuous terms without leading to a reinstatement of Meinong's subsistent entities or to a sudden population explosion.

We should recall that in Russell's theory "Hamlet killed his uncle" would become:

(A) The moody Dane killed his uncle.

where the definite description "The moody Dane," or some other description that uniquely identified Hamlet, replaces "Hamlet." But we ought to distinguish this sentence from a sentence that is syntactically similar to it:

(B) The present king of France is bald.

Both (A) and (B) have the same logical form except that (A) has a polyadic predicate while (B) has a monadic predicate. But these are not considered to be logically significant differences. (I could have used a sentence about Hamlet that was more isomorphic to (B), e.g., "The moody prince of Denmark was vengeful." But this would in no way affect the argument.) More significant is the fact that there are major differences in the truth conditions of (A) and (B). (B) can be false if there is no present king of France, or if there is a king of France and he is not bald. (B) can also be true if it were to turn out that there is a king of France and he is bald. To use Kripkean terminology there is nothing wrong in saying that in some possible world there could be someone who is the present king of France and is bald. But now compare this analysis with (A). Keeping in mind that we are not speaking of any moody Dane but of the one in Shakespeare's play, we can ask whether (A) could be false if there is no moody Dane. It could be if, as in the case of the present king of France, we are required to test empirically whether or not there is at present a moody Dane. But no such test ever occurs. No one ever looks to see if there really is a moody Dane. In any possible world in which Shakespeare wrote *Hamlet* (A) cannot be false on the grounds that no moody Dane was ever discovered. Even if all Danes were in fact happy it would not serve to show that (A) was false.

(B) can be falsified if we do not discover a substitution instance of "The present king of France." But no one ever looks for or ever expects to find a substitution instance of "The moody Dane." (A) can never be false merely because the description is never satisfiable. But could (A) be false in the sense that there may have been a moody Dane but he did not kill his uncle? Could there be a possible world in which the moody Dane, i.e., Shakespeare's Hamlet, might not have killed his uncle? Of course if we are thinking of some other Hamlet—say the one mentioned in Saxo Grammaticus' *Historia Danica* that Shakespeare used in writing *Hamlet*—then *that* moody Dane surely could have been the one who did not kill his uncle. Saxo Grammaticus might have been wrong. Historians might someday uncover evidence that *that* moody Dane never had an Ophelia to love. But this could not be the case with Shakespeare's moody Dane. In every possible world Shakespeare's moody Dane will kill his uncle, although we might always discover another play that Shakespeare wrote—something quite similar to *Hamlet*—in which Hamlet, the moody Dane, did not kill his uncle. But in the Shakespearean play *Hamlet*, Hamlet must always kill his uncle. Otherwise we are dealing with a different play. So this is the first distinction between (A) and (B). Both descriptions may be vacuous but there is a fundamental distinction in falsity conditions.

A second distinction relates to the truth of (A) and (B). For (B) there can be a possible world in which it is true. But (A) is true in *every* possible world, i.e., in every possible world in which Shakespeare's play *Hamlet* is performed. There could have been a possible world in which there was a king of France at a given time and he was bald. Even though it may never have occurred in the history of *this* world, there could have been a possible world in which one could truthfully assert, "There is presently a king of France and he is bald." But it would be wrong to say that this assertion must be true in every possible world. There is no necessary connection between a present king of France and his being bald. In fact, at this very moment a revolution might suddenly take place in France and a king acclaimed. Whether he has fifty million hairs or none would probably be of no matter. But now consider Shakespeare's moody Dane. Could there be a possible world in which the moody Dane did *not* kill his uncle? Could it turn out that we were mistaken and that is was not the moody Dane that killed his uncle but someone else? If "the moody Dane" is the Hamlet of *Hamlet* then these questions are preposterous, in the sense that they confuse fact with fiction. Hamlet—the moody Dane—will always and forever have killed his uncle. No historian will ever discover that he did not—unless, of course, he merely means that he has found a new Shakespearean play in which Hamlet did not commit such an act. In fact, we can always be sure that the moody Dane will be Hamlet. But we can be just as sure that in any world in which there is someone who is king of France he need not have any particular name. He could be named "Louis XX" or "Louis XXI," etc.

The conclusion to be drawn from the preceding discussion is that not all definite descriptions can be treated in the same way. (A) and (B) may have the same linguistic form, but they clearly do not have the same logical form if we take "logical form" to have a necessary connection to truth conditions. (A) apparently has a necessity about it that (B) does not have. How then are we to characterize this distinction? On first analysis it might be thought that we are adopting Donnellan's view of descriptions.[18] (A) is a referential use of the description; (B) reflects an attributive use. (A) is true by referring directly to Hamlet; (B) is made true by anyone who satisfies the various predicates. I think Donellan's distinction is an important one that surely entails a revision in Russell's theory of descriptions. But I do not think the distinction is fine enough to account for (A). The limitation of Donnellan's analysis can clearly be seen if we compare one of his examples to (A). Let us imagine a situation in which we discover that Smith, one of the most lovable persons in the world, has been brutally murdered. Even prior to the apprehension of any suspects one could say:

(C) The murderer of Smith is insane.

Here the description functions attributively. Someone or other—no one yet knows who—is the murderer of Smith and he is insane. This is Donnellan's first use of a description—a use that he believes exemplifies Russell's notion of a description. Donnellan does not state any of his descriptive statements formally, but I would assume that (C) could be stated formally, using obvious symbolism, as

$$(C') \quad (\exists x)(Mx \cdot (y)(My \supset (x=y)) \cdot Ix)$$

A second use of a description can occur when a suspect—Jones—has been apprehended and put on trial. Then one can say

(D) The murderer of Smith, namely, Jones, is insane.

This is the referential use of a description and it is the one which, according to Donnellan, Russell overlooked. In this instance it is not someone or other who is taken to be the insane murderer of Smith but a specific person—Jones. We can state (D) formally as

$$(D') \quad (\exists x)(Mx \cdot (y)(My \supset (x=y)) \cdot Ix \cdot x = J)$$

Here we specify the name that will replace the variable. Now let us consider (A) again. Is the description being used attributively or referentially? It is obviously not being used attributively. The moody Dane must have killed his uncle. Otherwise we would be dealing with someone other than the Hamlet of Shakespeare's play. Furthermore, the variables of (C') might have been satisfied by Roe or Doe or someone else. On the other hand, whatever variables there are in the formulation of (A) can only be satisfied by Hamlet. So Donnellan's first type of description is not applicable to (A). Shall we then say that (A) has the form of (D')? However, (D') is also synthetic. The fourth conjunct might not be true. If we translated (A) into the form exhibited in (D') we would be claiming that even though there is a moody Dane who killed his uncle, he might not have been Hamlet. But this is clearly not what we intend to assert when we state (A). The result then is that neither of Donnellan's uses for descriptions holds for (A).

In order to give a proper analysis of (A) I should like to introduce a third kind of description—one that I will call a definitional one—which will be reflected in the following formulation of (A):

$$(A') \ (y)((Dx \cdot (y)(Dy \supset (x=y)) \cdot Kx) \supset (x=H))$$

i.e., for anyone at all, if he is the one and only moody Dane (of Shakespeare's play) who killed his uncle, then he is Hamlet. The predicates of (A') do not fix a reference that can satisfy a variable, but they do fix the meaning of a name. Whoever takes on these predicates, i.e., whoever acts the role of Hamlet in *Hamlet,* is Hamlet. So Olivier, in so far as he took on himself the properties attributed to Hamlet was Hamlet. Gielgud, Chamberlain, and all the others who performed as Hamlets were Hamlets in so far as they adopted the required predicates. The predicates fix the meaning of the name in the same way that, in a beauty contest, anyone who best exhibits certain physical (and sometimes mental) properties becomes "Miss America." The name itself has no reference. It is attached to anyone who takes on some select, very specialized set of predicates under very special conditions. Hamlet, then, is anyone who plays the role of Hamlet, that is, takes on the properties attributed to Hamlet in the context of the famous Shakespearean play. (A'), it should also be noted, incorporates that feature of necessary truth that characterizes (A). If the antecedent is false, if it so happened that no one ever played the role of Hamlet, then (A') still remains true. If the antecedent is true and there is one who plays the role, who acts as the moody Dane who kills his uncle, then the consequent must be true. There is only one person who acts as the moody Dane and kills his uncle, and he turns out to be Hamlet. (A'), then, turns out to be not a false sentence as it would be on Russell's analysis, nor a possibly true sentence as it would be on Donnellan's referential use of descriptions, but rather a necessarily true sentence—and this accords with our intuitions of how (A) ought to be regarded.

The pragmatist then—in spite of many fundamental agreements—wants the formalist to make it possible to speak of characteristics of objects as well as of objects that do not exist. I have made some suggestions as to how such changes could be incorporated into a formal language. I think also that something ought to be done about modal terms so that they can be legitimately introduced into a formal system without falling prey to Quine's modal paradoxes and without suddenly expanding the population of the world to include various intensional entities. Some attempts have already been made to give extensional interpretations to modal systems.[19] The analysis of construction verbs is, of course, most crucial, but I believe that an understanding of such verbs depends upon the legitimate admission of modal and vacuous terms into a formal structure. Our view of what exists is not to be so sanitized that possible and actual man-made objects—artistic or technological—cannot be included. We want to be able to speak of ideal automobiles, of Hamlet, and of a table that I am in the process of making without bringing in intensions, ghosts, and bare particulars. Pragmatists such as James, Dewey, and Hook share that robust sense of reality that Russell eulogized. It is the Cheshire cat they want to see, not merely its smile.

NOTES

1. Perhaps the best statement of Quine's position on ontology is to be found in his *Ontological Relativity* (New York: Columbia University Press, 1969). But see also *Word and Object* (New York: Wiley, 1960), Chapter 7; *From a Logical Point of View,* 2nd ed. rev. (New York: Harper & Row, 1961), Chapters 1 and 6; "Designation and Existence," in H. Feigl and W. Sellars, eds., *Readings in Philosophical Analysis* (New York: Appleton-Century-Crofts, 1949), pp. 44-51.

2. *Word and Object,* p. 243n; *Set Theory and Its Logic* (Boston: Harvard University Press, 1963), Chapter 2.

3. At least in his paper with Nelson Goodman his nominalism seemed to be strong and unshakable. See Nelson Goodman and W. V. Quine, "Steps Toward a Constructive Nominalism," *Jour. of Symbolic Logic,* 12 (1947), 105-22.

4. *Methods of Logic,* 3rd ed. (New York: Holt, Rinehart & Winston, 1972), pp. 236-37.

5. See R. Carnap, "Testability and Meaning," in H. Feigl and M. Brodbeck, eds., *Readings in the Philosophy of Science* (New York: Appleton-Century-Crofts, 1953), pp. 53-62.

6. See Donald Davidson, "On Saying That," in D. Davidson and J. Hintikka, eds., *Words and Objections: Essays on the Work of W. V. Quine* (Dordrecht, Holland: D. Reidel, 1969), pp. 158-74.

7. *Logic: The Theory of Inquiry* (New York: Henry Holt, 1938), p. 14.

8. See *From a Logical Point of View,* Chapter 2.

9. See "Is Logic Empirical?" in R. S. Cohen and M. Wartofsky, eds., *Boston Studies in the Philosophy of Science* (New York: Humanities Press, 1969), pp. 216-41. See also criticisms of Putnam's view by Michael Dummett, *Truth and Other Enigmas* (Boston: Harvard University Press, 1978), Chapter 16.

10. S. Kripke, *Naming and Necessity* (Boston: Harvard University Press, 1980), pp. 48-49.

11. "Pragmatism and the Tragic Sense of Life," *Commentary,* 30 (1960), 148.

12. Bertrand Russell, *My Philosophical Development* (New York: Simon & Schuster, 1959), pp. 161-72.

13. *Word and Object,* pp. 21-25.

14. Thus in his paper "Facts of the Matter" Quine makes what he calls a "drastic ontological move," namely, "all physical objects go by the board—atoms, particles, all—leaving only pure sets" *(Essays on the Philosophy of W. V. Quine,* ed. R. W. Shahan and C. Swoyer [Norman: University of Oklahoma Press, 1979], p. 165).

15. William James, *Pragmatism* (New York: Longmans, Green, 1946), p. 259.

16. *Meaning and Necessity,* 2nd ed. (University of Chicago Press, 1956), p. 44.

17. Ibid.

18. "Reference and Definite Descriptions," in J. F. Rosenberg and C. Travis, eds., *Readings*

in the Philosophy of Language (Englewood Cliffs, N.J.: Prentice-Hall, 1971), pp. 195-211.

19. Cf. M. H. Lob, "Extensional Interpretations of Modal Logic," *Journal of Symbolic Logic,* 31 (1966), 23-45; also G. E. Hughes and M. J. Cresswell, *An Introduction to Modal Logic* (London: Metheun, 1968), pp. 291n, 318.

RALPH ROSS

A Glance at Experience

To celebrate a moment in the life of a man who hugely deserves celebration one can do a variety of things. If one is merely writing an essay, choice is narrowed to writing about the man or writing something else, something that might please him. I have already written, although too briefly, about Sidney Hook, who deserves a full-length appreciative study. Here I have written something I hope John Dewey would, and Sidney Hook will, approve. It is too small a thing to be a real tribute or to lend itself to genuine celebration, but it is offered with heartfelt thanks for what Sidney Hook is and what he has meant to me.

Much can be learned about ordinary experience from the experience of art. Philosophy has relied heavily on science—for ideas, method, and *Weltanschauung*—but has come *to* art *from* general philosophy, not using it as a way to come to philosophy, as it has used science. But a philosophy of experience that uses science as a base or a paradigm is relying on what is essentially nonexperiential, in that natural science depends on experience for verification but is quite nonexperiential in content. The world science describes is not the world we experience; at its best, it may be the conditions under which experience occurs, but those conditions are not themselves experienced directly.

Although science, in its content, is not a kind of experience, art is. And art is more compressed and more meaningful than ordinary experience, thus serving as a model or ideal. Perhaps the first thing to be learned about the experience of art is that its meanings sometimes do and sometimes do not refer beyond the work. When Hamlet says, "Imperious Caesar, dead and turned to clay / Might stop a hole to keep the wind away," Caesar is of course the same Julius who crossed the Rubicon with his troops, and thus beyond the play, although Alexander or Genghis Khan would have done as well to make the

291

point, and Hamlet used Alexander a moment before. Nor does stopping a hole matter literally. Yet Hamlet's reflection immediately precedes Ophelia's funeral and its meaning bears on that. The few simple words, most of them monosyllables, carry a multiplicity of meanings that could be paraphrased only at length. And the paraphrase, if one could write it, would not have the feeling that is part of the original meaning. Can a feeling be part of a meaning? No matter how often denied, it can be, and that is a second important thing to be learned about and from art. Meanings in art are felt, and the feeling is not separate from the meaning, as though first we knew an unfelt meaning and then, second, we responded to it in feeling.

In ordinary experience we feel meanings, too, which is something we can learn from imaginative literature. Some meanings are felt powerfully, while others are understood more than felt, but that is true in literature as well. A farewell can be poignant, not because of an action like a handshake, an embrace, or a verbal goodbye, but because they mean farewell. And without the poignancy the meaning of farewell is emptied to its definition, which covers farewell in general but is unencumbered by the felt qualities of particular farewells. Each farewell has its own felt qualities, which are part of its meaning and distinguish it from other farewells. Definitions offer less meaning than the particulars they encompass: indeed, that must be the case because definitions could not apply to particulars unless definitions stated only what is common to all their particulars, thus losing all individuality and perhaps all felt meaning. Words, of course, can be felt, often deeply: love, honor, justice, country are often warm with feeling; but when they are defined they are cooled. One has only to look at their definitions in a dictionary for this to be obvious.

By deciding to talk of the use of words rather than their meanings, Wittgenstein and others are able to avoid problems about the status of meaning. Actually, concern with how people use a word may be the best way to find out what they mean by it, as a concern with behavior rather than statement reveals value and belief. And the use of words is one kind of behavior. But experiential meanings, when they are not verbal, are a different matter: they are not symbols per se, although they may be thought of as symbolic; they are meaningful experiences. Such an experience is a farewell, which is sheer mummery if it is without meaning and slight in meaning if the meaning is not felt.

On occasion a meaning may be nonexistent when unfelt, but rich when felt. When Milton writes of Sin and Death in *Paradise Lost,* he first describes Sin and then refers to Death as "the other shape / If shape it might be called that shape had none." It is the feeling of Milton's lines, the awe or horror, that makes them profound and beautiful; without the feeling the second line is close to, or is, nonsense. The feeling is an indispensable part of the meaning. No wonder the lines were regarded as sublime, rather than beautiful. Paraphrase might yield "a shapeless shape" and be held up to the derision of analytic philosophers. Yet "shape" might have a different meaning in Milton's three uses of the word; the third use might mean sharp outline, and sharp outline is not our association with death. And on that reading of the lines they are not meaningless without the feeling, but surely the feeling of *that* shapeless shape adds meaning almost without measure.

My examples have been literary because the medium of literature is words, and words are too often thought of as discourse and thus identified with ideas and excluded from experience. The importance of citing literary art is to show that in it words are part of that experience which is art, and to establish that words in imaginative literature are elements in aesthetic experience, pregnant with meaning, association, and emotion. If that were not so there would be no poetry, and there is poetry as surely as there are apples; indeed, where there are no apples there is still poetry. But other arts serve the argument that there is felt meaning more easily than literature. What does Mozart's G-Minor Quintet mean? If we can ascribe it to more than its structure, we might say "sadness," as with almost all Mozart's writing in G minor. But the music does not refer to some floating abstraction named "sadness," nor to an emotion evoked in a listener by hearing the quintet. The *music* is sad. The listener may or may not be sad; he may very well be delighted and say, "The music is wonderfully sad."

What I have just said about art holds also of experiential situations. Sometimes meanings refer beyond a situation and sometimes they do not. Meanings often refer to other elements in a situation, perhaps one not yet perceived, as when a dog's growl warns of a stranger, an intruder, or the mailman. Yet meanings may emerge from a situation and illuminate something beyond it: much in experience is grist for the mill of a preoccupation. And, often enough, meanings are both in and beyond a situation.

Second, meaning is not just referential as with words in discourse, but is *in* experience, like the terror of a hurricane or the beauty of a landscape. Third, as in those instances, meaning is often felt as well as understood. I shall go on to treat the character of experience and, to some extent, the language we use to deal with it. Some of the conclusions I will come to (but not in this order) are: (1) emotions and sensations are ineffable, as are, perhaps, particulars, for which ostensive "definition" is necessary. (2) Sign-referent, stimulus-response, and means-ends are forms of cause-effect and, though used in different contexts, can function together in a single context and overlap. (3) Perception and response can be distinguished for various purposes but in an experience the response *is* the perception. (4) Values are not just responses or projections; they are experienced, and are often the dominant elements in an experience. As a consequence of these conclusions: it is not so much the case that we create meanings and values as it is that we discover and alter them, even within ourselves.

To wipe out some difficulties with the above quickly, the issue is experience and that assumes organisms. It is futile to ask whether things or events would have meaning in themselves if there were no people (the organisms we are concerned with), because if there were no people there might be no things or events, at least as we understand them. Those are kinds of experience, as atoms or wave frequencies are not, at least directly. And, if there were no things and events, they could scarcely have meaning. But, one may object, the way we perceive things and events depends on the culture we have inherited. And there are possible cultures in which people find Mozart's G-Minor Quintet joyous. However, *if* experience is culture-bound (how far that idea takes us is another question), it is still what it is to those in any one binding culture. And, if one finds the music joyous, that is because he hears joyous music, not because the emotionally meaningless music somehow evokes joy in him.

Another problem seems to be the widespread belief that we project our emotions into experience and then think we find them there. Santayana argued this brilliantly in *The Sense of Beauty,* in which beauty is objectified pleasure. But that is to misconceive the nature of experience. Where would we get the emotions we are supposed to project into experience? Presumably they are native and are evoked as a response to some stimulus. And then, if we cling to this sort of explanation, we have to explain why some stimuli evoke pleasure as a response and other stimuli do not. That is, the nature of the responder is not the only issue; another is the nature of the stimulus. What is there about those aesthetic stimuli, to stay with Santayana's concern, that give us pleasure as opposed to others that do not? The answer should be, "They are beautiful." But Santayana, and so many others, will not accept that. The golden Rembrandt gives pleasure, they think; and we project that pleasure on to the painting, thus giving it the quality of beauty.

I find it a mistake to equate beauty with pleasure, unless pleasure is defined in some special sense, for many things that are not beautiful give pleasure and there are sad and painful elements in beautiful things. More to the point is the question of why the golden Rembrandt gives pleasure if it is not because beauty gives pleasure? The painting is not to be eaten, drunk, or embraced; things that are may indeed give pleasure. If one answers by talking of the painting's forms, colors, spatial characters, draftsmanship, and meanings as giving pleasure, one has used the qualities of beauty but not its name. Our pleasure in it does not make a thing beautiful, but its beauty may give us pleasure.

There is no need to deny that things can be viewed and stated differently. Nor need one insist that there are no virtues to views other than one's own. Philosophy has offered a variety of ways of seeing and saying, and on occasion someone intimates that the great views (it is not easy to define "great" here) have an equal validity. That is like the early cultural relativism in this century, which found every culture, whatever its qualities, as good as every other culture. But there is no reason to come to that conclusion, because some views are more fruitful than others, explain more, and comport better with common experience. That is the kind of appeal I am making in denying the separation of perception from response. I think it is more adequate to human experience and more fruitful for thought to locate what has been called response in perception. We are frightened when a situation is frightening and are impelled to fight or flee, put ourselves at hazard or protect ourselves. A succulent meal is smelled as well as seen, and the juices flow. If it is argued that salivating is obviously part of the response of the organism — rather than contained in and continuous with the perception, as witness the hungry person salivating and the stuffed one perhaps nauseated — a first but adequate response is that *the perceiver and the perceived are both part of perception,* or part of a situation that may be called perceptual experience, and that the conditions of both as well as the relations between them and the larger context they are in are relevant to the perception.

Perhaps the reason for thinking that meanings and values are in responses, not in experiences, is the difficulty in grasping that the experiencer and his environment together are needed for experience and that they are not separable. When, analytically, we take them apart we must not forget that they do not and cannot *exist* apart, any more than the head and the body can. Of course, the man-nature dichotomy is an old one and it is comforting to slip back into it, but it is based on assumptions that we cannot hold. It is not that we invest things with meanings and values but that we are part of the perception of things, as the environment is, and the perception, or perceptual experience, or the thing perceived, contains meanings, values, and dysvalues.

If what is seen is obscured by dimness or fog or is brilliant with light, if an odor is wafted away by a breeze or blown directly to the perceiver, the conditions of perception are altered by and alter what is perceived, just as the hungry or stuffed person alters what is perceived. If the roast is enclosed in glass in a museum and is placed and lighted so as to be viewed as art, the conditions and the consequent perception are different. Perhaps the use of the term "percept" has misled us into thinking that what is perceived is not continuous with a perceptual experience, because "percept" has a neutral aura, as many technical words do. It may also seem like the culmination of a process which leaves the process behind. The difficulty in describing perception may come in the insistence that what is perceived, an element in experience, has the qualities so often referred to "response," when part of perception is how hungry the perceiver is. That seems to put response in the perceiver, not in what is perceived, even though the conditions of what is perceived be acknowledged as relevant to the perception. But the hunger of the perceiver is just another supposed condition of a perception, as light waves reflected from a surface to the eye are supposed conditions of seeing color. We do not perceive the light waves, which do impinge on us, but we perceive color. We may experience our hunger all by itself, perhaps as kinesthetic perception of stomach walls close to each other, or we may perceive it as part of the perceptual experience of a succulent roast. The whole complex of perceiving brings us into the presence of the perceived.

Perhaps I should not have taken this tack, because the answer to the problem is implicit in what went before. If a burly attacker appears suddenly on a dark street, he may be terrifying and his presumed victim may be terrified. If the "victim," however, is a specialist in the martial arts, always hoping for a chance to try his skills outside of a gymnasium with its padded mats and its injunction to break no bones, his assailant is still terrifying, and he somewhat terrified, but with a qualitative difference, because to him the assailant is welcome as a "legitimate victim." Brave soldiers are not without fear when they attack the fearful enemy. Just so, the roast may be wonderful or nauseating, depending on the perceiver's hunger, but it is a wonderful or nauseating roast; the perceiver is neither wonderful nor nauseating, although he may be nauseated. That is, the totality of the conditions under which perception takes place may alter the qualities of what is perceived, but the "percept" has the qualities it is perceived as having. There is not a neutral roast, with no qualities or values, to which I respond by projecting my responses on it.

The critic may not stop yet – why should he? He has a case. Don't we find that perception of the roast has the same explanation as color vision, that we project back a response to stimuli? Here there is probably no good parallel, for light waves, unlike roasts, are invisible and without odor or taste. But, if we try to meet the analogy anyway, can we not challenge orthodoxy with some success? We are told (there are of course many current criticisms in the psychology of perception) that light waves stimulate the rods of the eye, which are sensitive to brightness, and the cones, which are sensitive to regions of the spectrum; the resulting "color" in the brain is *projected* outward to the surface of the object from which the light waves were reflected, and we see it there. (In this fashion, our critic thinks we project succulence – and why not nauseousness – on to the roast.) But why do light waves from surface A stimulate blue and those from surface B stimulate red, both of which we project back? Must there not be some difference between surface A and surface B to cause this? Wave frequencies are different as light is reflected from different surfaces and those frequencies are conditions for seeing different colors. Are we not being over-rigid or over-subjective in calling the consequent projection red or blue, rather than calling the surfaces red or blue? The point is now made, but I shall go on, perhaps tediously, because so many traditional arguments exist. When we overstate the case thoroughly we call the wave frequencies themselves red or blue. And then we can say, as Rudolf Carnap did, that a physicist blind from birth can know all about color, as though Renoir did not know more, or as though there were no "knowledge" in the experience of color.

This overstatement removes color from the world of things seen. There is no point then in asking whether a rose is red in the dark because it is not even red in the light. An alternative open to so physicalist an argument is to say there are two senses of "color," one physical and one experiential. The implicit value falls on the physical, as though that were somehow more "real" than the experiential, although the "physical" is theory and the experiential is, in one sense of the word, fact. It still seems to me more reasonable and fruitful to call the experienced color "red" and to say that light waves are physical (as distinct from physiological) conditions for seeing red. The blind physicist, alas, has no notion of the quality of the red of a rose when seen against green leaves and stem.

It can easily be claimed, as so many scientists seem to, that in both senses of the word "red" there is no red (or any other color, of course) in the dark. Neither are there light waves nor are colors seen. All this may seem obvious until one asks whether a surface, seen as red in the light, is not still there in the dark. To be sure, one will be told, because it can be touched. Still, it first has to be found and that may not be easy in the dark. Yet we assume the surface is there, before we find and touch it. Is it less logical to assume the surface is red, before we turn the light on and see it? After all, if it was red before the lights went out, we are convinced it will be red, and not yellow, when the lights go on. Not touching a surface does not make its solidity and texture disappear; does not seeing it make its color disappear? Why should we not say that a surface regularly seen as red is red in the light or in the dark, and that seeing it is proof that it is red? If two people look at a red rose in bright noon and *one* closes his eyes, does the redness of the rose disappear? and if *both* people close their eyes does it, more surely, disappear? I have heard the answer that the redness does not then vanish, because *if* a third person came on the scene and looked in the right direction he would see a red rose. Is that logically different from saying that, when the people and the flower are in a dark room, *if* the lights went on they would see a red rose? Perhaps the answer to the stale question, "Is a rose red in the dark?" is "A red rose is."

This discussion removes "red" from wave frequencies and places it in the object or on its surface. It makes seeing red less a conjurer's trick that brings red into being *ex nihilo* than proof that a surface is red. Color blindness can be established so that one knows if he is color-blind, and that ceases to be an issue for scientific proof. It still raises a question that will interfere with the direct line of our discourse but that demands to be treated. We could use color blindness, like hunger, as a condition of perception and suppose that where one person sees a red rose another person sees a green one, because the conditions of the perceiver's eyes differed. One problem with this is where to stop. To the blind there are no colors at all. Perhaps it is better to treat these conditions as abnormal and thus outside the range of what we mean by conditions of perception. Otherwise I would have to say that the high C in the score did not come out of the mouth of the singer because I cannot hear a high C. Granted, my experience of the singing does not include that note, but I believe, knowing myself, that the note was sung. After all, I cannot maintain that, because I cannot read, Shakespeare could not write.

The same sort of thing probably holds of all abnormal conditions. The hallucination is undoubtedly experienced under conditions of high fever but, in a genuine sense, the hallucination is not there and is not perceived by people without high fevers. Indeed, it is probably not even perceived by other people with high fevers. For some, to say that the hallucination is not there and is not perceived by others is to say the same thing twice. For others, they are different statements and the latter is evidence for the former. But hallucinations, like dreams, are as natural as people and fevers and in some sense are there.

We may even learn from them, as we do from dreams. Yet in their very privacy they are not part of the common world. So it is with the persecution experienced by the paranoiac. And in both cases the perceiver may be genuinely injured by the delusion, but not, for example, by being stabbed, unless the wound is self-inflicted or brought about in strange ways, not by a nonexistent enemy lurking in dark hallways.

Now one may have to know other things before perceptions are meaningful, although the knowledge does not always have to be conscious and statable. Dark clouds mean rain, at least with some probability, but of course they mean it to someone and they mean it, further, only because he has at least a rudimentary knowledge of weather patterns. The meaning, however, granted these conditions, is not in some imagined (or real) response to dark clouds. The meaning is in the rain clouds and is perceived along with their darkness. The meaning may include seeking shelter or reaching for an umbrella before going outside. Perhaps the most forceful evidence of this is that, when the meaning is of some importance to us, we perceive meaning (or value) more strongly than physical characteristics. If the clouds are most threatening and one is at sea in a sailing vessel, life may be at stake and one glance at the clouds may bring fear and frantic activity. Meanwhile, the conformation and color of the clouds, as a painter might see them from a safe haven, are largely neglected in favor of their meaning. To an impressionable youth a maiden of great beauty glimpsed quickly yields above all the impression of her beauty, while the shape of her nose, her cheekbones, even the color of her eyes and the cut of her hair may evade him. We do not perceive the clouds or the lady in detail and respond with evaluations of doom or beauty; above all, we perceive doom or beauty in connection with clouds and people. Is it different with a great poetic line, where the shudder comes before a just prosodic appreciation of the words? "What is happening?" asks the novice who walks past the portrait and finds its eyes following him. The curious feeling and the technical device that embodied it, and caused it, are at one.

Wolfgang Koehler wrote a book with the interesting title *The Place of Values in a World of Fact,* yet from the standpoint of human experience it might have been better titled *The Place of Fact in a World of Value.* We experience values constantly; but it is difficult to find facts, especially when we must wash away values to do so. It is received philosophical wisdom in many "schools" of our time to stick with Koehler. We may perceive "things," but we impart value or dysvalue to them. Perhaps that is a necessary consequence of separating people sharply from an environment, a person-nature dichotomy. But the value is often the most powerful aspect of perceptual experience. It can erode "fact" as the Impressionists' color eroded form.

Most of the argument above recurs in other contexts.

Stimulus-Response

There are two different matters here, although they are usually treated as one.

The first is a presumed response of the organism to the invisible, silent, tasteless, odor free, unfelt, which is the world of physics. A response to waves or particles is the world of men, i.e., experience. We cannot perceive these stimuli; our response to them *is* perception. From at least Leucippus and Democritus on there have been some people who believed that their theories about the world are true descriptions of some kind of underlying reality. Because of this they conclude that the world we live and die in, the world of experience, is an illusion. It is a belief they share with some religions and poets, though their reasons differ. What must be pointed out in answer is the continuity of the "illusion," the rivers and trees and mountains and all the furniture of earth, and the discontinuity of the theories, which are intended to explain, and become scientific only when tested by, observation of that "illusion." Clearly, we start and end with experience whenever we try to explain the physical world; when we "explain" experience in terms of physics we are stating the physical conditions under which we experience. We may and do change our minds about those conditions, but not, in the same way, about experience.

The second matter about stimulus and response is its ordinary use in psychology and in the ways we apply it to countless items of experience. Here we are not explaining how it is that we experience what we do but how we behave and feel as we do. We are, it is usually taken for granted, stimulated by the odors of dinner and respond by a flow of saliva and gastric juices or we respond with laughter to the stimulus of a joke. It is this kind of explanation that is in question when we understand something of the nature of experience, because the explanation is not parsimonious; it adds another term to explanation and another dimension to experience, or at least to perception. We assume the stimulus is perceived, however peripherally; otherwise how could we be stimulated? Then, having perceived something, we respond to it in some fashion. This is, I think, a misunderstanding both of perception and of experience. It is a theory that assumes, without discussion or evidence, that perception does not include feelings, action, or meanings, and that these are evoked in us by the perception, the stimulus. It seems closer to the facts to say that *the response is the perception,* that it is not something that comes later, however quickly, and is in us as a result of perceiving something else.

Again, as in what amounts to a philosophic view, although not articulated systematically, we have a theory that divorces perception and response, making the former neutral and the latter emotional, active, and significant. "Beauty is in the eye of the beholder," "Man creates values in a neutral universe," "Behavior is a response to stimuli," are statements of received wisdom, taught to schoolchildren by adults who regard these statements as obvious truths in our scientific age. What limits perception to a neutered observation? Perhaps the answer is the age-old separation of matter and mind, nature and psyche, object and subject. Such separations insist on bare perceptions and then responses in the turmoiled or rational psyche, evaluations by the mind (with its own personal, which includes cultural, heritage), and rational or irrational action. Thus perception itself shrinks, but it acts as stimulus to trigger personal response and action.

Yet examination of the simplest instance of stimulus-response can lead to different conclusions. A hand flicked at the eyes causes them to blink. The movement of the hand signifies danger to the eyes and a part of the perception of danger is a movement of avoidance and protection. It does not change the case to say that blinking is here an involuntary action, because perception is not necessarily voluntary, nor is all sensible action. The human organism develops, even evolves, as part of an environment. The organism's senses have no more developed in order to have neutral perceptions than the mind has developed so it can know for the sake of knowing—although those functions can be developed. The senses, like the mind, function ordinarily to deal with the environment, to protect the organism, and to help it get what it needs and wants. Pure perception can exist to some extent, but it is not ordinary, or native; it is contrived and learned. In highly developed cultural activities the scientist and the artist come to perceive differently *qua* artist or scientist; the scientist learns to observe what is relevant to a hypothesis and remove his attention from what else is in front of him, but is not relevant. A red wheelbarrow on the white snow can become only rectangular red foreground against a white background when our concern is color vision.

The artist, too, can focus on form, rather than the entire perceptual situation. He can attend to triangles and circles. Like scientific observation, this is a trained capacity in which the focal, as defined by interest, is distinguished from the peripheral, and the latter is largely ignored. With different interests, of course, the focal and the peripheral might be interchanged.

In ordinary experience, attention is directed to what seems important at the moment, although almost everything else is suppressed by danger, as other feelings are suppressed when we feel pain. And what seems important is usually what contributes to the life and continuity of the human organism. Of course, this does not exclude the life of mind in science or art or any of its other manifestations, nor is the life of mind unconnected with human development. But in human perception as a whole, even when we include the trained minority that seeks to neutralize aspects of perception, feelings, actions, and meanings are probably part of perception itself. As the eyeblink is part of the perception of a sudden movement toward the eyes and is understanding of that movement's possible meaning, so feelings for what is observed by artist and scientist, a group of meanings, and an impulse to act (to draw or paint, to proceed toward a conclusion, seek a new observation, or create an experiment) are not a separate response but at one and continuous with sensory perception. Experience can only be truncated to sheer sensory neutrality by analysis for some purpose after the experience itself.

Such analysis is, obviously, legitimate and needed when our purposes make it so, but when analysis of perceptual experience into sensory elements is conceived consequent to the experience, those elements should not be treated as antecedents of the experience or as its building blocks, in the manner of the old structuralist theory of Wundt and Titchener. There has been too much conversion of intellectual consequents into experiential antecedents, a practice implicitly deplored by the new structuralists, but one into which they can slip when they nod, as even Homer did. They are concerned with reducing aspects of culture to their structural elements, somewhat like the phonemes and morphemes of a language, and then tracing relationships among these elements. One must be careful to view these as results of analysis and not as, somehow, the given in experience.

The stimulus-response relation is more suspect than the sign-referent relation. How much more sensible it really is to believe that some kinds of beauty, at least, include delight and that our pleasure in such cases *is* the experience of delightful-beautiful things. We are misled by a habitual use of a language of emotions to qualify "psychic states," and we may think it a fallacy to use words that are ordinarily attached to this "internal" realm when speaking of what we perceive. But it is not a fallacy to get rid of a mistake.

Some psychologists have been neglectful of the language of sign and referent, perhaps because it seems intellectual, not behavioristic. But is the language of stimulus and response anything but a translation of sign and referent into behavior, as both are normally viewed? A sign points to its referent. A stimulus evokes a response. In a way, the sign is neutral, empty in itself, for its meaning is its referent. And so with a stimulus, except that "meaning" is avoided. A stimulus is not itself a thing to be pondered or considered; its fulfillment is in response. Yet that is the meaning of the stimulus, namely, that it evokes this particular response. Conditioned response may seem different, as with Pavlov's dogs who finally salivate at the sound of a bell alone that was in the past rung simultaneously with feeding. But do we accept as utter fact that dogs have no sense of meaning? Anyone who has a dog knows better. Perhaps the tough-minded experimenter is trapped in medieval notions that creatures with souls have minds and creatures without souls do not. Wrathful denial of this by experimenters may end in reduction of men to dogs (as they conceive them): "Mind" vanishes, to be replaced by conditioning. The simple fact may be that the bell means "food's on," just as it does to people in institutions and farms. Do they salivate when they hear the bell? Perhaps.

There are, of course, simple reflex actions; one jumps, for example, when some loud and sudden noise startles him. These reflexes do not prove that meaning does not enter the situation simply because everything happens quickly. Nor does the distinction between stimulus and response mean that the two are fully separable in experience. Causal connections are too often treated as identical in inanimate and human matters, a part of the attempt to understand and control by constant reduction of the human to less than it is. Causal pattern has variations, which include stimulus-response, means-ends, and natural sign-referent (as when the year's first robin means spring). And even the symbol-referent relation mimics the cause-effect relationship, not in the purely conventional aspect of a word having an assigned meaning, but in the habitual response once the meaning relation has been established.

One can interchange some of these quasi-causal relationships, thus more clearly indicating their similarity. "Fire" is called a conventional sign; from the standpoint of logical analysis it is arbitrary and the same thing could just as easily be meant by "water," if everyone agreed. As such it is in a symbol-referent relation. But if one shouts "fire" in a crowded theater, he might cause panic. In such an instance, and in so many others, the word is a stimulus that triggers response. Yet when the order "fire" (meaning "shoot") is given in battle it is intended as a means to victory, or at least to bettering the military situation. And at one and the same time the command "fire" is a symbol, a stimulus, and a means. There is nothing wrong with this: our purposes will lead us to use of one or another of these relationships. But to think that the three relationships are totally distinct, or that all three differ from a traditional cause-effect relationship, is confusion.

It is also confusing to try to construct coherent experience out of relation-ships like these and the countless other bits and pieces that are put into the jigsaw puzzle of experience. The reason it is confusing is that all of these are subsequent to experience, a result of reflection with many purposes, and primary experience is there to begin with. Most puzzles about experience result from neglecting it, and putting something else in its place. What takes its place usually goes under the name "experience," but it is spurious. This spurious experience is sometimes thought of as purely external (and sometimes chiefly internal); often it is as though things and events were perceived by an unsocial-ized observer with no biography. Almost always the person who experiences and that which is experienced are treated (if not declared) as separate. And why not, one may ask: the same person might have had different experiences and the same experiences might have been had by other people. The seeming plausibility of this comment reveals an abyss of misunderstanding. If anyone had different experiences from those he in fact had, he would not be the same person. He would be similar in some ways because of his genes, but he would be enormously different. And if the same experiences were had by other people, those people, too, would be different.

Experience does not exist apart from organisms, and they have biographies. If people, they are part of a culture. Human experience contains biography and culture, and it is probably true that people in cultures quite alien to our own have experiences somewhat different from ours. Much anthropological data gives evidence of that. But differences are not so great that most experi-ences in different cultures are unrecognizable in ours, because environing con-ditions are not so different. A palm and an oak are dissimilar but they are trees. Still, what is enticing to some is frightening to others. This is not to be attributed simply to the differences among those having the experience, but to the experience they have. For the experience of huge, surging waves to one who has never before seen the ocean and the experience of those waves to the habitual surfer is quite a different experience. If the situation has a pervasive quality, John Dewey's term, it is not the same quality.

The argument above may seem a defense of Santayana, but it is not. For the answer to the question, Why do we respond differently? is not that the difference is in us and is projected on to the situation; rather the situation, which includes us, includes and colors our "responses." As an example, an Oriental who had never heard Western music might find his first Mozart eerie and disorganized. Mozart's extraordinary organization is nonetheless in the music, and can be found. Just so, the great ocean waves are dangerous and both the formerly land-locked viewer and the surfer know it. When a child ventures out carelessly and is swept away (a carelessness not so common except for toddlers who should be protected by their parents, because a pounding surf is frightening to even young children) we say, colloquially and properly, "The babe did not recognize the danger," never doubting that the danger is there to be recognized. Whether we contemplate the danger from a safe distance or are elated by it and try to ride a surfboard over it, the danger is there. It is not our fright that creates it. Why would we be frightened if we thought there were no danger? Indeed, Santayana's pleasure or delight "projected" on an object might be a way of defining beauty as the pleasurable or delightful; we are delighted by what is delightful. Santayana said he was using the psychology of his time to analyze the sense of beauty and his sparkling analysis depends on that erroneous psychology.

Words, of course, have some meaning, or we could not use them as we do. But until they are connected *in some way,* as in a sentence, words have meaning only as individual poker cards do when they are not in a hand of five. Words that stand for concepts, like "love," live in the sentences that define them. A thought does not exist in language until there is a relation — a commonplace observation. And a sentence does not function without a context, as we all know. The context lends meaning to sentences that they would not have without it, or in another context. Of course, sentences make up a language context, are indeed its parts; but the context, once attained, colors the meaning of the sentences. What has sometimes been overlooked is the similarity between a linguistic context and an experiential one. Just as the elements in an experienced situation make it what it is, the situation as some kind of whole gives the elements a quality they would not have without it. Parts are, of course, different from each other. If identical, they are at least in different places. The context, made up of its parts, must be different from any of them, and so imparts to them a quality no one of them possesses by itself. Imagine a nursery full of happy, playing children (for the moment no petty squabbles, no childhood heartbreak) and add, suddenly, the entrance of a hungry leopard. That leopard, caged in a zoo or seen afar in the jungle through binoculars, is not frightening; he is graceful, sinuous, beautiful. The children alone are surely not frightening. But the situation in which leopard and children are together is terrifying, and the leopard becomes predator and the children prey.

In all of this, ordinary experience and literary art are similar. Of course all discourse is similar to experience in the way elements are related in context, but literature is itself experience and so bears a closer resemblance to ordinary experience than discourse does. Literature is packed with meanings of an experiential sort. They may be, in the author's mind, the result of reflection on experience but, as they appear in his work, the meanings are put back into experiential situations and occur as they do or might in life. It is not that literature is an imitation of life, but that it is an intensified, denser, but imaginative version.

Literature makes it easy to understand how one can respond to an imaginary situation that is false, just as one responds to a real situation. The elderly woman who receives news that her daughter was killed in an automobile accident may sink into depression and then learn that the mangled body was identified incorrectly and her daughter is alive and well. Her response to an imagined situation is what happens in fiction regularly, except that the woman in a novel or short story is as imaginary as the situation. In life there are times when we are misinformed about the situation we are in, or we misread it. But that, too, is part of the nature of experience. Our situations are as we understand them , and controlled inquiry can move us from the misleading, the imaginary, the delusional, to the real, that is, a situation whose components have met reasonable tests and can be agreed on by a number of other people. But when a situation is misunderstood it is experienced as it is understood and it is felt and responded to in that fashion. For the paranoiac, for example, there is somewhat private experience, in that its dominant quality would not be experienced by a nonparanoiac who entered a *similar* situation. Such a situation would not be *identical* with the paranoiac's situation, because the person is part of each situation.

In general, existential situations, as distinct from imaginary or fictional situations, are influenced by others, who help determine the way in which they are experienced. A large social-science literature based on experiment shows that we tend to change initial responses as we learn what the responses of others are. A puzzling shape some distance off in the water may seem to be a ship until others identify it as a whale, and then we perceive the outline of a whale. Experience is social in this manner and in the entire learning process in which we become able to identify things and are habituated to feeling about them in one way or another. Each of us is constantly thus being socialized in feelings and socializing others, in an unceasing interplay which shapes and reshapes experience. Again appeal to the arts is useful and helps move the argument. The adolescent, enchanted by Rimsky-Korsakov or Swinburne, learns the opinions of others, which are often pressed on him strongly. He hears and reads things they prefer, and tries to see why they prefer what they do. As his taste moves toward Mozart and Milton, he has come to what many would call better taste, as indeed it is; but he also no longer experiences Rimsky-Korsakov and Swinburne as he once did, nor Mozart and Milton for that matter. It is artificial to think, as we commonly do, that those works of art are experienced as they always were in the past but that the experiencer has changed and so makes different evaluations. Experience is not like that.

LEE NISBET

Hook's "Pragmatism and the Tragic Sense of Life"

Sidney Hook writes with the worldly eloquence of William James and the logical acumen and wisdom of John Dewey. These traits render him perhaps the clearest, keenest spokesman for the pragmatic position, especially as it is brought to bear on important cultural issues. In his essay "Pragmatism and the Tragic Sense of Life," we find a clear and provocative statement of what philosophy is and is not, what the role of the philosopher is and is not, and an illuminating discussion of what Hook calls the tragic sense of life and its relation to moral experience.[1] In order to introduce, or to further acquaint, the reader with some of the important insights and implications of Hook's pragmatic vision, I will identify, develop, and reflect upon some of the meanings the eminent philosopher develops in that essay.

"Philosophy," Hook writes, is a "quest for wisdom," which means that philosophy is not "*proclaiming* solutions and programs on the basis of antecedent commitments which one shares with some faction of his fellowmen," but rather it is "analyzing specific and basic social problems and conflicts and clarifying the issues in dispute with all the tools at one's command." The philosopher is not one who merely imposes a ready-made program of what should be done on issues of value-conflict but "one who on the basis of what he knows, or believes he knows, makes fresh inquiry into the situations that define alternatives and exact their costs." The philosopher's task requires immersion in all the subject matter "out of which life's problems arise." Hook reminds us that we all have a right to voice an opinion but that this right implies the responsibility to know what we are talking about. The philosopher, "one who engages in a sustained, reflective pursuit of wisdom," is therefore one who must

305

"earn his title by the hard work of acquiring relevant knowledge and by hard thinking about it."

Sidney Hook's view of philosophy is unabashedly pragmatic. Philosophy is primarily (but not wholly) "normative social inquiry," which, he warns, is not the same thing as social reform. One misconstrues the role of the *philosopher as philosopher* unless the distinction is maintained between defining, analyzing, clarifying, and evaluating social problems and conflicts (normative social inquiry) and advocacy of some political program of action. Hook's view, as I read him, is that, although social inquiry may lead to some specific social or political action, that is not its aim. The aim, rather, is "to do intellectual justice to the varied and conflicting interests present or discovered." Philosophic or social inquiry is not separate from practice but is carried on in such a manner as to intellectualize practice—to enable us to become more aware of the alternatives in dealing with social problems and the probable costs of acting on those alternatives. In order to achieve such understanding, philosophic inquiry must be distinguished from a priori partisan imaginings about what choices and actions "should" be made and undertaken. Philosophic inquiry, Hook notes, is not value free, for it *is* the quest for wisdom; and precisely *because* it is such a quest the philosopher as philosopher can no more prescribe action than the therapist as therapist can direct his client's actions. The philosopher is an educator, not a propagandist. His job is to aid his clientele in making their *own* informed judgments as to what would be the better choice.

In sum, since the aim of all inquiry is to transform a conflicted situation into one free of inhibiting difficulties, those engaging in philosophic inquiry cannot decide before that inquiry what values and ideals are better or worse, what must be chosen and what must be set aside. In Hook's version of pragmatism, inquiry is central, and it is defined as a distinctive and autonomous phase of social action: distinctive and autonomous because, for Hook, the *process* of freeing action from ignorance and prejudice is what freedom is.

That Hook is correct in his view of the philosopher's role is borne out by the tragic mess that contemporary intellectual life has fallen into, especially as practiced in higher education and various forms of the persuasive media. Here, too often, we find intellectuality identified not with inquiry but with a particular political program. The word *tragic* is used for two reasons. First, the decision to politicize academia and intellectual activity in the media has led both to the discrediting of these institutions in the public eye and, worse yet, to the inability to carry out their critical intellectual functions. When professorial or priestly preachers of Left or Right denominations concoct political theologies to convert the heathen, effective thinking—thinking as a critical intellectual activity—is eliminated.

The word *tragic* is used for a second reason, which is related to the first. Dogmatism, the imposition of fixed ideals on unexamined situations in which choices have to be made, violates a primary quality of moral experience—the tragic quality, or tragic sense. Hook explains that, "every genuine experience of moral doubt and perplexity in which we ask 'What should I do?' takes place in a situation where good conflicts with good . . . No matter how we resolve the opposition some good will be sacrificed, some interest whose immediate craving for satisfaction may be every whit as intense and authentic as its fellow will be modified, frustrated, or even suppressed."

Goods and ideals that pull us in conflicting directions do so because they attract fundamentally important and now conflicting parts of our selves. When we are forced to choose the one over the other, tragically we choose what we will not become and what values we will not enjoy as much as we choose what we will become and enjoy. The more complex and intense the conflict, the more inherently tragic and difficult is the choice.

"If we have played it safe and made our existence apparently secure, the fascinating life of adventure and experience can never be ours . . . If we have scorned to put down roots . . . we have thrust from ourselves the warmth of sustained affection and comforting regularities which can best heal the bruised spirit."

This tragic quality of choice is at the heart of every intense and important juncture of our lives where we choose who we will become—and not become. The person with many lovers sacrifices the powerful intimacy and security of successful monogamy upon the altar of the tempestuous, soul-tingling novelty of uncommitted romance—*and* vice versa. Married lovers who seek the joys of the shared adventure of begetting a child sacrifice a treasured share of the effervescent spontaneity possible in a life where they have only each other to consider. The list of conflicts and sacrifices, great and small, is as long as there are goods in actual or possible conflict—the list is endless.

Hook's analysis of the tragic quality of moral experience becomes the central point of his moral and aesthetic vision of life. In his view, life can become free and harmonious, that is, beautiful, only on the condition that one affirms that the tragic quality is intrinsic to the moral experience. This point is rather significant when we consider that historically the mainline theological and philosophical traditions in our culture have attempted (and attempt) to rationalize away the tragic quality of moral experience with the claim that God will make up to us in the end what we have suffered and lost, or that every sacrifice is illusionary for it is only part of the necessary unfolding of a finalized world plan. In short, every sacrifice in a "necessary" world supposedly happens for the best. In Hook's words, "no monotheistic religion which conceives of God as both omnipotent and benevolent, no metaphysics which asserts that the world is rational, necessary and good has any room for genuine inescapable tragedy." There is a terrible price to be paid for this piece of intellectual dishonesty: the forfeiture of the possibilities of a free and harmonious life.

Dogmatism, whether philosophical, theological, or ideological, in its denial of the genuinely tragic quality of choice ends up denying that moral conflicts are amenable to negotiation. Dogmatism asserts that only one good or ideal is good or ideal and hence the alternative is automatically bad or evil. The free man understands that moral conflicts of good and good, good and obligation, and obligation and obligation are not necessarily contradictions, that there may be room for negotiation. Hence the task for inquiry is set. The free man is free to the extent that he has both the willingness and the ability to carry on such negotiations. In Hook's words, the free man, when "faced with a momentous conflict of value in which some value must give way if the situation is to be resolved," searches for "some encompassing value on the basis of some shared interest." Pragmatism as a philosophy of freedom is "melioristic, not optimistic." It therefore "focuses its analysis on the problems of normative social inquiry in order to reduce the costs of tragedy."

Acceptance of the tragic element as intrinsic to choice leads one to see that the aim of choice is, wherever possible, to produce harmony where before there was discord. Just *because* every important choice involves a tragic sacrifice of some part of oneself, the free man, in William James's words, "knows that he must vote always for the richer universe, for the good which seems most organizable, most fit to enter into complex combinations, most apt to be a member of the inclusive whole."[2]

When conflicts can be orchestrated into a harmony of the soul through selection of the more inclusive good or ideal, the free and beautiful life can be had. Pragmatism here is clearly revealed as an extension of the ancient Greek humanism that saw ethics and aesthetics as one. The Greeks knew, as Hook knows, that tragedy is an inescapable and real part of the human condition, and their philosophy as well as Hook's is the richer for it.

We see, then, that Hook's pragmatism, with its emphasis on the tragic, consistently affirms that choice exists. Choices can and do make a difference in our moral and aesthetic experience. The moral and aesthetic universe is not fully made and finalized. Genuine novelty exists not only in the unexpected but also in the difference made in our lives by intelligently negotiating conflicts of value— that is, by choosing through inquiry the more harmonizing good or ideal. A man who experiences his choice as making a difference experiences life as *being different,* changed, novel, freed from the conflicts that tied him down. The novelty of the difference is vitality—the vitality of the possibility of still more good coming his way.

Hook's pragmatic vision is an aesthetic vision. Dogmatism is wicked because it attempts to fictionalize tragedy through divine justice or some necessary world plan and therefore destroys essential ingredients in moral and aesthetic experience—risk and novelty. If choice is tragic, then there *is* risk, the risk of sacrificing the better to the worse, and if there is risk there is novelty. Without risk and novelty, moral choice would be meaningless and aesthetic life would be impossible. A world without novelty and risk, that is, precariousness, would be merely routine, stale, monotonous—a hell! When we realize that what we become and do not become are outcomes of what we choose, that we are responsible for the selves we choose to become or not to become, then our choices take on the greatest importance: the importance of fashioning our *own* becoming. To paraphrase Sidney Hook, we have the scintillating opportunity to live our own lives in our own reflective styles.

NOTES

1. Sidney Hook, "Pragmatism and the Tragic Sense of Life," in *Pragmatism and the Tragic Sense of Life* (New York: Basic Books, 1974).

2. William James, "The Moral Philosopher and the Moral Life," in *Pragmatism and Other Essays* (1910), by William James (New York: Washington Square Press, 1963), p. 232. ●

Compiled by Jo Ann Boydston and Kathleen Poulos

A COMPLETE BIBLIOGRAPHY
OF SIDNEY HOOK

1922

"The Philosophy of Non-Resistance." *Open Court* 36 (Jan. 1922): 1–5.
"A Philosophical Dialogue." *Open Court* 36 (Oct. 1922): 621–26.

1926

Review of Rebecca Cooper, *The Logical Influence of Hegel on Marx. Journal of Philosophy* 23 (18 Feb. 1926): 106–8.
"The Metaphysics of *Leading Principles*." *Journal of Philosophy* 23 (1 Apr. 1926): 169–83.
"Methodological Considerations in Primitive Art." *Open Court* 40 (June 1926): 328–39.

1927

The Metaphysics of Pragmatism. Chicago: Open Court Pub. Co., 1927.
Collected Works of Vladimir Ilyich Lenin, trans. Sidney Hook and David Kvitko. New York: International Publishers, 1927.
"The Ethics of Suicide." *International Journal of Ethics* 37 (Jan. 1927): 173–88.
"Freedom." *Open Court* 41 (Feb. 1927): 65–73.
"Categorial Analysis and Pragmatic-Realism." *Journal of Philosophy* 24 (31 Mar. 1927): 169–87.
"The Metaphysics of the Instrument, Part 1." *Monist* 37 (July 1927): 335–56. "Part 2: Thinking as Instrumental." Ibid. 37 (Oct. 1927): 601–19. "Part 3: The Ethics of the Instrument." Ibid., pp. 620–23.
"The Irrationality of *the Irrational*." *Journal of Philosophy* 24 (4 Aug. 1927): 421–37.

The final version of this Checklist has been compiled with the assistance of editors from the Center for Dewey Studies, Southern Illinois University at Carbondale, and the cooperation of Dale Reed, Assistant Archivist, Library of the Hoover Institution on War, Revolution and Peace. We are indebted to John Dennis Crowley, S.J., for his work on the "Bibliography of Sidney Hook," in *Sidney Hook and the Contemporary World,* ed. Paul Kurtz (New York: John Day Co., 1968), pp. 429–71.

1928

"Marx and Freud: Oil and Water." *Open Court* 41 (Jan. 1928): 20–25. See Max Eastman, "Karl Marx Anticipated Freud." *New Masses* 3 (July 1927): 11–12.

"The Philosophy of Dialectical Materialism, Parts 1 and 2." Review of Vladimir I. Lenin, *Materialism and Empirio-Criticism*. *Journal of Philosophy* 25 (1 Mar. 1928): 113–24; ibid. 25 (15 Mar. 1928): 141–55.

    Reply by Max Eastman, ibid. 25 (16 Aug. 1928): 475–76.

    Rejoinder by Hook, ibid. 25 (11 Oct. 1928): 587–88.

"Marxism, Metaphysics, and Modern Science." Review of Max Eastman, *Marx, Lenin, and the Science of Revolution*. *Modern Quarterly* 4 (May–Aug. 1928): 388–94.

    For the debate that ensued, see:

        Eastman, "As to Sidney Hook's Morals." Ibid. 5 (Nov. 1928–Feb. 1929): 85–87.

        Hook, "As to Max Eastman's Mentality." Ibid., pp. 88–91.

        Eastman, "Excommunication and Exorcism as Critical Methods, Part 1." Ibid. 7 (May 1933): 210–13.

        Hook, "The Engineering Conception of Marxism." Review of Max Eastman, *Karl Marx's "Capital" and Other Writings*. Ibid., pp. 248–50.

        Eastman, "A Master Magician, Part 2." Ibid. 7 (June 1933): 290–93, 307.

        Eastman, letter in reply to Hook's review of *Karl Marx's "Capital."* Ibid., p. 320.

        Eastman, "Man and History." Ibid. 7 (July 1933): 348–50.

        Hook, "A Note from Sidney Hook." Ibid., pp. 350–51.

        Eastman, letter in reply. Ibid. 7 (Aug. 1933): 447–48.

        Hook, response. Ibid. 7 (Sept. 1933): 510–11.

        V. F. Calverton, "To Max Eastman and Sidney Hook." Ibid., pp. 511–12.

        Eastman, letter. Ibid. 7 (Oct. 1933): 576.

"Freedom." *Archiv für systematische Philosophie und Soziologie* 31 (1928): 17–26. [Concluding chapter of *The Metaphysics of Pragmatism, 1927.*]

1929

"What Is Dialectic? Part 1." *Journal of Philosophy* 26 (14 Feb. 1929): 85–99. "Part 2." Ibid. 26 (28 Feb. 1929): 113–23.

Review of Julius Löwenstein, *Hegels Staatsidee*. *Journal of Philosophy* 26 (12 Sept. 1929): 526–30.

"A Pragmatic Critique of the Historico-Genetic Method." In *Essays in Honor of John Dewey*, pp. 156–74. New York: Henry Holt and Co., 1929.

1930

"A Critique of Ethical Realism." *International Journal of Ethics* 40 (Jan. 1930): 179–210. [Reprinted, with slight changes, in *Pragmatism and the Tragic Sense of Life, 1974.*]

"A Personal Impression of Contemporary German Philosophy." *Journal of Philosophy* 27 (13 Mar. 1930): 141–60.

    Reply by Dorion Cairns, "Mr. Hook's Impression of Phenomenology." Ibid. 27 (17 July 1930): 393–96.

    Rejoinder by Hook, "In Defence of an Impression." Ibid. 27 (6 Nov. 1930): 635–37.

"The Revolt against Dualism." Review of Arthur O. Lovejoy, *The Revolt against Dualism*. *New Republic* 63 (18 June 1930): 129–30.

"Husserl's Phenomenological Idealism." Review of Edmund Husserl, *Formale und transzendentale Logik*. *Journal of Philosophy* 27 (3 July 1930): 365–80.

"Contemporary American Philosophy." Review of *Contemporary American Philosophy: Personal Statements*, ed. George P. Adams and William P. Montague. *New Republic* 63 (16 July 1930): 237–39.

"The Philosophy of Morris R. Cohen." *New Republic* 63 (23 July 1930): 278–81.
"Capitalism and Protestantism." Review of Max Weber, *The Protestant Ethic and the Spirit of Capitalism. Nation* 131 (29 Oct. 1930): 476–78.
Review of George S. Counts, *The American Road to Culture. Current History* 33 (Oct. 1930): x–xiii.
"The Meaning of Marxism." *Modern Quarterly* 5 (Winter 1930–31): 430–35. [Part of a symposium on "Marxism and Social Change."]
"The Non-Sense of the Whole." Review of Waldo Frank, *The Re-Discovery of America: An Introduction to a Philosophy of American Life. Modern Quarterly* 5 (Winter 1930–31): 504–13. Reply by Frank, ibid., pp. 514–16.
Encyclopaedia of the Social Sciences, ed. Edwin R. A. Seligman. New York: Macmillan Co., 1930–35.
Contributions:
"Bauer, Bruno." Vol. 2, 1930, p. 481.
"Büchner, Ludwig." Vol. 3, 1931, p. 30.
"Determinism." Vol. 5, 1931, pp. 110–14.
"Dietzgen, Joseph." Vol. 5, 1931, p. 139.
"Engels, Friedrich." Vol. 5, 1931, pp. 540–41.
"Feuerbach, Ludwig Andreas." Vol. 6, 1931, pp. 221–22.
"Materialism." Vol. 10, 1933, pp. 209–20.
"Ruge, Arnold." Vol. 13, 1934, pp. 462–63.
"Violence." Vol. 15, 1935, pp. 264–67.

1931

Review of Henri DeMan, *The Psychology of Socialism. Current History* 33 (Jan. 1931): xxi–xxiii.
"The New Individualism." Review of John Dewey, *Individualism Old and New. Current History* 33 (Mar. 1931): xxii–xxiv.
"The Soviet Challenge." Review of George S. Counts, *The Soviet Challenge to America. Current History* 34 (May 1931): xiii–xiv.
"John Dewey and His Critics." *New Republic* 67 (3 June 1931): 73–74.
"Marx and Darwinism." *New Republic* 67 (29 July 1931): 290.
Reply by Robert Morss Lovett, ibid., pp. 290–91.
"Towards the Understanding of Karl Marx." *Symposium* 2 (July 1931): 325–67.
Review of Willy Moog, *Hegel und die Hegelsche Schule. Journal of Philosophy* 28 (27 Aug. 1931): 497–500.
"Experimental Logic." *Mind* 40 (Oct. 1931): 424–38.
Review of Edmund Husserl, *Ideas — General Introduction to Pure Phenomenology. Symposium* 2 (Oct. 1931): 531–40.
"The Metaphysics of Experience." Review of John Dewey, *Philosophy and Civilization. New Republic* 68 (4 Nov. 1931): 330–31.
"From Hegel to Marx, Part 1." *Modern Quarterly* 6 (Winter 1931): 46–62. "Part 2: Hegel and Marx in Continuity." Ibid. 6 (Summer 1932): 33–43. "Part 3: Dialectic in Hegel and Marx." Ibid. 6 (Autumn 1932): 58–67.

1932

"Reason and Nature: The Metaphysics of Scientific Method." Review of Morris Cohen, *Reason and Nature. Journal of Philosophy* 29 (7 Jan. 1932): 5–24.
Review of Theodor L. Haering, *Hegel, Sein Wollen und Sein Werk,* vol. 1. *Philosophical Review* 41 (Jan. 1932): 75–77.
"An Epic of Revolution." Review of Leon Trotsky, *The Overthrow of Tzarism. The History of the Russian Revolution,* vol. 1. *Saturday Review of Literature* 8 (27 Feb. 1932): 549–51.

"Pictures of the Past." Review of Michael N. Pokrovsky, *History of Russia,* vol. 1. *Saturday Review of Literature* 8 (30 Apr. 1932): 700.

Review of Dewitt H. Parker, *Human Values. International Journal of Ethics* 42 (Apr. 1932): 348–53.

Review of *Principles of Philosophy. Collected Papers of Charles Sanders Peirce,* ed. Charles Hartshorne and Paul Weiss, vol. 1. *Symposium* 3 (Apr. 1932): 248–56.

Review of *Principles of Philosophy. Collected Papers of Charles Sanders Peirce,* ed. Charles Hartshorne and Paul Weiss, vol. 1. *Current History* 36 (May 1932): 4–5.

"The Contemporary Significance of Hegel's Philosophy." *Philosophical Review* 41 (May 1932): 237–60.

"Half-baked Communism." Review of Robert Briffault, *Breakdown: The Collapse of Traditional Civilisation. Nation* 134 (8 June 1932): 654–55.

> Replies by M. F. Ashley-Montagu, Nelson Morris, and Briffault, ibid. 135 (13 July 1932): 36–37.
>
> Hook, "Rejoinder to Mr. Ashley-Montagu." Ibid. 135 (24 Aug. 1932): 170–71.

"Hegel's Phenomenology of Mind." Review of *Hegel's Phenomenology of Mind,* 2d rev. ed., trans. J. B. Baillie. *Journal of Philosophy* 29 (23 June 1932): 361–62.

"Myth, Fact, and Poetry of Soviet Russia." Review of Waldemar Gurian, *Bolshevism: Theory and Practice*; Joseph Freeman, *The Soviet Worker*; Waldo Frank, *Dawn in Russia*; George S. Counts, Luigi Villari, Malcolm Rorty and Newton D. Baker, *Bolshevism, Fascism, and Capitalism. Nation* 135 (14 Sept. 1932): 237–38.

Review of Vladimir I. Lenin, *What Is To Be Done? American Journal of Sociology* 38 (Sept. 1932): 315–17.

1933

Towards the Understanding of Karl Marx: A Revolutionary Interpretation. New York: John Day Co., 1933.

"Karl Marx and the Young Hegelians." *Modern Monthly* 7 (Feb. 1933): 33–44.

"Marxism—Dogma or Method?" *Nation* 136 (15 Mar. 1933): 284–85. Letter in reply by Leon Trotsky, with response by Hook, ibid. 137 (5 July 1933): 18–19.

"The Marxian Dialectic." *New Republic* 74 (22 Mar. 1933): 150–54.

"Russia in Solution." Review of Leon Trotsky, *The History of the Russian Revolution,* vols. 2 and 3, trans. Max Eastman. *Saturday Review of Literature* 9 (8 Apr. 1933): 521–22.

Review of August Faust, *Der Möglichkeitsgedanke Systemgeschichtliche Untersuchungen. Journal of Philosophy* 30 (13 Apr. 1933): 221–23.

"Against the Fascist Terror in Germany." *New Masses,* Apr. 1933.

"Karl Marx and Bruno Bauer." *Modern Monthly* 7 (Apr. 1933): 160–74.

"Education and Politics." Review of *The Educational Frontier,* ed. William Heard Kilpatrick. *New Republic* 75 (24 May 1933): 49–50.

"Why the German Student Is Fascist." *Student Outlook* 1 (May 1933): 4–6, 20.

"Science and the Crisis." Review of H. L. Levy, *The Universe of Science,* and *Science and the Changing World,* ed. Mary Adams. *Nation* 136 (21 June 1933): 705–6.

"Revolutionist's Symposium." Review of *Recovery through Revolution,* ed. Samuel D. Schmalhausen. *Nation* 136 (28 June 1933): 733–34.

"Kant and Political Liberalism," by Karl Marx, trans. Sidney Hook. *Modern Monthly* 7 (July 1933): 352–54.

"Arnold Ruge and Karl Marx, Part 1." *Modern Monthly* 7 (Aug. 1933): 409–21, 431; "Part 2." Ibid. 7 (Sept. 1933): 480–86.

"De Libris: Disputatio." *City College Alumnus,* Sept. 1933.

"On Hegel's 'Concrete Universal'," by Karl Marx, trans. Sidney Hook. *Modern Monthly* 7 (Sept. 1933): 496–97, 501.

"Karl Marx and Max Stirner." *Modern Monthly* 7 (Oct. 1933): 547–55, 569.

"Psychology: The Social Bias." Review of Edna F. Heidbreder, *Seven Psychologies*. *New Republic* 77 (29 Nov. 1933): 81-82.

"Social Psychology—Marxian Style." Review of Leon Samson, *Towards a United Front: A Philosophy for American Workers*. *Modern Monthly* 7 (Nov. 1933): 637-39.

"Theories of Social Determinism." *Scientia* 54 (Dec. 1933): 437-49.

1934

The Democratic and Dictatorial Aspects of Communism. Part 2. Worcester, Mass.: Carnegie Endowment for International Peace, 1934. [Part 1: Joseph Stalin, *The Political and Social Doctrine of Communism*.]

"The Meaning of Marx." In *The Meaning of Marx*, ed. Sidney Hook, pp. 47-82. New York: Farrar and Rinehart, 1934. [Symposium by Bertrand Russell, John Dewey, Morris R. Cohen, Sherwood Eddy, and Sidney Hook.]

"Towards the Understanding of Karl Marx." In Max Eastman, *Art and the Life of Action*, pp. 121-33. New York: Alfred A. Knopf, 1934.

"Is Marxism Compatible with Christianity?" *Christian Register* 113 (15 Feb. 1934): 103-6.

Reply to Francis A. Henson, "The Challenge of Marxism to Christianity." Ibid. 113 (18 Jan. 1934): 35-38.

Reply to Henry P. Van Dusen, "The Challenge of Christianity to Marxism." Ibid. 113 (1 Feb. 1934): 71-73.

"A Shot in the Dark." Review of Ralph Fox, *Lenin: A Biography*. *Saturday Review of Literature* 10 (24 Feb. 1934): 503.

"The Philosophy of Technics in the U.S.S.R." *Modern Monthly* 8 (Feb. 1934): 31-36.

"The Nature of Discourse." Review of Alfred Korzybski, *Science and Sanity: An Introduction to Non-Aristotelian Systems and General Semantics*. *Saturday Review* 10 (10 Mar. 1934): 546-47.

"Dewey on Thought and Action." Review of John Dewey, *How We Think*. *New Republic* 78 (21 Mar. 1934): 165.

"The Mythology of Class Science." *Modern Monthly* 8 (Mar. 1934): 112-17.

"What Is Materialism?" *Journal of Philosophy* 31 (26 Apr. 1934): 235-42.

Reply by R. W. Sellars, "Is Naturalism Enough?" Ibid. 41 (28 Sept. 1944): 533-44.

Rejoinder by Hook, "Is Physical Realism Sufficient?" Ibid., pp. 544-51.

"A Symposium on Communism: Why I Am a Communist (Communism without Dogmas)." *Modern Monthly* 8 (Apr. 1934): 143-65.

Bertrand Russell, "Why I Am Not a Communist." Ibid., pp. 133-34.

John Dewey, "Why I Am Not a Communist." Ibid., pp. 135-37.

Morris R. Cohen, "Why I Am Not a Communist." Ibid., pp. 138-42.

"Marxism and Democracy: Some Notes on the Draft Program of the A.W.P." *Labor Action*, 1 May 1934.

"Sidney Hook Replies." *Commonwealth College Fortnightly* 10 (15 June 1934): 2-3.

Reply to William Cunningham, "Misunderstanding Marxian Economics." Ibid. 10 (15 Feb. 1934): 2-3.

Response by Paul Evans, "On Sidney [sic] Hook's Reply." Ibid. 10 (15 July 1934): 2-3.

"Socialism at the Crossroads." Review of *Socialism, Fascism and Communism*, ed. Joseph Shaplen and David Shub. *Saturday Review of Literature* 11 (21 July 1934): 1-2.

"The Fallacy of the Theory of Social Fascism." *Modern Monthly* 8 (July 1934): 342-52.

"The Challenge of the Social Order to the Curriculum of the Liberal Arts College." In *Report of the 11th Annual Meeting of the Fellows of the National Council on Religion in Higher Education*, Colgate-Rochester Divinity School, Rochester, N.Y., 4-10 Sept. 1934.

"An Open Letter to Lincoln Steffens." *Modern Monthly* 8 (Sept. 1934): 486-92.

Review of *Systematic Sociology on the Basis of the Beziehungslehre and Gebildelehre of Leopold von Wiese*, adapted by Howard Becker. *Philosophical Review* 43 (Sept. 1934): 532-35.

Review of Theodore B. Brameld, *A Philosophic Approach to Communism. American Economic Review* 24 (Sept. 1934): 548–49.

"A Demonstration for Relief." *New Republic* 80 (31 Oct. 1934): 340. Letter, also signed by J. B. S. Hardman, James Burnham, Louis F. Budenz, and A. J. Muste.

"On Workers' Democracy." *Modern Monthly* 8 (Oct. 1934): 529–44.

Replies by Will Herberg: "Workers' Democracy or Dictatorship?: On Hook's Revival of Kautsky's Theories." *Workers Age* 3 (15 Dec. 1934): 3, 8; "Parties under Workers' Rule: An Answer to Sidney Hook's Concept of Parties in a Dictatorship." Ibid. 4 (4 May 1935): 5; "As to a Multi-Party Dictatorship: Hook Confuses Dictatorship with Bourgeois Democracy." Ibid. 4 (11 May 1935): 3.

Response by Hook, "Manners and Morals of Apache-Radicalism." *Modern Monthly* 9 (June 1935): 215–21.

Reply by Herberg, "Professor Hook Loses His Temper: Concluding Remarks on Hook's Misconception of Dictatorship." *Workers Age* 4 (6 July 1935): 3.

"The Importance of a Point of View, Part 1." *Social Frontier* 1 (Oct. 1934): 19–22. "Part 2." Ibid. 1 (Nov. 1934): 17–19.

"The Democratic and Dictatorial Aspects of Communism." *International Conciliation* 305 (Dec. 1934): 452–64.

"Karl Marx and Moses Hess." *New International* 1 (Dec. 1934): 140–44.

1935

"Experimental Naturalism." In *American Philosophy Today and Tomorrow,* ed. Sidney Hook and Horace M. Kallen, pp. 205–25. New York: L. Furman, 1935.

"Hegel and Marx." In *Studies in the History of Ideas,* vol. 3, pp. 329–404. New York: Columbia University Press, 1935.

"Marx's Criticism of 'True Socialism'." *New International* 2 (Jan. 1935): 13–16.

"A Philosophic Pathfinder." Review of George H. Mead, *Mind, Self and Society. Nation* 140 (13 Feb. 1935): 195–96.

"Interpreting Soviet Russia." Review of Julius Hecker, *Moscow Dialogues*; *Russian Sociology*; *Religion and Communism*; and *The Communist's Answer to the World's Needs*; James Bunyan and H. H. Fisher, *The Bolshevik Revolution, 1917–1918*; Maurice Parmelee, *Bolshevism, Fascism, and the Liberal-Democratic State. Saturday Review* 11 (16 Feb. 1935): 494–95.

"Marxism and Religion." *Modern Monthly* 9 (Mar. 1935): 29–35.

"Our Philosophers." *Current History* 41 (Mar. 1935): 698–704.

"Literature of Revolt: A Reply to Professor Cohen – II." *Student Outlook,* 3 (May 1935): 11–13.

"Philosophical Burlesque." *Modern Monthly* 9 (May 1935): 163–72.

"What Happened in Russia." Review of William Henry Chamberlin, *The Russian Revolution, 1917–1921. Saturday Review* (1 June 1935): 40–41.

"Pareto's Sociological System." Review of Vilfredo Pareto, *The Mind and Society. Nation* 140 (26 June 1935): 747–48.

"Saint Stalin." Review of Henri Barbusse, *Stalin. Saturday Review of Literature* 13 (16 Nov. 1935): 7.

"A Triumph of Scholarship." Review of *Encyclopaedia of the Social Sciences. Saturday Review of Literature* 13 (7 Dec. 1935): 38, 42.

"William James." Review of Ralph Barton Perry, *The Thought and Character of William James. Nation* 141 (11 Dec. 1935): 684–86.

"Ludwig Feuerbach." Part 1. *Modern Monthly* 9 (Dec. 1935): 357–69; Part 2: "Feuerbach's Psychology of Religion." Ibid. 9 (Jan. 1936): 430–36; Part 3: "Feuerbach's Philosophy of Anthropomorphism." Ibid. 9 (Mar. 1936): 493–501.

1936

From Hegel to Marx: Studies in the Intellectual Development of Karl Marx. New York: John Day Co., 1936; New York: Reynal and Hitchcock, 1936.

"Plato without the Legend." Review of Warner Fite, *The Platonic Legend. New Republic* 82 (27 Feb. 1936): 81.

"Revolutionary Mythology." Review of August Thalheimer, *Introduction to Dialectical Materialism. Nation* 142 (4 Mar. 1936): 288–90.

"The Faith of a Scientist." Review of Bertrand Russell, *Religion and Science. New Republic* 86 (1 Apr. 1936): 227.

"Marx's Life and Thought." Review of Franz Mehring, *Karl Marx: The Story of His Life. Saturday Review of Literature* 13 (18 Apr. 1936): 18–19.

"Radicals and War." A debate with Ludwig Lore. *Modern Monthly* 10 (Apr. 1936): 12–17.

"Ethereal Politics." Review of Richard Rothschild, *Three Gods Give an Evening to Politics. Nation* 142 (20 May 1936): 653–54.

"Social Masks and Social Facts." Review of Thurman Arnold, *The Symbols of Government. New Republic* 87 (20 May 1936): 51–52.

"On Rereading Veblen." Review of *What Veblen Taught*, ed. Wesley Clair Mitchell. *New Republic* 87 (17 June 1936): 182.

"Man behind Marx." Review of Gustav Mayer, *Friedrich Engels. Saturday Review of Literature* 14 (27 June 1936): 10.

"The Prophetic Trotsky." Review of Leon Trotsky, *The Third International after Lenin. Saturday Review* 14 (11 July 1936): 10.

"New Trend in Philosophy." Review of George H. Mead, *Movements of Thought in the Nineteenth Century. Nation* 143 (22 Aug. 1936): 220–21.

"The Uses of Opposition." *Modern Monthly* 10 (Aug. 1936): 13–15.

"Marxism as a Living Philosophy." *New Republic* 88 (30 Sept. 1936): 233–34.

Reply to Herman Simpson's review of *From Hegel to Marx,* ibid., pp. 232–33.

Rebuttal by Simpson, ibid. 89 (18 Nov. 1936): 75–76.

Rejoinder by Hook, ibid., p. 76.

"Philosophy in Action." Review of Horace M. Kallen, *The Decline and Rise of the Consumer. Opinion* 7 (Dec. 1936): 25, 27.

1937

"The Philosophical Implications of Economic Planning." In *Planned Society: Yesterday, Today and Tomorrow,* ed. Findlay Mackenzie, pp. 663–77. New York: Prentice-Hall, 1937.

Introduction to Richard Lowenthal, *What Is Folksocialism?* New York: League for Industrial Democracy, 1937.

"Marxism and Values." *Marxist Quarterly* 1 (Jan.–Mar. 1937): 38–45.

Review of Karl Joël, *Wandlungen der Weltanschauung. Journal of Philosophy* 34 (4 Mar. 1937): 131–33.

"Dialectic and Nature." *Marxist Quarterly* 1 (Apr.–June 1937): 253–84.

"A Philosopher on Movie Censorship." Review of Mortimer Adler, *Art and Prudence: A Study in Practical Philosophy. Saturday Review* 16 (15 May 1937): 17.

"Both Their Houses." *New Republic* 91 (2 June 1937): 104.

"History in Swing Rhythm." Review of Pitirim Sorokin, *Social and Cultural Dynamics. Nation* 145 (10 July 1937): 48–49.

"Socialism for a Democracy." Review of Harry W. Laidler, *American Socialism. Saturday Review* 16 (28 Aug. 1937): 20.

"Fantasia on the Left." Review of Albert Weisbord, *The Conquest of Power: Liberalism, Anarchism, Syndicalism, Socialism, Fascism, and Communism. Nation* 145 (11 Sept. 1937): 270–71.

"Discussion: Totalitarianism in Education." *Social Research* 4 (Sept. 1937): 401–4.

"Seeking Truth about Trotsky." Review of Preliminary Commission of Inquiry, *The Case of Leon Trotsky: Report of Hearings on the Charges Made against Him in the Moscow Trials. New York Herald Tribune Books,* 10 Oct. 1937.

"Worlds of Chance." Review of Edward Gleason Spaulding, *A World of Chance. Nation* 145 (23 Oct. 1937): 451–53.

"Promise without Dogma: A Social Philosophy for Jews." *Menorah Journal* 25 (Oct.–Dec. 1937): 273–88.

> Reply by Alvin Johnson, "A Social Philosophy for Jews." Ibid. 26 (Jan.–Mar. 1938): 1–6.
> Response by Hook, "A Note on Alvin Johnson's Article." Ibid. 26 (Winter 1938): 103–4.

"The Sociology of Knowledge." Review of Karl Mannheim, *Ideology and Utopia. Marxist Quarterly* 1 (Oct.–Dec. 1937): 450–54.

"The Technique of Mystification." Review of Kenneth Burke, *Attitudes Toward History. Partisan Review* 4 (Dec. 1937): 57–62.

> Reply by Burke, ibid. 4 (Jan. 1938): 40–44.
> Response by Hook, "Is Mr. Burke Serious?" Ibid., pp. 44–47.

"Ends and Means." Review of Aldous Huxley, *Ends and Means. Nation* 145 (11 Dec. 1937): 656–58.

"Liberalism and the Case of Leon Trotsky." *Southern Review* 3 (1937–38): 267–82.

> Correspondence by Hook, Frederick, Schuman, Carleton Beals, and James T. Farrell, ibid., pp. 406–16.

1938

"Violence As a (Marxist) Professor Sees It." *Common Sense* 7 (Jan. 1938): 22–23.

"The Ways of Philosophy." Review of Irwin Edman, *Four Ways of Philosophy. Nation* 146 (8 Jan. 1938): 48–49.

"Storm Signals in American Philosophy." *Virginia Quarterly Review* 14 (Winter 1938): 29–43.

"Zweiter Entfer oyf der Frage: Zie Leybt in sich Izt die Sowietische Arbeiter Besser, wic die Arbeiter in andere Lender?" *Der Tag,* 7 Feb. 1938.

"Broun v. Dewey." *New Republic* 94 (16 Feb. 1938): 48.

> Letter in reply to Heywood Broun, "Dr. Dewey Finds Communists in the C.I.O." Ibid. 93 (12 Jan. 1938): 280–81.

"Metaphysics and Social Attitudes: A Reply." *Social Frontier* 4 (Feb. 1938): 153–58.

> Reply to Brand Blanshard, "Metaphysics and Social Attitudes." Ibid. 4 (Dec. 1937): 79–81.
> Response by Porter Sargent, "Metaphysics and Social Attitudes: Some Forgotten Facts." Ibid. 4 (Mar. 1938): 178–79.
> Reply by Pitirim A. Sorokin, ibid., pp. 179–80.
> Rejoinder by Blanshard, "Metaphysics and Social Attitudes, A Rejoinder." Ibid. 4 (Apr. 1938): 219–21.
> Response by Hook, "Relevant Issues Restated." Ibid., pp. 221–23.

"Logic, Politics, and Plain Decency." *Social Frontier* 4 (Mar. 1938): 190–92.

> Response to Earl Browder, "Toward the American Commonwealth: 2. The Present Communist Position." Ibid. 4 (Feb. 1938): 161–64.

"Corliss Lamont: 'Friend of the G.P.U.'" *Modern Monthly* 10 (Mar. 1938): 5–8.

"The Baptism of Aristotle and Marx." Review of Mortimer J. Adler, *What Man Has Made of Man. Nation* 146 (9 Apr. 1938): 415–17.

"Some Social Uses and Abuses of Semantics." *Partisan Review* 4 (Apr. 1938): 14–25.

"The Politician's Handbook." Review of Thurman Arnold, *The Folklore of Capitalism. University of Chicago Law Review* 5 (Apr. 1938): 341–49.

> Reply by Arnold, "The Folklore of Mr. Hook—A Reply." Ibid., pp. 349–53.
> Rejoinder by Hook, "Neither Myth nor Power—A Rejoinder." Ibid., pp. 354–57.

"Thoughts in Season." *Socialist Review* 6 (May–June 1938): 6–7, 16.

"Democracy as a Way of Life." *Southern Review* 4 (Summer 1938): 45–57.

> Revised as "The Democratic Way of Life." *Menorah Journal* 26 (Oct.–Dec. 1938): 261–75.

"Science and the New Obscurantism." *Modern Quarterly* 11 (Fall 1938): 66–85.

"An Effective Logic." Review of Paul Weiss, *Logic: The Theory of Inquiry. New Republic* 97 (23 Nov. 1938): 79–80.

"Eduard Heimann on the 'Revolutionary Situation'." *Social Research* 5 (Nov. 1938): 464–71.

Response to Heimann, "The 'Revolutionary Situation' and the Middle Classes." Ibid. 5 (May 1938): 227–36.

Reply by Heimann, ibid. 5 (Nov. 1938): 471–73.

"The Tragedy of German Jewry." *New Leader* 21 (26 Nov. 1938): 8.

"Whitehead's Latest Phase." Review of Alfred North Whitehead, *Modes of Thought. Nation* 147 (10 Dec. 1938): 632–33.

"Critical Analysis as a Method of Radio Education." *School and Society* 48 (31 Dec. 1938): 858–59.

1939

John Dewey: An Intellectual Portrait. New York: John Day Co., 1939.

"Democracy as a Way of Life." In *Tomorrow in the Making,* ed. J. N. Andrews and C. A. Marsden, pp. 31–36. New York: McGraw-Hill, 1939.

"A Challenge to the Liberal-Arts College." *Journal of Higher Education* 10 (Jan. 1939): 14–23, 58.

"The Fetishism of Power." Review of Gaetano Mosca, *The Ruling Classes. Nation* 148 (13 May 1939): 562–63.

Letter by Hook introducing the Manifesto of the Committee for Cultural Freedom. Manifesto signed by Hook et al. *Nation* 148 (27 May 1939): 626.

Reply by Freda Kirchwey, "Red Totalitarianism." Ibid., pp. 605–6.

Response by Hook with rebuttal by Kirchwey, ibid. 148 (17 June 1939): 710–11.

"The Anatomy of the Popular Front." Essay review of Max Lerner, *It Is Later Than You Think. Partisan Review* 6 (Spring 1939): 29–45.

"Soviet Union a Totalitarian Dictatorship Just as Is Germany." Letter to the editor. *New York Post,* 7 June 1939.

"Hook Warns against Forgery Tactics of Totalitarian Agents." Letter to the editor. *New Leader,* 24 June 1939.

"Dialectic in Social and Historical Inquiry." *Journal of Philosophy* 36 (6 July 1939): 365–78.

"'The Totalitarian Mind'—and Those Who Hew to the 'Line'." *New York Post,* 2 Sept. 1939, p. 12.

"Salute to John Dewey!" *Call,* 27 Oct. 1939.

"John Dewey at Eighty." *New Leader,* 28 Oct. 1939.

"The Importance of John Dewey in Modern Thought." *Modern Quarterly* 11 (Fall 1939): 30–35.

"Upton Sinclair vs. Sidney Hook: The Debate on Russia Grows Warmer." *Call,* 18 Nov. 1939.

"Academic Freedom and 'The Trojan Horse' in American Education." *American Association of University Professors Bulletin* 25 (Dec. 1939): 550–55.

"Reflections on the Russian Revolution." Review of Leon Trotsky, *The Revolution Betrayed. Southern Review* 4 (Winter 1939): 429–62.

Review of Ernest Nagel, *Principles of the Theory of Probability. Philosophic Abstracts* 1 (1939–40): 8.

Review of Folke Leander, *The Philosophy of John Dewey, A Critical Study. Philosophic Abstracts* 1 (1939–40): 21–22.

"Abstractions in Social Inquiry." *Illinois Law Review* 34 (1939–40): 15–29.

1940

Reason, Social Myths and Democracy. New York: John Day Co., 1940.

"Unreconstructed Fellow-Travelers." *Call,* 13 Jan. 1940, p. 2.

Review of Theodor L. Haering, *Hegel: Sein Wollen und sein Werk,* vol. 2. *Philosophical Review* 49 (Jan. 1940): 87–88.

"An Attack on Freedom." *New York Herald Tribune Books,* 9 Mar. 1940, p. 14.

"Socialists Face Need of Unified Action." *New Leader* 23 (9 Mar. 1940): 7.

"Conceptions of Human Motivation: Socialism and the Motives of Men." *Frontiers of Democracy* 6 (15 Mar. 1940): 167.

"On Ideas." Review of Max Lerner, *Ideas Are Weapons. Partisan Review* 7 (Mar.–Apr. 1940): 152–60.

"What Stalin Wrote." Review of *Stalin's Kampf,* ed. M. R. Werner. *New York Herald Tribune Books,* 7 Apr. 1940, p. 6.

"Prof. Hook to Prof. Schuman." *Saturday Review* 21 (20 Apr. 1940): 9.

Reply to Frederick L. Schuman's review of *Stalin's Kampf,* ed. M. R. Werner, ibid., 6 Apr. 1940.

"What Is Living and What Is Dead in Marxism?" *Frontiers of Democracy* 6 (15 Apr. 1940): 218–20.

"The Integral Humanism of Jacques Maritain." Review of Jacques Maritain, *True Humanism. Partisan Review* 7 (May–June 1940): 204–29.

"Is Nazism a Social Revolution?" *New Leader* 23 (20 July 1940): 4, 6.

"How Has John Strachey Changed His Mind?" Review of John Strachey, *A Programme for Progress. New York Herald Tribune Books,* 21 July 1940, p. 5.

"Socialism, Common Sense and the War." *New Leader* 23 (31 Aug. 1940): 7.

"Alexander Goldenweiser: Three Tributes." With Ruth Benedict and Margaret Mead. *Modern Quarterly* 11 (Summer 1940): 31–32.

Review of James K. Feibleman, *Positive Democracy. Journal of Philosophy* 37 (26 Sept. 1940): 557–59.

"Thinkers Who Prepared for Revolution." Review of Edmund Wilson, *To the Finland Station: A Study in the Writing and Acting of History. New York Herald Tribune Books,* 29 Sept. 1940.

"Engels as Scientist." Review of Friedrich Engels, *Dialectics of Nature. Nation* 151 (5 Oct. 1940): 308.

"Planning—and Freedom." Review of Karl Mannheim, *Man and Society in an Age of Reconstruction. Nation* 151 (26 Oct. 1940): 398–99.

"The New Medievalism." *New Republic* 103 (28 Oct. 1940): 602–6. Hook's comments on Mortimer Adler's "God and the Professors." A paper delivered at the National Conference on Science, Philosophy, and Religion in their Relation to the Democratic Way of Life. Jewish Theological Seminary, New York City, 10–11 Sept. 1940. Adler's and Hook's papers reprinted in a special issue of the *Daily Maroon* (University of Chicago), 14 Nov. 1940, along with papers by Frank Knight, Quincy Wright, and Milton Mayer.

"Metaphysics, War, and the Intellectuals." Review of Waldo Frank, *Chart for Rough Water*; Archibald MacLeish, *The Irresponsibles*; and Lewis Mumford, *Faith for Living. Menorah Journal* 28 (Oct. 1940): 326–37.

"Despair on Mt. Olympus." Review of George Santayana, *The Realm of Spirit. Nation* 151 (2 Nov. 1940): 423–24.

"A Democratic Survival." Review of Emil Lederer, *State of the Masses. New York Herald Tribune Books,* 1 Dec. 1940, p. 38.

1941

"'Out of the Night' Uncovers Underworld of a Rotted Religion." Review of Jan Valtin, *Out of the Night. New Leader* 24 (15 Feb. 1941): 5.

"The Counter-Reformation in American Education." *Antioch Review* 1 (Mar. 1941): 109–16.

"The Basic Values and Loyalties of Communism." *American Teacher* 25 (May 1941): 4–6.

"Reason and Revolution." Review of Herbert Marcuse, *Reason and Revolution: Hegel and the Rise of Social Theory. New Republic* 105 (21 July 1941): 90–91.

"Moscow Order Dissolving Communist Party in U.S. Would Swing Wide Public Support to Aid for U.S.S.R." *New Leader* 24 (11 Oct. 1941): 4.

"Social Change and Original Sin: Answer to Niebuhr." Review of Reinhold Niebuhr, *The Nature and Destiny of Man* and Charles Sherrington, *Man and His Nature. New Leader* 24 (8 Nov. 1941): 5, 7.

"The Philosophical Presuppositions of Democracy." Abstract. *Journal of Philosophy* 38 (4 Dec. 1941): 685–86. Printed in full in *Ethics* 52 (Apr. 1942): 275–96.
"The Late Mr. Tate." *Southern Review* 6 (1941): 840–43.

1942

"Salvation by Semantics." Review of S. I. Hayakawa, *Language in Action: A Guide to Accurate Thinking. Nation* 154 (3 Jan. 1942): 16.
"Crisis of Our Culture." Review of Pitirim A. Sorokin, *The Crisis of Our Age: The Social and Cultural Outlook. New York Herald Tribune Books,* 11 Jan. 1942, p. 10.
"Russia's Military Successes Do Not Whitewash Crimes at Home." *New Leader* 25 (31 Jan. 1942): 5.
"National Unity and 'Corporate Thinking'." *Menorah Journal* 30 (Jan. 1942): 61–68. Comments on *Science, Philosophy and Religion: A Symposium* (New York: 1941).
"Milton Mayer: Fake Jeremiah." *New Leader* 25 (4 Apr. 1942): 5.
"Whitehead's Final Views." Review of *The Philosophy of Alfred North Whitehead,* ed. Paul Arthur Schilpp. Library of Living Philosophers, vol. 3. *Nation* 154 (4 Apr. 1942): 401–3.
"Two Views on Mortimer Adler and Milton Mayer." With Francis McMahon. *New Leader* 25 (16 May 1942): 5, 7.
"Sidney Hook Analyzes a New 'Faith' for the Businessman: A Review of Hocking's New 'Philosophical Healing'." Review of William Ernest Hocking, *What Man Can Make of Man. New Leader* 25 (5 Sept. 1942): 2, 7.
"The Function of Higher Education in Postwar Reconstruction." *Journal of Educational Sociology* 16 (Sept. 1942): 43–51.
"Theological Tom-Tom and Metaphysical Bagpipe." *Humanist* 2 (Autumn 1942): 96–102.

1943

The Hero in History: A Study in Limitation and Possibility. New York: John Day Co., 1943.
"The New Failure of Nerve, Part 1." *Partisan Review* 10 (Jan.–Feb. 1943): 2–23; "Part 2: The Failure of the Left." Ibid. 10 (Mar.–Apr. 1943): 165–77.
> Response by David Merian, "The Nerve of Sidney Hook." Ibid. 10 (May–June 1943): 248–57.
> Replies by Hook, "The Politics of Wonderland." Ibid., pp. 258–62; "Faith, Hope, and Dialectic: Merian in Wonderland." Ibid., 10 (Sept.–Oct. 1943): 476–81.
> Response by Malcolm Cowley, "Marginalia." *New Republic* 109 (12 July 1943): 50.
> Response by Isaac Rosenfeld, "The Failure of Verve." Ibid. 109 (19 July 1943): 80–81.
> Reply by Hook, "Experience and Intelligence." Ibid. 109 (6 Sept. 1943): 336–37.
> Responses by Cowley and Rosenfeld, ibid., pp. 337–38.
"Education for the New Order." Review of Alexander Mieklejohn, *Education between Two Worlds. Nation* 156 (27 Feb. 1943): 308, 310, 312.
> Response by Mark Van Doren, with reply by Hook, ibid. 156 (20 Mar. 1943): 430–31.
"Tribute to Carlo Tresca." *Il Martello* 28 (28 Mar. 1943): 44.
"Philosophy of Art and Culture." Review of Horace M. Kallen, *Art and Freedom. New York Herald Tribune Weekly Book Review,* 11 Apr. 1943, p. 20.
"Illusions of Our Time." Review of Harold Laski, *Reflections on the Revolution of Our Time. Partisan Review* 10 (Sept.–Oct. 1943): 442–47.
"Charles Beard's Political Testament." Review of Charles A. Beard, *The Republic: Conversation on Fundamentals. Nation* 157 (23 Oct. 1943): 474–76.
"The Perpetual Debate." Review of Henry Steele Commager, *Majority Rule and Minority Rights. Nation* 157 (11 Dec. 1943): 709–10.

1944

"Naturalism and Democracy." In *Naturalism and the Human Spirit,* ed. Y. H. Krikorian, pp. 40–64. New York: Columbia University Press, 1944.

"The Rebirth of Political Credulity." *New Leader* 27 (1 Jan. 1944): 4–5.

"Humanism and the Labor Movement." *New Europe,* Feb. 1944.

"Progressive Liberal Education." Review of Algo D. Henderson, *Vitalizing Liberal Education. Nation* 158 (11 Mar. 1944): 312–14.

"Hitlerism: A Non-Metaphysical View." Review of Konrad Heiden, *Der Fuehrer. Contemporary Jewish Record* 7 (Apr. 1944): 146–55.

"Ballyhoo at St. John's College—Education in Retreat." Part 1. *New Leader* 27 (27 May 1944): 8–9.

"Ballyhoo at St. John's—The 'Great Books' and Progressive Teaching." Part 2. *New Leader* 27 (3 June 1944): 8–10.

"God, Geometry and the Good Society." Review of Mark Van Doren, *Liberal Education. Partisan Review* 11 (Spring 1944): 161–67.

"Thirteen Arrows against Progressive Liberal Education." *Humanist* 4 (Spring 1944): 1–10.

"Is Physical Realism Sufficient?" *Journal of Philosophy* 41 (28 Sept. 1944): 544–51.
>   See Hook, "What Is Materialism?" Ibid. 31 (26 Apr. 1934): 235–42; and R. W. Sellars, "Is Naturalism Enough?" Ibid. 41 (28 Sept. 1944): 533–44.

"Heroic Vitalism." Review of Eric Bentley, *A Century of Hero-Worship. Nation* 159 (7 Oct. 1944): 412–14.

"If Only . . ." Review of Ludwig von Mises, *Omnipotent Government. Nation* 159 (28 Oct. 1944): 530.

"Planned Diversity." Review of Karl Mannheim, *Diagnosis of Our Time. Nation* 159 (11 Nov. 1944): 596.

"An Apologist for St. John's College." *New Leader,* 25 Nov. 1944.

"Schooling for Democrats." Review of Marie Syrkin, *Your School, Your Children. Nation* 159 (18 Nov. 1944): 621–22.

"The Ends of Education." *Journal of Educational Sociology* 18 (Nov. 1944): 173–84.

"Road to Freedom." Review of Bronislaw Malinowski, *Freedom and Civilization. New Europe,* Dec. 1944.

1945

The Authoritarian Attempt to Capture Education. By John Dewey, Sidney Hook, Arthur Murphy, Irwin Edman, and others. New York: King's Crown Press, 1945.

What Is the Future of Socialism? London, 1945.

"Proletariat." In *Encyclopaedia Britannica.* Chicago: Encyclopaedia Britannica, 1945.

"The Dilemma of T. S. Eliot." *Nation* 160 (20 Jan. 1945): 69–71.

"The Degradation of the Word." *New Leader* 28 (27 Jan. 1945): 7.

"Freedom and Socialism: Reply to Max Eastman." *New Leader* (3 Mar. 1945): 4–5.

"Democratic Faith and Puritan Piety." Review of Ralph Barton Perry, *Puritanism and Democracy. Nation* 160 (26 May 1945): 603–5.

"Total Condemnation: Denunciation of All Germans Held Unfair to Anti-Nazis." Letter by Hook et al. *New York Times,* 10 June 1945, p. 8.

"Man and the Universe of Symbols." Review of Ernst Cassirer, *An Essay on Man. Kenyon Review* 7 (Spring 1945): 335–38.

"The Case for Progressive Education." *Saturday Evening Post* 217 (30 June 1945): 28–29, 39, 41.

"A Discussion of the Theory of International Relations." *Journal of Philosophy* 42 (30 Aug. 1945): 493–95.

"Are Naturalists Materialists?" With Ernest Nagel and John Dewey. *Journal of Philosophy* 42 (13 Sept. 1945): 515–30.

Reply to Wilmon Henry Sheldon, "A Critique of Naturalism." Ibid. 42 (10 May 1945): 253-70.

For a continuation of the discussion, see Rudolph Allers, "Does Human Nature Change?" *Catholic University Bulletin* 14, no. 2 (1946): 6-9.

"Education for Vocation." *Antioch Review* 5 (Fall 1945): 415-28.

"The Signs of Aldous Huxley." Review of Aldous Huxley, *The Perennial Philosophy. Saturday Review of Literature* 28 (3 Nov. 1945): 12-13.

"Reflections on the Nuremberg Trial." *New Leader* 28 (17 Nov. 1945): 8, 14.

"Bertrand Russell among the Sages." Review of Bertrand Russell, *A History of Western Philosophy. Nation* 161 (1 Dec. 1945): 586, 588, 590.

"The Autonomy of Democratic Faith." *American Scholar* 15 (Winter 1945-46): 105-9.

Part 3 of a forum on "The Future of Religion." For parts 1 and 2, see Raphael Demos, "The Need for Religion and Its Truth," pp. 97-102; and Paul Tillich, "Vertical and Horizontal Thinking," pp. 102-5. See rejoinders by Demos and Tillich, pp. 109-12, and by Hook, pp. 112-13.

1946

Education for Modern Man. New York: Dial Press, 1946.

"Illustrations." In *Theory and Practice in Historical Study: A Report of the Committee on Historiography,* pp. 108-30. New York: Social Science Research Council (Bulletin 54), 1946.

"Introduction." In *Social Democracy versus Socialism,* by Karl Kautsky, ed. David Shub, trans. Joseph Shaplen, pp. 7-20. New York: Rand School Press, 1946.

"Problems of Terminology in Historical Writing." With Charles A. Beard. In *Theory and Practice in Historical Study: A Report of the Committee on Historiography,* pp. 105-8. New York: Social Science Research Council (Bulletin 54), 1946.

"Role of Science in Determination of Democratic Policy, A Symposium." In *Papers: Science for Democracy,* ed. Jerome Nathanson, pp. 109-70. New York: King's Crown Press, 1946.

"Fin du Mondisme: The Birth of a New World Mood in Face of Atombomb." *New Leader,* 23 Feb. 1946, pp. 8-9.

"Toward Intellectual Teamwork: Notes on the Evolution of a Conference." *Commentary* 1 (Feb. 1946): 81-85.

"What Is Philosophy?" Review of Brand Blanshard, Curt J. Ducasse, Charles Van Hendel, Arthur E. Murphy, and Max C. Otto, *Philosophy in American Education: Its Tasks and Opportunities. Nation* 162 (30 Mar. 1946): 375-77.

"Moral Values and/or Religion in Our Schools." *Progressive Education* 23 (May 1946): 256-57, 278-79.

"The Philosophic Scene: Scientific Method on the Defensive." *Commentary* 1 (June 1946): 85-90.

"Russia's Foreign Policy." Letter to the editor. *New York Times,* 17 Oct. 1946, p. 22.

"The Laws of Dialectic." *Polemic* no. 6 (Nov.-Dec. 1946): 9-29.

"Synthesis or Eclecticism?" *Philosophy and Phenomenological Research* 7 (Dec. 1946): 214-25.

The National council of Jewish women on the present-day Jewish scene. New York, 1946.

1947

"Intelligence and Evil in Human History." In *Freedom and Experience: Essays Presented to Horace M. Kallen,* ed. Sidney Hook and Milton R. Konvitz, pp. 24-45. Ithaca: Cornell University Press, 1947.

"Education for Vocation." In *American Thought,* with an introduction by Philip Wylie, pp. 133-47. New York: Gresham Press, 1947.

"The Future of Socialism." *Partisan Review* 14 (Jan.-Feb. 1947): 23-36.

"Philosophy and the Police." Review of John Somerville, *Soviet Philosophy: A Study of Theory and Practice. Nation* 164 (15 Feb. 1947): 188–89.

    Reply by Somerville with Hook's response, ibid., 10 May 1947, pp. 550–52.

"Totalitarian Liberalism." *Time* 49 (17 Feb. 1947): 28.

"What Exactly Do We Mean by 'Democracy'?" *New York Times Magazine,* 16 Mar. 1947, pp. 10, 48, 49.

"Intelligence and Evil in Human History." *Commentary* 3 (Mar. 1947): 210–21.

"From Question to Assertion: A Rejoinder to Professor Demos." *Philosophy and Phenomenological Research* 7 (Mar. 1947): 439–45.

"Mr. Fly's Web of Confusions: A Problem of Contemporary Liberalism." *New Leader* 30 (18 Oct. 1947): 8, 9, 15.

    Reply by James Lawrence Fly, "On the Befuddlement of Sidney Hook." Ibid. 30 (22 Nov. 1947): 8.

    Rejoinder by Hook, "Mr. Fly Entangles Himself More Deeply." Ibid., pp. 9, 15.

"Is the U.S. a Republic or Democracy?" *New York Times Magazine,* 19 Oct. 1947, pp. 17, 49, 50, 51.

"The U.S.S.R. Views American Philosophy." *Modern Review* 1 (Nov. 1947): 649–53. Foreword to M. Dynnik, "Contemporary Bourgeois Philosophy in the U.S."

"The Source of Value." Review of Clarence I. Lewis, *An Analysis of Knowledge and Valuation. New York Times Book Review,* 16 Nov. 1947, p. 16.

"Moral und Politik." *Amerikanische Rundschau* 3 (1947): 3–18.

"An Unanswered Letter to the American Jewish Congress." *New Leader* 30 (1947): 15.

"Portrait . . . John Dewey." *American Scholar* 17 (Winter 1947–48): 105–10.

Letter to the editor. *Philosophical Review* 56 (1947): 608–9.

1948

"The Autonomy of Democratic Faith." In *Living, Reading, and Thinking,* ed. J. R. Chamberlain, W. B. Pressey, and R. E. Watters, pp. 649–60. New York: Scribners, 1948.

"Humanism and the Labor Movement." In *European Ideologies,* ed. Feliks Gross, pp. 1057–63. New York: Philosophical Library, 1948.

"Meeting of Logic and the Arts." Review of F. S. C. Northrup, *The Logic of the Sciences and the Humanities. New York Times,* 11 Jan. 1948, p. 7.

"On the Casting Out of Devils." Review of Norman Angell, *The Steep Places. New York Times Book Review,* 25 Jan. 1948, pp. 1, 33.

"The Communist Manifesto 100 Years After." *New York Times Magazine,* 1 Feb. 1948, pp. 6, 36, 38.

"On Historical Understanding." *Partisan Review* 15 (Feb. 1948): 231–39.

"The State—Servile or Free?" *New Leader* 31 (13 Mar. 1948): 1, 12.

"Academic Freedom." Letter to the editor. *New York Times,* 23 Mar. 1948, p. 24.

"Why Democracy Is Better." *Commentary* 5 (Mar. 1948): 195–204.

"Mr. Toynbee's City of God." Review of Arnold Joseph Toynbee, *Civilization on Trial. Partisan Review* 15 (June 1948): 691–99.

    Replies by C. Roland Wagner and E. G. Gallagher, ibid. 15, Aug. 1948, pp. 940–41.

    Response by Hook, ibid., pp. 941–42.

Letter to the editor. *American Scholar* 17 (Summer 1948): 360–61.

"Russia's Slave Labor." Letter to the editor, by Sidney Hook et al. *New York Times,* 2 Nov. 1948, p. 24.

"Drei Grundzüge westlichen Denkens." *Der Monat* 1 (Nov. 1948): 8–17.

1949

"Academic Freedom and Communism." In *People Shall Judge,* by the Social Science Staff, pp. 705–14. Chicago: University of Chicago Press, 1949.

"Nature and the Human Spirit." In *Proceedings: 10th International Congress of Philosophy,* pp. 153–55. Amsterdam: North Holland Publishing Co., 1949.

"Should Communists Be Permitted to Teach?" *New York Times Magazine,* 27 Feb. 1949, pp. 7, 22, 24, 26, 28, 29.

"Communism and the Intellectuals." *American Mercury* 68 (Feb. 1949): 133–44.

"Die Zukunft der demokratischen Linken." *Der Monat* 1 (Feb. 1949): 13–17.

"International Communism." *Dartmouth Alumni Magazine* 41 (Mar. 1949): 13–20.

"John Dewey: Ein Porträt." *Der Monat* 1 (Mar. 1949): 40–46.

"The Philosophy of Democracy as a Philosophy of History." *Philosophy and Phenomenological Research* 9 (Mar. 1949): 576–87.

"On the Battlefield of Philosophy." *Partisan Review* 16 (Mar. 1949): 251–68.

"Stand of the Liberals." With George S. Counts. *New York Times,* 13 Apr. 1949, p. 28.

"The Fellow-Traveler: A Study in Psychology." *New York Times Magazine,* 17 Apr. 1949, pp. 9, 20, 21, 22, 23.

"Dr. Hook Protests." *Nation* 168 (30 Apr. 1949): 511.

"Reflections on the Jewish Question." Review of Jean-Paul Sartre, *Anti-Semite and Jew. Partisan Review* 16 (May 1949): 463–82.

"Science, Freedom and Peace." *New Leader* 32 (25 June 1949): 6.

"A Gallant American Rebel." Review of Ray Ginger, *The Bending Cross: A Biography of Eugene Victor Debs. New York Times Book Review,* 17 July 1949, p. 7.

"Report on the International Day Against Dictatorship and War." *Partisan Review* 16 (July 1949): 722–32.

"What Shall We Do about Communist Teachers?" *Saturday Evening Post* 222 (10 Sept. 1949): 33, 164–68.

"The Literature of Political Disillusionment." *American Association of University Professors Bulletin* 35 (Autumn 1949): 450–67.

"John Dewey at Ninety: The Man and His Philosophy." *New Leader* 32 (22 Oct. 1949): S-3, S-8.

"Academic Integrity and Academic Freedom." *Commentary* 8 (Oct. 1949): 329–39.

    Reply by Helen Lynd, ibid. 8 (Dec. 1949): 594–95.

    Response by Hook, "Professor Hook Replies." Ibid., pp. 598–601.

"U.S.S.R. Distorts Theories to Fit 'Party Truth'." *New York Times,* 18 Nov. 1949, p. 28.

"Academic Freedom—Academic Confusions." *Journal of Higher Education* 20 (Nov. 1949): 422–25.

1950

From Hegel to Marx. With a new introduction by Hook. Ann Arbor: University of Michigan Press, 1950.

"The Desirable and Emotive in John Dewey's Ethics." In *John Dewey: Philosopher of Science and Freedom,* ed. Sidney Hook, pp. 194–216. New York: Dial Press, 1950.

"John Dewey and His Critics." In *Pragmatism and American Culture,* ed. Gail Kennedy, pp. 92–94. Boston: D. C. Heath and Co., 1950.

"The Place of John Dewey in Modern Thought." In *Philosophic Thought in France and the United States,* ed. Marvin Farber, pp. 483–503. Buffalo: University of Buffalo Press, 1950.

Contribution in *Religion and the Intellectuals.* A symposium with John Dewey, Hook, and others. New York: Partisan Review, 1950.

"Democracy—Minus the Rhetoric." Review of R. M. MacIver, *The Ramparts We Guard. New York Times Book Review,* 26 Feb. 1950, pp. 3, 31.

"Religion and the Intellectuals." *Partisan Review* 17 (Mar. 1950): 225–32.

    Reply by Ernest van den Haag, ibid. 17 (July–Aug. 1950): 607–12.

    Rejoinder by Hook, ibid., pp. 612–16.

"Mr. Hook Replies." *Commentary* 9 (Mar. 1950): 286–87.

"The Scientist in Politics." *New York Times Magazine,* 9 Apr. 1950, pp. 10, 25, 27, 28, 30.
"Communists in the Colleges." *New Leader* 33 (6 May 1950): 16–18.
"Lenin—oder Die Rolle des Einzelnen." *Der Monat* 2 (May 1950): 174–89.
"Heresy, Yes—But Conspiracy, No." *New York Times Magazine,* 9 July 1950, pp. 12, 38–39.
"The Berlin Congress." Letter to the editor on comments by H. R. Trevor-Roper on the Congress for Cultural Freedom. *Manchester Guardian Weekly,* 7 Sept. 1950.
"Past and Present of the Case That Shook the Nation." Review of Alistair Cooke, *A Generation on Trial: U.S.A. v. Alger Hiss. New York Times Book Review,* 24 Sept. 1950, p. 7.
"The Berlin Congress for Cultural Freedom." *Partisan Review* 17 (Sept.–Oct. 1950): 715–22.
"The University of California and the Non-Communist Oath." Review of George R. Stewart, *The Year of the Oath. New York Times Book Review,* 1 Oct. 1950, p. 6.
"Encounter in Berlin." *New Leader* 33 (14 Oct. 1950): 16–19.
"How to Stop Russia without War." Review of Boris Shub, *The Choice. New York Post,* 22 Oct. 1950.
"Why They Switch Loyalties." *New York Times Magazine,* 26 Nov. 1950, pp. 12, 26, 28, 30.
"U.N. Stand on Korea." Letter to the editor. *New York Times,* 15 Dec. 1950, p. 30.

1951

"Bertrand Russell's Philosophy of History." In *Philosophy of Bertrand Russell,* ed. Paul A. Schilpp, pp. 643–78. New York: Free Press, 1951.
"General Education: Its Nature and Purpose." In *General Education in Transition,* ed. Horace T. Morse, pp. 68–82. Minneapolis: University of Minnesota Press, 1951.
"Nature and the Human Spirit." In *Freedom and Reason,* ed. Salo Baron, Ernest Nagel, and K. S. Pinson, pp. 142–56. New York: Free Press, 1951.
"The Danger of Authoritarian Attitudes in Teaching Today." *School and Society* 73 (20 Jan. 1951): 33–39.
"Communists: Authoritarians in the Schools." *Socialist Call,* 26 Jan. 1951, pp. 3, 5.
"Prof. Hook and the Loyalty Oaths." *Socialist Call,* 26 Jan. 1951, p. 3.
    Reply to S. M. Lipset, ibid., 12 Jan. 1951.
"Coverage of Rousset Trial." Letter to the editor, by Sidney Hook et al. *New York Times,* 15 Feb. 1951, p. 30.
"To Counter the Big Lie—A Basic Strategy." *New York Times Magazine,* 11 Mar. 1951, pp. 9, 59, 60, 61, 62, 63, 64.
"A Case Study in Anti-Secularism." Review of Eliseo Vivas, *The Moral Life and the Ethical Life. Partisan Review* 18 (18 Mar. 1951): 232–45.
"Liberty, Society and Mr. Santayana." Review of George Santayana, *Dominations and Powers. New York Times Book Review,* 6 May 1951, pp. 1, 20.
"Academic Freedom." Letter to the editor. *New York Times,* 27 May 1951, p. 8.
"Interpreting the Madison Incident." Letter to the editor. *New York Times,* 21 Aug. 1951, p. 26.
"Bread, Freedom, and Businessmen." *Fortune* 44 (Sept. 1951): 117, 176–88.
"The Dangers in 'Cultural Vigilantism'." *New York Times Magazine,* 30 Sept. 1951, pp. 9, 44, 46, 47.
"The Use and Abuse of Words." Review of *Democracy in a World of Tensions,* ed. Richard Mckeon. *New Leader* 34 (15 Oct. 1951): 20–21.
"Russia by Moonshine, Part 1." *New Leader* 34 (12 Nov. 1951): 15–18. "Part 2." Ibid. 34 (19 Nov. 1951): 12–14.
    Reply. Ibid. 34 (26 Nov. 1951): 28–29.
    Reply. Ibid. 34 (3 Dec. 1951): 28.

1952

Democracy and Desegregation. New York: Tamiment Institute, 1952.

Heresy, Yes—Conspiracy, No. New York: American Committee for Cultural Freedom, 1952; New York: John Day Co., 1953.

"Academic Freedom and Its Values for Higher Education." In *Current Issues in Higher Education,* by the National Conference on Higher Education, pp. 70-75. Washington, D.C.: Association for Higher Education, 1952.

"Atheism." In *Collier's Encyclopedia,* vol. 2, p. 418. New York: P. F. Collier and Son, 1952.

"The Philosophical Basis of Marxian Socialism in the United States." In *Socialism and American Life,* ed. Donald Drew Egbert and Stow Persons. Princeton: Princeton University Press, 1952.

"Why Democracy Is Better." In *My Life, My Country, My World,* ed. H. M. Gloster, W. E. Farrison, and N. Tillman, pp. 514-33. Englewood Cliffs, N.J.: Prentice-Hall, 1952.

"Kann man die Freiheit essen?" *Der Monat* 4 (Jan. 1952): 339-44.

"Perennial and Temporal Goals in Education." *Journal of Higher Education* 23 (Jan. 1952): 1-12.

"Mindless Empiricism." *Journal of Philosophy* 49 (14 Feb. 1952): 89-100.

> See Victor Lowe, "A Resurgence of 'Vicious Intellectualism'." Ibid. 48 (5 July 1951): 435-47.

> Response by A. O. Lovejoy, "On a Supposed Resurgence of Vicious Intellectualism." Ibid. 49 (14 Feb. 1952): 85-89.

> Reply by Lowe, "In Defense of Individualistic Empiricism: A Reply to Messrs. Lovejoy and Hook." Ibid., pp. 100-111.

> Rejoinder by Lovejoy, "Rejoinder to Mr. Lowe." Ibid., pp. 111-12.

> Rejoinder by Hook, "Not Mindful Enough." Ibid., pp. 112-21.

"Is America in the Grip of Hysteria?" *New Leader,* 3 Mar. 1952.

"Cultural Freedom and Starving Men: A Case for Democracy." *Bharat Jyoti,* 16 Mar. 1952.

"Degrees of Soviet Scholars." Letter to the editor. *New York Times,* 28 Apr. 1952, p. 18.

"The Faiths of Whittaker Chambers." Review of Whittaker Chambers, *Witness. New York Times Book Review,* 25 May 1952, pp. 1, 34-35.

> Letters by Herman F. Reissig et al., ibid., 22 June 1952, p. 17.

> Hook reply to Reissig letter, ibid.

"RuBland im Mondenschein." *Der Monat* 4 (May 1952): 172-78.

"Academic Manners and Morals." *Journal of Higher Education* 23 (June 1952): 323-26, 342-43.

"One Hit, One Miss." Review of Paul Blanshard, *Communism, Democracy and Catholic Power. Twentieth Century* 152 (July 1952): 45-48.

"Our Country and Our Culture." *Partisan Review* 19 (Sept. 1952): 569-74.

"Some Memories of John Dewey." *Commentary* 14 (Sept. 1952): 245-53.

"Letter to an English Friend." *New Leader* 35 (13 Oct. 1952): 16-18.

"The Fall of the Town of Usher." *New Leader* 35 (27 Oct. 1952): 16-19.

"John Dewey and Dr. Barnes." *Commentary* 14 (Nov. 1952): 504.

"Lattimore on the Moscow Trials." *New Leader* 35 (10 Nov. 1952): 16-19.

"What Is 'Guilt by Association'?" *American Mercury* 75 (Nov. 1952): 37-43.

> Reply to James Burnham, "The Case against Adlai Stevenson." Ibid. 75 (Oct. 1952): 11-19.

> Response by Burnham, ibid. 75 (Nov. 1952): 69.

"A Trans-Atlantic Dialogue." *New Leader* 35 (8 Dec. 1952): 15-20.

"The Job of the Teacher in Days of Crisis." *New York Times Magazine,* 14 Dec. 1952, pp. 9, 62, 63, 65.

1953

"Philosophy of Democracy as a Philosophy of History." In *Vision and Action,* ed. Sidney Ratner, pp. 133-47. New Brunswick: Rutgers University Press, 1953.

"The Ethics of Academic Freedom." In *Academic Freedom, Logic and Religion,* 1953. Symposium with George Boas.

"The Quest for Being." In *Proceedings of the 11th International Congress of Philosophy, Brussels, 1953*. Amsterdam: North Holland Publishing Co., 1953.

Letter to the editor. *Life* 34 (12 Jan. 1953): 7. On Communism in the United States.

"Soviet Anti-Semitism." Letter to the editor. *New York Times,* 30 Jan. 1953, p. 20.

"Does the Smith Act Threaten Our Liberties?" *Commentary* 15 (Jan. 1953): 63–73.
  "Mr. Hook Replies." Ibid. 15 (Mar. 1953): 308–9.

"Education: Campuses Unlimited." *New York Times Magazine,* 1 Feb. 1953, p. 70.

"Sidney Hook Replies to British Critic of United States Foreign Policy." *New Leader* 36 (2 Feb. 1953): 27.

"The Place of the Public School in American Life." Review of James Conant, *Education and Liberty. New York Times Book Review,* 15 Feb. 1953, p. 3.

"Should We Stress Armaments or Political Warfare?" *New Leader* 36 (23 Feb. 1953): 17–19.

"Indoctrination and Academic Freedom." *New Leader* 36 (9 Mar. 1953): 2–4.

"A Reply to the Editors' 'In Justice to Mr. Conant'." *New York Times Book Review,* 15 Mar. 1953, p. 28.

"Science et materialismé dialectique." In *Science et Liberté,* pp. 22–30. A supplement to *Preuves,* no. 37, Mar. 1954.

"Freedom in American Culture." *New Leader* 36 (6 Apr. 1953): S3–S16.

"Can We Trust Our Teachers?" *Saturday Review* 36 (18 Apr. 1953): 11, 12, 45–47.
  Replies by Gwynne Nettler, William Couch, and Stanley Cooperman, ibid. 36 (23 May 1953): 21.

"Mr. McCarthy Criticized." *New York Times,* 8 May 1953, p. 24.

"The Words Came Easily." Review of Kingsley Martin, *Harold Laski (1893–1950). New York Times Book Review,* 17 May 1953, pp. 7, 33.

"The Party Line on Psychology." Review of Brian H. Kirman, *This Matter of Mind. New Leader* 36 (25 May 1953): 23–24.

"Firing Teachers for Communist Membership." *New Leader* 36 (5 Oct. 1953): 27–29.

"The Fifth Amendment — A Moral Issue." *New York Times Magazine,* 1 Nov. 1953, pp. 9, 57, 59, 60, 62, 64, 66.

"The Quest for 'Being'." *Journal of Philosophy* 50 (19 Nov. 1953): 709–31.
  Reply by J. H. Randall, Jr., "On Being Rejected." Ibid. 50 (17 Dec. 1953): 797–805.

1954

"Modern Education and Its Critics." In *American Association of Colleges Yearbook,* pp. 139–60. Oneonta, N.Y.: American Association of Colleges, 1954.

"The Problem of the Individual in a Totalitarian Society." In *The Contemporary Scene.* Symposium by the Metropolitan Museum of Art, 28–30 Mar. 1952. New York: New York Metropolitan Museum of Art, 1954.

"The Ethics of Controversy." *New Leader* 37 (1 Feb. 1954): 12–14.

"Symposium: Are Religious Dogmas Cognitive and Meaningful?" *Journal of Philosophy* 51 (4 Mar. 1954): 165–68.

"The Techniques of Controversy." *New Leader* 37 (8 Mar. 1954): 15–18.

"Articles of the Bolshevik Faith." Review of Nathan Leites, *A Study of Bolshevism. New York Times Book Review,* 28 Mar. 1954, p. 10.

"Reply to A. J. Muste." *New Leader* 37 (5 Apr. 1954): 29–30.

"Robert Hutchins Rides Again." *New Leader* 37 (19 Apr. 1954): 16–19.

"Rigors of Heresy." Review of Norman Thomas, *The Test of Freedom. Saturday Review* 37 (24 Apr. 1954): 16–17.

"Myths of Marx." Review of Granville Hicks, *Where We Came Out. Saturday Review* 37 (15 May 1954): 11–12.

"Unpragmatic Liberalism." Review of Henry Steele Commager, *Freedom, Loyalty and Dissent. New Republic* 130 (24 May 1954): 18–21.

"The Substance of Controversy: A Reply." *New Leader* 37 (24 May 1954): 18–19.
"Uncommon Sense about Security and Freedom." *New Leader* 37 (21 June 1954): 8–10.
"Security and Freedom." *Confluence* 3 (June 1954): 155–71.
"The Problem of the Ex-Communist." *New York Times Magazine,* 11 July 1954, pp. 7, 24–27.
"Should Our Schools Study Communism?" *New York Times Magazine,* 29 Aug. 1954, pp. 9, 24, 26.

> Response by Howard Selsam, ibid., 26 Sept. 1954, p. 6.

> Reply by Hook, ibid., 10 Oct. 1954, p. 6.

"Why Some Sign Up." Review of Gabriel A. Almond et al., *Appeals of Communism. New York Times Book Review,* 19 Sept. 1954, pp. 3, 28, 29.
"Sikkerhed og Frihed." *Det Danske Magasin* 2 (1954): 441–58.

1955

Dialectical Materialism and Scientific Method. Manchester, England, 1955.
Marx and the Marxists: The Ambiguous Legacy. Princeton, N.J.: Van Nostrand, 1955.
"Science and Dialectical Materialism." In *Science and Freedom,* pp. 182–95. Boston: Beacon Press, 1955.
"Historical Determinism and Political Fiat in Soviet Communism." *Proceedings of the American Philosophical Society* 99 (1955): 1–10.
"Fallacies in Our Thinking about Security." *New York Times Magazine,* 30 Jan. 1955, pp. 15, 33, 35.
"A Question of Means and Ends in a World Threatened by Evil." Review of Bertrand Russell, *Human Society in Ethics and Politics. New York Times Book Review,* 30 Jan. 1955, p. 3.
"Marx in Limbo." *New Leader* 38 (2 May 1955): 14–17.
"Tyranny through the Ages." Review of George W. Hallgarten, *Why Dictators? New Leader* 38 (6 June 1955): 18–19.
"A Steady Light." Review of *John Dewey: His Contribution to the American Tradition,* ed. Irwin Edman. *New York Times Book Review,* 24 July 1955, pp. 3, 20.
"The Grounds on Which Our Educators Stand." Review of Richard Hofstadter and Walter P. Metzger, *The Development of Academic Freedom in the United States* and Robert M. MacIver, *Academic Freedom in Our Time. New York Times Book Review,* 30 Oct. 1955, pp. 6, 28.
"The Teaching and the Taught." Review of E. Merrill Root, *Collectivism on the Campus. New York Times Book Review,* 6 Nov. 1955, p. 58.
"A Reply." *New York Times Book Review,* 27 Nov. 1955, pp. 52–53.
"Introduction" to *Communism's Postwar Decade. New Leader* 38 (19 Dec. 1955): S2–S4.
"A Reply." *New York Times Book Review,* 25 Dec. 1955, p. 12.

1956

"Naturalism and First Principles." In *American Philosophers at Work,* ed. Sidney Hook, pp. 236–58. New York: Criterion Books, 1956.
"The Ethics of Controversy Again." *New Leader* 39 (16 Jan. 1956): 16–18.
"Prophet of Man's Glory and Tragedy." Review of *Reinhold Niebuhr—His Religious, Social, and Political Thought,* ed. Charles Kegley and Robert W. Bretall. *New York Times Book Review,* 29 Jan. 1956, pp. 6, 7, 22.
"The Strategy of Truth." *New Leader* 39 (13 Feb. 1956): 21–24.
"Six Fallacies of Robert Hutchins." *New Leader* 39 (19 Mar. 1956): 18–28.

> Responses, ibid. 39 (2 Apr. 1956): 28–29; ibid. 39 (9 Apr. 1956): 22; ibid. 39 (16 Apr. 1956): 29; ibid. 39 (23 Apr. 1956): 28–29; ibid. 39 (14 May 1956): 29.

> Replies by Hook, ibid. 39 (16 Apr. 1956): 29–30; ibid. 39 (23 Apr. 1956): 28–29.

"Exposing Soviet Purges." *New York Times,* 1 Apr. 1956, p. 8.

"Prospects for Cultural Freedom." *New Leader* 39 (7 May 1956): Sec. 2, p. 5.
"The AAUP and Academic Integrity." *New Leader* 39 (21 May 1956): 19-21.
>   Response by Cormac Philip, ibid. 39 (4 June 1956): 29.
>   Rejoinder by Hook, ibid., p. 29.
>   Response by Ralph F. Fuchs, ibid. 39 (25 June 1956): 28-29.
>   Rejoinder by Hook, ibid., pp. 29-31.
>   Responses by Pierre Aubeuf and Arthur O. Lovejoy, ibid. 39 (2 July 1956): 21-22.
>   Response by William Edel, ibid. 39 (16 July 1956): 13.
>   Response by Sam Lambert, ibid. 39 (13 Aug. 1956): 22.
"Portrait and Definition of Academic Freedom." *Time* 67 (11 June 1956): 69.
"Education and Creative Intelligence." *School and Society* 84 (7 July 1956): 3-8.
"Wanted, an Ethics of Employment for Our Time." Review of John Cogley, *Report on Blacklisting. New York Times Book Review,* 22 July 1956, pp. 6, 14.
>   Letters in response with Hook's reply, ibid., 19 Aug. 1956, p. 22.
"The Jurisdiction of Intelligence." *School and Society* 84 (4 Aug. 1956): 35-39.
"Common Sense and the Fifth Amendment." Review of Erwin N. Griswold, *The Fifth Amendment.* "Logic and the Fifth Amendment." *New Leader* 39 (1 Oct. 1956): 12-22; "Psychology and the Fifth Amendment." Ibid. 39 (8 Oct. 1956): 20-24; "Ethics and the Fifth Amendment." Ibid. 39 (15 Oct. 1956): 16-24; "Politics and the Fifth Amendment." Ibid. 39 (22 Oct. 1956): 16-23.
>   Reply by Griswold, "The Individual and the Fifth Amendment." Ibid. 39 (29 Oct. 1956): 20-23.
>   Rejoinder by Hook, "Logic, History and Law: A Rejoinder to Dean Griswold." Ibid. 39 (5 Nov. 1956): 12-15.
"Philosophy Must Provide Synthesis of Thought and Action." *Indian Express,* 11 Oct. 1956.
"Right to Equal Treatment." Letter to the editor. *New York Times,* 7 Nov. 1956, p. 30.
"Sense and Salvation." Review of Colin Wilson, *The Outsider. Commentary* 22 (Nov. 1956): 479-80, 82.
"Man as a Whole." Letter to the editor. *Listener* 56 (27 Dec. 1956): 1076-77.
>   Reply to John Nef, "Man as a Whole." Ibid. 56 (29 Nov. 1956): 875-76.
>   Reply by John Nef, "Man as a Whole." Ibid. 57 (7 Feb. 1957): 233, 235.
"Filosofien i den moderne verden." *Perspektiv* 4 (Dec. 1956): 28-30.
"A Joint Statement on a Matter of Importance." With Ralph F. Fuchs. *AAUP Bulletin* 42 (Dec. 1956): 692-95.
"Scope of Philosophy of Education." *Harvard Educational Review* 26 (1956): 145-48.

1957

Common Sense and the Fifth Amendment. New York: Criterion Books, 1957.
"Outlook for Philosophy." In Arnold Toynbee et al., *New Frontiers of Knowledge,* pp. 18-21. Washington: Public Affairs Press, 1957.
"The Monolithic State." Review of Carl J. Friedrich and Zbigniew K. Brzezinski, *Totalitarian Dictatorship and Autocracy. New York Times Book Review,* 20 Jan. 1957, pp. 3, 36.
"Liberalism and the Law." Review of Zechariah Chafee, *The Blessing of Liberty. Commentary* 23 (Jan. 1957): 46-56.
>   Response by C. Rajagopalachari, ibid. 23 (Apr. 1957): 380.
"From Opera Bouffe to Treason." Review of Theodore Draper, *The Roots of American Communism. Saturday Review of Literature,* 16 Mar. 1957, pp. 14-15.
"Abraham Lincoln, American Pragmatist." *New Leader* 40 (18 Mar. 1957): 16-18.
>   Reply by Max Eastman, "Lincoln Was No Pragmatist." Ibid. 40 (23 Sept. 1957): 19-20.
>   Response by Hook, "Marx, Dewey and Lincoln." Ibid. 40 (21 Oct. 1957): 16-18.
>   Responses by Bernard Herman and Martin Gardner, ibid. 40 (18 Nov. 1957): 28-29.
>   Reply by Hook, "Pragmatism." Ibid. 40 (9 Dec. 1957): 29-30.

Response by Eastman, "A Debate on Pragmatism: Marx, Dewey and Hook." Ibid. 41 (10 Feb. 1958): 16-18.
> Reply by Hook, "Marx, Dewey and Eastman." Ibid., pp. 18-19.

"The Fifth Amendment: A Crucial Case." *New Leader* 40 (22 Apr. 1957): 18-20.
"Use of Fifth Amendment Discussed." *New York Times*, 10 May 1957, p. 26.
> Reply by Irving Mariash, ibid., 17 May 1957, p. 24.

"A Fateful Chapter of Our Times." Review of Alger Hiss, *In the Court of Public Opinion. New York Times Book Review*, 12 May 1957, pp. 1, 28, 29.
"Scientific Knowledge and Philosophical 'Knowledge'." *Partisan Review* 24 (Spring 1957): 215-34.
"The Atom and Human Wisdom." *New Leader* 40 (3 June 1957): 8-10.
"The Old Liberalism and the New Conservatism." *New Leader* 40 (8 July 1957): 7-10.
"The Affair Hiss." *Encounter* 9 (July 1957): 81-84.
"Moral Judgment and Historical Ambiguity." *New Leader* 40 (19 Aug. 1957): 16-19.
"Socialism and Liberation." *Partisan Review* 24 (Fall 1947): 497-518.
"The Red Lodestar." Review of Raymond Aron, *The Opium of the Intellectuals. Saturday Review* 40 (23 Nov. 1957): 18-20.
"Justice Black's Illogic." *New Leader* 40 (2 Dec. 1957): 17-20.

1958

"Necessity, Indeterminism and Sentimentalism." In *Determinism and Freedom in the Age of Modern Science*, ed. Sidney Hook, pp. 180-93. First Symposium, New York University Institute of Philosophy, 9-10 Feb. 1957. New York: New York University Press, 1958.
"The Missing Link in American Science." *New Leader* 41 (6 Jan. 1958): 16-19.
> Replies by Susan Bodan, Sol Feinstone, Edward Rozek, E. Burton, and A. M. Wallach, ibid. 41 (3 Feb. 1958): 28-29.

"Befreiung Durch Evolution." *Der Monat* 10 (Feb. 1958): 10-25.
"A Foreign Policy for Survival." *New Leader* 41 (7 Apr. 1958): 8-12.
> Response by Bertrand Russell, "World Communism and Nuclear War." Ibid. 41 (26 May 1958): 9-10.
> Reply by Hook, "A Free Man's Choice." Ibid., pp. 10-12.

"Democracy and Desegregation." *New Leader* 41 (21 Apr. 1958): Sec. 2, pp. 3-19.
"A Look at the Evidence in a Famous Case." Review of Fred J. Cook, *The Unfinished Story of Alger Hiss. New York Times Book Review*, 4 May 1958, pp. 4, 20.
> Letters in response, ibid., 1 June 1958, p. 14.

"Bureaucrats Are Human." *Saturday Review* 41 (17 May 1958): 12-14, 41.
"Moral Freedom in a Determined World." *Commentary* 25 (May 1958): 431-43.
"Bertrand Russell Retreats." *New Leader* 41 (7-14 July 1958): 25-28.
"Brotherhood Aim Held Impractical." *New York Times*, 15 July 1958, p. 27.
"Die Letzte Entscheidung: Ein Streitgespräch über die Atombombe." *Der Monat* 10 (July 1958): 11-16.
> Reply by Bertrand Russell, "Keine Despotie währt ewig." Ibid., pp. 16-18.
> Response by Hook, "Grenzen der Nachgiebigkeit." Ibid., pp. 18-21.
> Response by Russell, "Die Freiheit zu überleben." Ibid. 10 (Sept. 1958): 81-84.
> Reply by Hook, "Mehr als zu überleben." Ibid., pp. 84-89.

"Socialism and Democracy." *New Leader* 41 (3 Nov. 1958): 17-18.
"Education in Japan." *New Leader* 41 (24 Nov. 1958): 8-11.

1959

John Dewey: His Philosophy of Education and Its Critics. New York: Tamiment Institute, 1959.
Political Power and Personal Freedom: Critical Studies in Democracy, Communism, and Civil Rights. New York: Criterion Books, 1959.

"Science and Mythology in Psychoanalysis." In *Psychoanalysis, Scientific Method and Philosophy,* ed. Sidney Hook, pp. 212–25. Second Symposium, New York University Institute of Philosophy, 28–29 Mar. 1958. New York: New York University Press, 1959.

"John Dewey, 1859–1952." In *Philosophy in Mid-Century,* vol. 4, ed. Raymond Klibansky, pp. 210–14. International Institute of Philosophy, 1958–1959. Florence: La Nuova Italia, 1959.

"The Philosophical Basis of Education." In *Proceedings of the Summer Conference,* ed. Western Washington College of Education, pp. 13–15. Bellingham: Western Washington College of Education, 1959.

"Philosophy for a Time of Crisis." In A. Koch, *Naturalism and Democracy,* pp. 302–19. New York: E. P. Dutton and Co., 1959.

"The Philosophy of Reading." In *Science and the Philosophy of Reading,* pp. 20–34. Newark: University of Delaware Press, 1959.

"Proletariat." In *Encyclopaedia Britannica,* 14th ed., p. 576. Chicago: Encyclopaedia Britannica, 1959.

"The Psychological Basis of Education." In *Proceedings of the Summer Conference,* ed. Western Washington College of Education, pp. 22–36. Bellingham: Western Washington College of Education, 1959.

"The Social Basis of Education." In *Proceedings of the Summer Conference,* ed. Western Washington College of Education, pp. 39–50. Bellingham: Western Washington College of Education, 1959.

"What Is Education?" In *Education in the Age of Science,* ed. Brand Blanshard, pp. 1–52. New York: Basic Books, 1959.

"Conscience and Consciousness in Japan." *Commentary* 27 (Jan. 1959): 59–66.

"Which Way Japan?" *New Leader* 42 (9 Feb. 1959): 3–7.

"The Impact of Ideas." Review of H. Stuart Hughes, *Consciousness and Society: The Reorientation of European Social Thought, 1890–1930. New York Times Book Review,* 29 Mar. 1959, p. 22.

"The Philosophy of Reading." *Proceedings of the 41st and 42nd Annual Education Conferences,* University of Delaware School of Education 8 (Mar. 1959): 20–34.

"Grim Report: Asia in Transition." *New York Times Magazine,* 5 Apr. 1959, pp. 11, 104, 106, 108.

"J. H. Randall, Jr., on American and Soviet Philosophy." *Journal of Philosophy* 56 (23 Apr. 1959): 416–19.

    Reply to Randall, "The Mirror of U.S. Philosophizing." Ibid. 55 (6 Nov. 1958): 1019–28.

"Man and Nature: Some Questions for Mr. Mitin." *Journal of Philosophy* 56 (23 Apr. 1959): 408–16.

"A Talk with Bhave." *New Leader* 42 (4 May 1959): 10–13.

"A Talk with Vinoba Bhave." *Encounter* 12 (May 1959): 14–18.

"Hannah Arendt's Reflections." Letter to the editor. *Dissent* 6 (Spring 1959): 203.

    Reply by Arendt, "Hannah Arendt Replies." Ibid., pp. 203–4.

"What's Left of Karl Marx?" *Saturday Review* 42 (6 June 1959): 12–14, 58.

"Pragmatism and Existentialism." *Antioch Review* 19 (Summer 1959): 151–68.

"'Common Sense' in Japan." *New Leader* 42 (5 Oct. 1959): 10–12.

"John Dewey: His Philosophy of Education and Its Critics." *New Leader* 42 (2 Nov. 1959): Sec. 2.

"What Is Education?" *Science Teacher* 26 (Nov. 1959): 462–67, 516–21.

"John Dewey: Philosopher of Growth." *Journal of Philosophy* 56 (17 Dec. 1959): 1010–1018.

"The Ends and Content of Education." *Daedalus* 88 (Winter 1959): 7–24.

"Two Types of Existentialist Religion and Ethics." *Partisan Review* 26 (Winter 1959): 58–63.

1960

"A Pragmatic Note." In *Dimensions of Mind,* ed. Sidney Hook, pp. 202–11. Third Symposium,

New York University Institute of Philosophy, 15–16 May 1959. New York: New York University Press, 1960.

"The Centrality of Method." In *The American Pragmatist,* ed. Milton R. Konvitz and Gail Kennedy, pp. 360–69. New York: Meridian Books, 1960.

"To Free Gold and Sobell." *New York Times,* 16 Feb. 1960, p. 36. [Letter with Nathan Glazer, Irving Kristol, and Dwight Macdonald.]

"Of Tradition and Change." Review of F. A. Hayek, *The Constitution of Liberty. New York Times Book Review,* 21 Feb. 1960, pp. 6, 28.

"Modern Knowledge and the Idea of God." *Commentary* 29 (Mar. 1960): 205–16.

"A Handbook for the Years Ahead." Review of Robert L. Heilbroner, *The Future as History. Saturday Review* 43 (2 Apr. 1960): 22–23.

"Distrust of Soviet." *New York Times,* 5 Apr. 1960, p. 36.

"A New Ism for Socialism." *New York Times Magazine,* 10 Apr. 1960, pp. 13, 62, 64, 66, 69.

"Second Thoughts on Peace and Freedom." *New Leader* 43 (11 Apr. 1960): 8–12.

"Carte-Blanche Legislative Authority." Review of Charles L. Black, Jr., *The People and the Court. Saturday Review* 43 (30 Apr. 1960): 19–20.

"Bertrand Russell's Political Fantasies." *New Leader* 43 (9 May 1960): 15–17.

"Pragmatism and the Tragic Sense of Life." *Commentary* 30 (Aug. 1960): 139–49.

Letter by George Kimmelman with Hook's reply, ibid. 30 (Dec. 1960): 536.

"A Recollection of Berthold Brecht." *New Leader* 43 (10 Oct. 1960): 22–23.

"Scapegoat for Tyranny." Review of Clinton Rossiter, *Marxism: The View from America. Saturday Review* 43 (12 Nov. 1960): 25–26.

" 'Welfare State'—A Debate That Isn't." *New York Times Magazine,* 27 Nov. 1960, pp. 27, 118–19.

    Response by Marjorie H. Schefler, ibid., 11 Dec. 1960, p. 4.

    Reply by Hook, ibid.

"Philosophy and Human Conduct." *Kenyon Review* 22 (Fall 1960): 648–66.

"Visionary or Man of Vision?" *New Leader* 43 (12 Dec. 1960): 22–23.

"Political Pretenders and How to Tell Them." *Saturday Review* 43 (31 Dec. 1960): 6–8, 29.

"Was hat uns Karl Marx heute noch zu sagen?" *Politische Studien* 11 (1960): 364–70.

1961

The Quest for Being, and Other Studies in Naturalism and Humanism. New York: St. Martin's Press, 1961.

"The Atheism of Paul Tillich." In *Religious Experience and Truth: A Symposium,* ed. Sidney Hook, pp. 59–65. Fourth Symposium, New York University Institute of Philosophy, 21–22 Oct. 1960. New York: New York University Press, 1961.

"Diderot's Great Legacy." Review of *A Diderot Pictorial Encyclopedia of Trades and Industry. New Leader* 44 (2 Jan. 1961): 25–26.

"In Memoriam: S. M. Levitas." *New Leader* 44 (16 Jan. 1961): 3–4.

"The Ethics of Controversy: Rejoinder to Julius Stone." *Observer,* 18 Mar. 1961.

"The Death Sentence." *New Leader* 44 (3 Apr. 1961): 18–20.

    Reply by Hugo Adam Bedau, ibid. 44 (8 May 1961): 28.

Review of Ayn Rand, *For the New Intellectual: The Philosophy of Ayn Rand. New York Times Book Review,* 9 Apr. 1961, p. 3. Correction, ibid., 23 Apr. 1961, p. 44.

    Letters in response with Hook's reply, ibid., 7 May 1961, p. 35.

"The Couch and the Bomb." *New Leader* 44 (24 Apr. 1961): 6–9.

    Replies by Zbigniew Brzezinski, Bernard Herman, and Paul Lauter, ibid. 44 (8 May 1961): 27–28.

    Reply by Erich Fromm, ibid. 44 (29 May 1961): 10–12.

    Response by Hook, "Escape from Reality." Ibid., pp. 12–14. [Correction to Hook's "Escape from Reality" appears in ibid. 44 (5 June 1961): 22.]

Response by Maximilien Rubel, ibid. 44 (12 June 1961): 30.
Reply by Hook, ibid., p. 30.
B. K. Harper in response to Fromm, ibid. 44 (19 June 1961): 29.
Response by Maximilien Rubel, ibid. 44 (31 July-7 Aug. 1961): 29.
Response by Hook, ibid., p. 29.
"Growth of Pacifism Noted." *New York Times,* 2 May 1961, p. 36.
"In League with the Kremlin." Review of Sandor Voros, *American Commissar. Saturday Review* 44 (20 May 1961): 38-39.
"Split Decisions." Review of Wallace Mendelson, *Justices Black and Frankfurter. New York Times Book Review,* 23 July 1961, pp. 6, 26.
"For Stand at West Berlin." Letter to the editor. *New York Times,* 28 Aug. 1961, p. 24.
Reply to letter by Erich Kahler, ibid., 18 Aug. 1961, p. 20.
"Enlightenment and Radicalism." *Encounter* 17 (Aug. 1961): 44-50.
"The New Revisionism." Review of John Lukacs, *The History of the Cold War. East Europe* 10 (Aug. 1961): 19, 48-49.
Letter by Hook, ibid. 10 (Oct. 1961): 39.
"Symposium on Capital Punishment." *New York Law Forum* 7 (Aug. 1961): 249-319. [Hook's contribution, pp. 278-83, 296-99, 300.]
"Questions of Conformity." Letter to the editor. *New Republic* 145 (21 Aug. 1961): 30-31.
"Unless We Resist." *Time,* 8 Sept. 1961, p. 22.
"Western Values and Total War." *Commentary* 32 (Oct. 1961): 277-304. [A panel with H. Stuart Hughes, Hans J. Morganthau, and C. P. Snow.]
See William F. Rickenbacker, "Schism of the Left." *National Review* 11 (15 July 1961): 8.
"After Berlin—What Next?" *Nation's Business* 49 (Oct. 1961): 59-60.
"Marx and Alienation." *New Leader* 44 (11 Dec. 1961): 15-18.

1962

Paradoxes of Freedom. Berkeley: University of California Press, 1962.
Political Power and Personal Freedom: Critical Studies in Democracy, Communism and Civil Rights. Collier Macmillan paperback, 1962.
World Communism, ed. Sidney Hook. Princeton, N.J.: Van Nostrand, 1962.
"Enlightenment and Radicalism." In *History and Hope,* pp. 59-67. Congress for Cultural Freedom, Berlin, 1960. New York: Praeger, 1962.
"Hegel and the Perspective of Liberalism." In *A Hegel Symposium,* ed. Don C. Travis, pp. 39-62. Austin: University of Texas, 1962.
"The Humanities and the Taming of Power." In *The Role of the Humanities in Ordering a Peaceful World,* pp. 5-21. New Britain: Central Connecticut State College, 1962.
"The Import of Ideological Diversity." In *Problems of Communism: Russia under Khrushchev,* ed. Abraham Brumberg, pp. 554-70. New York: Praeger, 1962.
Introduction to R. R. Abrahamovich, *The Soviet Revolution.* New York: International University Press, 1962.
"Philosophy and Human Culture." In *Philosophy and Culture—East and West,* ed. C. A. Moore, pp. 15-32. Honolulu: University of Hawaii Press, 1962.
"Better Red Than Dead, or Lord Russell's Guide to Peace." Review of Bertrand Russell, *Has Man a Future? New York Times Book Review,* 14 Jan. 1962, p. 44.
Letters in response with Hook's reply, ibid., 18 Feb. 1962, pp. 42-43.
"Revisionism at Bay." *Encounter* 19 (Sept. 1962): 63-67.
"Communism: What Lies Ahead." *Nation's Business* 50 (Oct. 1962).
"The Map Was Redrawn to Make Man's Agony a Part of the Geography." Review of Martin Heidegger, *Being and Time. New York Times Book Review,* 11 Nov. 1962, pp. 6, 42.

"The Politics of Science Fiction." Review of Eugene Burdick and Harvey Wheeler, *Fail-Safe*. *New Leader* 45 (10 Dec. 1962): 12–15.
"The Impact of Expanding Research Support on the Universities." *Journal of Medical Education* 37 (Dec. 1962): 230–46.
"The Cold War and the West." *Partisan Review* 29 (Winter 1962): 20–27.

1963

Education for Modern Man: A New Perspective. New York: Alfred A. Knopf, 1963.
The Fail-Safe Fallacy. New York: Stein and Day, 1963.
"Objectivity and Reconstruction in History." In *Philosophy and History,* ed. Sidney Hook, pp. 250–75. Fifth Symposium, New York University Institute of Philosophy, 11–12 May 1962. New York: New York University Press, 1963.
"Democracy and Equality." *In Quest of Value,* ed. Frederick C. Dommeyer, pp. 60–70. San Francisco: Chandler Publishing Co., 1963.
"Heresy and Conspiracy." *In Quest of Value,* ed. Frederick C. Dommeyer, pp. 485–99. San Francisco: Chandler Publishing Co., 1963.
"Intelligence and Human Rights." In *Memorias del XIII Congreso Internacional de Filosofía,* VII, pp. 101–2. México: Universidad Nacional Autónoma de México, 1963.
"Philosophy and Social Welfare." In *Health-Care Issues of 1960.* New York: Group Health Insurance, Inc., 1963.
Introduction to Eric Hoffer, *The True Believer.* New York: Time-Life Books, 1963.
"'Lord Monboddo' and the Supreme Court." Review of *One Man's Stand for Freedom,* ed. Irving Dilliard. *New Leader* 46 (13 May 1963): 11–15.
"Do the People Rule and Can They?" Review of Walter Lippmann, *The Essential Lippmann. New York Times Book Review,* 14 July 1963, pp. 1, 24, 25.
    Letters in response with Hook's reply, ibid., 8 Sept. 1963, p. 32.
"Why the U.S. Needs a Freedom Academy." *Think* 29 (Sept. 1963): 6–9.
"Challenging Study: Challenge of Communism." *New York Times Magazine,* 13 Oct. 1963, pp. 25, 33, 34, 38, 41.
    Reply by Louis Fischer and response by Hook, ibid., 27 Oct. 1963, p. 12.
"Accused Assassin Belied Tenets of Marxism, Experts Here Agree." *New York Times,* 27 Nov. 1963, p. 21.
"Religious Liberty from the Viewpoint of the Open Society." *Cross Currents* 13 (Winter 1963): 65–75.
"American Philosophy Today." *America* 68 (1963): 27–34.

1964

"Law, Justice and Obedience." In *Law and Philosophy,* ed. Sidney Hook, pp. 55–60. Sixth Symposium, New York University Institute of Philosophy, 10–11 May 1963. New York: New York University Press, 1964.
"Conversations by Professors Hook, Dallin and Bell." In *World Politics,* ed. Mahir Nasim. Cairo: Dar Al-kurrnek, 1964.
"The Death Sentence." In *The Death Penalty in America,* ed. Hugo Adam Bedau, pp. 146–54. Chicago: Aldine, 1964.
"Historical Determinism and Political Fiat in Soviet Communism." In *Political Thought since World War II,* ed. W. J. Stankiewicz, pp. 159–74. New York: Free Press, 1964.
Introduction to Walter Lippmann, *A Preface to Morals,* new ed. New York: Time-Life Books, 1964.
"Religious Liberty from the Viewpoint of a Secular Humanist." In Earl Rabb, *Religious Conflict in America,* pp. 138–51. Garden City, N.Y.: Doubleday, 1964.
"Liberalism and the Negro." With James Baldwin, Nathan Glazer, and Gunnar Myrdal. *Commentary* 37 (Mar. 1964): 25–42.

"Fulbright's Rights Stand." *New York Times,* 8 Apr. 1964, p. 42.
    Reply by J. A. Fabro, ibid., 13 Apr. 1964, p. 28.
"Pornography and the Censor." *New York Times Book Review,* 12 Apr. 1964, pp. 1, 38–39.
    Response and Hook's reply, ibid., 10 May 1964, pp. 32–33.
"The Cunning of History." Review of Isaac Deutscher, *The Prophet Outcast. New Leader* 47 (11 May 1964): 15–18.
"Common Sense and Disarmament." *Yale Political* 3 (Spring 1964): 16, 29–30.
"There's More Than One Way to Teach." *Saturday Review* 47 (18 July 1964): 48–49, 59.
"Thinking about Thinkers of the Unthinkable." Review of Anatol Rapoport, *Strategy and Conscience. New York Times Book Review,* 19 July 1964, pp. 6, 25.
    Responses and Hook's reply, ibid., 6 Sept. 1964, p. 18.
"A Search Here and Beyond." Review of Whittaker Chambers, *Cold Friday. New York Times Book Review,* 8 Nov. 1964, pp. 3, 32.
"Faces of Betrayers." Review of Rebecca West, *The New Meaning of Treason. New York Times Book Review,* 29 Nov. 1964, pp. 1, 60–61.
"Hegel e le prospettive del liberalismo." *De Homine,* nos. 9–10 (1964): 115–40.
Review of John F. Boler, *Charles Peirce and Scholastic Realism: A Study of Peirce's Relation to John Duns Scotus. Bibliography of Philosophy* 11 (1964): 100.
Review of Sören Halldén, *True Love, True Humour and True Religion: A Semantic Study. Bibliography of Philosophy* 11 (1964): 208.
Review of Emil L. Fackenheim, *Metaphysics and Historicity. History and Theory* 3 (1964): 389–92.

1965

Reason, Social Myths and Democracy. With a new introduction by Hook. New York: Harper and Row, 1965.
"Academic Freedom and the Right of Students." In Seymour Martin Lipset, *The Berkeley Student Revolt,* pp. 432–42. Garden City, N.Y.: Anchor Books, 1965.
"The Political Aspects of General and Complete Disarmament." In *The Prospects for Arms Control,* ed. James E. Dougherty and John F. Lehman, Jr., pp. 153–63. Philadelphia: Macfadden Books, 1965.
"Second Thoughts on Berkeley." In *Revolution at Berkeley,* ed. Michael V. Miller and Susan Gilmore, pp. 116–59. New York: Dial Press, 1965.
Introduction to Paul Edwards, *The Logic of Moral Discourse.* New York: Free Press of Glencoe, 1965.
Introduction to Rebecca West, *The New Meaning of Treason,* new ed. New York: Time-Life Books, 1965.
"Hegel Rehabilitated?" *Encounter* 24 (Jan. 1965): 53–58.
    Reply by Shlomo Avineri, "Hook's Hegel." Ibid. 25 (Nov. 1965): 63–66.
    Letters in reply by Paul Goodman, Lawrence D. Hochman, Harold Leitenberg, and Kay Boyle, ibid., 17 Jan. 1965, pp. 6, 21.
    Response by Hook, ibid., p. 21.
"Defends Protests to Russia on Jews." *New York Times,* 13 Feb. 1965, p. 20.
    Response to Stephen P. Dunn, "Anti-Semitism in Soviet." Ibid., 25 Jan. 1965, p. 36.
"Changing Values in Higher Education in a Changing Society." *New York State Education* 52 (Feb. 1965): 7–9.
"Reply to Dr. Oppenheimer." *Denver Post,* 27 July 1965, p. 19.
    Reply to Frank Oppenheimer's letter on U.S. policy toward communism, ibid., 6 June 1965, p. 51.
"The Philosophy of American Pragmatism." *Span* 6 (Aug. 1965): 21–28.
"Friends and Enemies." Review of Haakon Chevalier, *Oppenheimer. New York Times Book Review,* 22 Aug. 1965, pp. 3, 28.

Reply by Chevalier and response by Hook, ibid., 19 Sept. 1965, pp. 52–53.
"Radicalism in America." *New Leader* 48 (27 Sept. 1965): 34–35.
"Second Thoughts on Berkeley." *Teachers College Record* 67 (Oct. 1965): 32–63.
"The Conflict of Freedoms." *Common Factor* 1 (Autumn 1965): 36–42.
"Thoughts after Knopfelmacher." *Minerva* 4 (Winter 1965): 279–85.

1966

"Are There Universal Criteria of Judgments of Excellence in Art?" In *Art and Philosophy,*
    ed. Sidney Hook, pp. 49–55. Seventh Symposium, New York University Institute of Philos-
    ophy, 23–24 Oct. 1964. New York: New York University Press, 1966.
"The Content of Education." In *The Education of Modern Man,* ed. Margaret Starkey, pp. 138–
    43. New York: Pitman Publishing Corp., 1966.
"Man's Quest for Security: A Philosopher's View." In *Man's Quest for Security,* ed. E. J. Faulkner,
    pp. 3–17. Lincoln: University of Nebraska Press, 1966.
"Marxism in the Western World: From 'Scientific Socialism' to Mythology." In *Marxist Ideology
    in the Contemporary World—Its Appeal and Paradoxes,* ed. Milorad M. Drachkovitch, pp. 1–
    36. Palo Alto, Calif.: Stanford University Press, 1966.
"Pragmatism and the Tragic Sense of Life." In *Moderns on Tragedy,* ed. Lionel Abel, pp. 227–49.
    New York: Fawcett Publishers, 1966.
"Pragmatism and the Tragic Sense of Life," and "Naturalism and First Principles." In *Amer-
    ican Philosophy in the Twentieth Century,* ed. Paul Kurtz, pp. 522–44. New York: Macmillan,
    1966.
"In Reply to Dr. Hutchins." Letter to the editor. *Santa Barbara News-Press,* 27 Feb. 1966.
"U.S. Policy and Communism." Letter to the editor. *Santa Barbara News-Press,* 20 Mar. 1966.
"Writer Buttresses His Previous Criticism of Tax-Exempt Center." Letter to the editor. *Los Angeles
    Times,* 4 Apr. 1966, pt. 2, p. 4.
"Liberal Catholic Thought." Review of Michael Novak, *Belief and Unbelief. Commentary* 41
    (Apr. 1966): 94–100.
"Speaking of Books: Karl Marx's Second Coming." *New York Times Book Review,* 22 May 1966,
    pp. 2, 44–45.
    Response by L. Marcus, ibid., 10 July 1966, p. 50.
    Reply by Hook, ibid., pp. 50–51.
"Hegel and His Apologists." *Encounter* 26 (May 1966): 1–8.
"Neither Blind Obedience nor Uncivil Disobedience." *New York Times Magazine,* 5 June 1966,
    pp. 52–53, 122–28.
"Lord Russell and the War Crimes 'Trial'." *New Leader* 49 (24 Oct. 1966): 6–11.
    Reply by Ralph Schoenman, "Lord Russell's 'Tribunal'." Ibid. 49 (19 Dec. 1966): 27–28.
    Response by Hook, ibid., p. 28.
"Liberties in Conflict." Review of Thomas I. Emerson, *Toward a General Theory of the First
    Amendment. Book Week,* 6 Nov. 1966, pp. 5, 10.
"Some Educational Attitudes and Poses." *Harvard Educational Review* 36 (Fall 1966): 496–504.

1967

Religion in a Free Society. Lincoln: University of Nebraska Press, 1967.
"Basic Values and Economic Policy." In *Human Values and Economic Policy,* ed. Sidney Hook.
    Eighth Symposium, New York University Institute of Philosophy, 13–14 May 1966. New
    York: New York University Press, 1967.
"The Outlook for Philosophy." In Arnold Toynbee et al., *New Frontiers of Knowledge,* pp. 18–
    21. Washington, D.C.: Public Affairs Press, 1967.
"On the Couch." Review of Meyer A. Zeligs, *Friendship and Fratricide. New York Times Book
    Review,* 5 Feb. 1967, pp. 4, 40, 41.

Response by Zeligs with Hook's reply, ibid., 19 Mar. 1967, pp. 59–60.
Response by Marshall A. Best, ibid., 2 Apr. 1967, p. 44.
"Le Deuxième avénement de Marx." *Le Contrat Social* 11 (Mar.–Apr. 1967): 91–94.
"Whither Russia? Fifty Years After." *Problems of Communism* 16 (Mar.–Apr. 1967): 76–79.
"Lessons of the Hungarian 'October'." *Scope,* Spring–Autumn 1967.
"Crisis for White, Negro Leadership." *Los Angeles Times,* 28 July 1967, Part 2, p. 5.
"Cruel Deception." Letter to the editor. *New Leader* 50 (14 Aug. 1967): 26–27.
"Is There a Legal 'Right' to Revolt?" *Los Angeles Times,* 15 Aug. 1967, Part 2, p. 5.
"Fluff on the Sleeve of History." Review of C. P. Snow, *Variety of Men. New Leader* 50 (28 Aug. 1967): 16–18.
"Fulbright's Colossal Gall." *Providence Journal,* 4 Sept. 1967.
Letter to the editor. *New Republic* 50 (25 Sept. 1967): 27.
Response to comments by M. S. Arnoni on the Vietnamese conflict, ibid., pp. 26–27.
Reply by Arnoni, ibid. 50 (23 Oct. 1967): 34.
Rejoinder by Hook, ibid., pp. 34–35.
"Liberal Anti-Communism Revisited: A Symposium." With Lionel Abel et al. *Commentary* 44 (Sept. 1967): 44–48.
"Social Protest and Civil Disobedience." *Humanist* 27 (Sept.–Dec. 1967): 157–59, 192–93.
"The Human Cost [of Soviet Industrialization following the 1917 Revolution]." *New Leader* 50 (6 Nov. 1967): 16–20.
"Does Philosophy Have a Future?" *Saturday Review* 50 (11 Nov. 1967): 21–23, 62.
"A Right Way to Remedy a Wrong, a Wrong Way to Remedy a Right." *New York Times Magazine,* 26 Nov. 1967, pp. 124, 126.

1968

Contemporary Philosophy. Chicago: American Library Association, 1968.
"Experimental Naturalism." In *American Philosophy Today and Tomorrow,* ed. Sidney Hook and Horace M. Kallen, pp. 205–25. Freeport, N.Y.: Books for Libraries Press, 1968.
"In Defense of 'Justice' (A Response)" and "Reflections on Human Rights." In *Ethics and Social Justice,* ed. Howard E. Kiefer and Milton K. Munitz, pp. 75–84, 252–81. Vol. 4 of *Contemporary Philosophic Thought: The International Philosophy Year Conferences at Brockport.* Albany: State University of New York Press, 1968.
"The Democratic Challenge to Communism." In *Fifty Years of Communism in Russia,* ed. M. M. Drachkovitch, pp. 284–92. Hoover Institution Publication no. 77. University Park: Pennsylvania State University Press, 1968.
"Human Rights and Social Justice." In *Social Justice and the Problem of the Twentieth Century,* ed. Sidney Hook, Tom Wicker and C. Van Woodward. Raleigh, N.C., 1968.
"The University Law School." In *The Law School of Tomorrow,* ed. D. Haber and J. Cohen. New Brunswick: Rutgers University Press, 1968. [Speech by Robert M. Hutchins with comment by Sidney Hook.]
"Ethics of Political Controversy (and Discussion)." In *Proceedings of the First Annual Symposium on Issues in Public Communications,* June 1968, pp. 50–85.
"The Enlightenment and Marxism." *Journal of the History of Ideas* 29 (Jan.–Mar. 1968): 93–108.
"The Human Costs of Revolution." *Survey* 66 (Jan. 1968): 129–37.
"Public Strikes." *New York Times,* 9 Feb. 1968, p. 26.
"Student Revolts Could Destroy Academic Freedom." *New York University Alumni News,* May 1968, pp. 8–9.
"America Must Erase the Cult of Violence." *Newsday,* 6 June 1968.
"Civil Liberties Issue in Appointment." *New York Times,* 1 Aug. 1968, p. 30.
Reply by Donald D. Schack, "Academic Freedom Called Issue." Ibid., 6 Aug. 1968, p. 36.
"Political Thinking beyond Politics." Review of Leszek Kolakowski, *Toward a Marxist Humanism. New York Times Book Review,* 1 Sept. 1968, pp. 8, 25.

"Hook Favors Bigger Role for Faculty." *New York Times,* 29 Sept. 1968, p. 52.

"N.Y.U. vs. Hatchett." *New York Times,* 28 Oct. 1968, p. 46.

"Marcusian Values." *New York Times Magazine,* 10 Nov. 1968, p. 22.

> Reply to Herbert Marcuse, "Marcuse Defines His New Left Line." Ibid., 27 Oct. 1968.
> Letters by others, ibid., 17 Nov. 1968, p. 12.

"Sidney Hook Replies." Letter to the editor. *New York Post,* 19 Nov. 1968.

1969

The Essential Thomas Paine, ed. Sidney Hook. New American Library, Mentor paperback, 1969.

"Empiricism, Rationalism, and Innate Ideas." In *Language and Philosophy: A Symposium,* ed. Sidney Hook, pp. 160-67. Ninth Symposium, New York University Institute of Philosophy, 1968. New York: New York University Press, 1969.

"Absolutism and Human Rights." In *Philosophy, Science, and Method: Essays in Honor of Ernest Nagel,* ed. Sidney Morgenbesser, Patrick Suppes, and Morton White, pp. 382-99. New York: St. Martin's Press, 1969.

"Social Protest and Civil Disobedience." In Paul Kurtz, *Moral Problems in Contemporary Society,* pp. 161-72. Englewood Cliffs, N.J.: Prentice-Hall, 1969.

"Brecht." *New Leader* 52 (3 Feb. 1969): 34.

> Reply to Eric Bentley's review of Robert Conquest, *The Great Terror.* Ibid. 51 (2 Dec. 1968): 6-8.
> Reply by Robert Conquest, ibid. 52 (3 Mar. 1969): 35.
> Rebuttal by Eric Bentley, ibid. 52 (17 Mar. 1969): 34-35.
> Responses by Hook and Henry M. Pachter, ibid. 52 (28 Apr. 1969): 34-35.

"Prof. Hook Replies to His Critics." *Connecticut Daily Campus,* 4 Feb. 1969. Letter to the editor relating to comments by Jerome Shaffer and others on Hook's speech "The Trojan Horse in American Higher Education."

"Professor Hook Replies." *Connecticut Daily Campus,* 24 Feb. 1969. Letter to the editor relating to comments by Jerome Shaffer and others on Hook's letter to the editor "Prof. Hook Replies to His Critics."

"The War against the Democratic Process." *Atlantic* 223 (Feb. 1969): 45-49.

"Reason and Violence: Some Truths and Myths about John Dewey." *Humanist* 29 (Mar.-Apr. 1969): 14-16.

"Who Is Responsible for Campus Violence?" *Saturday Review* 52 (19 Apr. 1969): 22-25, 54-55.

"Help Wanted—Superman." Review of Herbert Marcuse, *An Essay on Liberation. New York Times Book Review,* 20 Apr. 1969, p. 8.

"Mr. Hook Replies." *Atlantic* 223 (Apr. 1969): 46-47.

"Barbarism, Virtue, and the University." *Public Interest,* no. 15 (Spring 1969): 23-39.

"The Real Crisis on the Campus: A Noted Educator Sounds a Warning—Exclusive Interview." *U.S. News and World Report,* 19 May 1969, pp. 40-44.

"Democracy's Survival Problematic." *Antioch College Record,* 23 May 1969.

"The Barbarism of Virtue." *PMLA* 84 (May 1969): 465-75.

"*Modern Quarterly,* A Chapter in American Radical History: V. F. Calverton and His Periodicals." *Labor History* 10 (Spring 1969): 241-49.

"Labor Sit-Ins and University Sit-Ins: The Crucial Differences." *Measure,* June 1969.

"John Dewey and the Crisis of American Liberalism." *Antioch Review* 29 (Summer 1969): 218-32.

"The Crisis of Our Democratic Institutions." *Humanist* 29 (July-Aug. 1969): 6-7.

"The Architecture of Educational Chaos." *Phi Delta Kappan* 51 (Oct. 1969): 68-70.

Review of Henri Lefebvre, *The Sociology of Marx.* Trans. from French by N. Guterman. *American Historical Review* 75 (Oct. 1969): 148-49.

"The Trojan Horse in American Higher Education." *Educational Record* 50 (Winter 1969): 21-29.

"Some Reflections on the Encyclopedia of Philosophy." *Religious Humanism* 3 (Winter 1969): 4-7.

"Harold Taylor's Evasions." *Phi Delta Kappan* 51 (Dec. 1969): 197–98.
    Response to Harold Taylor, "Students, Universities, and Sidney Hook." Ibid., pp. 195–97.

1970

American Freedom and Academic Anarchy. New York: Cowles Book Co., 1970.
"Conflict and Change in the Academic Community." In *Papers of the Fifty-second Annual Conference,* National Association of Student Personnel Administrators, 1970.
"Paradise Lost: The Tragedy of Whittaker Chambers." Review of Whittaker Chambers, *Odyssey of a Friend: Whittaker Chambers' Letters to William F. Buckley, Jr., 1954–1961. Chicago Sun-Times,* 1 Feb. 1970.
"Justice Douglas." *New York Times,* 19 Apr. 1970, p. 17.
"The Ideology of Violence." *Encounter* 34 (Apr. 1970): 26–29, 31–38.
"What Student Rights in Education?" *Current* no. 117 (Apr. 1970): 21–27.
"Philosophy and Public Policy." *Journal of Philosophy* 67 (23 July 1970): 461–70.
"A Plan to Achieve Campus Peace." *Los Angeles Times,* 30 Aug. 1970.
"From the Platitudinous to the Absurd." *Philosophic Exchange* (Summer 1970): 21–30.
"Hook's Views on Riots." *New York Times,* 30 Sept. 1970, p. 42.
"Points of Confusion." *Encounter* 35 (Sept. 1970): 45–53.
"The Survival of the Free University." *Humanist* 30 (Sept.–Oct. 1970): 26–28.
Contribution to a symposium on William O. Douglas, *Points of Rebellion. Brooklyn Law Review* 37 (Fall 1970): 16–22.
    Panel Discussion, ibid., pp. 22–32.
"Corporate Politics on Campus." *Freedom at Issue,* Sept.–Oct. 1970.
"Campus Terror: An Indictment." *New York Times,* 22 Oct. 1970, p. 47.
    Reply by Lipman Bers, ibid., 30 Oct. 1970, p. 40.
"The Political Fantasies of Noam Chomsky." *Humanist* 30 (Nov.–Dec. 1970): 26–29.

1971

In Defense of Academic Freedom, ed. Sidney Hook. New York: Pegasus, 1971.
"Academic Freedom and the Supreme Court: The Court in Another Wilderness." In *On Academic Freedom,* ed. Valerie Earle. Washington: American Enterprise Institute for Public Policy Research, 1971.
"How Democratic Is America? A Response to Howard Zinn." In *How Democratic Is America? Responses to the New Left Challenge,* ed. Robert A. Goldwin. Chicago: Rand McNally, 1971.
"Ideals and Realities of Academic Tenure." In *Proceedings of the Twenty-eighth Annual Utah Conference on Higher Education.* Logan: Utah State University, 1971.
"Ideologies of Violence and Social Change." In *Peaceful Change in Modern Society,* ed. E. B. Tompkins, pp. 112–27. Stanford, Calif.: Stanford University Press, 1971.
"The Place of John Dewey in Modern Thought." In *Philosophical Thought in France and the United States,* pp. 483–503. Buffalo: University of Buffalo Publications in Philosophy, 1971.
"The Knight of the Double Standard." *Humanist* 31 (Jan.–Feb. 1971): 29–34.
    Response by Noam Chomsky, ibid., pp. 23–29.
"Knight Comes a Cropper." *Humanist* 31 (Mar.–Apr. 1971): 34–35.
"A Sentimental View of Crime." Review of Ramsey Clark, *Crime in America. Fortune* 83 (Feb. 1971): 140–41.
"Comments on Professor Nelson's Address." *Personalist* 52 (Spring 1971): 335–42.
"The Snare of Definitions." *Humanist* 31 (Sept.–Oct. 1971): 10–11.
"An American Verdict on Star-Spangled Australia." *Sunday Australian,* 31 Oct. 1971.
"Discrimination, Color Blindness and the Quota System." *Measure,* Oct. 1971.
"Discrimination against the Qualified?" *New York Times,* 5 Nov. 1971, p. 43.
    Reply by Martha Burke-Hennessy and Myra L. Skluth, ibid., 24 Nov. 1971, p. 34.

Response by J. Stanley Pottinger, "Come Now, Professor Hook." Ibid., 18 Dec. 1971, p. 29.
Response by Frank Askin, ibid., 19 Dec. 1971, p. 10.
"John Dewey and His Betrayers." *Change* 3 (Nov. 1971): 22–26.
Discussed by Albert Shanker in his weekly column, "Where We Stand," *New York Times,* 3 Oct. 1971, p. 9.
"Authority and Democracy in the University." *Quadrant,* Nov. -Dec. 1971, pp. 42–48.
"Epilogue: Democracy and the Open Society." *Humanist* 31 (Nov.-Dec. 1971): 29–31.
"HEW Regionals—A New Threat to Educational Integrity." *Freedom at Issue* no. 10 (Nov.-Dec. 1971): 5–7.

1972

Introduction to Marvin Zimmerman, *Contemporary Problems of Democracy.* New York: Humanities Press, 1972.
"The Freedom Shouters." *New York Times,* 17 Jan. 1972, p. 30.
Reply by Barry Commoner, ibid., 28 Jan. 1972, p. 44.
Preface to Ernest van den Haag, "Civil Disobedience." *National Review* 24 (21 Jan. 1972): 29.
"Illich's De-Schooled Utopia." Review of Ivan Illich, *De-schooling Society. Encounter* 38 (Jan. 1972): 53–57.
"Democracy and Genetic Variation." *Humanist* 32 (Mar.-Apr. 1972): 9.
"The Road to a University 'Quota System.'" *Freedom at Issue* no. 12 (Mar.-Apr. 1972): 2, 21–22.
Response by Jack Hirshleifer, ibid., p. 23.
"The Rights of the Victims." *Encounter* 38 (Apr. 1972): 11–15.
"Adrienne Koch: Student and Colleague." *Maryland Historian* 3 (Spring 1972): 5–8.
"HEW's Faculty 'Quotas' Inspire Semantic Evasions." *Freedom at Issue* no. 14 (July–Aug. 1972): 12–14.
"An Open Letter to Senator George McGovern." *Los Angeles Times,* 15 Oct. 1972.
"Uncertain Progress." *Measure* no. 20 (Oct. 1972): 1–2.

1973

Education and the Taming of Power. La Salle, Ill.: Open Court Pub. Co., 1973.
Education for Modern Man: A New Perspective. New Enlarged Edition. Atlantic Highlands, N.J.: Humanities Press, 1973.
Heresy, Yes—Conspiracy, No. With new introduction. Westport, Conn.: Greenwood Press, 1973.
Foreword to *Radical School Reform, Critique and Alternatives,* ed. Cornelius J. Troost. Boston: Little, Brown and Co., 1973.
See also Hook, "John Dewey and His Betrayers," pp. 57–66; "Illich's De-Schooled Utopia," pp. 67–73; "The Teaching of Values," pp. 190–95.
"Higher Education and Morality." In *Private Higher Education: The Job Ahead.* Papers delivered by Ernest van den Haag et al. of the American Association of Presidents of Independent Colleges and Universities, Annual Conference, Scottsdale, Ariz., Dec. 1972. [c 1973].
"Marxism." In *Dictionary of the History of Ideas,* ed. Philip P. Wiener, vol. 3, pp. 146–61. New York: Charles Scribner's Sons, 1973.
"The Relevance of John Dewey's Thought." In *The Chief Glory of Every People,* ed. Matthew Bruccoli, pp. 53–75. Carbondale: Southern Illinois University Press, 1973.
"Lenin and the Communist International." Review of Branko Lazitch and Milorad M. Drachkovitch, *Lenin and the Comintern,* vol. 1. *Russian Review* 32 (Jan. 1973): 1–14.
"The Politics of Irresponsibility." Review of Richard King, *The Party of Eros: Radical Social Thought and the Realm of Freedom. Virginia Quarterly Review* 49 (Spring 1973): 274–82.
"Make the Punishment Fit the Criminal." *New York Times,* 6 Apr. 1973, p. 40.
"The Academic Mission and Collective Bargaining." *Proceedings of the First Annual Conference,*

National Center for the Study of Collective Bargaining in Higher Education, New York City, Apr. 1973.

"Myth and Fact in the Marxist Theory of Revolution and Violence." *Journal of the History of Ideas* 34 (Apr.–June 1973): 271–80.

"Semantics and Politics." *Measure,* May 1973.

"Solzhenitsyn and the Western Liberals." *New York Times,* 19 Sept. 1973, p. 46.

"John Reed, the Romantic." Review of Barbara Gelb, *So Short a Time. New Republic* 169 (29 Sept. 1973): 23–25.

"Have We Reached Shore?" *Measure* no. 24 (Sept. 1973): 1–3.

"Humanist Manifesto II," by Sidney Hook et al. *Humanist* 33 (Sept.–Oct. 1973): 4–9.

"Materials for a Biography." Review of George Dykhuizen, *The Life and Mind of John Dewey. New Republic* 169 (27 Oct. 1973): 38–39.

"For Louis Althusser." Review of Louis Althusser, *For Marx. Encounter* 41 (Oct. 1973): 86–92.

"William James and George Santayana." *ICarbS* 1 (Fall–Winter 1973): 34–39.

"Professing the Truth: An Exchange." *Columbia Forum,* Winter 1973.

"The Attack on Objectivity." *Measure* no. 26 (Dec. 1973): 1–2.

1974

Pragmatism and the Tragic Sense of Life. New York: Basic Books, 1974.

"Democracy and Higher Education." In *The Idea of a Modern University,* ed. Sidney Hook, Paul Kurtz, and Miro Todorovich, pp. 33–40. Buffalo, N.Y.: Prometheus Books, 1974.

"The Modern Quarterly: Baltimore and New York, 1923–1932, 1938–1940. The Modern Monthly: New York, 1933–1938." In *The American Radical Press,* vol. 2, ed. Joseph R. Conlin, pp. 596–605. Westport, Conn.: Greenwood Press, 1974.

"A Dawning Light—Belated but Welcome." *Measure* no. 27 (Jan. 1974): 4.

"Reflections on the Disorder of Our Times." *Alternative* 7 (Jan. 1974): 5–7.

"Humanism and the Human Experience." *Humanist* 34 (Jan.–Feb. 1974): 6–7.

"Violence Usually Frustrates or Delays Reform." *Los Angeles Times,* 27 Feb. 1974, p. 7.

"Letter from New York." *Encounter* 42 (Feb. 1974): 44–45.

"Anyone for Objectivity?" *Encounter* 42 (Mar. 1974): 94–95.

"The Education of an Auto-Didact." Review of James D. Koerner, *Hoffer's America. Change* 6 (Mar. 1974): 60–61.

"John Dewey's *Democracy and Education." New York University Education Quarterly* 5 (Spring 1974): 26–29.

"Stalin—Mystery and Legacy." Review of Ronald Hingley, *Joseph Stalin: Man and Legend*; Robert Tucker, *Stalin as Revolutionary*; and Adam B. Ulam, *Stalin: The Man and His Era. New Republic* 171 (20 July 1974): 21–24.

"The Bias in Anti-Bias Regulations." *Measure* no. 30 (Summer 1974): 1–2, 4–6.

"Congressional Testimony: On Discrimination." *Measure* no. 31 (Sept. 1974): 1, 2, 5, 6.

"A Quota Is a Quota Is a Quota." *New York Times,* 12 Nov. 1974, p. 39.

　　Reply by Peter J. Wilson, ibid., 27 Nov. 1974, p. 36.

　　Reply by Nancy Alderman Ransom, ibid., 2 Dec. 1974, p. 32.

"Will to Illusion." Review of Ernest Fisher, *An Opposing Man. New Republic,* 16 Nov. 1974, pp. 27–28.

"A Bolshevik Reconsidered: The Case of Comrade Bukharin." Review of Stephen Cohen, *Bukharin and the Bolshevik Revolution, 1888–1938. Encounter* 43 (Dec. 1974): 81–92.

1975

Revolution, Reform, and Social Justice—Studies in the Theory and Practice of Marxism. New York: New York University Press, 1975.

The Philosophy of the Curriculum: The Need for General Education, ed. Sidney Hook, Paul Kurtz, and Miro Todorovich. Buffalo, N.Y.: Prometheus Books, 1975.

"Higher Education and Morality." In *Private Higher Education: The Job Ahead,* vol. 4, pp. 1-6. American Association of Presidents of Independent Colleges and Universities Annual Meeting Talks, Scottsdale, Arizona, 1975.

Preface to John Dewey, *Moral Principles in Education.* Carbondale and Edwardsville: Southern Illinois University Press, Arcturus Books, 1975.

"For An Open Minded Naturalism." *Southern Journal of Philosophy* 13 (1975): 127-36.

"In the Forefront." *New York Post,* 1 Feb. 1975.

    Response to Carl Rowan, "The War on Quotas," ibid., 20 Jan. 1975.

"Education: The Wrong Affirmative Action." Letter by Sidney Hook et al. *New York Times,* 29 Mar. 1975, p. 22.

"What the Cold War Was About." *Encounter* 44 (Mar. 1975): 62-67.

"A Humanist Philosophy of Life." Review of Paul Kurtz, *The Fullness of Life. Humanist* 35 (Mar.-Apr. 1975): 36-37.

"University Women: An Exchange." *New York Review of Books,* 3 Apr. 1975, pp. 36-37.

    Reply by Gertrude Ezorsky, ibid., pp. 37-38.

"The Issue Redefined." *Freedom at Issue.* May-June 1975, pp. 17-19.

"America Now: A Failure of Nerve? — A Symposium." *Commentary* 60 (July 1975): 41-43.

"The Hiss Ruling's Contradictions." *Wall Street Journal,* 25 Aug. 1975, p. 6.

    Response by John F. Burke, ibid., 29 Sept. 1975, p. 11.

    Reply by Hook, ibid.

"The Promise of Humanism." *Humanist* 35 (Sept.-Oct. 1975): 41-43.

    Response to Jerome Frank, "The Limits of Humanism." Ibid., pp. 38-40.

    Reply by Albert Ellis, "Comments on Frank's 'The Limits of Humanism'." Ibid., pp. 43-45.

    Response by Frank, ibid. 35 (Nov.-Dec. 1975): 34.

    Rejoinder by Hook, ibid., pp. 34-35.

"In Defense of Terminological Sobriety: A Reply to Professor Kellner." *Journal of Politics* 37 (Nov. 1975): 912-16.

    See Menachem Marc Kellner, "Democracy and Civil Disobedience." Ibid., pp. 899-911.

"The Tyranny of Reverse Discrimination." With Miro Todorovich. *Change* 7 (Dec. 1975-Jan. 1976): 42-43.

1976

Ethics, National Ideology, Marxism and Existentialism: Discussions with Sidney Hook. Ed. Harsja W. Bachtiar. Jakarta, Indonesia: Djambatan, 1976. In Indonesian and English.

Foreword to James Gouinlock, *The Moral Writings of John Dewey.* New York: Macmillan Co., Hafner Press, 1976.

Introduction to *The Middle Works of John Dewey, 1899-1924,* ed. Jo Ann Boydston, vol. 2. Carbondale and Edwardsville: Southern Illinois University Press, 1976.

"The Strange Case of Whittaker Chambers." *Encounter* 46 (Jan. 1976): 78-89.

Review of John P. Diggins, *Up From Communism. New Republic* 174 (21 Feb. 1976): 24-27.

    Reply by Diggins, ibid. 174 (12 June 1976): 31-32.

    Response by Hook, ibid., p. 32.

"Alger Hiss: The Continuing Whitewash." Review of John Chabot Smith, *Alger Hiss: The True Story. Wall Street Journal,* 22 Mar. 1976, p. 14.

"Intelligence, Morality and Foreign Policy." *Freedom at Issue,* no. 35 (Mar.-Apr. 1976): 3-6.

    Condensed in *New York Times,* 1 May 1976, p. 23.

"The Legacy of 1776 — and a New Call for Freedom." *American Views* 1 (5 July 1976): 1-2.

"Bertrand Russell the Man." *Commentary* 62 (July 1976): 52-54.

Review of Michael Harrington, *The Twilight of Capitalism: A Marxian Epitaph. New Republic* 175 (7 and 14 Aug. 1976): 34-37.

"Morris Cohen—Fifty Years Later." *American Scholar* 45 (Summer 1976): 426-36.
    Reply by Diggins, ibid. 174 (12 June 1976): 31-32.
    Response by Hook, ibid., p. 32.
"The Social Democratic Prospect." *New America* 13 (Aug.-Sept. 1976): 8-9, 14.
"The Big Casino in the Sky." *New York Times,* 3 Sept. 1976.
"It's All in the Cards, My Dear. (Luck plays important role in life.)" *Fort Worth Star-Telegram,* 19 Sept. 1976.
"Can the University Survive Equal Access?" Review of *On The Meaning of the University,* ed. Sterling M. McMurrin. *Change* 8 (Sept. 1976): 59-61.
"A Symposium: What Is a Liberal—Who Is a Conservative?" *Commentary* 62 (Sept. 1976): 69-70.
"Is Secular Humanism a Religion?" *Humanist* 36 (Sept.-Oct. 1976): 5-7.
"The Hero and Democracy." *Gandhi Marg* 21 (Oct. 1976): 226-34.
"A Voice from Another Shore." Review of Lev Navrozov, *The Education of Lev Navrozov.* *Humanist* 36 (Nov.-Dec. 1976): 47, 50.
"An Interview with Sidney Hook." *Forum* (Austin, Texas) 1 (Dec. 1976): 6-7.
"Letters from George Santayana." *American Scholar* 46 (Winter 1976-77): 76-84.
Letter to editor. *American Scholar* 46 (Winter 1976-77): 142-43.

1977

"Academic Freedom and Professional Responsibility." In *The Ethics of Teaching and Scientific Research,* ed. Sidney Hook, Paul Kurtz, and Miro Todorovich, pp. 117-23. Buffalo, N.Y.: Prometheus Books, 1977.
"Dr. Hibbs and the Ethics of Discussion." *The Ethics of Teaching and Scientific Research,* ed. Sidney Hook, Paul Kurtz, and Miro Todorovich, pp. 187-90. Buffalo, N.Y.: Prometheus Books, 1977.
"How Democratic Is America? A Response to Howard Zinn." In *How Democratic Is America? Responses to the New Left Challenge,* ed. Robert A. Goldwin, pp. 61-75. Chicago: Rand McNally & Co., 1977.
"The Books That Shape Lives: Book Choices of Henry David Aiken and Sidney Hook." *Christian Century* 94 (5-12 Jan. 1977): 20.
"The New Religiosity." *Humanist* 37 (Jan.-Feb. 1977): 38-39.
Part of a symposium entitled "The Resurgence of Fundamentalism."
"Lillian Hellman's *Scoundrel Time.*" *Encounter* 48 (Feb. 1977): 82-91.
"Racial and Sexual Quotas: They're Not Only Illegal, They're Immoral." *New York Daily News,* 27 Mar. 1977.
"To Teach the Truth without Let or Hindrance." *Chronicle of Higher Education* 14 (4 Apr. 1977): 40.
    Reply by Leonard Marsak, ibid., 2 May 1977, p. 16.
    Response by Hook, ibid., 23 May 1977.
"Marxists and Non-Marxists." *Times Literary Supplement* 88 (29 Apr. 1977): 522.
    Reply to Ghita Ionescu review, ibid., 8 Apr. 1977, p. 427.
"An Outstanding Symbol of Free Trade Unions." *New America* 14 (May 1977): 8.
"Fanaticism and Absolutism." *Intellect* 105 (May 1977): 387-88.
"Marxism and Crypto-Marxism." *New York Times,* 26 Oct. 1977, p. 27.
"The Bias in Public Media Programs." *Measure* no. 44 (Oct. 1977): 3-5.
"Socialism Means Freedom." *New America,* Oct. 1977.
"Reflections on the Metaphysics of John Dewey: *Experience and Nature.*" *Revue Internationale de Philosophie* (*La Pensée Philosophique Américaine 1776-1976*) no. 121-22 (1977): 313-28.

1978

The Hero in History: Myth, Power, or Moral Ideal? Stanford University: Hoover Institution on War, Revolution and Peace, 1978.

The University and the State, ed. Sidney Hook, Paul Kurtz, and Miro Todorovich. Buffalo, N.Y.: Prometheus Books, 1978.

"Bernstein's Contribution to Social Democracy." *New America* 15 (Jan. 1978): 2, 8.

"Of I.Q. Tests and the Desire to Succeed." Letter to the editor. *New York Times,* 3 Mar. 1978, p. 24.

"Politics on the Obituary Page." *National Review* 30 (28 Apr. 1978): 514.

"Capitalism, Socialism and Democracy." *Commentary* 65 (Apr. 1978): 48-50.

"Civil Discourse and Editorial Responsibility." *Measure* no. 46 (Apr.-May 1978): 3, 8.

"Above All, Freedom." *Time,* 26 June 1978, p. 22.

> Response to speech by Alexander Solzhenitsyn, Harvard Yard, June 1978.

Review of John G. Gurley, *Challengers to Capitalism: Marx, Lenin, and Mao. Slavic Review* 37 (June 1978): 307-8.

Review of Eugen Loebl, *My Mind on Trial. Slavic Review* 37 (June 1978): 323-25.

"Beyond Freedom Lies Terror." *Business and Society Review* no. 26 (Summer 1978): 15.

"Imaginary Enemies, Real Terror." Review of James Atlas, *Delmore Schwartz: The Life of an American Poet. American Scholar* 47 (Summer 1978): 406-12.

Review of Kostas Axelos, *Alienation, Praxis, and Techne in the Thought of Karl Marx. Journal of Economic History* 38 (Summer 1978): 744-46.

"The Case of Alger Hiss." Review of Allen Weinstein, *Perjury: The Hiss-Chambers Case. Encounter* 51 (Aug. 1978): 48-55.

> Reply to Eric Jacobs and Margaret Stern, ibid., Mar. 1979, pp. 85-90.

"Letter to the editor." *Contemporary Sociology,* Sept. 1978. On review by Jerome H. Skolnick of Ernest van den Haag, *Punishing Criminals.*

"Home Truths." Review of Yvonne Kapp, *Eleanor Marx. Commentary* 66 (Sept. 1978): 82-86.

"*Bakke*—Where Does It Lead? The Triumph of Racism?" *Freedom at Issue* no. 47 (Sept.-Oct. 1978): 3-6.

> Reply by Nathaniel R. Jones, "Marshall Points the Way." Ibid., pp. 3-6.
>
> Rejoinders by Hook and Jones, ibid., pp. 7, 12.

"Solzhenitsyn and Secular Humanism: A Response." *Humanist* 38 (Nov.-Dec. 1978): 4-6.

1979

"Alternatives to Collective Bargaining." In *Proceedings of the Seventh Annual Conference on Collective Bargaining in Higher Education,* New York City, 24 Apr. 1979.

"The Conceptual Structure of Power: An Overview." In *Power: Its Nature, Its Use, and Its Limits,* ed. Donald W. Harward. Boston: G. K. Hall, 1979.

Introduction to *The Middle Works of John Dewey, 1899-1924,* ed. Jo Ann Boydston, vol. 8. Carbondale and Edwardsville: Southern Illinois University Press, 1979.

"Solzhenitsyn and Western Freedom: How Serious a Challenge?" In *Conference on Issues in Liberal Education,* University of Oklahoma, Norman, 28 Mar. 1979.

"Anti-Semitism in the Academy: Some Pages of the Past." *Midstream* 25 (Jan. 1979): 49-54.

"David Caute's Fable of 'Fear and Terror'." Review of Caute, *The Great Fear: The Anti-Communist Purge under Truman and Eisenhower. Encounter* 52 (Jan. 1979): 56-64.

"Social Democracy Means Human Freedom: A Response to the Conservatives." *New America* 16 (Jan. 1979): 6, 12.

"Cosmology and Ethics." Letter to the editor. *New Republic* 180 (5 May 1979): 7.

Letter to the editor. *Russian Review* 38 (July 1979): 412-14.

> On review by Andrzej Korbonski of J. K. Zawodny, *Nothing but Honour.*

"The True Meaning of the Pumpkin." *Warbler,* Aug. 1979.

"Political Wish-Thinking and the Eurocommunist Myth." Review of Roy Godson and Stephen Haseler, *Eurocommunism: Implications for East and West. Policy Review,* Summer 1979.

"Remembering Max Eastman." *American Scholar* 48 (Summer 1979): 404-5.

"Rebuff to Jane Fonda Logical." *Dallas Morning News,* 23 Nov. 1979.

"Trotsky: The Prophet Who Failed." *New America* 16 (Dec. 1979): 6–7.
    Letter by Otto Nathan with Hook's reply, ibid. 18 (Jan.–Feb. 1981): 4.

1980

Philosophy and Public Policy. Carbondale and Edwardsville: Southern Illinois University Press, 1980.

Introduction to *The Middle Works of John Dewey, 1899–1924,* ed. Jo Ann Boydston, vol. 9. Carbondale and Edwardsville: Southern Illinois University Press, 1980.

Introduction to James H. Wentzel, *Countdown 1984: A Review of Federal Government "Minority" Group Preference in Small Business and Public Works Programs,* Jan. 1980. Pamphlet.

"On Western Freedom." In *Solzhenitsyn at Harvard,* ed. Ronald Berman, pp. 85–97. Washington, D.C.: Ethics and Public Policy Center, 1980.

"Liberalism and the Jews." *Commentary* 69 (Jan. 1980): 46–47. Symposium contribution.

"Memories of John Dewey Days: An Autobiographical Fragment." [St. John's] *College,* Jan. 1980.

"The Soviet Britannica: An Intellectual Obscenity." *Midstream* 26 (Feb. 1980): 21–22.

"Isaiah Berlin's Enlightenment." Review of Isaiah Berlin, *Against the Current. Commentary* 69 (May 1980): 61–64.

"The 'Radical' Tilt against Academic Freedom." *Measure* no. 50 (Spring 1980): 1–2.

"Spectral Marxism." Essay review of Leszek Kolakowski, *Main Currents of Marxism: Its Rise, Growth, and Dissolution: The Founders; The Golden Age; The Breakdown. American Scholar* 49 (Spring 1980): 250–71.

"Marx for All Seasons." Review of Robert L. Heilbroner, *Marxism: For and Against. Commentary* 70 (July 1980).

"The Institute for Social Research—Addendum." *Survey* 25 (Summer 1980): 177–78.

"Academic Freedom in Jeopardy—Time to Strike the Alarm Bell." *Measure,* supp. to no. 53, Sept. 1980.

Review of Norman Podhoretz, *The Present Danger. American Spectator,* Sept. 1980.
    Hook letter, ibid., Jan. 1981.

"Reflections on Tenure and Confidentiality." *Measure* no. 54 (Oct. 1980): 1, 3.
    Reply by Philip Groth, ibid. no. 57 (Summer 1981): 2, 6.
    Rejoinder by Hook, ibid., p. 2.

"Disremembering the Thirties." Review of Malcolm Cowley, *The Dream of the Golden Mountain. American Scholar* 49 (Autumn 1980).

"Call to Conscience." *New York Times,* 14 Dec. 1980, p. 7. Letter signed by Hook et al.

"The Ground We Stand on: Democratic Humanism." *Free Inquiry* 1 (Winter 1980–81): 8–10.

1981

Introduction to *The Later Works of John Dewey, 1925–1953,* ed. Jo Ann Boydston, vol. 1. Carbondale and Edwardsville: Southern Illinois University Press, 1981.

Review of Stanley Moore, *Marx on the Choice between Socialism and Communism. Russian Review* 40 (Jan. 1981): 55–56.

"A Critique of Conservatism." *National Forum* (Phi Kappa Phi Journal) 61 (Spring 1981): 21–24.

"The Secular Humanist Declaration: Pro and Con." *Free Inquiry* 1 (Spring 1981): 6–12.
    [Hook, "The Autonomy of Moral Judgment," p. 7.]
    [See "A Secular Humanist Declaration, ibid. 1 (Winter 1980–81): 3–7.]

"Misrepresentation." *New York Times Book Review,* 12 Apr. 1981, p. 39.
    Reply to Alfred Kazin letter, ibid., 15 Mar. 1981.

"Jacobo Timerman." Letter to the editor. *New York Times Book Review,* 2 Aug. 1981, p. 24.

"'The Future Danger.'" *Commentary* 72 (Aug. 1981): 4.

Popper/Skinner Debate. *Free Inquiry* 1 (Summer 1981): 3.

Response to letters by Karl Popper and B. F. Skinner on the Secular Humanist Declaration, ibid. 1 (Spring 1981): 3–4.

Reply by Corliss Lamont, ibid. 1 (Fall 1981): 3.

Reply by Dora Black, ibid. 2 (Spring 1982): 5.

Hook's rejoinder to Lamont, ibid. 2 (Winter 1981–82): 39–40.

"Communism and the American Intellectuals: From the Thirties to the Eighties." *Free Inquiry* 1 (Fall 1981): 11–15.

Reply by Lawrence Cranberg, "Is Marx Refutable?" Ibid. 2 (Winter 1981–82): 5, 44.

"So Schoen War's Frueher Mal in Kalten Krieg." *Die Welt,* 12 Sept. 1981.

"A Million-Dollar Gift's Forbidding Proviso." Letter to the editor. *New York Times,* 10 Oct. 1981, p. 24.

"Human Rights and American Foreign Policy: A Symposium." *Commentary* 72 (Nov. 1981): 25–63.

"The Worldly Ways of John Kenneth Galbraith." Review of Galbraith, *A Life in Our Times. American Spectator* 14 (Oct. 1981): 7–12.

"Communism and the American Intellectuals from the Thirties to the Eighties." *Free Inquiry* 1 (Fall 1981): 11–15.

"To President of Amherst College." *Measure* no. 58 (Fall 1981): 1.

"Books for Christmas." *American Spectator,* Dec. 1981.

1982

"Soviets Won't Honor Freeze." *Stanford Daily,* 23 Apr. 1982.

Comments by Joe Walder, ibid., 13 May 1982.

"Nuclear Freeze Talk Needs a New Focus." *Peninsula Times Tribune,* 26 Apr. 1982. [Interview.]

"Rights for Potential Crime Victims." *Newsday,* 13 May 1982.

"A Call for the Critical Examination of the Bible and Religion." Signed by Hook et al. *Free Inquiry,* 2 (Spring 1982): 1, 48.

"Out of the Depths." Review of Anton Antonov-Ovseyenko, *The Time of Stalin. American Scholar* 51 (Spring 1982): 291–95.

"My Running Debate with Einstein." *Commentary* 74 (July 1982): 37–52.

"A Dissent on Kohrmon." *Brattleboro* (Vt.) *Reformer,* 4 Aug. 1982.

"An Interview with Sidney Hook at Eighty." *Free Inquiry* 2 (Fall 1982): 4–10.

[Interviewed by Paul Kurtz.]

"The Battle Continues." *Measure* no. 59 (Winter 1982): 1, 3–4, 6.

REVIEWS OF SIDNEY HOOK'S WORKS

1927

The Metaphysics of Pragmatism. Chicago: Open Court Pub. Co., 1927.
  Reviewed in *Dial* 85 (Oct. 1928): 360; *Journal of Philosophy* 25 (21 June 1928): 356–59 (Scott Buchanan).

1933

Towards the Understanding of Karl Marx: A Revolutionary Interpretation. New York: John Day Co., 1933.
  Reviewed in *American Economic Review* 23 (Dec. 1933): 687–89 (Joseph J. Senturia); *American Political Science Review* 27 (Aug. 1933): 657–58 (Selig Perlman); *Boston Transcript,* 12 Apr. 1933, p. 2; *Commonweal* 18 (18 Aug. 1933): 390–91 (Ross J. S. Hoffman); *Current History* 38 (Aug. 1933): VI; *Journal of Philosophy* 30 (9 Nov. 1933): 634–37 (George H. Sabine); *Modern Monthly* 7 (Oct. 1933): 571–73 (Harry Slochower); *Nation* 136 (12 Apr. 1933): 414; *New Republic* 75 (28 June 1933): 186–87 (Harold J. Laski); *New York Herald Tribune Books,* 16 Apr. 1933, p. 6 (Max Eastman); *North American Review* 236 (Dec. 1933): 570; *Saturday Review of Literature* 9 (22 Apr. 1933): 550 (Felix Morrow); *Student Outlook* 3 (Nov.–Dec. 1934): 31–34 (Morris R. Cohen); *World Tomorrow* 16 (Aug. 1933): 476.

1934

The Meaning of Marx, ed. Sidney Hook. Symposium by Bertrand Russell, John Dewey, Morris R. Cohen, Sherwood Eddy, and Sidney Hook. New York: Farrar and Rinehart, 1934.
  Reviewed in *Saturday Review of Literature* 11 (2 Mar. 1935): 522 (Fabian Franklin).

1935

American Philosophy Today and Tomorrow, ed. Sidney Hook and Horace M. Kallen. New York: L. Furman, 1935.
  Reviewed in *New Scholasticism* 10 (July 1936): 292–94 (Henry A. Lucks).

1936

From Hegel to Marx: Studies in the Intellectual Development of Karl Marx. New York: John Day Co., 1936.
Reviewed in *American Sociological Review* 3 (June 1938): 295-97 (Howard Becker); *Boston Transcript,* 1 Aug. 1936, p. 4; *Christian Century* 54 (3 Mar. 1937): 291; *Economist* 124 (29 Aug. 1936): 395; *International Journal of Ethics* 47 (Apr. 1937): 405-6 (Harold D. Lasswell); *Journal of Philosophy* 34 (21 Jan. 1937): 47-49 (V. J. McGill); *Nation* 143 (15 Aug. 1936): 188-89 (Harold J. Laski); *New Republic* 88 (30 Sept. 1936): 232-33 (Herman Simpson); *New Statesman* 65 (4 Jan. 1963): 16 (George Lichtheim); *New Statesman and Nation,* n.s. 11 (6 June 1936): 897; *New York Herald Tribune Books,* 23 Aug. 1936, p. 2 (Max Lerner); *New York Times Book Review,* 6 Dec. 1936, p. 40 (Fabian Franklin); *Saturday Review of Literature* 14 (15 Aug. 1936): 11 (Max Eastman); *Slavic and East European Journal* 7 (Winter 1963): 437-38 (Donald S. Carlisle); *Spectator* 156 (12 June 1936): 1090; *Tablet* 168 (19 Dec. 1936): 878; *Times* (London) *Literary Supplement,* 11 July 1936, p. 574.

1939

John Dewey: An Intellectual Portrait. New York: John Day Co., 1939.
Reviewed in *Booklist* 36 (1 Dec. 1939): 125; *Journal of Higher Education* 11 (Apr. 1940): 226-29 (Boyd H. Bode); *Journal of Philosophy* 36 (7 Dec. 1939): 695 (Herbert Schneider); *Nation* 150 (6 Jan. 1940): 22-23 (Eliseo Vivas); *New Republic* 10 (6 Dec. 1939): 206-7 (Paul Weiss); *New York Herald Tribune Books,* 5 Nov. 1939, p. 2 (Ernest Sutherland Bates); *Philosophical Review* 50 (Jan. 1941): 86-87 (Everett Wesley Hall); *Saturday Review of Literature* 21 (11 Nov. 1939): 12-13 (Robert Bierstedt); *Thought* 15 (June 1940): 365-67 (Ruth Byrns).

1940

Reason, Social Myths and Democracy. New York: John Day Co., 1940.
Reviewed in *Annals of the American Academy of Political and Social Science* 213 (Jan. 1941): 199-200 (Hans Kohn); *Ethics* 52 (Apr. 1942): 386-87 (Glenn Negley); *Journal of Philosophy* 38 (24 Apr. 1941): 243-49 (V. J. McGill); *Library Journal* 65 (15 Oct. 1940): 873 (Felix E. Hirsch); *Living Age* 359 (Feb. 1941): 593-95 (Albert Lippman); *Nation* 151 (19 Oct. 1940): 370 (Reinhold Niebuhr); *New Republic* 103 (2 Dec. 1940): 762-64 (Irwin Edman); *New Yorker* 16 (7 Dec. 1940): 105; *New York Herald Tribune Books,* 22 Dec. 1940, p. 6 (A. N. Holcombe); *Saturday Review of Literature* 23 (11 Jan. 1941): 15 (Jacques Barzun).

1943

The Hero in History: A Study in Limitation and Possibility. New York: John Day Co., 1943.
Reviewed in *Annals of the American Academy of Political and Social Science* 229 (Sept. 1943): 197-98 (Glenn R. Morrow); *Atlantic Monthly* 172 (July 1943): 129; *Booklist* 39 (1 June 1943): 385; *Catholic Historical Review* 30 (Apr. 1944): 59 (Geoffrey Bruun); *Ethics* 54 (Jan. 1944): 152-53 (Albert W. Levi); *Foreign Affairs* 22 (Oct. 1943): 155 (Robert Gale Woolbert); *Historical Bulletin* 34 (May 1956): 246; *Journal of Philosophy* 40 (14 Oct. 1943): 575-80 (John Herman Randall, Jr.); *Nation* 157 (18 Sept. 1943): 326-28 (Jacques Barzun); *New Republic* 108 (21 June 1943): 834-35 (C. Wright Mills); *New Yorker* 19 (1 May 1943): 67; *New York Times Book Review,* 27 June 1943, p. 23 (Joseph Freeman); *Saturday Review of Literature* 26 (1 May 1943): 6 (Robert Pick); *School and Society* 57 (24 Apr. 1943): 484; *Social Studies* 34 (Dec. 1943): 376 (Walter H. Mohr); *Tablet* 185 (26 May 1945): 250; *Time* 41 (17 May 1943): 90, 92; *Weekly Book Review,* 6 June 1943, p. 16 (Adrienne Koch).

1945

The Authoritarian Attempt to Capture Education. By John Dewey, Sidney Hook, Arthur Murphy, Irwin Edman, and others. New York: King's Crown Press, 1945.
Reviewed in *Journal of Philosophy* 42 (27 Sept. 1945): 548–50 (H. A. L.); *Saturday Review of Literature* 28 (23 June 1945): 37 (Ordway Tead).

1946

Education for Modern Man. New York: Dial Press, 1946.
Reviewed in *Best Sellers* 6 (15 May 1946): 27–28; *Booklist* 42 (15 May 1946): 293; *Catholic Educational Review* 44 (Sept. 1946): 442–45 (George F. Burnell); *Chicago Sun Book Week,* 21 Apr. 1946, p. 5 (Wendell Johnson); *Commentary* 2 (Oct. 1946): 397–98 (Sidney Morganbesser); *Current History,* n.s. 11 (July 1946): 49; *Ethics* 58 (Jan. 1948): 133–37 (Donald Meiklejohn); *Journal of Philosophy* 43 (7 Nov. 1946): 629–36 (Mason W. Gross); *Kirkus* 14 (1 Apr. 1946): 171; *Library Journal* 71 (15 Apr. 1946): 584 (Thelma Brackett); *Nation* 162 (20 Apr. 1946): 476, 478 (Irwin Edman); *New Republic* 114 (10 June 1946): 840–41 (Jerome Nathanson); *New Yorker* 22 (18 May 1946): 110; *New York Times Book Review,* 26 May 1946, p. 6 (Howard Mumford Jones); *Partisan Review* 13 (Nov.–Dec. 1946): 595–96 (Delmore Schwartz); *Review of Politics* 9 (Oct. 1947): 502–4 (Leo R. Ward); *Saturday Review of Literature* 29 (20 Apr. 1946): 22 (Eric Bentley); *School and Society* 65 (22 Mar. 1947): 209–10 (William Sener Rusk); *Time,* 6 May 1946, p. 88; *U.S. Quarterly Book List* 2 (Sept. 1946): 210; *Weekly Book Review,* 11 Aug. 1946, p. 10 (Albert Guerard).

1947

Freedom and Experience: Essays Presented to Horace M. Kallen, ed. Sidney Hook and Milton R. Konvitz. Ithaca: Cornell University Press, 1947.
Reviewed in *Annals of the American Academy of Political and Social Science* 257 (May 1948): 207–8 (W. H. Sheldon); *Journal of Higher Education* 19 (Nov. 1948): 436 (Ordway Tead); *Modern Schoolman* 26 (Mar. 1949): 257–61 (James Collins).

1950

John Dewey: Philosopher of Science and Freedom, ed. Sidney Hook. New York: Dial Press, 1950.
Reviewed in *Booklist* 46 (15 June 1950): 310; *Ethics* 61 (Oct. 1950): 89 (Alan Gewirth); *Humanist* 10 (Oct. 1950): 223 (Rubin Gotesky); *Journal of Philosophy* 48 (15 Mar. 1951): 192–95 (Harold A. Larrabee); *Journal of Symbolic Logic* 16 (Sept. 1951): 209 (Carl G. Hempel); *Modern Schoolman* 47 (Nov. 1969): 132–33 (Kenneth L. Becker); *New Leader* 33 (29 July 1950): 22 (Ordway Tead); *New York Times Book Review,* 23 Apr. 1950, p. 6 (Thomas Vernor Smith); *San Francisco Chronicle,* 6 Aug. 1950, p. 18; *Saturday Review of Literature* 33 (19 Aug. 1950): 35 (Robert Bierstedt); *Thought* 26 (Summer 1951): 288–91 (James Collins).

1952

Heresy, Yes—Conspiracy, No. New York: American Committee for Cultural Freedom, 1952; New York: John Day Co., 1953.
Reviewed in *America* 89 (6 June 1953): 282 (M. D. Reagan); *American Mercury* 77 (Aug. 1953): 143 (Frank Meyer); *Booklist* 49 (15 June 1953): 334; *Books* 11 (June 1953): 343 (F. Steggert); *Chicago Sunday Tribune Magazine of Books,* 31 May 1953, p. 2 (Alfred C. Ames); *Christian Science Monitor,* 11 Sept. 1953, p. 9 (Saville R. Davis); *Commentary* 16 (July 1953): 86–88 (Robert E. Fitch); *Commonweal* 58 (15 May 1953): 155–56 (John Cogley); *Foreign Affairs* 31

(July 1953): 677-78 (Henry L. Roberts); *Freeman* 3 (18 May 1953): 600-601 (Max Eastman); *Journal of Higher Education* 25 (Mar. 1954): 166-67 (A. Cornelius Benjamin); *Library Journal* 78 (1 June 1953): 992 (James Heslin); *Nation* 176 (6 June 1953): 484-85 (John W. Ward); *New Leader* 36 (8 June 1953): 21-22 (Ordway Tead); *New Republic* 128 (15 June 1953): 20 (Henry Bamford Parkes); *New York Herald Tribune Book Review,* 10 May 1953, p. 7 (August Heckscher); *New York Times Book Review,* 10 May 1953, p. 3 (Everett N. Case); *Saturday Review* 36 (13 June 1953): 13-14 (Arthur M. Schlesinger, Jr.); ibid. 36 (20 June 1953): 13, 38 (John K. Sherman); *School and Society* 77 (2 May 1953): 286; *Thought* 28 (Winter 1953-54): 528-46 (Charles Donahue); *United Nations World* 7 (June 1953): 61-62 (George W. Shuster); *U.S. Quarterly Book Review* 9 (Sept. 1953): 328-29.

1955

Marx and the Marxists: The Ambiguous Legacy. Princeton, N.J.: Van Nostrand, 1955.
Reviewed in *American Sociological Review* 21 (June 1956): 397-98 (Paul W. Massing); *Library Journal* 80 (15 Sept. 1955): 1904 (H. H. Bernt); *Review of Politics* 18 (Apr. 1956): 254-56 (Gerhart Niemeyer).

1956

American Philosophers at Work, ed. Sidney Hook. New York: Criterion Books, 1956.
Reviewed in *Booklist* 53 (15 Jan. 1957): 236-37; *Commentary* 24 (Nov. 1957): 454-60 (Kathleen Nott); *New Leader* 40 (1 Apr. 1957): 23-24 (R. G. Ross); *New Republic* 136 (17 June 1957): 16-18 (Robert E. Fitch); *New York Herald Tribune Book Review,* 27 Jan. 1957, p. 12; *New York Times Book Review,* 23 Dec. 1956, pp. 3, 14 (Reinhold Niebuhr); *Thought* 32 (Winter 1957-58): 620-21 (W. Norris Clarke).

1957

Common Sense and the Fifth Amendment. New York: Criterion Books, 1957.
Reviewed in *Bookmark* 16 (June 1957): 210; *Chicago Sunday Tribune Magazine of Books,* 19 May 1957, p. 3 (Willard Edwards); *Cleveland Open Shelf,* Nov. 1957, p. 20; *Critic* 16 (Aug.-Sept. 1957): 16 (Albert H. Miller); *Kirkus* 25 (1 Mar. 1957): 203; *Library Journal* 82 (15 Apr. 1957): 1053 (Louis Barron); *New Leader* 40 (10 June 1957): 22-23 (Carl A. Auerbach); *New Yorker* 33 (11 May 1957): 163-64; *New York Herald Tribune Book Review,* 9 June 1957, p. 6 (William H. Edwards); *New York Times Book Review,* 26 May 1957, pp. 3, 12 (John B. Oakes); *Saturday Review* 40 (10 Aug. 1957): 32-33 (Harry Kalven, Jr.); *Time* 69 (27 May 1957): 111-12; *Yale Review,* n.s. 47 (Autumn 1957): 117-25 (Charles L. Black, Jr.).

1958

Determinism and Freedom in the Age of Modern Science, ed. Sidney Hook. First Symposium, New York University Institute of Philosophy, 9-10 Feb. 1957. New York: New York University Press, 1958.
Reviewed in *Heythrop Journal* 5 (Jan. 1964): 116-17; *International Philosophical Quarterly* 1 (Sept. 1961): 516-32 (Joseph F. Donceel); *Journal of Philosophy* 56 (9 Apr. 1959): 369-73 (Arthur C. Danto); *Library Journal* 83 (1 Apr. 1958): 1081 (Robert W. Henderson); *Modern Schoolman* 37 (Mar. 1960): 246-47 (Joseph F. Collins); *New York Times Book Review,* 16 Nov. 1958, p. 47 (Charles Frankel); *Philosophical Quarterly* 10 (July 1960): 282 (H. J. N. Horsburgh); *Ratio* 5 (Dec. 1963): 213-23 (D. F. Pears); *Review of Politics* 23 (Jan. 1961): 96-97 (Karl Kreilkamp); *Revue philosophique de louvain* 60 (Nov. 1962): 622-37 (Gérard Deledalle).

1959

John Dewey: His Philosophy of Education and Its Critics. New York: Tamiment Institute, 1959.

University Institute of Philosophy, 21–22 Oct. 1960. New York: New York University Press, 1961.
Reviewed in *Church Quarterly Review* 164 (Jan.–Mar. 1963): 106–7 (W. R. Matthews); *Commonweal* 75 (2 Mar. 1962): 599–601 (Daniel Callahan); *Journal for the Scientific Study of Religion* 2 (Oct. 1962): 130–31 (Kirtley F. Mather); *Jubilee* 9 (Mar. 1962): 52; *Library Journal* 87 (15 Feb. 1962): 775 (LaVern Kohl); *Life of the Spirit* 17 (Jan. 1963): 293; *New York Times Book Review,* 28 Jan. 1962, p. 42 (Reinhold Niebuhr); ibid., 28 Jan. 1963, p. 14 (H. Smith); *Philosophical Quarterly* 14 (Apr. 1964): 186–87 (Basil Mitchell); *Saturday Review* 45 (3 Feb. 1962): 23, 35 (Huston Smith); *Tablet* 216 (31 Mar. 1962): 307; *Theology Today* 20 (Jan. 1964): 583–85 (P. L. Holmer).

1962

Paradoxes of Freedom. Berkeley: University of California Press, 1962.
Reviewed in *Annals of the American Academy of Political and Social Science* 350 (Nov. 1963): 211–12 (John D. Lewis); *Commentary* 35 (Mar. 1963): 260–62 (Lewis A. Coser); *Forum Service* no. 585 (16 Mar. 1963): 1–4 (Daniel Bell); *Humanist* 24 (Jan.–Feb. 1964): 19–20 (Van Meter Ames and William Van Alstyne); *Jewish Social Studies* 27 (Oct. 1965): 262 (J. L. Blau); *Journal of Church and State* 6 (Winter 1964): 90–94 (William G. Toland); *Journal of Philosophy* 62 (29 Apr. 1965): 241–46 (Arnold S. Kaufman); *Library Journal* 87 (15 Sept. 1962): 3053 (Thomas M. Bogie); *New Statesman* 65 (4 Jan. 1963): 16 (George Lichtheim); *New York Times Book Review,* 7 Oct. 1962, pp. 6, 34 (John Cogley); *Progressive* 27 (Mar. 1963): 43–44 (David Fellman); *Saturday Review* 46 (13 Apr. 1963): 80 (Charles A. Madison).

1963

The Fail-Safe Fallacy. New York: Stein and Day, 1963.
Reviewed in *Book Week* 1 (27 Oct. 1963): 4 (Gerald Wendt); *Library Journal* 88 (15 Oct. 1963): 3856 (Bernard Poll); *National Review* 15 (19 Nov. 1963): 444–45 (Jameson G. Campaigne, Jr.); *New York Times,* 14 Oct. 1963, p. 27 (Harrison E. Salisbury); *New York Times Book Review,* 6 Oct. 1963, p. 3 (Mark S. Watson); *Virginia Quarterly Review* 40 (Winter 1964): xlii.
Philosophy and History, ed. Sidney Hook. Fifth Symposium, New York University Institute of Philosophy, 11–12 May 1962. New York: New York University Press, 1963.
Reviewed in *American Historical Review* 69 (Oct. 1963): 83–84 (William Gerber); *Bibliographie de la Philosophie* 11 (1964): 199–200 (Paul Kurtz); *Christian Century* 80 (20 Nov. 1963): 1436 (William A. Sadler, Jr.); *Ethics* 74 (July 1964): 302–4 (Frank H. Knight); *History and Theory* 4 (1965): 328–49 (Marvin Levich); *International Philosophical Quarterly* 4 (Feb. 1964): 320–22 (Eugene Fontinell); *Journal of the History of Ideas* 25 (Oct.–Dec. 1964): 587–98 (Frank H. Knight); *Mind* 74 (July 1965): 434–38 (W. H. Walsh); *Mississippi Valley Historical Review* 50 (June 1963): 155; *Personalist* 44 (Autumn 1963): 549–50 (William H. Werkmeister); *Wisconsin Magazine of History* 48 (Summer 1965): 327–28 (William Fletcher Thompson, Jr.).

1964

Law and Philosophy, ed. Sidney Hook. Sixth Symposium, New York University Institute of Philosophy, 10–11 May 1963. New York: New York University Press, 1964.
Reviewed in *Catholic Lawyer* 11 (Summer 1965): 263–64 (Patrick J. Rohan); *Choice* 2 (May 1965): 192; *Christian Century* 81 (4 Nov. 1964): 1372; *International Philosophical Quarterly* 5 (May 1965): 311–16 (Thomas F. McGann); *Nation* 200 (12 Apr. 1965): 398–401 (Hugo Adam Bedau); *New York Times Book Review,* 22 Nov. 1964, p. 10 (Fred Rodell; letters with Rodell's reply, ibid., 20 Dec. 1964, p. 12).

1966

Art and Philosophy, ed. Sidney Hook. Seventh Symposium, New York University Institute of

Philosophy, 23–24 Oct. 1964. New York: New York University Press, 1966.

Reviewed in *British Journal of Aesthetics* 6 (July 1966): 303; *Dalhousie Review* 46 (Autumn 1966): 390–91 (Geoffrey Payzant); *Foundations of Language* 5 (Nov. 1969): 567–68 (J. J. A. Mooij); *Journal of Aesthetics and Art Criticism* 35 (Summer 1967): 478 (David Thoreau Wieck); *Journal of the History of Philosophy* 6 (Oct. 1968): 416–17 (John M. Walker); *Music and Letters* 47 (July 1966): 269 (F. H.); *New Statesman* 72 (1966): 367–68 (Richard Wollheim); *Philosophy and Phenomenological Research* 28 (Sept. 1967): 137–38 (Jerome Stolnitz); *Review of Metaphysics* 20 (Sept. 1966): 163 (R. J. Woods); *Saturday Review* 49 (11 June 1966): 60, 62 (George W. Linden); *Southern Review* 4 (Summer 1968): 766 (R. Hollander).

1967

Religion in a Free Society. Lincoln: University of Nebraska Press, 1967; Don Mills, Ontario: Burns and MacEachern, 1967.

Reviewed in *Ave Maria* 105 (13 May 1967): 11 (D. McDonald); *Booklist* 63 (15 July 1967): 1168–69; *Choice* 5 (Mar. 1968): 70; *Christian Century* 84 (30 Aug. 1967): 1104 (John M. Swomley, Jr.); *Journal of Church and State* 12 (Autumn 1970): 497–500 (William G. Toland); *Journal of Value Inquiry* 2 (Winter 1968): 308–14 (Marvin Fox); *Religion and the Public Order* no. 5 (1969): 183–84 (Thomas J. O'Toole); *Review of Religious Research* 11 (Fall 1969): 92–93 (Eugene A. Mainelli); *Saturday Review* 50 (21 Oct. 1967): 82 (John Calam); *Stanford Law Review* 20 (Nov. 1967): 146–47 (Walter F. Berns).

Human Values and Economic Policy, ed. Sidney Hook. Eighth Symposium, New York University Institute of Philosophy, 13–14 May 1966. New York: New York University Press, 1967.

Reviewed in *American Economic Review* 58 (Dec. 1968): 1384–85 (Kurt Klappholz); *Choice* 6 (June 1969): 550; *Critique* 35 (Apr. 1969): 359–76 (B. Cazes); *Economic Journal* (London) 80 (Mar. 1970): 122–23 (C. W. Guillebaud); *Library Journal* 92 (1 Oct. 1967): 3413 (Richard A. Gray).

1969

Language and Philosophy: A Symposium, ed. Sidney Hook. Ninth Symposium, New York University Institute of Philosophy, 1968. New York: New York University Press, 1969.

Reviewed in *Canadian Journal of Linguistics* 14 (Spring 1969): 142–43 (Zeno Vendler); *Dialogue* 8 (Dec. 1969): 523–26 (Douglas Odegard); *Forum for Modern Language Studies* 7 (Oct. 1971): 413; *Journal of Linguistics* 6 (Feb. 1970): 134–36 (L. Jonathan Cohen); *Journal of Value Inquiry* 4 (Fall 1970): 235–37 (G. Benjamin Oliver); *Linguistics* 111 (1 Sept. 1973): 99–115 (Venera Mihailescu-Urechia); *Philosophischer Literaturanzeiger* 25 (1972): 115–17 (Gharati Agehananda); *Queen's Quarterly* 77 (Winter 1970): 653–54 (P. W. Rogers); *Times* (London) *Literary Supplement* 616 (18 June 1971): 717.

1970

Academic Freedom and Academic Anarchy. New York: Cowles Book Co., 1970.

Reviewed in *Choice* 7 (Sept. 1970): 906; *Christian Century* 87 (7 Jan. 1970): 22; *Christian Science Monitor,* 22 Oct. 1970, p. 9 (C. Michael Curtis); *Humanist* 30 (May–June 1970): 42–43 (Edward Chalfant and Gordon W. Keller); *Library Journal* 95 (1 Jan. 1970): 57 (Henry J. Steck); *Minnesota Law Review* 55 (1971): 1275–85 (Nelson W. Polsby); *Modern Age* 15 (Winter 1971): 96–99 (C. P. Ives); *National Review* 22 (27 Jan. 1970): 91–92 (Russell Kirk); *New York Review of Books* 14 (12 Feb. 1970): 5–11 (Henry David Aiken); *New York Times Book Review,* 8 Mar. 1970, pp. 25–29 (Edgar Z. Friedenberg); *Philosophical Forum* (De Kalb) 11 (Summer 1972): S77–S87 (Paul Kurtz and Gail Kennedy); *Review for Religious* 29 (May 1970): 483 (V. Bourke); *Saturday Review* 53 (24 Jan. 1970): 67–68 (Lewis B. Mayhew).

1971

In Defense of Academic Freedom, ed. Sidney Hook. New York: Pegasus, 1971.
Reviewed in *Choice* 8 (Sept. 1971): 880; *Library Journal* 96 (1 Nov. 1971): 3604 (James Ranz).

1973

Education and the Taming of Power. La Salle, Ill.: Open Court Pub. Co., 1973.
Reviewed in *AAUP Bulletin* 61 (Oct. 1975): 248–51 (Ronald M. Johnson); *Change* 6 (Apr. 1974): 58–60 (John K. Jessup); *Educational Studies* 5 (Winter 1974–75): 246–47 (Richard Gambino); *Library Journal* 98 (15 Nov. 1973): 3373 (Adeline Konsh); *Modern Age* 19 (Fall 1975): 423–25 (Hugh Mercer Curtler); *National Review* 26 (30 Aug. 1974): 992 (Aram Bakshian, Jr.); *New Republic* 170 (9 Feb. 1974): 30 (Joseph Featherstone); *News From Open Court,* 25 Nov. 1973, pp. 29–30; *Review of Education* 1 (May 1975): 298–302 (Terry Nichols Clark and Priscilla P. Clark); *Saturday Review/World* 1 (27 July 1974): 52 (John Calam).

1974

The Idea of a Modern University, ed. Sidney Hook, Paul Kurtz, and Miro Todorovich. Buffalo, N.Y.: Prometheus Books, 1974.
Reviewed in *Bibliographie de la Philosophie* 22 (1975): 243–44 (Loy Littlefield); *Change* 6 (Sept. 1974): 56–57 (Sol Cohen); *Choice* 11 (Nov. 1974): 1362; *Commonweal* 101 (4 Oct. 1974): 18–22 (Dennis O'Brien); *Educational Studies* 6 (Fall–Winter 1975): 217–18 (Milton K. Reimer); *Humanist* 35 (Mar.–Apr. 1975): 33–35 (David Sidorsky); *International Philosophical Quarterly* 16 (June 1976): 248–51 (John Donnelly); *Library Journal* 99 (Aug. 1974): 1944 (Adeline Konsh); *Review of Education* 1 (May 1975): 298–302 (Terry Nichols Clark and Priscilla P. Clark).
Pragmatism and the Tragic Sense of Life. New York: Basic Books, 1974.
Reviewed in *Commentary* 59 (June 1975): 86, 88 (Michael Novak); *Encounter* 45 (Oct. 1975): 37–45 (Lewis S. Feuer); *Humanist* 35 (July–Aug. 1975): 39 (Steven M. Cahn); *Journal of the History of Ideas* 36 (Oct.–Dec. 1975): 739–46 (Philip P. Wiener); *Journal of Philosophy* 74 (Mar. 1977): 172–76 (Frederick A. Olafson); *Library Journal* 100 (15 Feb. 1975): 396 (Robert Hoffman); *Midstream* 21 (Dec. 1975): 70 (Reuben Abel); *National Review* 28 (23 Jan. 1976): 44–46 (Frederick L. Will); *New Republic* 175 (18 Sept. 1976): 35–37 (William K. Frankena); *Philosophy and Phenomenological Research* 36 (Dec. 1975): 275 (Henry W. Johnstone, Jr.); *Review for Religious* 34 (May 1975): 491 (P. Reardon); *St. Croix Review* 8 (June 1975): 48.

1975

Revolution, Reform, and Social Justice—Studies in the Theory and Practice of Marxism. New York: New York University Press, 1975.
Reviewed in *Choice* 13 (Mar. 1976): 104; *Economist* 262 (8 Jan. 1977): 101–2; *Humanist* 36 (May–June 1976): 36–37 (Marvin Kohl); *Journal of Economic Issues* 11 (Dec. 1977): 904–6 (Howard Sherman); *New Republic* 174 (14 Feb. 1976): 24–25 (Irving Howe); *Political Studies* 25 (Dec. 1977): 629 (David Miller); *Review of Metaphysics* 29 (June 1976): 737–38 (Michael P. Malloy); *Sociology* 12 (Jan. 1978): 180–81 (Peter Lassman); *Studi internazionali di filosofia* 9 (1977): 193–95 (Donald Weiss); *Times* (London) *Literary Supplement,* 8 Apr. 1977, p. 427 (Ghita Ionescu).
The Philosophy of the Curriculum: The Need for General Education, ed. Sidney Hook, Paul Kurtz, and Miro Todorovich. Buffalo, N.Y.: Prometheus Books, 1975.
Reviewed in *Change* 7 (Sept. 1975): 58–59 (Maurice Hungiville); *Choice* 12 (Nov. 1975): 1215; *Chronicle of Higher Education* 14 (11 Oct. 1976): 17 (Leon Botstein); *College and University* 52 (Winter 1977): 240 (Robert A. Scott); *Encounter* 45 (Oct. 1975): 37; *Higher Education*

(Netherlands) 5 (1976): 349-50 (Samuel E. Kellams); *Humanist* 35 (Nov.-Dec. 1975): 38-39 (Robert Simon).

1977

The Ethics of Teaching and Scientific Research, ed. Sidney Hook, Paul Kurtz, and Miro Todorovich. Buffalo, N.Y.: Prometheus Books, 1977.
   Reviewed in *Contemporary Psychology* 23 (May 1978): 371 (Dennis Regan); *National Association of Secondary School Principals Bulletin* 62 (Mar. 1978): 114 (Weldon Beckner); *New Scientist* 75 (7 July 1977): 30 (Tim Robinson); *Religious Studies Review* 7 (Jan. 1981): 53; *Review of Metaphysics* 31 (Dec. 1977): 320 (Milton Goldinger); *Science Books and Films* 13 (Mar. 1978): 197 (Rachelle D. Hollander).

1978

The University and the State, ed. Sidney Hook, Paul Kurtz, and Miro Todorovich. Buffalo, N.Y.: Prometheus Books, 1978.
   Reviewed in *Booklist* 75 (1 Sept. 1978): 6; *Change* 10 (Oct. 1978): 60 (Joseph Barbato); *Choice* 15 (Dec. 1978): 1419; *Educational Studies* 11 (Spring 1980): 77-80 (M. M. Chambers); *Journal of Church and State* 22 (Autumn 1980): 540-41 (Timothy J. Hansen); *Journal of Higher Education* 51 (Sept.-Oct. 1980): 569-72 (Jerry A. May); *Library Journal* 103 (Aug. 1978): 1505-6 (Carol Eckberg Wadsworth); *New England Law Review* 14 (Summer 1978): 144-45; *Publishers Weekly* 214 (3 July 1978): 56.

1980

Philosophy and Public Policy. Carbondale and Edwardsville: Southern Illinois University Press, 1980.
   Reviewed in *America* 142 (31 May 1980): 464-65 (Robert F. Drinan); *American Spectator* 13 (Aug. 1980): 40-41 (Arnold Beichman); *Choice* 18 (Sept. 1980): 161-62; *Christian Century* 97 (23 Apr. 1980): 476; *Commentary* 70 (Oct. 1980): 74, 76-77 (Werner J. Dannhauser); *Educational Studies* 11 (Fall 1980): 315 (Walter P. Krolikowski); *Encounter* 55 (Nov. 1980): 71-73 (Constantine FitzGibbon); *Horizons* 8 (Spring 1981): 191-92 (Joseph W. Devlin); *Library Journal* 105 (15 May 1980): 1169 (Peter Vari); *Modern Age* 25 (Summer 1981): 308-10 (J. Brooks Colburn); *Nation* 231 (20 Dec. 1980): 680-81 (Philip Green); *National Review* 32 (31 Oct. 1980): 1335-36 (Jeanne Wacker Sobran); *New Oxford Review* (Jan.-Feb. 1981): 26-28 (Erazim Kohák); *New York Times Book Review,* 30 Nov. 1980, p. 9 (Nathan Glazer); ibid., 8 Feb. 1981, pp. 7, 24-25 (Hilton Kramer); *Perspectives in Religious Studies* 8 (Summer 1981): 175-79 (R. M. Helm); *Philosophical Books* 22 (Oct. 1981): 232-34 (Antony Flew); *Time* 115 (28 Apr. 1980): 92 (Stefan Kanfer); *Wall Street Journal,* 3 Sept. 1980, p. 26 (Carl Gershman).

CONTRIBUTORS

DANIEL BELL is Henry Ford II Professor of Social Sciences at Harvard University. His career has spanned journalism and politics. In the early 1940s, he was managing editor of *The New Leader* (where he first met and published Sidney Hook). He has taught at the University of Chicago and Columbia. His books include *The End of Ideology, The Coming of Post-Industrial Society, The Cultural Contradictions of Capitalism,* and *The Winding Passage: Sociological Essays and Journeys 1960-1980.*

JO ANN BOYDSTON, Director of the Center for Dewey Studies, Southern Illinois University at Carbondale, is the general editor of *The Collected Works of John Dewey, 1882-1953,* of which twenty-one volumes have now been published. She is also the editor of *The Poems of John Dewey* and author of a number of other works on Dewey's life and thought.

JOHN H. BUNZEL is a Senior Research Fellow at Stanford University's Hoover Institution. A political scientist and author of several books and many articles, he received the San Francisco Board of Supervisor's Certificate of Merit in 1974 for "dedicated efforts looking to the elimination of racial and religious bigotry and discrimination." He served as president of San Jose University from 1970-1978.

STEVEN M. CAHN, Adjunct Professor of Philosophy at the University of Vermont, is Director of the Division of General Programs at the National Endowment for the Humanities. Among his books are *Fate, Logic and Time, The Eclipse of Excellence,* and *Education and the Democratic Ideal.*

NICHOLAS CAPALDI, Professor of Philosophy at Queens College, is an internationally known Hume scholar. He has also published widely on topics in the philosophy of the social sciences and on public policy issues.

LEWIS S. FEUER is University Professor of Sociology and Government at the University of Virginia. Author of *Einstein and the Generations of Science* and *Ideology and the Ideologists,* he was formerly Professor of Philosophy at the University of California, Berkeley, and at the University of Vermont.

ANTONY G. N. FLEW is Professor of Philosophy at the University of Reading, England. He has held many visiting appointments elsewhere, including one in 1958 at New York University. His books include *Hume's Philosophy of Belief, An Introduction to Western Philosophy, Crime or Disease?, A Rational Animal,* and *The Politics of Procrustes.*

NATHAN GLAZER is Professor of Education and Sociology at Harvard University and co-editor of *The Public Interest.* He is the author of *American Judaism, Beyond the Melting Pot, Remembering the Answers,* and *Affirmative Discrimination.* He was born in New York City in 1923, attended the City College of New York, the University of Pennsylvania, and Columbia University, and in his teens regularly went to hear Sidney Hook lecture at Cooper Union.

JACK KAMINSKY is Professor of Philosophy at the State University of New York at Binghamton, where he served as Chairman of the Philosophy Department from 1953 to 1963. He received his B.S. in 1944 from the City College of New York and his Ph.D. in 1950 from New York University. His books include *Essays in Linguistic Ontology, Language and Ontology,* and *Hegel on Art.*

MARVIN KOHL teaches ethics and philosophy at the State University of New York College at Fredonia. He is the author of *The Morality of Killing* (1974) and is a Contributing Editor of *Free Inquiry* magazine.

MILTON R. KONVITZ is Professor of Industrial and Labor Relations, and Law, Emeritus, Cornell University. He is the author of *The Constitution and Civil Rights* (1946), *Fundamental Liberties of a Free People* (1957), *Expanding Liberties* (1966), *Religious Liberty and Conscience* (1968), *Judaism and the American Idea* (1979), and other books, and editor of *The Recognition of Ralph Waldo Emerson* (1972), *Bill of Rights Reader* (1954), and other works.

IRVING KRISTOL is Professor of Social Thought at the Graduate School of Business at New York University and is co-editor (with Nathan Glazer) of *The Public Interest.* He has previously been an editor of *The Reporter, Encounter,* and *Commentary.*

PAUL KURTZ is Professor of Philosophy at the State University of New York at Buffalo. He studied with Sidney Hook as an undergraduate at New York University and has been associated with Professor Hook as editor of *The Humanist* and *Free Inquiry.* He is the author of *Exuberance* (1977), *The Fullness of Life* (1973), *Decision and the Condition of Man,* and other books. He edited an earlier *Festschrift* on Sidney Hook entitled *Sidney Hook and the Contemporary World: Essays on the Pragmatic Intelligence* (1968). Professor Kurtz is also Editor-in-Chief of Prometheus Books.

DAVID S. LICHTENSTEIN was the Supervising Attorney for the International Communications and Satellite Division of the Federal Communications Commission. Subsequent to government service, he became General Counsel to Accuracy in Media and has written numerous articles on the Fairness Doctrine in broadcasting.

SEYMOUR MARTIN LIPSET is the Caroline S. G. Munro Professor of Political Science and Sociology and a Senior Fellow at the Hoover Institution, Stanford University. A past president of the American Political Science Association and the International Society of Political Psychology, he is currently President-elect of the World Association for Public Opinion Research. He is the author of many books, including *Political Man, Revolution and Counterrevolution, The First New Nation,* and most recently *The Confidence Gap.*

ERNEST NAGEL, born in 1901 in what is now Czechoslovakia, came to the United States in 1911, attended New York City public schools, and received his B.S. in social studies from the City College of New York, where he was a classmate of Sidney Hook, and his M.A. and Ph.D. from Columbia University. He was a member of the Columbia University Department of Philosophy from 1930 until his retirement in 1974 as University Professor Emeritus. He is the author of several books, including *The Structure of Science.*

LEE NISBET is Associate Professor of Philosophy at Medaille College, Buffalo, where he is Chairman of the Humanities Department. He is Associate Editor of *Free Inquiry* magazine.

KATHLEEN POULOS is a Senior Editor at the Center for Dewey Studies and co-author with Jo Ann Boydston of the *Checklist of Writings About John Dewey* (1974, 1978).

RICHARD RORTY is Kenan Professor of Humanities at the University of Virginia. He is the author of *Philosophy and the Mirror of Nature* (1979) and *Consequences of Pragmatism* (1982).

RALPH ROSS, Hartley Burr Alexander Professor of Humanities and Professor of Philosophy, Emeritus, Scripps College, the Claremont Colleges, is author or co-author of seven books and has edited many others. He has also written many articles and reviews.

PAUL SEABURY is Professor of Government at the University of California at Berkeley. He is Vice Chairman of the University Centers for Rational Alternatives and Chairman of the Board of the International Council on the Future of the University. Among the many books he has written and edited are *Bureaucrats and Brainpower: Government Regulation of the Universities* (1979) and *America's Stake in the Pacific* (1981).

EDWARD SHILS is Distinguished Service Professor of Social Thought and Sociology at the University of Chicago and Honorary Fellow of Peterhouse, Cambridge. He is the founder and editor of *Minerva, a Quarterly of Science, Learning and Policy.*

DAVID SIDORSKY is Professor of Philosophy at Columbia University. He has written articles in moral and political philosophy for the *Journal of Philosophy, Mind, Social Philosophy,* and *New Literary History,* among other journals, and has authored, edited, or contributed to *The Nature of Disagreement in Social Philosophy, The Essential Writings of John Dewey, The European Tradition in Liberal Thought,* and *Essays in Human Rights.*

ERNEST VAN DEN HAAG is the John M. Olin Professor of Jurisprudence and Public Policy at Fordham University. He taught for many years at New York University and at the New School for Social Research. His two most recent books are *Punishing Criminals: Concerning a Very Old and Painful Question* (1975) and *Capitalism: Sources of Hostility* (1979). His *Death Penalty: Pro and Con* (with John Conrad) will be published in 1983.

MARVIN ZIMMERMAN is Professor of Philosophy at the State University of New York at Buffalo. He is the author of *Contemporary Problems of Democracy.*